THE
SECRET
CODE
BREAKERS

ALSO BY SARAH VALENTINE

When I Was White

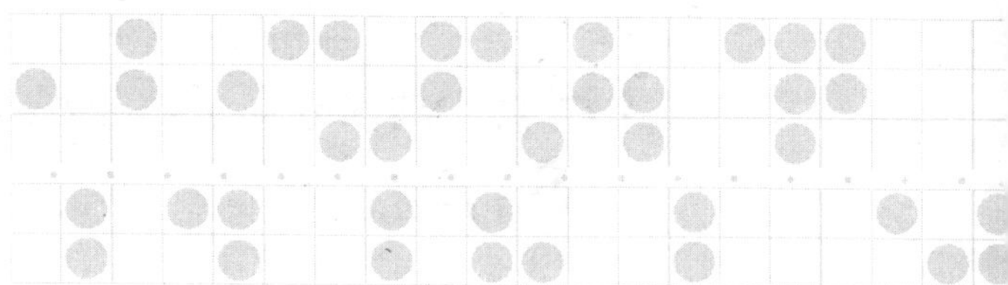

THE SECRET CODE BREAKERS

THE UNTOLD STORY OF BLACK WOMEN CRYPTOLOGISTS AND THE WAR AGAINST STALIN'S BOMB

SARAH VALENTINE

ROBINSON

ROBINSON

First published in the United States of America as *Decoding the Devil: Black Women Codebreakers and the Secret War Against Stalin's Bomb* in 2026 by Harper, an imprint of HarperCollins Publishers

First published in Great Britain in 2026 by Robinson

1 3 5 7 9 10 8 6 4 2

A CIP catalogue record for this book
is available from the British Library.

ISBN: 978-1-47214-810-0 (hardback)
ISBN: 978-1-47214-811-7 (trade paperback)

Designed by Nancy Singer
Printed and bound in Great Britain by Clays Ltd, Elcograf S.p.A.

Papers used by Robinson are from well-managed forests
and other responsible sources.

Robinson
An imprint of
Little, Brown Book Group
Carmelite House
50 Victoria Embankment
London EC4Y 0DZ

The authorised representative
in the EEA is
Hachette Ireland
8 Castlecourt Centre, Dublin 15,
D15 XTP3, Ireland
(email: info@hbgi.ie)

An Hachette UK Company
www.hachette.co.uk

www.littlebrown.co.uk

This book is dedicated to federal employees past and present, whose work and patriotism are invaluable.

God is on your side? Is He a Conservative? The Devil's on my side. He's a good Communist.

—Joseph Stalin to Winston Churchill,
Tehran Conference, 1943

Colored women are the only group in this country who have two heavy handicaps to overcome, that of race as well as that of sex.

—Mary Church Terrell,
A Colored Woman in a White World (1940)

CONTENTS

INTRODUCTION

On Iris's first day at the National Security Agency, a white lieutenant marches her down to the basement of Operations Building A. The underground facility is even hotter than the sunbaked rooms upstairs. Before Iris sees the room, she feels it—the floor rumbles like she's standing on empty tracks. As she approaches, the rumbling grows into a sound of a hundred teletype machines thundering like a freight train. Outside the door, she smells perspiration and machine oil, hints of the furious operation to break Stalin's war machine.

When Iris opens the door, she finds scores of women in lace-collared blouses and men in smart suits working in controlled chaos: One group wrangles clunky machines that hiss, jam, and clatter out messages in Cyrillic. Another speed-reads continuous strips of Russian telegrams—raw intelligence from Soviet ministries on atomic production, weapons shipments, delayed deliveries. A third stamps and routes printouts to a dizzying list of branches, sections, and subsections—all working on the Russian problem.

In the long, windowless wing, like the belly of a whale, Iris takes her place amid the throng. She puts on a rubber apron and stands at an industrial ink press to stamp serial numbers on outgoing messages—for eight hours straight. She is a cryptologic clerk, grade 3, a role assigned to hires with high-school educations. With her master's degree and aced training exams, she should be a cryptanalyst, grade 7. But it's 1950, and Iris is Black. Her credentials don't count.

Iris is part of Traffic Processing Division, the outfit that handles all the Agency's Russian-language telegrams. The Agency's white professionals won't touch this kind of work—it's too dirty, too tedious, too labor-intensive. But it's the bedrock on which almost all the Agency's Russian operations rely. The Black cryptologic clerks, most of them college educated like Iris, process more than one hundred thousand Soviet telegrams a day under crushing quotas and constant surveillance.

The only white person in the room is the armed Air Force guard at the door.

Everyone at the Agency knows the nickname for this division: "the plantation."

But no one talks about it.

This story was never meant to be told.

The Black codebreakers who kept America's intelligence machine running during and after World War II were hidden in plain sight—segregated, overworked, and written out of the official histories because they revealed an uncomfortable truth. For decades, their contributions were buried under layers of classified secrecy and institutional neglect—and no one outside the intelligence world knew they existed.

Now, as the intelligence community reckons with its past—and as our country continues to confront how race and labor have shaped every American institution—the Black codebreakers' story demands attention. The Cold War may be over, but its infrastructure is still with us. The enmity between the United States and Russia, the legacy of nuclear weapons production. The surveillance systems, federal workforce structure, hierarchies of access and recognition all have roots in places like Arlington Hall and in stories like these.

This book tells the story of the National Security Agency's most secret wartime and Cold War operations from the point of view of the Black codebreakers who made the operations possible. It follows the creation of America's surveillance state from the back rooms and basement wings where Black workers toiled under harsh conditions, doing work that shaped the future of global intelligence. It reveals the long-ranging impact of the early civil rights movement amid the rise of nuclear weapons, the Red Scare, and the Korean War.

This is not a story about a few exceptional individuals breaking barriers. It's a story about a system—one that depended on Black labor while denying Black talent—and about the people who endured and resisted, who carved out careers, rose above expectations, and refused to disappear.

The majority of Black codebreakers in this book are women, but available research overrepresents the men. Though they too must overcome racial injustice, they do benefit from being men in a male-dominated era in a male-dominated institution. Some have less education and experience than the women but are promoted to leadership roles within the segregated branches. The military establishment assumes the one man in the group will be the leader, a pattern revealed in many of the cryptologists' firsthand accounts. Having more of their stories about the men makes them feel more present than the hundreds (maybe thousands) of Black women among whom they worked. While their contributions are no less important, this book highlights the legions of Black women whose work has gone unrecognized until now.

Contrary to what movies want us to believe, not all codebreakers look like Benedict Cumberbatch. Intelligence is not just the province of geniuses like Alan Turing (played by Benedict Cumberbatch), undercover agents like Grenville Wynne (played by Benedict Cumberbatch), or hacktivists like Julian Assange (played by you-know-who). Before the era of high-speed computers, codebreaking was mostly grunt work done by hand. Pencil, paper, eraser, codebook, coffee, cigarette, repeat. File, sort, type, microfilm, index, repeat. Analysts scratched slanted matrices on graph paper, used informed trial and error to see if their hunches about an enemy's cipher were correct. They usually weren't. So it was back to the drawing board, day after day, or night after night, if they worked the night shift.

During World War II and after, cryptologic clerks and mid-level code-breakers kept the wheels of intelligence turning. Many women in this story could have been more; they had the brilliance, tenacity, passion, and creativity that characterizes some of codebreaking's most renowned figures. But their contributions matter at every level. Their stories are just as thrilling—and at times more terrifying—because in a Jim Crow world, every move a Black woman makes is weighted with implications.

Recently, major works on codebreaking have taken note of the Black cryptologists. *Code Girls* by Liza Mundy and *Code Warriors* by Stephen Budiansky include sections on the all-Black World War II and Cold War operations. However, neither goes into enough detail to convey the true impact of the Black cryptologists' work or the awfulness of their circumstances. Studies like *The Invisible Cryptologists* and *Candle in the Dark* provide more detailed accounts, but these are NSA publications, and they don't paint the whole picture.

The story begins in the early 1940s when the United States enters World War II. To meet a racial hiring quota, a handful of Black workers—mostly women—join the Army's secret codebreaking programs in Washington, DC. What starts as a small wartime unit grows into a much larger workforce as the Cold War intensifies and the government races to collect intelligence on the Soviet Union. Throughout the 1950s, hundreds of educated Black women and men are hired to support the Agency's most critical surveillance project—the Russian plaintext operation. These intelligence professionals often perform highly skilled, high-stakes work while being paid and classified as clerks.

The story follows this workforce through its transformations: from World War II through the Korean War, from pencil-and-paper codebreaking to early automation, from Army barracks and segregated buses to desegregation and the vast machinery of Cold War surveillance. It's told through the lives of real people—codebreakers, translators, traffic processors, file clerks, and data specialists—who kept the US intelligence engine running while being systematically denied the right to rise within it.

The Black codebreakers' work was essential, but their stories have been neglected. They joined the Agency at different times from different places. All of them entered the dark heart of American intelligence—working in the shadows of a system that needed—but never fully saw—them. There are too many codebreakers to go into detail about each of their lives. More than thirty Black codebreakers worked in the Commercial Code Unit during World War II, and over a thousand worked in different departments of the Agency's Cold War operation. Most of their names remain unknown, and even when their names are known, documentation about their work and lives can be scarce. I chose several noteworthy individuals to guide the narrative. Their breakthrough work suggests that many other women made similar, if not greater, contributions that remain uncredited.

The book opens with Naomi McElwaine, a sophomore at Purdue in 1941, who is unaware that the government is about to draft her into a world of secrecy and silence. Next is Martha McWatt, a University of Minnesota graduate and decoder, who finds out what happens when someone breaches the Agency's strict security protocols. Sixty-year-old Ethel Just, a translator and an Ohio native, fights to keep her job as an analyst as the Agency reduces its workforce after the war. In the postwar years, Iris Carr, a schoolteacher from Texas, leaves a secure job to serve her country. Minnie Kenny, a sharp-witted Philadelphian, joins the Agency after the war and refuses to accept the racial status quo. These women stand out because they never give up—on their work, on their country, or on themselves. They maintain their commitment to justice while working for the very system that legislates the injustices they experience daily. For the rest of their lives, they keep their successes a secret, observing the oath of loyalty they signed when entering into duty.

They begin in a hopeful era. The United States is recovering from the Depression, supporting its allies overseas. The war pulls the nation into a new world—technology advances, women enter the workforce, Black Americans fill government roles in Washington. For a moment, Americanness overshadows race. Black newspapers proclaim the "Double V"—victory over fascism abroad and over racism at home.

Too soon reality muscles in. During the war, industry and tech companies mostly hire whites. Japanese Americans are interned. The military is segregated. The federal government—soon to be Naomi's employer—doubles down on the systems that keep Black workers from advancing. When Naomi is chosen for the wartime codebreaking program, it feels like an opportunity. It is also a test: of her endurance, skill, loyalty, and ability to thrive in a system designed to hold her back.

The institutions that shape the Black codebreakers' careers—first the Army's Signal Corps, then the intelligence agencies that evolve into NSA—exist in a contradiction. On the surface, they fight to uphold democracy. At the same time, they enforce segregation and undermine the ideals they claim to defend. It is America's contradiction: to perfect its democracy while maintaining racial hierarchy. The goals are incompatible, and the Black cryptologists' story shows the consequences of prioritizing the second goal over the first.

The anxiety of not knowing whom to trust pervades this era, from the Red Scare's spy trials to blacklisting "subversive" actors and activists. The same thing happens at Arlington Hall. Spies move in the secret halls of the "Russian problem" unseen, even as analysts race to decrypt their identities. At times, inherent trust in whiteness compromises national security. White spies can blend in and become trusted friends and coworkers. Because they're insiders, suspicious characters avoid background checks; supervisors don't report irregularities. Unauthorized people slip through Agency checkpoints and nobody lifts an eyebrow. After every major leak, there are calls to increase security—but nothing really happens. Looking back, it's amazing the consequences weren't worse.

KEY TERMS

Codebreaking uses unique terminology, so a discussion of key terms is helpful. Disagreement surrounding these terms drives most of the story's conflicts. A detailed glossary provides further discussion of these topics, and readers will find descriptions of key terms in the book.

Intelligence

Intelligence is information related to a target. Information that's not related to a target is just information. To be of value, intelligence must be accurate, timely, and actionable. If you know in advance that an enemy will be at the top of the hill at sundown, you can use that intelligence to plan an ambush or raid their camp. You get to the hill a little early, they come, thinking they have the upper hand, and you blast them into oblivion. Well done.

If you go to the hill and find the enemy there already, ready to ambush *you*, you'll know the message was a trap! False intelligence, or misinformation, is used to make an enemy act wrongly and become vulnerable.

If you receive the same intelligence three weeks after the fact, and three weeks ago you fought the enemy on that hill, you'll know the message was authentic, but it won't be actionable.

If you solved a code or cipher to reveal that message, even if the message is no longer actionable, having solved the code provides valuable intelligence, provided the enemy uses that code again.

In this story, the Agency and its allies don't always know what to do with the intelligence they gather from Russian plaintext. It's disparate and fragmentary, but there's a lot of it, and connecting the dots leads to some great insights. The argument remains: Is it intelligence or just information? That doubt leads to a lack of full support for the project even though it's the best source of intel they have for many years.

Plaintext

This is the most important term in the book. Plaintext is simply readable language. After you decode a message, you reveal its plaintext. This book is written in plaintext. Right now, you are reading plaintext.

Using plaintext as an intelligence source is controversial because unencrypted messages usually doesn't contain secrets. At some point, plaintext telegrams from the Soviet Union are the only intelligence source the Agency has. This causes problems, but it also creates opportunities. The Black cryptologists are the first line readers and processors of these messages.

High-Level

The principle of codebreaking is that when information is important, it is well concealed. The better something is concealed, the higher its value—both to its intended recipient and to the person who's trying to steal it. Cryptanalysis as a profession and as an institution is based on this idea.

Cryptanalysts must solve a complex set of problems to figure out what a concealed message says. Only a select group of people have the skills to do this, and the Intelligence Community values them highly.

In wartime, the most important kinds of information are an enemy's plans, ability, and means of attack. If a message is well concealed, it is assumed to contain this kind of "high-level" or "high-value" intelligence and comes from a high-level source, like a senior official or high-ranking political figure, with access to top secret operations.

Complex ciphers are "high-level" or "high-echelon" systems. If an enemy is very dangerous, they are a "high-value" target. Ideally, cryptanalysts want high-level intelligence on high-level targets, which usually means breaking high-level codes and ciphers.

Low-Level

"Low-level" describes information of minimal value, codes that are easy to break, and targets that don't pose much of a threat. Low-level intelligence may be "nice to have" (of secondary value) but it's not "need to have" (mission critical). Low-level communications are often sent by minor officials or the rank and file, who don't have the clearance to participate in top secret operations.

When codes and ciphers are easy to break—or when they're absent, as in the case of plaintext—the Agency assumes the information they contain is not important. This assumption leads to many conflicts and missed opportunities throughout the book.

Baudot Code

Baudot (baw-DOH), like Morse, is an alphabetic code used for long-distance communication in the early to mid-1900s. In Baudot code, each letter is a string of five 1s and 0s, where 1 is a pulse (+) and 0 is no pulse (-). The Soviet telegraph system uses Baudot code, so the Agency needs linguists who can read Cyrillic *and* its Baudot equivalents to scan Soviet telegrams for intelligence. This is what the Black cryptologists do.

From a cryptanalysis perspective, messages sent in Morse or Baudot are considered "plaintext" because the code is a one-for-one substitution. For most people, reading Morse or Baudot code at speed is a complex skill to master—especially in a foreign language—but the Agency considers this easy, low-level work.

WHAT ARE THE STAKES?

In a moment of global crisis, leaders in the Agency's world of strict hierarchies have to decide whether low-level intelligence can have high-level value. This question may not seem earth-shattering, but the cognitive dissonance it creates shakes the Agency's principles to their core.

Ultimately, the Agency straddles the fence on this question: They throw nearly all their resources into Russian plaintext, making it the country's main source of Soviet intelligence from 1948 to 1955. The CIA, FBI, State Department, British, and Canadians all need it, and many agencies aid the operation. The Atomic Energy Council and the National Security Council need it. In the dark postwar years, the safety of the free world relies on intelligence drawn from Russian plaintext.

But the Agency can't let go of its prejudices. They treat the intelligence they gain from plaintext as high-level, but they treat the source—and the people who work on it—as low-level. That means they never develop the plaintext workforce to its full extent or accord it the same importance as high-level Russian codebreaking operations even though it yields far greater results.

Most plaintext operations is data processing, and without automation the monotonous, time-consuming work is done by hand. The Agency needs a large, underpaid workforce to do this, so instead of treating the Black cryptologists like linguists and codebreakers—as many of them are—the Agency treats them as manual laborers.

Arlington Hall spends half a billion dollars a year on plaintext, but almost none of it goes to the cryptologists. They train hundreds of Russian linguists and analysts, but they bar the Black women from these programs. They don't have full security clearance, so most don't know where the messages they process are going.

The white analysts and the Black clerks are in different buildings, and it makes for an awkward, disjointed operation. Because of this, plaintext intelligence struggles to fulfill its goal of uncovering the Soviet nuclear weapons program. The Agency races to fix the problem as tensions mount—from an escalating arms race with the Soviet Union to war with Korea. The Black cryptologists are the key to solving the intelligence problem, but Russian plaintext's success spells career death for many of them, keeping hundreds of Black workers on "the plantation" long after segregation ends.

COLD WARCRAFT

What is the Cold War? While this might seem like an obvious question, it's more nuanced than it appears. Generally, the Cold War is considered the period of political hostility between the United States and the Soviet Union from the end of World War II in 1945 to the Soviet Union's dissolution in 1991. "Cold" because nuclear war—that is, a "hot" war—between the only two countries with atomic weapons is always threatened but never waged. Instead, Russia and the US fight proxy wars in smaller countries that represent the worldwide clash between capitalism and communism, democracy and socialism. The US can't afford for countries around the world to side with the Soviet Union, which would give them a strategic advantage in future wars. The Soviet Union is a closed society, and there's little communication between the two world powers. Each races to build an arsenal of nuclear weapons to deter the other from even thinking about planning a surprise attack. In the US, the Cold War is characterized by widespread fear: of atomic annihilation, communist infiltration, and society's moral collapse.

The tensions that create the Cold War between Russia and the United States begin much earlier than history describes. From the moment the last tsar abdicates the throne in 1917, enmity rises between the new wild state and the Western giant. Imperial Russia was a US ally in World War I, and it supported the Union in America's Civil War. Later in 1917, when the October Revolution strikes and the Russian Civil War begins, the United States backs the moderate Whites—the Menshevik, or minority, Party.

Unfortunately for the United States, the Reds—the Bolshevik, or majority, Party—wins. Russia enters World War I under the banner of the golden eagle but ends it under the red star of communism. With Belarus, Ukraine, and Transcaucasia, Russia forms a new nation on the principles of socialism and communal ownership—the Union of Soviet Socialist Republics.

By siding with the Whites, the United States declares itself an enemy of the Soviet Union, an imperial nation like Great Britain, France, and Germany that colonizes people around the world and profits from their labor. The Western powers don't see themselves that way—they believe they are democracy's defenders—but the Soviets see only blood-hungry capitalists, economic vampires draining the working classes, just like the Russian dynasty they fought to overcome. The Russians make a separate peace with Germany and emerge from World War I righteous and battle-scarred, ready to show the world where they stand.

Before the ink dries on the Soviet Constitution, V. I. Lenin—the

Communist Party leader—sends a letter to the workers of America: Comrades! Do not believe the multimillionaires—"Modern slaveholders"—who blame the Bolsheviks for concluding peace with Germany. It is a sacrifice to preserve the world's first Socialist Republic. America's bourgeois puppets and *capitalist sharks* fear our dictatorship of the proletariat—government by and for the people—"Without the bourgeoisie." Just as you fought to overthrow Negro slavery, fight with us to overthrow capitalist *wage slavery*. Every billionaire's dollar is stained with blood. "Slowly but surely, the workers of the world are adopting communist, Bolshevik tactics and are marching towards the proletarian revolution, which alone is capable of saving mankind."

Newspapers from New York to Paris print the manifesto, and it galvanizes the US Socialist Left. They join the Communist International, and Communist Party USA is born—its goal: to spread Marxist-Leninism across the United States. Labor reform and workers' rights are first on its agenda. This spooks US politicians, who begin a communist witch hunt that never lets up.

Lenin's successor is Joseph Stalin, a wily Georgian with a knowing smile. Stalin is a Socialist, but he's also a businessman. And enemies can do business.

He sets up the American Trading Corporation ("Amtorg") in New York City to be the Soviet Union's trade representative. Its headquarters are in a huge building on Broadway, and it scores contracts with Ford, RCA, and General Electric. Amtorg exports lumber, furs, and caviar and imports industrial machinery and raw materials. Not a bad trade. The United States doesn't recognize the Soviet Union as a country until 1933. Until then, Amtorg is the Soviets' de facto embassy in the US.

There is no war on, but Stalin knows there will be, and he begins a campaign of commercial warfare that transforms the Soviet military. He does business with another enemy—Germany—setting up covert industrial operations all over Russia under the guise of international trade. The German-Russian joint stock company Bersol manufactures poison gases in Trotsk and Samara. German engineers produce ammunition at plants in Zlatoust, Tula, and Petrograd. Stalin establishes the Lipetsk Aviation School, where dozens of German pilots train to become the Luftwaffe, the feared German air force of World War II. At a tank-training school near Kazan, they develop the *Panzerwagen*. In 1926, Russian boats quietly deliver three hundred thousand shells, gunpowder, and fuses to the German War Ministry—disguised as shipments of aluminum and pig iron.

Economic warfare is a theme in this book. At a time when war is fought on seas and battlefields, the industry that produces war's machinery itself is weaponized. Secret partnerships form between enemy governments. Contracts are leveraged like diplomacy. Stalin's tactic of disguising war preparations as open trade hides the scale and scope of his operations from the outside world—putting Soviet military technology decades ahead of what anyone expects. The holy grail is atomic weapons technology, and KGB spies begin sniffing around the United States for it as early as 1939.

Before the Cold War, the US is fighting a political battle with socialism; its chief concern is keeping communist ideas out of the labor force and government. Once the Cold War begins, the battle becomes moral and ideological—with each side believing the other is evil. Stalin wasn't an evil genius or a demonic force, as some texts portray him, but he did rule with absolute brutality and disregard for human life. In 1941, when asked about his decision to ally with the Soviet Union, which he so deplored, Winston Churchill said, "If Hitler invaded hell, I would at least make a favourable reference of the Devil in the House of Commons." In the United States, the fight against communism took on the tone of a holy crusade to root out evil—mostly as an excuse to crush dissent. Stalin wasn't the devil, but to his allies turned enemies that was what he represented—and it was a part he gladly played.

SOURCES AND METHODS

As an academic, I specialized in Soviet-era Russian literature, so I was primed to take an interest in this story. I first came across the Black cryptologists in 2010 while researching another project. At the time, I was working on a memoir and teaching Russian literature, but the secret operation of Black Americans breaking Russian codes lodged itself in my mind. Whenever I had a break, I researched persistent questions: Who were these people? Where did they learn Russian? What exactly was their mission? I found breadcrumbs here and there—a profile on a university blog, a Wikipedia entry. My encounter with the obscure government study—*The Invisible Cryptologists*—and the lack of information elsewhere made clear how little of their story had been preserved.

Out of curiosity, I started digging through archival photos of Arlington Hall Station, the Agency's wartime headquarters in Virginia. I was struck by the photos' overwhelming whiteness: rows of codebreakers at their desks, groups posing in uniform, women laughing on the softball field—white faces, every one. It unsettled me because these photos looked just like the images I'd seen in stories about World War II—the celebrations, the battles, the victory—only white faces told the story. The presence of Black Americans and the reality of segregation are details the narrative leaves out.

One photo showed a small wartime office with Black codebreakers—fifteen people at their desks, neatly dressed, hardworking, professional. It was the only image that told a different story—and hinted at how much had been left off the official record. Other photos showed Black workers laboring in the Agency's storage facilities, construction sites, and cafeterias. Photos from the 1950s showed a kind of integration: group photos of white people with a single Black face—maybe two—in the crowd. A bus trip to Fort Meade, an officers' luncheon, a Christmas charity committee, an engineer training class, a "Miss NSA" pageant. Sports teams, men's glee club. Some photos exude tension—stiff postures, watchful eyes—while others show camaraderie and ease. The images revealed the careful whitewashing of history. Black codebreakers, mathematicians, and engineers took part in all aspects of Agency life, from major operations to volunteer work and social activities. Erasure often avoids the discomfort of acknowledging racism, but here even positive stories about Black codebreakers had been erased. The photos showed that the lack of representation doesn't reflect history; it reflects the pieces of history that have been selected to tell the official story. What's been labeled, preserved, and published.

Looking through the photos was surprisingly emotional. I know what it feels like to be "the only one" in the frame. In most of my Russian courses from college through graduate school, I was the only person of color in the room. In language and literature classes, in Moscow and the Czech Republic, at conferences and speakers' panels, as a student and as a professor—me in a classroom full of white faces. I remember a workshop for graduate teaching assistants called When You Are the Diversity in the Room. I didn't go. Much like the Black codebreakers, I had plenty of experience in that scenario.

That resonance fueled my desire to recover this story—and the more I searched, the more I saw how much was missing. The National Cryptologic Museum highlights the Agency's Black pioneers, but the profiles were brief, the stories disconnected. Many documents about the Russian plaintext operation were still classified or redacted. Some gaps in the record were simply unexplained—stretches of history never recorded because the people who lived them didn't write the reports.

My background in Russian studies gave me an unusual advantage: I could read the untranslated Soviet messages these workers processed and see, line by line, the kind of intelligence they were pulling out of what looked like noise to everyone else. I now had a window into their day-to-day work and gained a perspective on how much intelligence history still relies on their labor. Poring over histories on the Soviet atomic program, reading Stalin's prewar messages to Kim Il Sung—these sources gave me special insight into the stakes of Black cryptologists' work for US Soviet intelligence. Even with this mine of knowledge, it was still the people that kept me going—their life stories, their spirit, their overlooked brilliance.

Over time, I built a research archive that spans technical manuals, organizational charts, personnel records, oral histories, and much more. The archive became the foundation for this book. But it's not just about what I found. It's about what is still missing, and why that matters.

Intelligence is an insider's world. Most books about it are written by or for the people who lived it—or by those with security clearances and technical backgrounds. I come to the subject differently: as a story-driven researcher with a deep investment in uncovering histories that institutions choose not to preserve.

This book tells the story of postwar intelligence from the inside out. It blends rigorous research with vivid storytelling to bring readers into the secret rooms where these workers toiled. It shows their lighter moments too—where they found joy and friendship despite their exclusion. I've had over a thousand documents—including firsthand accounts from the cryptologists—released from the National Archives or declassified by NSA. I've conducted interviews—both formal and informal—with intelligence professionals and historians. Where the record is silent, I mark that silence and ask what it reveals. Where conjecture is necessary, I label it clearly.

Until now, NSA's 2001 study *The Invisible Cryptologists* has been the best—and really the only—public source of information on this group. Because it was written for a narrow audience, it avoids the story's larger implications and leaves out details that underscore just how complex their work was, and how critical it was to Cold War intelligence. In the two decades since its publication, the Black cryptologists have remained—true to form—almost entirely invisible.

This story sheds light on unknown parts of a story we think we know well. Some readers are encountering this pocket of Cold War history for the first time. Others know the wars, leaders, and movements the book recounts. Still others are cryptology experts from the field's earliest days to the latest in cybersecurity. No expertise is needed to enjoy this book. I've included glossaries to explain technical and historical terms, and I note definitions throughout the book when they are relevant.

Wound through the codebreakers' stories is the story of labor, power, and secrecy—forces that shaped their world and continue to define America as a nation and an ideal. The cost of advancement: the technology they helped create that gradually replaced them.

The cost of being hidden in plain sight.

NOTE ON TERMS

This book requires special terminology because of its subject matter, and a lot of the terms vary and evolve over time. In the 1940s and 1950s, America's racial dynamics are hugely volatile, and there's a lot of terminology associated with American constructions of race. This is a note about the way some of the most common terms—and the offensive ones—are used in the book.

The National Security Agency restructures many times in the course of this story: The country's first intelligence agency was MI8, founded in Washington as part of the Army's Military Intelligence Division during World War I. It was replaced by the Signal Intelligence Service (SIS) in 1930, a new part of the Army Signal Corps staffed by civilians. During World War II, the SIS became the Signal Security Service (SSS) and then the Signal Security Agency (SSA), both of which remained part of the Signal Corps and added military personnel to their staff. A new Cold War configuration, the Army Security Agency (ASA), emerged in 1945, no longer under Signal Corps control. Finally, the Armed Forces Security Agency (AFSA), a joint military operation, spun off from ASA in 1949. AFSA's failure in 1952 led to the creation of the National Security Agency (NSA), an independent civilian organization, as is known today. This history can get confusing, so I call the organization "the Agency," with a capital *A*, throughout most of the book. I note the organizational shifts when they are relevant, especially when the Agency becomes AFSA (pronounced "AF-sa").

Similarly, the Soviet secret police is the NKVD, MVD, and MGB—not the KGB—for most of this story. They encompass both domestic and international surveillance, like the FBI, CIA, and NSA rolled into one. I generally use NKVD and note when that changes to KGB in 1954. I also refer to them broadly as the "Soviet secret police." The Soviets have half a dozen other intelligence services, including one for the Red Army (GRU) and Navy (GRU Naval). They also operate spy rings in the United States, so I refer to them by name when needed.

In literature about the American Intelligence Community, sometimes NSA and CIA are preceded by the definite article "the" but mostly, they're not. I follow suit and refer to NSA and CIA though at times I use "the NSA" or "the CIA."

Abbreviations for different kinds of intelligence appear throughout the book. COMINT stands for "communications intelligence," a general term for the kind of intelligence the Agency collects. SIGINT stands for "signals intelligence," the exploitation of any transmitted communication intercepted from an enemy source. HUMINT stands for "human intelligence," meaning intelligence gained from human sources like spies and informants. OSINT stands for "open source intelligence," or intelligence gleaned from freely available sources like publications. ELINT stands for "electronic intelligence," which becomes more prevalent at the Agency as technology develops in the 1950s. The glossary discusses these terms and more, so readers can get as much or as little information about them as they want.

The women in this book hold positions from cryptanalyst to translator to machine operator to document stamper. The term "cryptologist" encompasses all these roles, meaning someone who works in signals intelligence. Job titles like "cryptographic clerk" can also mean "codebreaker," depending on the work the person does, so I use these terms pretty much interchangeably, except when specified.

The US federal government uses grades and steps for its employees, and I refer to these frequently throughout the book. Grade 1 is the lowest, while 18 is the highest. Grade 5 is the lowest professional grade. A disturbing theme in the book is that even the most highly qualified Black women are stuck between grades 2 and 5 for much of their careers. Each grade has ten steps, which means an employee can get consistent raises based on seniority but unless they're promoted to a higher grade, they might stay a 4 or 5 for most of their careers. Directors and division heads retire between 15 and 18, for context. Before 1949, the federal government uses "Crafts, Protective, and Custodial" (CPC) for service positions like custodian and messenger. "Clerical, Administrative, and Financial" (CAF) denotes clerical roles. So a Black woman codebreaker may be a CAF-3, that is, a cryptographic clerk, grade 3. A Black man usually starts government work as a CPC-3 in one of the labor roles. Codebreakers and analysts are in the Subprofessional "SP" and Professional "P" grades. Junior cryptanalysts may begin at SP-5 or P-1. Top cryptanalysts who aren't management hover around P-5. In 1949, all these abbreviations change to General Schedule "GS," without distinguishing between custodial, clerical, and professional roles.

One of the most important intelligence terms in the book is "plaintext," which means readable, unenciphered language. English, Russian, Japanese—the result of any decoded or decrypted text before translation (in its original language) is plaintext.

Some sources use "plain language" or "language in the clear" to express the same idea. Sometimes "plaintext" is written as one word when used as an adjective and two words ("plain text") when used as a noun, but even that varies. For simplicity's sake, I use the standard one-word term "plaintext" throughout the book to refer to the messages and operation that is Russian.

Racial dynamics are fraught in the 1940s and '50s, and white supremacy guided most American laws and culture at this time. "Negro" and "colored" were neutral terms used to refer to Black Americans. "Nigger" appears often in this book as reported speech.

Most of the time, I don't censor it because people were subjected to this harmful, violent slur regularly. White society used the term to demean and dehumanize Black Americans. It was part of the lynching culture meant to terrorize Black people into silence. In the South among racist white people, this was the most common way people referred to Black people. It even appears in a professional setting. Some Black Americans quoted in the book recall how the word was used against them, and I don't censor their speech.

"Nigger" was mainly a harmful slur at this time, not a term Black people reappropriated or used to self-identify. Though some Black laborers used the term as an identity and class marker beginning in the early nineteenth century, in the era of Black social mobility, whites deployed the word "nigger" to remind Black people of their enslaved past and keep them in their place.

Race terms were used as nouns at this time; "whites" and "blacks" or "a white" and "a black" were common phrases. I generally use the contemporary terms "Black Americans" and "white Americans," or "Black people" and "white people," and maintain current norms for capitalization: "Black" is usually capitalized now while "white" remains lowercase. Some Black people preferred the term "Black" to "Negro" or "colored" during this time; some found "Negro" offensive or inaccurate.

"Afro-American" and "African American" were advocated by intellectuals and activists but not widely used. These terms focused on heritage and national identity rather than race. Skin color was often referenced as a marker of class and privilege among Black people. "Tans" and "Lights" were lighter-skinned people. The "one-drop rule" was a Jim Crow law in the United States that stated even a person with "one drop" of African blood was considered Black. This was important because segregation was legal. Even an "invisible Black" or a white-passing Black person could not use white facilities.

On the other side, many Southern states had "racial integrity laws." They stated that only a "pure white" or "lily white" person could be part of their community. This came into play with restrictive housing covenants and the other social and civic privileges whites enjoyed during segregation.

THE
SECRET
CODE
BREAKERS

1

CHANGE OF PLANS

1941–1942

On a windy fall morning, wrapped in a pressed wool coat and kerchief, sophomore Naomi McElwaine walks five blocks to the bus stop at Twenty-Eighth and Ferry Street to begin her journey from segregated Lafayette to Purdue University's campus across the river. The short three-mile journey is an odyssey. After fighting her way to the back of the city bus, she's jostled through twelve stops before reaching the end of the city line, where she transfers to the West Lafayette bus, 4B, which takes her across the Wabash River to the whites-only college town. As if to deter city folks from crossing the river, the 4B comes by only once an hour. If Naomi is late, even by a minute, she'll have to wait for the next bus or walk thirty minutes across the pedestrian bridge to campus. The bus (or bridge) takes her as far as the student union, but Naomi has another ten-minute walk to get to the northeast corner of campus for her first class—Organic Chemistry. After that, it's back across campus to the southwest corner for Experimental Foods in her home department of Home Economics.

From Naomi's front door to campus is only an eight-minute drive, but the bus trip takes thirty-five minutes or more. This is daily life for Naomi, who is one of the handful of Purdue's Black students. The school is 85 percent male, and the other 15 percent is almost entirely white women, so Naomi is outnumbered on two fronts. These numbers mean that even at such a large school, Naomi's options are limited. Some women at Purdue enroll in the General Science Department, but most find themselves in the Home Economics Department, which offers degrees in Textiles, Design, Industrial Food Management, and Education. Naomi does not want to be a homemaker—she wants a career in science, particularly biology. She chooses Education because like many Black women, Naomi sees teaching as the best career path. She channels her love of science into becoming a high school Biology teacher. The department is still Home Economics, and half of Naomi's coursework is devoted to female-coded tasks like running a household, childrearing, and nursing the elderly. She gets to slice tissue samples and dissect invertebrates, but she must also learn to choose fabrics in a course called Clothing.

Naomi's department isn't the only compromise. For Black women at a predominantly white school, education comes with a cost.

When Naomi steps off the bus, the tree-lined sidewalks meet but do not welcome her. To passersby, she might blend in with the other students—she's inherited her Scottish great-grandmother's light skin tone, slim mouth, and determined jaw. Her rounded features and dark, textured hair mark her as Black to some, but gray eyes and olive skin make her hard to place. Naomi may by white-passing, but in America, she is less-than for being Black. Indiana isn't the Jim Crow South, but it practices segregation. In West Lafayette, Black people cannot eat, live, or work in town. They can study on Purdue's campus, but they cannot step foot in the surrounding city. Signs warn homeowners against renting to anyone who isn't a "pure white Caucasian." This includes students of color, foreign students, and non-Christians of any race. The town has only four Black residents; they are white families' live-in servants.

Purdue doesn't have to segregate, but it does. University policy forbids Black men and women from living on campus, in the residence halls and co-ops that most students call home. Naomi lives with her family. Other Black students have to find housing in Lafayette, which can be expensive.

And exhausting. If they miss the last bus home from campus, they have to walk. Dates, dinners, dances, war bond drives—off-campus students miss these college experiences. Unburdened by the boundaries of race, Purdue's white students live five minutes from their lecture halls, can pop in to grab forgotten notes or textbooks. Sleeping in may cost them a reprimand, but not a grade. They have more time for late-night library and gab sessions—those memories with friends that last a lifetime.

As a local, Naomi is what the university calls a "town girl." Almost three hundred town girls—Black and white—live in Lafayette. They miss the campus social life, but they also have less access to the university's resources. If they can't attend office hours or group study sessions, they don't get extra help. With transportation restrictions, many can't participate in student clubs, and with the town-gown class distinction, on-campus students may avoid townies, even if they happen to attend Purdue.

Instead of scurrying for the bus after classes end, Naomi heads to the union to write scripts with the Scriveners, debate social issues in Religious Council, and share global perspectives in the Cosmopolitan Club. On an unwelcoming campus, the Memorial Union where these clubs meet is her second home—a safe space to eat, work, and socialize in a town that excludes her.

Naomi's insistence on being seen is a family value. At Purdue, Black students exist "on the edge" of student life, but Naomi's folks are serious about making the most of their opportunities. Her mother, Ethel, is a Denver University graduate and educator. Her father, Sterling, is one of Indiana University's first Black graduates and a public scholar. As a school principal, he's taught generations of Black students—including Naomi and her younger brother, Sterling Jr.—about the importance of education. Where there are no opportunities—you make them yourself.

In the Black community education has always been "for the race." As soon as she could read, her parents taught her that education was the best way, the only way, to help her people rise and achieve the success that America affords. Throughout her studies, Naomi has known that her professional life won't just be about forwarding her own goals and interests.

As a Black woman, she's been taught to put her community's needs first even when planning her own future.

But what if there were another option?

Naomi is engaged in world politics because forces that fight injustice, whether in Hitler's camps or in campus housing, don't belong to only one country. Connecting across borders, faiths, and races is the only way to ensure these principles remain intact—in this war and in all the wars to come. It's why she joined the Cosmopolitan Club. On Friday evenings, Naomi must sit on the edge of her chair with the cluster of other pledges eager to trade their whitewashed days for an hour of cultural exchange. A league of nations that learns from one another's differences rather than suppresses them. Naomi loves the club's motto—"Above all nations, humanity"—and the pink and gray ribbons the pledges wear as symbols of the dawn of fulfillment of friendship. They'll be inducted soon, and Naomi makes sure to attend every meeting until the semester's end.

On a frosty November evening, Naomi listens, rapt, as a Turkish student concludes her presentation on the Soviet Union's role in the war: Turkey is neutral, but they have a stake in the Soviets' victory or defeat. Sitting elbow to elbow, the students trade ideas about what happens next. The Nazis have invaded Moscow; the fighting is still overseas. But it is a world war—touching cities and neighborhoods far from Europe's battlefields. Naomi's thoughts must drift to what happens if—or when—America enters the war. What her role might be, and how she can contribute.

After the meeting, a few members stay behind, sparring over some point in the debate. Naomi and her friends—Jane from West Lafayette and Gloria from Mexico City—slip away together, coats in hand, their conversation shifting easily from club business to finals, then to winter break. They're all looking forward to the Cosmo Club's national convention just before Christmas—a festive gathering beyond exams and headlines. It's one of the few places where they can exist side by side: They don't see each other off campus. Only in integrated spaces like the Memorial Union, club meeting rooms, or the cafeteria at lunch.

Bright and familiar, "O Come All Ye Faithful" drifts down from phonograph speakers, echoing off the high ceilings, as the girls make their way to the first floor. The lobby is dressed for the season: fir trees glitter with glass ornaments, and garlands wind around the colonnades—red and blue instead of red and green, a show of patriotism and a harbinger of war.

The girls might linger in the entryway, reluctant to say good night. Here, they're just three young women conspiring under the twinkling lights.

When they step into the night, the spell breaks. Jane crosses the street on foot. Her house is nearby; no need to check the bus schedule.

Gloria turns back toward the hill, her path lit by rows of windows in dormitories Naomi is not allowed to enter. When Gloria returns, South Hall II will be warm and full of activity, with lights glowing in the common room until curfew.

Naomi heads for the bus stop, just in time to catch the 4B. On the bumpy ride home, she might stare out the window as the campus recedes, questions lingering in her mind about what comes next. There's change in the air—a buzz between fear and excitement on campus. War correspondents speak to packed auditoriums. Male students debate compulsory military training. The university opens high school correspondence courses in math and science—training the engineers of tomorrow. The United States isn't in the war yet, but the war is on everyone's minds.

At the kitchen table, long after everyone else has gone to bed, Naomi might run through her four-year plan again and again—flip through the course catalog, swap out electives, rearrange requirements. She hasn't settled on a new plan yet, but she knows the old one may not survive.

BREAKING GROUND

In the frenzied months after Germany invades Russia, Washington, DC, becomes a war machine. Offices flood with military personnel, and the

War Department scrambles to keep up. The solution is to ramp up the already mammoth construction effort of federal buildings. They need the world's biggest office building—and they need it fast. Within days, blueprints are drafted for what becomes the Pentagon: a five-sided colossus designed to house the growing army of bureaucrats needed to wage global war.

Construction kicks off on September 11, 1941, just across the Potomac River in Arlington, Virginia. The site, mostly flat and farmland, looks ideal, but it isn't empty. It's home to Black families, churches, and communities that have lived there for generations. Among them is Queen City, a tight-knit Black neighborhood established by the US government as Freedman's Village at the end of the Civil War. Located next to Robert E. Lee's family plantation, Freedman's Village was meant to be a symbol of freedom and protection for the families who resided there.

Queen City residents own their homes, raise families, and have jobs nearby. It isn't paradise. Independence for Black communities comes at a price. Arlington County refuses to provide plumbing, running water, sidewalks, streetlights, or electricity, but schools, churches, gathering places, and employment make the town a safe and relatively comfortable place to live. The Pentagon changes that.

With little to no warning, hundreds of residents are forced out. The new construction gobbles up land, paying people pennies on the dollar, leveling their homes, and forcing them into shanty towns. These thrown-together Army trailers the government provides are reeking cesspools, no running water, no plumbing. Children live there. Men, women, the elderly. They can get sick from these conditions. The government doesn't care. They were in the way, and now they're not. That's all that matters.

Queen City is razed to make way for the Pentagon's parking lots. At a time when Black Americans are fighting for basic rights at home, the federal government destroys one of their few footholds of property and security in the name of national defense.

In the meantime, the behemoth rises—6.5 million square feet of office space, five concentric rings, and more than seventeen miles of corridors. To manage the labor shortage caused by the war, the government employs thousands of workers, including Black laborers, who are paid less and assigned the dirtiest, most dangerous jobs. Segregation is in full force: Black workers use separate facilities, and even when the building opens, it initially follows Jim Crow codes, with separate bathrooms, cafeterias, and seating areas. Hearing of this, President Franklin D. Roosevelt signs Executive Order 8802 demanding nondiscrimination in federal buildings. The Pentagon stops segregating, but the rest of the military doesn't. The order helps Black employees, but it doesn't change the loss of Queen City. To the government, it's all just procedure:

> Condemnation proceedings affected as many as 150 homes and a number of small commercial tracts in the path of roads and approaches . . . Families required to move from their homes on very short notice were offered the use of nearby trailers for a reasonable period of time at no cost to them.

The official report doesn't tell the whole story. A Black resident recounts:

> Where the Pentagon building is, there used to be a Hot Shoppe and an airfield. There was a "colored" area right there called Queen City. The Pentagon took all the property these people had. Then they built houses for the people that they had thrown out. This is when I saw the first low-income housing—right off Columbia Pike, near Arlington—right near the Navy Department. It was called Johnson Hill. The people had to have some place to live, however, some of these buildings were like shanties, and they had cesspools, no plumbing. But it was their homes. You can't pay somebody $200 or $250 for a house and replace it for that kind of money, but that's what the government did. Just like they did in Southwest [District of Columbia]. Many of those houses in Southwest had no plumbing. They had a big truck to come around and pick up the sewage from

the houses in big buckets. They used to call it the "honey wagon," and you could smell it for blocks.

The United States isn't in the war yet, but they are fighting an enemy at home. Two-faced agents that loiter in offices and classrooms. That infiltrate factories and consulates, rallies and bake sales. Saboteurs of democracy known as the Nazi "fifth column." Rampant in Europe and gaining ground in America, the Axis spies are clearing the way for a stateside Nazi attack.

No one's sure if the threat is real. The fifth column witch-hunter is Congressman Martin Dies, who leads the House Un-American Activities Committee (HUAC). Dies is fighting a holy war to root out enemy agents in New York, Chicago, Los Angeles—all hubs of espionage, he claims. In laboratories and labor unions across the country, Dies believes "foreign subversive elements" are undermining the defense industry.

HUAC unmasks pro-fascists in white supremacist groups like the Ku Klux Klan, the Silver Legion, and the Knights of Camellia, but most of the time, their evidence is flimsy—circumstantial at best, at worst fabricated. President Roosevelt, the Justice Department, and the FBI see Dies as a sideshow, but others say the threat is real; the fifth column is out there, breeding its Trojan Horses and strengthening Nazi support. Hitler's invaded the Soviet Union—the United States could be next.

The fifth column may indeed be real, but it's not the greatest threat. America's new ally, the Soviet Union, does not believe its partner can be trusted. Since the 1920s, they've had spy rings throughout the US, based in their New York import-export company, Amtorg (the American Trading Corporation). From its headquarters in Manhattan, Amtorg does business with major companies like Ford Motors and General Electric. The United States buys Russian furs and caviar, and the Russians buy industrial components, cars, machinery. Under the Lend-Lease Act, the US supplies the Soviets with more than a billion dollars in tires, locomotives, food, boots, cotton, steel, aluminum, explosives, 400,000 trucks, 12,000 armored vehicles, 7,000 planes—everything the Red Army needs to win a war. As bombs whistle toward Leningrad, NKVD spies fan out across

America, looking for Stalin's holy grail—plans for America's atomic bomb. Research is ramping up: American chemists have discovered plutonium, and physicist Robert Oppenheimer is making waves at Berkeley. Amtorg's engineers enter industrial research and production facilities. Scientists-turned-agents plant themselves in the Manhattan Project. Couriers pose as low-level bureaucrats, ready to pass information when needed. The FBI investigates leads, but they always come up short. The US needs a bigger intelligence agency to combat the Soviet threat.

PEARL HARBOR

On December 7, 1941, Naomi's breath rises in a vapor cloud as she and her family filter out of the morning service at Second AME Baptist Church. The devil finds work for idle hands, her father likes to say, so like every other day, Naomi's Sunday schedule is packed. From here, she'll go to the Lincoln School to teach 4-H Club youngsters how to can pears and sweet potatoes. After lunch, she'll help her mom make toffee and gingerbread for the Mary L. Service Club's Christmas fundraiser. The Scriveners have an important meeting tonight. An announcement at the last meeting requested that all officers be present, and there was another reminder in the *Exponent* this morning. They might be announcing the contest winners. Naomi doesn't want to miss it.

As the McElwaines pile into the car, Naomi might ask her dad to let her drive to the meeting that evening—she doesn't want to endure the bus ride, not in this cold, not on a weekend. Sterling isn't easygoing—his word is law. His pupils—and his children—fear him. But a gruff "maybe" lets Naomi know the answer is "yes."

The meeting doesn't happen.

Around 2 p.m., as the warmth of cinnamon and nutmeg fills the kitchen, Sterling walks in, looking grave. Naomi turns, wiping her hands on her apron; her mother half turns, still stirring a bubbling pot of caramel. Sterling Jr. tiptoes in and peers around his father. At thirteen, he's old enough to know something is wrong.

Less than an hour ago, in a surprise attack, more than three hundred Japanese planes bombed a US naval base off the coast of Oahu. Diplomats from Tokyo have flown to Washington, but the situation is beyond diplomacy. Japan has cast the die, and President Roosevelt and Congress are ready to declare war. All military personnel must report to work tomorrow in uniform.

Naomi might not notice the eye-watering smoke from the sugar burning on the stove until Ethel pushes open a window to let in a rush of cold air.

That's it.

America is at war.

Over break, Purdue becomes a military base camp. The university shaves months off its academic calendar, launching a "speed-up" program that pushes students toward their degrees in under three years. Classrooms once filled with Shakespeare and French conversation now teach military readiness. The civil engineering department drills students in topographical surveys and engineering astronomy. Chemistry veers into weapons research; mechanical and aeronautical engineering merge courses on airplane design and thermodynamics. Hundreds of Army and Navy men flood engineering labs and chemistry classrooms for special training in technical fields. Sailors train as naval electricians, ensigns become diesel engine experts. Cadets take flying classes at the university's airport, which is already home to the Boilermaker Flying Squadron. In their huge goggles and rubber aprons, servicemen bound for ammunitions plants learn to handle powder and explosives. The Signal Corps recruits radar technicians to locate enemy aircraft. Every department of the US Armed Forces sets up shop on campus like barkers on a fairground.

The War Department itself quietly moves into the library, away from the crowded labs and swelling lecture halls. They call it the Information Center—a data collection project—but they are also looking for recruits. Under the direction of the head librarian, the center checks in with faculty and staff, writes down names, takes notes.

While Naomi's head might be spinning, she is ready. She completed her training as a Red Cross Gray Lady in October. In her white peaked cap and long gray veil, she will assist the nurses in greater Lafayette's "colored" wards and hospitals. Here, soldiers won't be coming in with battle wounds—they'll be coughing, feverish, barely able to sit up. The flu epidemic is ripping through barracks like Hitler's buzz saw. A physiology student, she knows what fever looks like, how skin turns cold and clammy when the body starts to fail. Wringing out old compresses, filling syringes, preparing trays of medicine, helping nurses change vomit-covered or sweat-soaked sheets—all of this is well within her reach.

Naomi is one of only four Black women who have their veils, but more are on their way. Women throughout Lafayette—not just students—take on these roles. The Red Cross doesn't allow Black people to donate blood, but that doesn't stop Naomi from giving the war effort her all. She can see past race even if the country's largest volunteer organization cannot.

Black soldiers won't just be coming into hospitals—they'll be housed at Cary Hall. The nation's needs—and a federal mandate—overshadow the cries of West Lafayette's racists who protest having Black people (who aren't servants) live in their city for the first time. Along with white cadets and ensigns, Black men and women will train as mechanics.

While Purdue women scramble to enroll in first aid training and bandage rolling sessions, Naomi takes a breath. The war is a crisis but not a surprise. Now her wheels are turning again: A change of plans is no longer just a possibility—it's her reality. The only question is in which new direction she'll go.

In the melee, Naomi doesn't forget the Cosmo Club's national convention. As if the flurry on campus weren't enough, ten thousand students from across the country descend on Purdue to address the theme of humanity and democracy—the aims of cosmopolitanism. The three-day event features the usual dancing, banquets, meetings, and assemblies, but this time, the goal is to establish guidelines for foreign and American student interaction. The club includes white, Black, and Japanese Americans. Germans, Argentinians, and Chinese. Some of these groups are "enemies," and as the war deepens, the spirit of global citizenship might not withstand the pull of nationalism—or propaganda. No one knows what the next four, five, or six years will bring.

Naomi is committed to her values as ever. Reunited with Gloria and Jane, local problems feel suddenly small against the drama of the world stage. As eager visitors fill the union, Naomi and her friends take in the cultural rooms, each decorated to display a different country's traditions. The food and festivity belie tensions roiling beneath the surface. The business meetings are somber, the elections subdued. Something remains unspoken—a question, maybe, about what will happen to the spirit of fraternity when the convention ends. The war can't wait, but for the next few days, Naomi wants to enjoy what might be the club's last celebration of unity.

ARLINGTON HALL STATION

Purdue isn't the only campus transforming for wartime. Far across the country, in the oak groves of Northern Virginia, Arlington Hall Junior College for Women is feeling the post-Depression squeeze. An exclusive boarding school, Arlington Hall recovered from bankruptcy but has struggled to stay afloat. The one-hundred-acre campus houses three hundred daughters of DC's elite who study liberal arts, math, and science if they are college bound; home economics, clerical studies, and the arts if not. The ladies swim, play tennis, golf, learn archery, and most of all—ride. Ribbons, trophies, and photographs of the school's equestrian stars— horses and riders—line the colonial hall's display cases.

The setting is bucolic. A network of bridle paths flow past the riding arena and gymnasium. Willow groves, gardens, and manicured lawns give a fairy-tale feel; irises and peonies line flagstone paths, rustic bridges cross meadow streams, and visitors are greeted by a circular pool and fountain. Four sheer stories of yellow brick and a central colonnade whisper of grand plantations. Black housemen serve and clean—Black gardeners maintain the grounds. Black handymen repair. While the first Black servicemen and women cautiously enter Purdue's residence halls for training,

Arlington Hall prepares to welcome a new set of tenants much like its last: hundreds of young white women and a Black support staff that stays out of sight.

Before the United States enters the war, its codebreakers are a clique of analysts working out of the Munitions Building in Washington, DC. They are the Signal Intelligence Service, a branch of the Army Signal Corps and successor to the World War I codebreaking operation, Military Intelligence Section 8 (MI8). Better known as the Black Chamber. The government shut that program down in 1929, finding its practice of snooping through private correspondence a bridge too far. With that, the Black Chamber was dissolved.

That kind of attitude doesn't win wars, and the Signal Corps brings in codebreaking heavyweight William Friedman to lead a new SIGINT operation. Through the 1930s, Friedman and three junior cryptanalysts work on breaking Russian codes with limited success. Its other code-breaking operations fare better. Nearby, the Navy works Japanese naval codes in its own cryptanalytic outfit, OP-20-G. Army-Navy rivalry prevents cooperation, but it doesn't matter: By mid-1940, Friedman's team has broken "Purple," the Japanese crypto machine, and the resulting messages—called "Magic"—reveal Japan's strategic war plans.

Codebreaking needs are growing fast. The Signal Intelligence Service decides to leave its cramped quarters in DC in search of a larger, more secluded headquarters—close to the action in Washington, but remote enough to disappear behind barbed wire.

Arlington Hall blooms in April, with young women on horseback and flowers nestled amid the green. A party of Signal Corps officers chances upon this spectacle when they turn down the lush drive on their way back from scouting other sites. They quickly agree—this is the place. By June, the students and horses are gone, leaving the service staff and the school's property—furniture, office, and kitchen equipment—which the government adds to the sale. Within days, the Supply Unit—fifty men strong—descends on the campus.

Their first order of business is plumbing.

Arlington Hall's students lived in small two-bedroom suites with shared bathrooms, but a growing workforce of five hundred men and women need better accommodations. Even now, 1,500 enlisted men ready for their transfers complete cryptanalysis correspondence coursework. Turning to a new hiring pool—white civilian women—the Army recruits schoolteachers from small Southern towns, commuter schools, and farms. The Navy's marked the Seven Sisters as its turf, and it easily scouts standouts from Wellesley and Radcliffe, holding secret codebreaking courses on college campuses. The University of Illinois, just a stone's throw from Purdue, sets up the first full program in cryptology, and Signal Corps officers swarm to reel in recruits. As the top brass moves into its new headquarters, plans to expand Arlington Hall's campus are already underway.

These aren't the only bathrooms that need building. The men in the Supply Unit are Black; they can't use Arlington Hall's facilities. A gymnasium with an indoor swimming pool, three faculty housing units, a boiler house, and a power plant are the other buildings on campus. There's even an old log cabin called the Tea House, which the school tears down before its new owners move in.

The Agency puts the Supply Unit in the riding arena—the horse training ring with a dirt floor and stables. It may be a showplace for horses, but it is no place for men. While the laborers and Supply Unit sweep, paint, stock, and lift to convert Arlington Hall Junior College into Arlington Hall Station, they must lay a concrete floor, build offices, and install bathrooms in the riding hall. They can work—but not eat—in the cafeteria. There's no running water. Until their bathrooms are complete, they must use the outdoors for nature's calls.

By executive order, the defense industry may not discriminate against employees. Even if a federal defense agency builds facilities in a segregated area, like Arlington, Virginia, they are not bound by local law. The Pentagon is also in Arlington, and they follow the nondiscrimination policy. The Agency's leaders, William Friedman, Solomon Kullback, and

Abraham Sinkov, are civilians—linguists, academics, and mathematicians. They have no stake in upholding America's racial hierarchy—but they're not in charge anymore. A new generation of Army men—Southern men—lead the Agency. Their hierarchy is strict—in rank and in race. Without question, they maintain Virginia's status quo.

Jim Crow.

WHITE CADETTES, BLACK ROSIES

Women like Naomi are just the sort the Agency wants to hire—educated, creative, science-minded—but the Agency doesn't consider Black Americans for any but the most menial roles. Necessity forces the Agency to hunt for white female codebreakers; as the war wears on, they have to pull from yet another talent pool. Naomi is entering her junior year, still focused on her clubs and coursework. She wants to fight on the home front, but she won't drop everything and head to Washington, as tempting as that may be.

The women leaving their enclaves for Arlington Hall have a new mission: "Free a man to fight" now means taking on technical—not just physical—work. The war has plunged women into factories and shipyards, but now they are entering deeper waters. In addition to filling the Army's codebreaking offices, they are moving into the engineering shops and laboratories once reserved for men.

At Purdue, these new recruits are "engineering cadettes"—young women enrolled in the first training programs of their kind. Aircraft giant Curtiss-Wright and radio manufacturer RCA will hire women from across the country to train as engineering assistants. Announcements stress that these women won't replace male engineers—they'll "assist with details that take much of the engineer's time." The companies still expect men to take the lead, but women have proved they can do more than line work.

For ten months, nearly two hundred cadettes will live in the Women's Residence Halls, don flannels, and take crash courses in mathematics, electronics, aerodynamics, and structural analysis. They'll draft blueprints, calibrate instruments, and operate the iron leviathans in Michael Golden Labs. They'll enter as coeds and emerge to guide production as drafters, inspectors, computers, and technicians. The cadettes can make or break the war: Curtiss-Wright's Helldiver can't make it off the runway, and RCA has more military contracts than it can handle. Male engineers are shipping out in droves, and without fully staffed departments, production could halt.

Curtiss-Wright is in danger of going under, but RCA has the opposite problem: The Army, the Navy, and the Allies have laundry lists of radio electronics they need ASAP. At the same time that RCA is recruiting cadettes, it's growing its production workforce. RCA's manufacturing arm—the Victor Division—has factories across Indiana that churn out hit records and the latest broadcasting equipment. Now they've stopped pressing vinyl and started building transmitters, receivers, and radar equipment. RCA may be recruiting cadettes, but like many companies, they believe women are best suited to repetitive line work, their smaller hands more adept at the delicate surgery of crafting cathodes and wiring transistors. These roles require intricacy and precision, but RCA doesn't advertise for them at Purdue: The jobs don't require a college degree, and even two years of satisfactory coursework qualify coeds to become cadettes. As the local hiring pool runs dry, RCA begins hiring Black women to fill these roles, but they're not always welcome. At some plants, white workers walk off the line when they arrive; often, they're treated like the help.

Interviews for the cadette programs begin in April 1943 and women flock to campus from plants and universities across the country. The corridors buzz—not with professional respect but barely concealed amusement. Newspaper articles frame the cadettes as a visiting sorority, not engineers in training.

In the spring of her junior year, Naomi has dashed through most of the science, psychology, and education courses she needs to earn her speed-up degree. She could graduate in August, but she decides to get some real-world experience before finishing her degree. She's a strong candidate for the cadette training program, but as always, there is a catch. Even when gender isn't a barrier, race is. White women are tolerated in the engineers' boys' club, but Black and Jewish women don't make it past the door. In a crowd huddled around the job post boards in the union, Naomi might overhear that Curtiss-Wright rejected a Jewish applicant in favor of her blond friend. She was just tagging along, someone may whisper. The blond girl didn't know she was being interviewed until the recruiter handed her the contract.

Maybe Naomi applies for the program, or maybe she doesn't. But as scores of hopeful coeds delight and confuse Purdue's young men, Naomi stops by the Registrar's Office, withdraws from her studies, and steps onto the production line at RCA. Before she goes, she gives a talk on India's caste system for the International Relations Club.

As an electronics assembler, Naomi makes wiring harnesses at the Victor Division's factory in Indianapolis. While the cadettes play softball and sweat over thermodynamics, Naomi stands on the line for eight hours a day bundling cables with a needle and waxed twine. She must tune out the parade marches booming over the loudspeakers, the roar of propeller-size industrial fans. She might sigh on her way to the cafeteria as she passes banners and signs bearing the slogans Don't Be a Bottleneck! and Beat Your Promise! RCA's pledged to overfulfill its war contract quotas, and it's the Rosies' job to make that happen. Days and nights of cramped hands and sore feet don't deter Naomi or the other Black Rosies—RCA's "soldiers of production"—from meeting the challenge.

RCA is one of the few plants that freely hires Black women. Mary McLeod Bethune, the only Black woman on the president's Black advisory committee, founded the National Council of Negro Women to advocate for fair wartime practices in hiring, housing, and crafting policy. Along with the National Non-Partisan Council of Public Affairs—the federal lobbying arm of the Black sorority Alpha Kappa Alpha—the National Council of Negro Women advocates to end discrimination in defense plants and force compliance with the president's executive order banning nondiscrimination.

Even when their lobbying efforts work, white workers don't always comply. At nearby Allison, the engine manufacturer, white workers walk off the line when Black hires arrive. At Western Electric in Baltimore, twenty-two white women strike when Black women enter their department. They believe the Black women carry venereal disease and refuse to return until management builds a separate "colored" bathroom.

Rosie the Riveter, Wendy the Welder, Uncle Sam's Nieces, Government Girls—all the wartime mascots of female empowerment are white. From Norman Rockwell's Rosie in smudged coveralls to the "We Can Do It!" Rosie in a polka dot kerchief flexing her slim bicep. Brochures and film reels celebrate the white Rosies, who trade skirts for pants to the horror of their families, and proudly step onto the production line. Young, smiling, and determined, they symbolize patriotism and progress. The six hundred thousand Black women who work alongside them are rarely acknowledged.

In response, Black women fund their own campaigns: *The Aframerican Women's Journal* publishes its Summer 1943 issue with a cover illustration featuring three smartly dressed Black women war workers. The issue, subtitled "The Negro Woman Serves America," features stories about Black women's contributions to the war effort. These publications encourage Black women to join in the war effort as volunteers, factory workers, and service women, to show they're just as patriotic as any other American, even against staggering odds. Dr. Dorothy I. Height, a member of the National Council of Negro Women, recalls the segregation in Washington, DC: "It was so segregated that you felt like you were in a foreign country." The premier Black newspaper, *The Pittsburgh Courier*, coins a slogan for Black Americans, who are fighting two wars: the "Double V"—victory against fascism abroad and racism at home. Black women are really fighting for the "Triple V"—against fascism, racism, and sexism—a fight with too few allies.

Naomi may or may not endure prejudice at RCA, but all over the country, Black women who join in the war effort experience harassment and violence for their patriotism. College women like Naomi are often light-skinned, a trait that makes white people accept them more easily, and they have some level of economic privilege. Most Black women who join the wartime workforce do not. Ninety-eight percent of Black women work as maids, cooks, and sharecroppers; they care for their employers' white children alongside their own, and they do not finish high school.

When these women arrive on the job, white Americans refuse to see them as equals. "Colored women don't get the first jobs or the best jobs." They operate "dangerous machinery in dangerous working conditions around predatory bosses." They don't return that hate, but living and working in these conditions isn't easy. Birdia Whitfield Bush, a house-keeper turned allowances and allotments clerk in the War Department, says, "I never would not teach my daughter to hate anyone. If I hated some-one, I certainly wouldn't have them cooking for me. You know, they could poison you." One live-in maid says, "All my life I've followed rules, and when they call you a nigger, boy, that hurts. You do want to fight." One by one, their brothers and cousins go off to fight, knowing the military is seg-regated. Marian Elean Todd-Reid, a sharecropper from North Carolina, says, "It was a sad time for my family, but I decided I wouldn't let myself cry for anything. I was going to be strong and brave."

In engravers' offices and munitions factories, Black women suffer harm from chemical toxicity. In government offices, they type, file, and distribute documents, but unlike their white counterparts, they don't get breaks or promotions. Some supervisors don't give Black women real work, forcing them to type the same manual again and again. Black Rosies tow the freight of sexual and racial intimidation. Willie Mae Govan, a maid turned gunpowder processor at DuPont from Alabama, feels like America belongs to her too—but her bosses don't. "We were niggers. And we [were] treated like a nigger . . . But I just didn't have sense enough to be a nigger." She pauses as if there's a story she wants to tell but thinks better of it. "They were cruel to us," she sums up. "We were people."

Battle-scarred Black Rosies don't give up on the Double—or the

Triple—V. They plant Victory Gardens, buy ration books and war bonds, join carpools, dance with soldiers at the USO. Like Naomi, Birdia, Marian, and Willie Mae, they roll up their sleeves, and step onto the assembly lines. They volunteer to support their country. Many get their first paychecks, open bank accounts, and find new independence as breadwinners. Some remain in their work and become supervisors, others return to school to finish their education. They make futures for themselves and their families—and prove America doesn't belong to the white hoods and little Hitlers.

Black Rosies rewrite the rules.

2

TRADE SECRETS

1943–JUNE 1944

Across the Atlantic, the British are fast at work breaking the German Enigma. At Bletchley Park, a country estate in Buckinghamshire, the Government Code and Cypher School (GCCS) is cracking Axis messages almost faster than they come in. Despite the frenzy, they keep calm: Bletchley Park's operation is shaped by military urgency and centuries of spycraft.

Behind the manor and tennis courts, rows of wooden buildings—known as huts—house hives of codebreaking teams. From the outside, they look like modest shacks. Inside, mathematicians, linguists, bankers, and crossword prodigies turned codebreakers race against the clock. They have different roles but work in synchrony. Hut 1 is packed with radio equipment. Hut 3 translates Enigma's Army and Air Force decrypts. Hut 11 builds Bombes, and in Hut 8, Alan Turing demolishes German U-boat codes—the Naval Enigma. Hut 2 serves tea and sandwiches, and Hut 14's communications hub keeps everyone connected. Jean Nissan recalls learning traffic analysis by osmosis. "By working in Hut 4 you just picked up what was going on."

Nearby the huts stand the "blocks," plain operations buildings, like the ones going up at Arlington Hall. The buildings have the same footprint, but that's where the similarities end.

The British run this show as civilians. GCCS reports to the Foreign Office, not the War Office. The codebreakers are mostly women in uniform, but there are no barked orders here. Just brilliant, eccentric, efficient people trusted to do the job. Collaboration happens on and off the clock—over tea and under fire. Codebreaking here is a less regimented operation, more high-stakes salon.

And it works.

The United States has a wartime spy service, but it stays far away from the codebreakers. British intelligence runs on integration. Signals and human intelligence feed each other. MI6, the Foreign Office, and Bletchley stay in constant contact. No data point is too small: a weather report, a trade deal, a vague diplomatic cable—everything is a lead. There's no rigid line between high and low—all sources matter. All information has value.

Meanwhile, Arlington Hall is finding its footing. The Army's increasing military management of its civilian-run program without a plan of attack. In the absence of method, they fall back on what they know: rank, chain of command, and rigid divisions of labor. At the moment they should be innovating, they fall back on tradition—inertia. Everyone does their job—decrypt, decode, translate, publish—and nothing more.

Cracks in the operation show when Arlington Hall puts twenty young codebreakers on Japan's secondary diplomatic system, J20. Bletchley Park has two elderly civil servants—"Practically palsied," by one account—doing the same work, and they get results faster. Why? Communication. Their analysts talk to their spies, who talk to their diplomats, who feed the results to Berkley Street and back to the analysts. Reports circulate to all departments. Everyone gets input and feedback. The Americans keep their departments siloed—each operation reinvents the wheel.

Instead of working with the spy service, Arlington Hall fights with it for resources. The Office of Strategic Services (OSS) is the United States' newly formed human intelligence service. They're not the only ones elbowing their way to Uncle Sam's bank vault. Every agency in Washington has a stake in the intelligence boom. The Pentagon's a shark tank, and Arlington Hall is the smallest fish. Instead of cooperating, everyone's angling for control.

The British skip the fight and steal the win. When MI6 needs a Spanish diplomatic key, they don't grind through a onetime pad—they just lift it out of a diplomat's pouch. Communications intelligence (COMINT) and human intelligence (HUMINT) work together. That kind of coordination saves weeks. It lets Bletchley tackle the toughest ciphers with speed while Arlington Hall argues over who does what.

When US Army intelligence finally sees its first decrypts from Arlington Hall, they're shocked—in a bad way. The messages are translated, but no one's even tried to analyze them. They expected intelligence. They got raw data. At this point, Arlington Hall has no authority. No prestige in intelligence gathering at home or abroad.

No idea how to take the data a step further.

They need a crash course, and the solution is simple: Send a delegation to London. Officially, it's a liaison. Unofficially, it's study abroad. The Americans need to see how the pros do it. Arlington Hall has talent—they have machines—but no system.

ALDFORD HOUSE

In Mayfair, a flat overlooking Hyde Park houses Britain's Commercial and Diplomatic Section, the codebreaking team that tracks embassies and trade. Like Berkley Street, the operation is named after its address: Aldford House, the fashionable mansion block on Park Lane that conceals Berkley Street's outpost.

The British break codes in style. The Commercial Code Section's flat is a seven-room expanse with enough workspace to fit fifty codebreakers and typists. When the ladies need a break, they can take a brisk walk to Marble Arch or step out onto the balcony and admire the greenery.

Jean Nissan, a twenty-two-year-old analyst who works in the "flying squad"—a trio of codebreaking troubleshooters—moves to Aldford

House to help out on some sticky Italian codes. It's 1943, and one night, she takes a break on that balcony, only to see the flash of anti-aircraft gunfire rise out of Hyde Park. The quaint attraction Speakers' Corner is a defense base for German air raids. In London, even codebreakers on the home front are on the front lines. With stakes this high, they know to make every piece of intelligence count.

Soon, a young American officer visits. He's not a tourist; Brigadier Telford Taylor is the US Army's Special Intelligence liaison in London, Arlington Hall's man on the inside to scope out the British operation. Taylor's mission is twofold: first, to discover intelligence the British are getting that the Americans aren't; and second, to spy on the Navy, who are already ensconced at Bletchley. Taylor is not an ordinary officer. A Harvard law grad, before the war he was general counsel for the FCC (Federal Communications Commission), a senior post not often given to a thirty-two-year-old.

Arlington Hall chose Taylor because he is that rare type of American who can blend well with Britain's cultural elite. He can hobnob with Bletchley Park's Oxbridge academics, his "powerful intellect" tempered by an easygoing manner. He's "sensitive and curious," looks younger than his age, and delights worn-out colleagues with impromptu concerts, flaunting his skill as a classical pianist. In short, Telford Taylor can get any HUMINT and SIGINT that information-starved Arlington Hall needs to flesh out its operation and gain crucial Axis intelligence.

From his arrival in April 1943, Taylor sends endless reports to the Agency, beginning with his post in the Commercial and Diplomatic Section. When he gets to Aldford House, he's stunned by the robust operation. The United States has diplomatic intelligence, but commercial intelligence is a new frontier.

Taylor may have expected a sleepy office, but the section moves more like a trading floor. Everywhere he turns, clerks, translators, and typists scramble in controlled chaos, producing a stream of intelligence that Arlington Hall can only dream of.

Sheaves of intercept pour in from Bletchley Park and Berkley

Street—sixty thousand daily. Clerks clear the baskets as quickly as they fill, passing the slips to language specialists, who sort them with practiced speed, deciding what to translate and what to set aside. Even the discards aren't wasted: They're summarized in a different series, seeds for intelligence that might be revealed months later. Translations move to the scriveners, clerks whose sharp pencils catch errors, mark urgent phrases. They batch these messages in the Confidential Series, slip them into folders bound for senior hands. The French and German desks each generate hundreds of reports before nightfall, their typists' keys clattering in relentless rhythm. Alongside them, cryptanalysts grind away at Italian, Portuguese, and even Tibetan trade codes. By now, Jean might be pale with fatigue, leaning over her Italian notes, looking for repetitions in the ciphers that others missed. Taylor watches the unit work, struck by how nothing seems too small, too obscure, to be pressed into meaning.

The trust between branches is absolute, and the Commercial Code Section is wired into the Ministry of Economic Warfare at every level. The section receives a constant flow of reports—weekly digests of global developments, daily shipping indexes, long-term special studies on contraband and relief, even Far Eastern summaries charting broadcasts and trade. Taylor stops trying to count the series; there are far too many. What strikes him is their integration: Each report feeds into the next, forming a complete picture of the enemy's economic life.

The British understand the commercial codes' unique value. They may be readily available and easy to break, but they're legally binding. They define shipment details in such precise terms that, written out, would take several sentences to describe—and manufacturers are held to their terms. The section translates this commercial jargon into plain English, so Berkley Street knows how much oil Italy is buying from Romania, how much mohair they're shipping to Turkey. The section tracks suspect German contraband deals like blips on a radar screen.

At the top, the supervisor sifts through the translations, correcting trade jargon and cross-referencing with other intercepts. By the time the packets leave Aldford House, they are polished intelligence reports—the

"Comm Series"—circulated to the Foreign Office, the prime minister, and other war ministries. The scale is staggering: ten thousand reports a year, each one processed at lightning speed.

Amid this whirlwind, Taylor notes a surprising trend: The Allies have restricted the use of codebooks, and some markets may have to abandon their codes altogether. As the war goes on, Aldford House gets more and more messages in plaintext—and the number steadily rises. Soon, only one in seven thousand messages received is in code.

As Jean and her team plug away at the Italian codes, her supervisor, whom Jean describes as a "wizened old spinster," gets an idea. The Americans have "machines." Jean hasn't seen them—no one knows what they look like—but she does know they speed up codebreaking. Right now, they need help with Hungarian codes.

As soon as Taylor leaves the room, Jean's supervisor looks at her slyly.

"You know, if you offered to sleep with him, I am sure he would let us use their machines!"

Jean is a patriot, and Taylor is charming—but the request is beyond the call of duty.

Jean tells her supervisor the work is almost finished—they don't need the Americans' machines. Besides, both Jean and Taylor are married. Despite what might have been, this particular US-British liaison doesn't happen.

"A SUBSTANTIAL OPERATION OF OUR OWN"

Before Taylor heads to Bletchley Park for the next phase of his assignment, he sends two long telegrams to Arlington Hall about Aldford House. He's read thirty Comm Series reports a day—nearly five hundred altogether. Each contains five hundred translations, mostly from Japanese, Portuguese, German, Spanish, and Swiss, but also from Italian, French, and Turkish. Persian. South American. Bulgarian. So many languages, it's alarming.

The United States needs British commercial intelligence because it needs to evaluate the same information, especially from the German buying corporation, Hisrowak, in Berlin to its counterpart, Sofindus, in Spain. Why? Because Sofindus-Hisrowak is busting the British blockade of Germany's foreign trade, affecting the Americans' Lend-Lease deal with Britain. The Hong Kong–based Melchers and Co. is stocking Japan and Manchuria with raw materials, and many Axis trading groups in Mexico and South America are using a handful of variations on the *Rudolph Mosse* codebook. The US Coast Guard has picked up some of the Mosse traffic, but there's so much more. Taylor reports the British have all of it.

Thanks to Jean and her team, the British have broken the Italian trade cipher used between Rome and Lisbon and another used by Mussolini's commercial attaché, Romolo Angelone. They've discovered that the Japanese are enciphering JIG trade messages, helping them uncover Japanese shipping routes. Spanish naval attaché messages between Berlin and Madrid prove that Hitler is supplying the Spanish Navy.

The United States needs all this intelligence—but they have no one to read it, let alone produce it. A liaison operation won't work; even the resourceful Taylor can't summarize these reports. "It seems to me," he concludes,

> either we must rely on the British and accept their intelligence based on this mass of material, or else we must start a very substantial operation of our own. It would be impossible for us to process or digest this material even with several assistants. Maybe twenty.

With Normandy looming and the Pacific war gathering steam, commercial codes are barely on the American intelligence radar. Britain has armies of codebreakers who can tear through packing lists, missives, and shipping receipts—in a dozen languages—but the United States doesn't have that kind of manpower. Besides, even though commercial—or trade—codes are in the US's top five areas of cryptanalytic work, no one knows which operation should break them. The Army, Navy, and FBI want diplomatic and military enciphered traffic, not shipping manifests and bank statements.

When Taylor's report reaches Arlington Hall, the Agency has only four people working on commercial codes in a subsection of the Romance Language Unit. They read and translate "a few German and Spanish texts" and decode English-language messages from South America. Sometimes, their work helps other sections, but the unit produces no intelligence of its own. When the officer in charge transfers to a bigger mission, the unit gets shuffled into the Cipher Section, where a series of officers supervises them part-time. By the end of 1943, commercial intercept slows to a trickle, and the unit shuts down, its staff reassigned to more important projects.

Instead of heeding Taylor's advice, the Agency goes in the opposite direction—dismantling the small unit they have instead of building a bigger one. They're not getting commercial intelligence from London, and they don't seem to see it as a loss.

Soon, the empty unit comes in handy.

"WOULD YOU LIKE TO DO SECRET WORK?"

The Agency has a personnel problem. They can't pay as well as other government agencies and have a hard time recruiting candidates. Those they do recruit don't stay: In early 1944, the average turnover in the Payroll Office is two to five clerks per month. They're hiring people with no experience in accounting positions, paying them grade 3 wages, working them hard with tight deadlines and few vacations . . . It's a nightmare. They upgrade these clerks to grade 4, but other agencies steal the most experienced ones, beckoning them with the promise of grade 5. There's no clear system of promotion, and the Agency lacks support programs, like employee counseling, health care, recreation, and housing placement. Once new employees get a feel for life at Arlington Hall, the intrigue of doing secret government work fades.

Their low-grade employees have low attendance rates across the board: Patriotism isn't enough to keep bright young men and women in this hell of a work environment. It's so hot in the summer that sometimes the Agency has to let employees go home midday. People are transferred between sections and branches, rotated on a three-shift schedule, and put in pressurized scenarios. The payroll clerks complain their work "carries heavy responsibilities and requires constant and concentrated attention."

The enlisted personnel fare no better. Men in the Second Signal Service Battalion, which staffs technical posts at Vint Hill Farms, are paid less than they would be in other Signal Corps posts. Their commanding officer writes to the Signal Corps' chief officer to plead for better working conditions: If they face "no prospect of advancement and watch other men on all sides progress rapidly, it can only destroy morale." Personnel turnover burdens the remaining employees, who can't take leave and must take on extra work. "Few men," he concludes, "are willing to enter such an organization." Most men qualified radiomen don't reenlist, taking their talents to other divisions.

Enlisted women also give the Agency a wide berth. In early 1944, the Agency has nowhere near its allotment of 1,250 Women's Army Corps (WAC) employees. Between the Farm and the Hall, there are less than three hundred.

The Agency needs bodies. In early 1944, a hiring push aims to double the workforce—from around 3,500 to 7,000. They aren't just looking in the South, targeting rural schoolteachers. They have recruiters stationed across the country, especially on college campuses. The Agency has schools like Purdue—with high-performing science and engineering students—in its crosshairs.

In January 1944, Naomi McElwaine is halfway through her senior year and applying for jobs. The Agency doesn't advertise in the *Purdue Exponent*, but Naomi may have read about the university-sponsored program to train women for jobs in the Army Signal Corps. Like the Curtiss-Wright cadettes, they'll be engineering assistants, studying radio engineering at Wright Field Aircraft Laboratory in Ohio. After their twenty-four-week course, they're slated to work in Signal Corps' aircraft radio operation, but the Agency likely has its eye on these recruits. Likewise, RCA cadettes may also be poached by a handsome Signal Corps officer offering the intriguing proposition of doing "secret work."

Naomi may not even notice the ROTC officers on the lookout, the faculty members recruited to sniff out candidates. The Signal Corps recruiters set up in hotel lobbies and rec centers—any community space that sees student traffic. She passes them every day.

Until one day, she catches someone's eye. It could be her education professor, Mr. Wilkening, who's known Naomi since she was a first-year student. He organized a group of students to spend the summer building war housing in Vallejo, California, and Naomi was one of them. It could be her former supervisor at RCA or one of the Army recruiters slowly circling the campus like sharks.

Whatever bait they throw—she bites. The thing Naomi loved most about RCA is that her work contributed to something greater. Even if Naomi hadn't considered working for the War Department before, this job—whatever it is—gives her the opportunity to contribute in a new way. Not everyone can keep a secret—but Naomi can. The intensity and allure of secret work, coupled with the all-expenses-paid cross-country move to Washington, DC, is an offer she can't refuse.

Teaching has always been Naomi's mission, but now she has a new one.

She sends in her federal employment application, and in a few weeks' time, an application from the War Department arrives. It's a long questionnaire, far more detailed than the first.

Naomi fills it out, mails it in, and waits to see what happens next.

Unlike previous hiring campaigns, this one has a racial quota. For the past year, the War Department has been pressuring the Army to increase Black enlistment with little success. In 1943, the Army struggled to reach its 10 percent requirement, peaking at 10.46 percent in July and hovering around 8 percent thereafter. The Fair Employment Practices Committee is investigating racial discrimination in the federal government. Including civilians, the Army and Navy employ between 12–15 percent, the federal workforce 12 percent, but only at the lowest grades.

Before the war, the federal government had two systems to screen out Black workers. The "rule of three" dictated that a federal agency had to hire one of the top three candidates for a position, but not necessarily the top candidate: "This rule permitted the arbitrary passing over of any Negro who stood highest on a list of eligibles." Requiring a photo of applicants meant personnel officers could easily discard most Black applications. The National Association of Colored Women and other civil rights groups lobbied to remove the photo requirement and have race-blind federal applications. From 1941 onward, the only racial category to check was "Indian."

The War Department's application, which Naomi filled out, is called the civilian questionnaire. It requires detailed personal information, including race and skin color. The directive comes down from "someone in a high place" that 12–15 percent of the Signal Corps hires must be Black "and gainfully employed." Presumably, this means they can't be hired into custodial or service positions, as is the Army's norm; they must be added to the professional workforce. As a branch of the Signal Corps, the Agency must meet this requirement. If they don't comply, precious funding could be at stake.

Agency chief Colonel Preston Corderman decides to place them in the General Cryptanalytic Branch. They work all codes except for Germany and Japan with operations in manual codebreaking, machine processing, traffic analysis, and weather. With more than eight hundred civilians in the branch, adding about one hundred new Black workers shouldn't be a problem.

The chief of the Cryptanalytic Branch is Lieutenant Colonel Earle Cook, a young Army intelligence officer. Smart but lacking tact. He has neither the time nor the patience to be a personnel officer—and certainly not for Black people. Cook only knows one Black employee: a messenger from Virginia named William "Bill" Coffee. Bill was one of the laborers hired from Arlington Hall when the Army took over. He has two years of college, but in the Jim Crow South, Bill could only find unskilled or domestic work. At the Agency, Bill moved from laborer to janitor to classified messenger. He's personable, a good manager, eager to help. Cook likes him.

He calls Bill into his office and tells him, "I got to have about a hundred and some odd niggers. You're my personnel officer to see that I get the right ones."

Cook promotes Bill from grade 3 to grade 5 and changes his title to cryptographic clerk. In early 1944, Bill moves out of the Messenger Department and into the Cryptanalytic Branch.

There's no record of how Bill responds to Cook's comment. He's likely learned to endure racist language and focus on the task at hand. Contrary to lore, Bill does not rush out and whisper a secret message about a secret Agency to an Underground Railroad of Black job candidates. Nor does he liaise with the Personnel Office on Cook's behalf. Black people get jobs in the federal government the same way everyone else does—through the Civil Service Commission. They go to the post office, fill out a federal employment application, and mail it in.

Black hires are on their way before Cook has his crisis.

The small Commercial Code Unit sits abandoned, and Cook decides it is just what he needs. He can move the new hires in there, and they can do mission-related work tracking international trade—segregated from the other codebreakers. No need to integrate an all-white unit—that could get messy, and Cook does not want that job.

Black messengers deliver mail to the back of the building: They don't use the front door. For the first time since his hiring two years earlier, Bill trades his work clothes and messenger bag for a suit and walks in the front door of Operations Building B. The guard must be surprised—maybe he does a double take. Bill's ID badge shows that he's cleared for top secret work, so the guard lets him through. Bill enters with the flow of white workers—the Agency's first Black codebreaker.

But not its last.

On a cold January morning, Bill sets up in the unit's empty office with a file box of backlogged traffic. Soon, veteran stenographer Annie Briggs joins Bill from the Messenger Department as the unit's administrator, and the first hires trickle in. Audrey Fox, a Howard prelaw graduate, transfers from the Agency's New York office in April. She's a cryptologic clerk grade 4, a French translator, and an analyst. She's already trained; Bill and Annie likely attend the two-week training program for cryptologic clerks at Arlington Hall, which includes geography, signal communications, cryptanalysis, and decoding. As internal hires, all are security cleared, so they quickly get to work.

Far away in Lafayette, Naomi tears open an official envelope from the Signal Corps. Her hands pause on the letterhead. She's been selected—subprofessional grade 5, salary $1,800. But the letter doesn't say what the job is—or even where she'll be working.

The mystery is part of the hook. The blank more telling than any detail.

Naomi's no stranger to secrecy. At Purdue, she saw professors fingerprinted and research labs restricted for cleared personnel only. At RCA, her coworkers whispered about the vacuum tubes and transistors—where they were going, how they would be used—but the projects were classified.

Now it's her turn to keep a secret.

The process takes weeks. A medical exam—clean. A date of arrival—June 27. Then, a reward: The Agency sends her a first-class train ticket, all expenses paid, for her journey from Lafayette to Washington, DC. As a recruiting strategy, the Agency covers travel expenses for its out-of-state hires and finds them housing on arrival. But for single Black women, the choices are restricted. Only lobbying by the Black sorority Alpha Kappa Alpha convinces the government to build the same dormitory-style housing available for white women. Eleanor Roosevelt oversees the construction of Slowe Hall, Wake Hall, and Midway, all located throughout

Washington. The Phyllis Wheatley branch of the YWCA also houses single Black women in the city, since the organization doesn't allow Black women in their white facilities. With the new dorms, Naomi and thousands of Black women like her can live safely and respectably while serving their country.

Then comes the real test. A sealed packet arrives at Naomi's house, marked "Confidential." Inside is a correspondence course in Elementary Military Cryptography. It must feel almost illicit, paging through symbols, codes, and ciphers at the kitchen table with her family in the other room. Page after page of strange alphabets, transpositions, substitutions. Instructions warn that no one—not her professors, friends, even family—can know she's taking the course. It is "of a confidential nature." The letter's officialese hides an intoxicating secret. From now on, no one can know what she does from sunrise to sundown. For now, it's just homework. Soon, it will be much more.

Naomi begins a double life. Instead of hanging around the union after club meetings, she heads straight home: a family engagement, not feeling well—she might use any excuse to cover her change of schedule. The first thing that hires learn is anonymity. The less the outside world knows about intelligence work, the better. Naomi must read at night, her lamp the only light in the house, symbols spreading across the page like a map of another world.

As she solves the puzzles, the reality of her work must start to sink in. Unlike her friends, who discuss their summer plans, interviews, and new jobs, Naomi cannot give away details. She tells family and friends that she will be working in the War Department. If they press for more, she can say the job is in "communications." Every lesson reminds her she is being initiated into a hidden war, with enemies even the president and the military can't see. A battle of wills and wits that can only have one winner. To everyone else, she is a senior finishing her coursework, headed for an ordinary government job.

But Naomi knows: She is preparing to become a codebreaker.

DEPARTURE

A whiff of engine grease and coal dust greets Naomi on the platform at Lafayette Station. It is late June, and her proud parents—and restless little brother—are seeing her off on her journey to the nation's capital. The trip is one-way—no return ticket. Travelers clamor as the ground rumbles with the approaching train, and the world seems to shift beneath Naomi's feet. Her heartbeat quickens with the urgency—the mystery—of the arrival instructions folded neatly in her bag. The war casts a long shadow, but in the uncertainty, Naomi finds a flicker of hope—and adventure.

At Union Station, she'll go to the Civilian Reception booth marked "Army Service Force." She'll leave her luggage at the station and take a special car to Arlington Hall. There, she'll receive an address and further instructions.

Her gray eyes betray a mixture of nerves and resolve that her parents know well. Standing back from the crowd, side by side, they must wish they could go with her. The world isn't kind to young Black women, even those as bright and capable as Naomi. But she must make this journey on her own. They'll be here to cheer her return on the holidays. Sterling Jr. tugs at his mother's hand, bringing lightness back to the almost somber goodbye. Naomi clutches her smart leather bag, a gift from her parents for the occasion. She fishes out her ticket for a final check: one lower standard berth in first class. A uniformed Pullman porter arrives to collect her luggage. Quick and courteous, he lifts her bags onto the cart, tips his cap, and disappears in a cloud of steam from the arriving train.

As the train screeches and hisses to a stop, Naomi and her parents have one last goodbye hug. Even Sterling Jr. gives his sister a big hug, and Naomi smiles. She promises her parents that she'll write, and soon they are jostled by the flood of arriving passengers. The conductor begins to call out destinations, and Naomi listens for hers. She will take the New York Central Railroad to Cincinnati, where she'll transfer to the C&O and on to Washington. After the monthslong correspondence, the giddy acceptance letter, and the secret course of study, the new life that felt impossibly far from Lafayette is about to become a reality. She might still feel bad that she can't tell her friends and parents exactly what she's doing. Might still think about her major in education. Did she make the right choice? Even she's not sure what she'll be doing in the Agency. The secrecy is exciting, but . . . She shrugs off the doubt. She can always return to teaching after the war. After all, the war can't last forever. She has been offered a chance to contribute her skills to the war effort, a once-in-a-lifetime opportunity she can't refuse.

"All aboard!"

The call jolts Naomi out of her reverie, and she turns toward the train, its doors beckoning like another world. She finds her car—her parents follow on the platform at a distance—and climbs aboard. She makes her way to her cabin, finds a seat by the window, and tucks her bag beneath her berth. Adjusts her hat and blouse, greets her cabinmates. As the doors close and the locomotive chugs to life, Naomi waves to her parents. Their hands stay raised in parting until they disappear from view.

Soon the station slips away, and the train bursts into a future green with possibilities. Naomi leans back, the train's rhythm marking her new life. A city brimming with action awaits, the gateway to her final destination—Arlington Hall.

3

BREAKING CODE

JUNE–DECEMBER 1944

On Naomi's first day at the Agency, a young lieutenant walks her up the stairs to the inner sanctum of cryptanalysis. It's a new kind of building for Naomi—all doors. Like Alice in Wonderland, she follows the lieutenant—her white rabbit—through a series of black staircases and white corridors, as they push through door after wooden door, each opening into a new section of offices exactly like the last. Naomi follows the lieutenant through the crowd. Being among so many white people reminds Naomi of her days at Purdue. Every class began and ended with a stampede. Now they disappear behind closed doors to steal enemy secrets. Not exactly Home Management.

Footsteps and chatter fade as the last codebreakers join their units. Two steps behind the lieutenant, Naomi shifts her lunch bag to her other hand and discreetly tugs at her blouse—*Is it always this hot?* Even empty, the corridor feels like an oven.

Pushing through the last door, the lieutenant takes Naomi to a small office on the far end of the building. Inside, Naomi sees something new: an office of women—college-educated, professional, well-dressed, and Black like her—doing work that has always been reserved for whites. She shakes hands with the manager, a short, energetic man, who introduces himself as Mr. Coffee. Mr. Coffee—Bill to his friends—shows Naomi to her desk in the Research section, behind the tall, bespectacled Herman Phynes, a Howard graduate who leads the section. He and Naomi will work on decipherments. With a reassuring nod, Bill leaves Naomi to meet the messenger who has just arrived from the Traffic Coordination office with the day's messages. Bill takes the large stack of pages and, after some quick sorting, hands them out to each section.

Each day the unit handles thousands of messages from more than a dozen different countries, including Japan, Germany, Great Britain, and Russia. The United States is not supposed to spy on its allies, but the Agency sees commercial traffic more as recordkeeping, not intelligence. Countries that use codes aren't trying to keep secrets. If they are, the unit flags anything that doesn't look like routine trade.

Russia shouldn't be on this list—President Roosevelt already shut down a secret project that was working to crack Amtorg's cables to Moscow. But Amtorg's commercially coded cables? They're going to US companies. Some may even be in plaintext. Every message that uses *ABC*, *Acme*, or any other common codebook is fair game. The decoded Russian cables travel to the Foreign Economic Administration with the rest of the unit's messages and make a pit stop at the Military Intelligence Service on the way.

While the sections get to work, Herman introduces Naomi to the woman seated in the front row of the second aisle. Petite and dignified with a neat gray bun, Ethel Just is the multilingual analyst who heads the Translation section. Naomi has a couple of years of high school German, but Ethel grew up speaking it. She taught German literature at Howard University before Herman was born, then taught foreign languages in the Washington, DC, high school system. Raised in Ohio when Queen Victoria was still on England's throne, Ethel has a formal demeanor. And high standards. Some might find her intimidating, but Naomi may see a spark of her own mother—also named Ethel—in the fifty-nine-year-old. Naomi turns to greet the last section head, Annie Briggs, a light-skinned woman and former stenographer, in the back row. Her section, Production, occupies half of the room, flanked by file cabinets, typewriters, and some mysterious equipment Naomi has never seen. These women do the critical work of identifying codes, decoding, transcribing, and keeping the complex file system up-to-date.

Production houses the most important feature of the unit—the permutation tables. Charts posted on a large board show the most frequently used commercial systems. Shipping, trade, banking, mining, and other industries all have their own codes designed to save money and move business. These codes pack a lot of meaning into short cryptic phrases. In *Bloomer's Commercial Cryptograph*, "2952" means "Panic in the market. If you want to sell, telegraph immediately" while "2951" conveys a more general disaster: "Panic in all stocks." Some books, like the *ABC Telegraphic Code*, use letters instead of numbers. An import-export dealer might be alarmed to receive "EBNET" in a cable from his merchant vessel ("Captain is insane") or "PAASG" ("Encountered a severe gale and heavy seas, which carried away boats and wheel, stanchions and bulwarks, broke mast and jib-boom, all sails gone"). Each code has a system of permutations—or sequence of transformation—that helps identify it, such as the *International Police Telegraph Code*, where "hht" is "warehouse keeper," "hhu" is "coal porter," and "hhx" is "furniture packer." If a codebreaker sees "hhy" in a telegram, they'll know it belongs to this system. After consulting the permutation table, they'll learn it means "horse broker." Codes skip combinations that can lead to errors (like "hhv" or "hhw"), but codebreakers always have to look out for slipups.

Commercial codes are the only codes the Allies are allowed to use. Encoded communication was banned when war broke out in 1939, but since they're vital to international trade, nine standard commercial codebooks, including *Bentley's Complete Phrase Code*, *ABC Telegraphic Code*, and *Acme Code and Supplement*, were approved for use. If a company wants to create a private code, they must submit it to Allied censors for approval and print fifteen copies for distribution.

The unit doesn't deal only with Allied communications. Modified, unknown, and enciphered codes still appear. To identify these, they look for common features in the messages. Then they set about reconstructing parts of the codebooks from clues. This is called bookbreaking.

A subtle science, bookbreaking reconstructs a key from clues in coded messages—like using a partly completed *New York Times* crossword puzzle to back engineer the questions. The science of bookbreaking involves painstakingly applying logic and method to unlock the code's pattern, deduce its variations, and match the deduced codewords with their plaintext meanings.

The science requires creativity. Branch chief and analyst Frank Rowlett, who oversees the group, considers bookbreakers the artists of cryptanalysis. In addition to logic, the "honorable art" demands sharp language ability, patience, and vision to invent new techniques when the old ones don't fit. "It's just like painting. Nobody can train somebody to be an artist. What you do is sort of tell them how to do it and they go ahead and become an artist themselves." The unit's bookbreakers figure it out. They reconstruct six more permutation tables to make up the fifteen that Naomi now examines.

When new messages come in, the processing staff checks them against the charts. They've likely memorized the basics of each code and can sort most of them on sight. If they match the known codes, the message gets passed to Annie's decoders, who break it down using books. If they don't match, Ethel, Herman, and now Naomi begin frequency studies—counting the number of times a letter, number, or group of letters or numbers appears. They compare the patterns to previous frequency studies. If there's still no luck, they begin deciphering, a tedious, intensive process that uses their brains, skills, experience, and luck to unearth the codes' secrets.

Finally, Naomi's ready to begin. A fresh stack of indecipherable letter and number combinations waits on her desk. Bright morning sun pours through the windows, spotlighting maps of Japan, North Africa, and the Atlantic. The hanging lights and wooden desks make the office feel more like a classroom than a government office, but Naomi is no longer among students. The people working around her, with their intensity and expertise, are the professors. She's studied elementary cryptanalysis and a gauntlet of other courses in training, but this isn't practice. It's the real thing. The code work Naomi does today and the next day will help the Allies win the war. Help *end* the war, which is what she wishes most. The Pentagon, State Department, and Foreign Economic Administration will read the intelligence they provide. Only she and the others will know what happens in this room—the breakthroughs and frustrations, challenges and triumphs.

Today, Naomi joins a secret sisterhood, the first of its kind—Arlington Hall's Black codebreakers.

SEPARATE BUT EQUAL-ISH

The Agency is still uncomfortable at having a professional all-Black unit. To assuage their discomfort, Corderman separates the unit administratively—grouping it with the Service and Supply staff. The move conveys that the unit may be equal in name, skill, and qualifications to other codebreaking operations, but it will never be equal in substance. Whiteness is capital the unit can't earn. No one mentions segregation, but a memo notes that the Commercial Code Unit has been placed with the service staff "for reasons of policy." Everyone reading the memo knows what that means.

The unit's chief mission covers everything from Morse telegrams to unknown or enciphered codes to plaintext. Ethel's section translates messages in German, Spanish, French, Portuguese, or Italian. Their work not only tracks foreign trade; they also sniff out military secrets and pick up diplomatic chatter from around the globe.

Bill Coffee runs a tight ship. The larger codebreaking operations are noisy, messy, smoky, sweaty, crowded, frantic affairs, long tables at odd angles, women's chairs practically overlapping, elbows barely missing each other as pencils and typewriters run nonstop, Army men squeezing in to work wherever they can, within the lines of propriety. That's the Agency's norm, but the Commercial Code Unit cannot afford to be seen as anything less than perfect. Bill walks the regimented rows of wooden desks, making sure each workstation is up to snuff. Folders neat, papers stacked. Blotters clean, ashtrays empty. Outfits crisp, jewelry modest. Pocket squares sharp, badges visible. The posters, maps, and directories on the walls—straight as arrows. Brass-knobbed card catalogs, file cabinets, desk lamps—not a speck of dust.

Women with sleek pompadours and men in polished suits work with quiet intensity, pencils scratching across paper, pages rustling, typewriters clacking away. They decrypt, decode, translate, tabulate, and while they're at it, they build a complex filing system that cross-references every cracked message, cipher, and code for instant access. About half of their cracked codes bear intelligence—mostly diplomatic and economic, some military and strategic. Copies of those messages are whisked away to the Pentagon and State Department to help shape Allied policy.

The other half? Those go in the burn bag—from there, the incinerator.

The unit's most stunning achievement is that they clear almost all the traffic they receive. No backlog. Tens of thousands of messages per week—not one goes unsorted, unsolved, unbroken, untranslated, unread. They don't have personnel to spare, but they do the work of a group twice their size.

THE OFFICE OF CENSORSHIP

Most of the unit's traffic comes from the Office of Censorship. Created for the war, its first mission is to unmask spies and saboteurs. To make sure secrets aren't leaked to the press, on the radio, or in personal mail. Its operation is even bigger than Arlington Hall's, with more than ten thousand personnel strong to the Hall's three thousand. Its staff reads every piece of mail, listens to every phone call, and intercepts every telegram coming into or leaving the country. They check handwritten messages for secret ink and magnify typed texts to uncover microfilm embedded in the print. They can legally inspect international mail, but domestic mail is off-limits, even in wartime.

Arlington Hall does similar work: snooping in the name of patriotism. But it can be hard to see beyond the paperwork. A supervisor notes, "Too often we are apt to go along on our daily routine and we see nothing but the papers that pass across our desks. We would like to bring to your attention that it is all part of a big picture." To help workers understand their role in the war, the Agency invites the director of the Office of Censorship, Byron Price, to give a talk.

Price used to be the chief news editor of the Associated Press and sees his office's paradox: "Everything you do in censorship is wrong. Everything is backward. Everything we do contradicts everything you've been taught about what's right and proper in a democracy." They only compromise these values because of the war. "A censor must always remember that what he is doing is part of the war. What does not concern the war does not concern censorship."

The Office has a deal with RCA, ITT, and Western Union that lets them read foreign cables before they reach their recipients. All shipping information in and out of the country passes the censors' desks—and much of it goes straight to the Commercial Code Unit. The Office also hands over intelligence to the FBI. Embassies, corporations, and anyone who has dealings abroad might have valuable information—or be selling secrets to the enemy. The Office works as discreetly as possible. Most of the time, people never know that censors have been crawling all over their mail.

For Price, the Office's staff and Arlington Hall's codebreakers share a sense of responsibility: Their work is anonymous and temporary, vital only in wartime. The job is monotonous, but each individual knows they might either let a crucial message slip through or uncover one that could win the war. Most of the material they process ends up in the trash, but he hopes they understand: "It takes a lot of people to win a big war."

Domestic censorship is illegal, and Price assures the Hall's staff that he only restricts information, not opinions: "In no case have we ever objected to any editorial expression, to any criticism of any part of the government."

This isn't strictly true. Information that aids the enemy includes criticism of the American government. The Office pressures news outlets to focus only on positive aspects of the war effort. Public support is essential to keep the economy strong and the troops funded. Here, censorship gets a boost from the Office of Public Information—the US government's propaganda machine. Positive propaganda campaigns with catchy lines and colorful posters encourage rationing, war bonds, and frugality. Posters like "Loose Lips Might Sink Ships" remind citizens to avoid gossip or "loose talk" that might give sensitive information away. Even weather forecasts are banned to prevent aiding the enemy.

These campaigns work only if Americans wholeheartedly commit to the war effort. Patriotism must outweigh critical thinking. Organizations that report problems or question the war's legitimacy are labeled "defeatist" and "subversive." The government fears they will damage morale and spread anti-American ideas.

The Black press is one of the Office of Censorship's main targets. Every week from early 1941 onward, the FBI and Office of Public Information have filed detailed reports on the stories running in Black newspapers. They track over thirty but focus on Washington's *Afro American, The Pittsburgh Courier,* and *The Chicago Defender.* Reports include clipped articles and statistical breakdowns so the office can nip disturbing trends in the bud. Black press outlets, such as the *Pittsburgh Courier* and *Chicago Defender,* are pressured to stop reporting on racial unrest. The government is concerned that such stories can fuel enemy propaganda, which is apparently more important than whether they are true. Even British newspapers are censored, with reports of Black American soldiers dating white British women suppressed to avoid racial tension.

Early in the war, the papers reported on systemic racism in the war effort. In 1942, Atlanta's *Daily World* reported that Black Army enlistees were being classed as "mentally deficient" for opposing segregation and relayed that the American Medical Association considered it "stupid and unscientific" for the Red Cross to segregate "white" and "Black" blood. The paper also reported that white Southern soldiers were trying to establish Jim Crow laws in England. Cleveland's *Call & Post* warned that the war's outcome may depend on the US racial equality. Black women were denied defense work despite having sons fighting abroad. New York's *People's Voice* wrote, "The white press should realize that it can't destroy Japanese propaganda unless it deplores undemocratic practices . . . Democracy for Negroes is anti-Japanese propaganda." *The Chicago Defender* added that Black people didn't want to fight in a Jim Crow military but wanted the right to fight "as any German, Japanese, or Italian citizen" can in their own countries.

Such stories can fuel enemy propaganda, which is more important to the government than righting the wrongs they describe. By 1944, Black newspapers focus almost entirely on the heroism of Black soldiers, community fundraising, and the Double V campaign. Articles about discrimination in the military still appear, but articles expressing compassion for the Japanese, denouncing internment, or comparing the United States to the Axis powers disappear.

In the US, World War II is a race war—and it needs to stay that way. The government relies on Americans' belief that the Japanese are evil and subhuman. Combatants or not, they cannot—and should not—be trusted. Grotesque faces with yellow skin, slanted eyes, and fanged buck teeth taunt from propaganda posters. "Don't Save His Face!" reads one, as a fist marked "American Labor" punches a caricatured Japanese person in the jaw. Production posters written in broken English thank American workers for wasting scrap metal and taking time off. Even Dr. Seuss stokes racist hate in his cartoon "Waiting for the Signal from Home," where thousands of Japanese Americans line up along the West Coast to collect dynamite from a booth labeled "Honorable 5th Column."

US propaganda depicts the Japanese as rats, snakes, and apes. In a poster captioned "This Is the Enemy," a beast-like Japanese man attacks a white woman with a knife. In American culture, the racialized "other" is always portrayed as attacking white women, the American symbol of pride and purity. The Black press doesn't support the Japanese, but it doesn't villainize them either—and that deviation is dangerous. Propaganda is "the direct manipulation of social suggestion." Mass hypnotism to align public views. Psychological warfare. If Americans weren't anti-Japanese before the war, they are now.

Black Americans are immune to the government's race-baiting propaganda. They've been the subject of such campaigns since colonial times. Images of white women under attack don't rouse the righteous anger or protective instinct that they do in white men. The government knows this and strains to keep the Black press on a leash. It can't, of course, so the next best thing is making sure Black viewpoints never reach the population most vulnerable to propaganda: the military.

The Army and Office of Censorship cut off soldiers' access to "subversive" media. Absentee voting laws allow soldiers to vote while stationed abroad, but the Army doesn't want them to be influenced by the "radical" press. Black newspapers—along with *Time, The Nation*, and *The Atlantic*—are banned from military bases. They might influence soldiers' political views, especially when they're far from home and struggling to keep faith in their cause. Losing that faith can lead to desertion, surrender, or worse. American soldiers are fighting to protect democracy. They're willing to die for it. With its lynchings, segregation, and internment camps, America can't call itself a democracy—but it needs the world to believe that it is one. Support for anti-racism undermines that narrative; it shows how far the United States needs to go to achieve equality. Axis propaganda seizes on this inconsistency.

To fight claims that Black soldiers are fighting "a white man's war," the government launches a positive propaganda campaign reinforcing racial unity. Posters show white and Black workers side by side, building tanks and supporting the war. The campaign doesn't change anyone's mind, but it does show that American racism can make or break the war.

Price wraps up his talk with a note on individual responsibility. In Arlington Hall, as in the Office of Censorship, they work anonymously at tedious tasks for which they will never be thanked. But they each have a duty: "It takes a lot of people to win a big war . . . And any one of us has it in our power to wreck it."

This is what the government fears. Any report of racial violence at home or abroad can be the tipping point, turning public opinion against the United States. Instead of fixing the problem, the US dispatches the four horsemen of propaganda—Censorship, Public Information, FBI, and the Agency—to cover it up.

ENDLESS TRAFFIC

The daily tedium Price describes is even worse in traffic processing. For a message to get to Naomi's desk, it goes through multiple levels of scanning, sorting, routing, and management before codebreaking even begins. The intercept station at Vint Hill Farms snatches enemy radio waves and prints them out in long paper strips. These go to the Message Center—a labyrinthine operation where messages are sorted, labeled, and categorized. From there, the Teletype Section transcribes the messages, and the Distribution and Exchange Section routes them to the Cryptographic (codemaking) or Cryptanalytic (codebreaking) Branch. There, a Traffic Coordination Section separates encrypted from plaintext messages and parcels them out to the appropriate units.

Each cryptanalytic unit sorts its own traffic further. They scan or speed-read the strips to determine what's worth analyzing; these are stamped with dates and serial numbers and cut from the strip. Clerks distribute them to the correct subsection, and only then do codebreakers get to work analyzing and decoding them. Linguists translate and check messages for errors, and processing clerks copy, file, and enter them into the unit's records. Recordkeepers send notable translations to the Agency bulletin for circulation.

Processing traffic is endless; cryptanalysts play a small part in the messages' life cycle. Analysts know this and want to avoid as much early-stage grunt work as possible. It's monotonous, time-consuming, and can involve heavy lifting—a cross between clerical work and manual labor.

Traffic processors have to work quickly—they handle tens of thousands of messages per day. They're hired at the lowest grades as 2s and 3s. These jobs have the highest turnover rates but are the most crucial for the Agency to keep churning out intelligence.

Often seniority solves the problem. In codebreaking units, new hires get stuck doing dreaded tasks like stamping serial numbers, scanning, or slicing tapes with a paper guillotine. Soon, most get their bearings and move on to more exciting tasks.

But they still grumble. Traffic processing isn't brainy work, and many feel it's beneath them. A report notes: "Personnel have been trained to a high degree . . . Personnel have been required to do the same job day in and day out. Personnel have been required to do the same job for weeks on end. Certain personnel [feel] that their capacity is greater than the position they are now in." Supervisors lobby for better pay and incentives for their staff, but they rarely succeed. Meanwhile, workers forget Price's message about individual responsibility. They show up late, or don't show up at all.

When they do show up, it's chaos. Japanese codebreaker Ann Caracristi writes: "We who worked in the bowels of the organization were constantly asking ourselves, 'Where is the real work being done?'" Even in the Japanese branch, the endless busywork convinces Caracristi that she and her fellow codebreakers aren't doing the "real work." When she does get to analyze, "it's like doing crossword puzzles every day and getting most of the answers."

The Agency strives to balance the tedium with fun activities. A softball league, a chorale, theater group, and film series. The top brass stay for the night shift in solidarity. Some of the codebreakers buy a sailboat and float down the sunlight-dappled channels of the Potomac. Others save up their ration coupons and buy gasoline for weekend trips to the Blue Ridge Mountains. With morale this precarious, the Agency tries its best to make Arlington Hall a warm, lively community. The work can be monotonous, but they are part of something great—and that's what matters.

None of the activities include the Black codebreakers. Outside of their work, they're not part of life at the Hall. The lecture series in which Price speaks is called "This Is Our War." Nothing at the Hall is integrated at this point, and the Black codebreakers likely aren't invited. For them, the Hall is a maze of restrictions—just like the world outside.

Joseph Grew, the former US ambassador to Japan, is the next speaker in this series. He puts the morale problem another way: "In carrying on our War work on the home front, there is only one thing to guide us and that is our conscience. 'Am I contributing my maximum efforts according to my capacity in the circumstances in which I find myself?' If we can't answer that question in the affirmative, I'm afraid our consciences are going to trouble us." There are no troubled consciences at Arlington Hall. Some bite the bullet and do their jobs, but many must be cajoled into working.

The Japanese, Grew says, believe Americans are "flabby" and "undisciplined." Too caught up in labor strikes and luxuries to succeed in making total war. Grew often speaks to young people on the home front who don't think their work is important. He reminds them that they're precision instruments; if one instrument fails, the whole machine suffers. He warns them not to believe in stereotypes about the weak Japanese: They are fierce fighters who won't be easily beaten. Each war worker, no matter what they're doing, needs to give that work their all.

Meanwhile, producing intelligence becomes more urgent, and the Agency needs a reliable way to get this traffic processing done. They add a few clerks to the Commercial Code Unit, and then add a few more. Black women, transfers from other departments. Grades 2 and 3. Soon the unit holds thirty people, more than half of them clerks. By November 1944, the Cryptanalytic Branch restructures, and the unit is no longer labeled a service operation. They're officially a codebreaking unit, but they've merged with Traffic Coordination. The new Black clerks take those unpopular jobs while the white workers transfer to other tasks.

Each month, the unit sorts and routes between 175,000 and 200,000 plaintext messages—at emergency room–triage speed. They sort plaintext, enciphered, and encoded messages by address, heading, signature, and any other clue they can find. Straight commercial messages go in one box; commercial traffic from diplomatic sources in another. Romance-language and German traffic separate from plaintext in other languages. Diplomatic cables on government business, not trade, get their own category. Red Cross plaintext yet another. They are precision instruments, dispatching reports, queries, orders, missives, confessions, contracts, and receipts—thousands of lifelines—across the Agency every day.

THE RUSSIAN PROBLEM

The Commercial Code Unit is supposed to flag anything that isn't routine trade—but with the Soviets, it's routine trade that hides the action. For Stalin, open trade is covert warfare. His goal is to reach and surpass the United States' atomic weapons technology: "Either we do it," he says, "or they crush us." The plan's been in motion since the 1920s and is gaining steam. Every scrap of commerce tied to heavy industry matters, but at the Agency, studying low-level trade data isn't a priority.

The main Russian codebreaking effort is happening in a back wing of B Building. Secretly launched in 1943, the "Russian problem" technically doesn't exist. The analysts work enciphered Amtorg cables for prime diplomatic intelligence. Like everything commercial, the messages come through RCA and are spirited back to the secret section toiling away in B Building.

This is illegal. The Americans are not supposed to spy on allies. As wary as they are about the Soviets, they are technically allies—and the Americans can't afford to risk that relationship. However, everyone who needs to know knows that Amtorg is an NKVD front. If the United States doesn't spy on Russian trade, they could miss crucial information.

They work through five thousand telegrams with little luck, until one reveals a critical flaw: A few onetime pads—the notebook keys to the cipher system—have been duplicated, exposing a system once thought unbreakable. The analysts uncover five: One is for trade—Lend-Lease, Amtorg, and the Soviet Government Purchasing Commission. The rest belong to diplomats, NKVD agents, and Red Army and Navy Intelligence (GRU). This break begins the top secret operation called Venona, and the section begins to wrench the lid off of Stalin's black box of secrets.

4

SECURITY BREACH

MARCH–JULY 1945

At Arlington Hall, secrecy is of the highest order. The mission depends on keeping the outside world unaware of its existence. The ten-thousand-person operation needs supplies and transportation; streams of deliveries and shuttle buses are bound to draw attention. Near the Pentagon, Washington, DC, and the region's military bases, high levels of daily activity might be considered normal, but fully staffed round-the-clock shifts mean that this activity never stops. Even food deliveries are camouflaged.

Personnel security is an even greater concern. Recruits must sign a Civil Service Oath of Office—standard for government employees—and a special oath of secrecy for the Agency. The Army's security clearance process is lengthy, designed to cull all but the most loyal citizens. Excellent character, temperate habits, and adequate finances ensure that Agency employees won't be tempted by spies. Officers conducting background checks don't just call an applicant's references: They ask a reference for three other names to vouch for the applicant and call them too.

The clearance process is effective, but it's not always clear-cut. Erring on the side of caution means that even a recruit who's studied with a professor suspected of holding communist views can be rejected. Having family or friends in foreign countries may also raise alarms, even though only having "enemy" connections can disqualify an applicant. Some investigations turn up information that places an applicant in a gray area. The Army Adjutant's Office might reject an applicant while the Agency's Personnel Office approves them, or vice versa. With a military and civilian workforce, who has the final say isn't always clear. This puts the two sides at odds. The civilians think the Army Security process is too harsh, robbing the Agency of much-needed talent. The Army does not want to act suspicious toward its own people, so sometimes its background checks of Army personnel are lax.

Identification badges are the mainstay of Arlington Hall security. They bear the employee's photo and must be worn on the left lapel. Color-coded backgrounds show the clearance level. The badges can't be duplicated, and there are stiff, if shifting, penalties for forgetting them. Leaving badges where they can be taken—pinned to coats, in pockets, on desks—is risky but common. They're checked at the main gate and at the entrance to the Operations buildings and other secure areas.

Naomi never forgets her badge, and neither does Martha McWatt, who sits two seats behind Naomi in the decoding section. Martha is twenty-five, a psychology and child welfare major from the University of Minnesota. She lives in Wake Hall, a dormitory for Black women in DC. Like Naomi, Martha was politically active in college—a member of St. Paul's Junior Farmer-Labor Club and the Urban Youth League. The labor club's meetings about cooperatives, religion, and propaganda might strike an Agency background checker as "subversive" activity, so she leaves it off her résumé. She leaves the Urban Youth League off her application too, in favor of listing her membership in the YWCA's Girl Reserves and social clubs.

Martha knows she has to tread carefully; having foreign relatives can cast doubt on Agency applicants. Her father, Arthur, is a recently naturalized US citizen from British Guiana, South America. The tiny country sandwiched between Venezuela and Suriname is still home to three sets of Martha's aunts, uncles, and cousins. British Guiana is an ally, but it shares a border with Brazil, which made secret arms deals with Mussolini and Hitler before the war. Her uncles might be working for the British merchant navy or in plants refining bauxite for the US aircraft industry; most of the aluminum used in Allied aircraft comes from British Guiana. She wants to know, but she hasn't written. Her telegrams would be checked by the Office of Censorship, and she can't afford to have a report sent to the Agency: If you're caught spilling secrets, you'll be shot by firing squad—so she's heard. Even a hint of suspicion could be deadly.

In late March 1945, Arlington Hall is energized. The war's end is in sight, and they're wrapping up a Red Cross War Bond drive. In the Operations buildings, codebreakers join the last-minute rush to sign clipboards and make donations. People talk about their postwar plans and how their codebreaking adventures would make a great story.

Martha's chatty too, but not about war secrets. She sits at a table at the back of the room. There are no codes in front of her, no pencil poised over message traffic, but her hands are busy as she chats with a woman from the Production staff.

At his desk near the front, Bill Coffee checks his watch: five minutes until his daily inspection round. He wears his authority in the unit like a starched collar—straight and unbending. Pride and politics: The unit is under a microscope, and Bill can't afford a disturbance in their work or a blemish on their image. He hopes to advance his own career and banks on a promotion after the war.

Murmurs of conversation prick his attention. At the back of the room, he spies Martha, partly obscured by the woman sitting in front of her. He notices her busy hands. A few minutes early, he stands, smooths his jacket, and makes the short walk across the room.

"Miss McWatt, what are you doing back here?"

Martha doesn't glance up. "What does it look like I'm doing?"

The other woman hurries back to her seat and reveals the truth:

Martha is tearing paper into tiny pieces. Absently, strip by strip. The wastebasket beside her fills with shredded scraps. She doesn't say why—whether something happened or whether it's just an off day. Methodical, determined, like it's a new mission, she just keeps tearing strips.

Bill blinks but keeps his tone measured. "Miss McWatt, that trash is classified. You cannot destroy it."

He glances at his watch again, annoyed that he's three minutes late for his rounds. Heads turn and pencils hover above their papers. "You had better get back to your desk." He walks off in a slight huff to salvage the inspection.

Two hours later, the woman is back, and Martha is still chatting—still shredding. Whether it's decoding notes or doodles, every piece of discarded paper in the unit goes into the burn bag—a large paper bag for classified trash that's checked at the end of the day before being taken to the incinerator and destroyed.

This time Bill doesn't bother asking. He leaves the room and returns shortly with a young lieutenant.

"That's enough, Miss McWatt," the lieutenant says.

Without responding, Martha stands, leaves the trash on the table, and returns to her desk. The rest of the unit continues their work; no one wants to risk the lieutenant noticing anything out of order. He's their officer in charge, though they've seen him a handful of times. When they do, it's usually bad news.

Bill could let the incident slide. It was a small lapse from a productive, dependable worker. Martha gets good employee reviews: They highlight her skill, accuracy, and attention to detail. But she's made Bill look bad in front of his white supervisor, and that takes precedence over showing solidarity or being a gentleman.

Before the day ends, Bill's fired off a formal reprimand recounting the incident, and it goes up the chain to the Personnel Office. A few days later, Martha receives a letter from the Separations Officer: She's being suspended. "Your country is now facing its greatest crisis, and your record leads this office to believe you are not aware of the seriousness of the effort in which you are engaged. It is hoped this suspension will bring pointedly to your attention the need for you to be at all times at your work."

It's only for one day, but the suspension stings. Martha has always been aware of the war's seriousness. It's a harsh punishment for a small infraction. While not a security infraction, being AWOL (absent without leave) can raise security concerns. But like a security check, there is latitude. Managers decide which infractions to report and which to let slide.

COMFORT TO THE ENEMY

With such strict security enforcement, Arlington Hall should be a locked box. An alarmed security fence surrounds it, and only four guarded gates provide access. Once inside, barbed-wire fences, gates, and checkpoints ensure that only people with proper clearance enter restricted areas. Visitors, messengers, and maintenance staff follow special security procedures. They have their own security badges, which must be worn at all times.

Despite the measures, word gets around that secret papers aren't being guarded as safely as they should. And then something else happens.

To the nation's shock, President Roosevelt dies of a cerebral hemorrhage. Rumors of sabotage and conspiracy swirl. Fifth columnists. Communists! The administration is crawling with spies . . .

Amid the chaos, Vice President Harry S. Truman takes over the White House. At the Agency, rumors of infiltration raise concerns about security. A check is suggested but never followed up.

In early May 1945, Germany surrenders. Unconditionally. The mood at Arlington Hall is high. The rumors, fears, and conspiracy theories feel like a distant memory.

A couple of weeks later, two young women walk out of a hotel in downtown Washington and step onto a morning bus filled with government workers. Soon, they learn that a certain government agency badly needs workers. The jobs are secret—and exciting. Critical to the war effort. The employees can't tell the two women more, but they heartily suggest they look into it.

When the stream of Arlington Hall's workers steps off the bus and makes their way to Arlington Hall's gates, two young women step off with them. In civilian dress with purses looped over their shoulders, they blend easily into the crowd. At the front gate, two uniformed guards flank the entrance, checking badges.

"Morning, ladies," one says. "Let's see your badges."

The first woman smiles. "We're actually here about a job," she says. "They told us to check in with Personnel?"

The guard glances toward his partner, who keeps scanning badges. Then he steps into the gatehouse and returns with two temporary visitor passes and a clipboard.

"Sign in here, ladies."

They sign, pin the badges to their coat lapels, and thank the guard.

"Personnel's the first building on the right," he says, gesturing down the road. "You can't miss it."

A few hours later, the two women find the cafeteria. Inside, they notice that many employees leave their coats on hooks in the hallway—without removing their ID badges from the lapel. The women drift through the crowd like regulars, chatting easily as they move through the line. After some casual inquiries, they learn what the colors on the badges mean and which provide the highest level of access.

After a few minutes, they move to the coatroom. Dozens of coats hang unattended. Inside pockets and on loose lapels: the badges. Dozens of them. They work quickly. Checking pockets on the coat fronts, they find two that are a perfect match. It takes almost twenty minutes, but one seems to notice them searching the coats. They slip the matching badges into their handbags and slip out the door with the crowd.

Back at the hotel that night, they make a workstation on the bed and clip strips of colored paper to fit the ID badges around the photos. Covered with cellophane, the fake badges look just like the Hall employees'. They must smirk, thinking, *This is too easy.*

The next morning, as birdsong flutters in the treetops, the women join the flow of Arlington Hall workers. They wear new outfits, new hairstyles, and—most important—new badges.

One by one, employees pause before the guard. A glance at the badge. A nod. They pass through.

The women do the same. No questions. No resistance. Once through, they head straight for the most classified building on campus: Operations Building B.

The badges open every door.

The women move from corridor to corridor, office to office, unchallenged. Past armed guards. Past security officers. Past supervisors who barely glance up. They browse desks, flip through folders, scan bulletin boards, slip papers into their bags.

CONFIDENTIAL. SECRET. TOP SECRET.

From the basement to the top floor, in every wing, they steal from unlocked drawers, orphaned folders, unattended reports and notebooks. They do the same in A Building, quietly harvesting state secrets. If anyone finds the women suspicious, they don't report them. Employees might be used to seeing unfamiliar faces: With the personnel shortage, uncleared employees are often allowed to enter restricted areas to do unclassified work.

The night shift proves even easier. Half-empty offices, tired employees, laxer security. They don't even bother to check the burn bags—there's enough classified stuff in the open.

The perimeter's four entrances are guarded and set with alarms, but the women enter and exit gates at random, never detained or detected.

In the cafeteria, seated like regular employees, they sip hot coffee and chat. Around them mill WACs, Army men, civilians from all divisions. A few familiar faces. A young officer strolls past and nods.

Beneath their table, tucked into a canvas tote, badges, memos, worksheets, key books, decrypts, operations lists, intercepts, personnel records, stamped with TOP SECRET in red ink.

They exit with the night shift, heading to the line of buses just as the early comers on the day shift filter in. The doors hiss closed. The engine rumbles. As Arlington Hall recedes into the distance, the women disappear once again into the city.

The guard they met on their first morning reports two visitors' badges missing to the Personnel Office, but no one in Security follows up. No one reports their badges missing.

Two weeks later, an article appears in *The Washington Post*. Instead of submitting to a security evaluation, the chief of a secret government agency conducted an experiment. He recruited two WACs from another post to approach the Agency as civilians and collect as much classified material as they could, using any means at their disposal. Each night, the WACs took their bounty to the Agency's Security Office, so the material never left the premises. The WACs did no harm, but they lifted enough intelligence "to give aid and comfort to the enemy" and embarrass some high-ranking officials.

The exercise was supposed to remain a secret; the Agency staff didn't know it was taking place. Only Colonel Corderman, the two WACs, and select Security personnel knew about the project. Somehow, the story was leaked to the press within days.

At the Agency, the story spurs alarm—and paranoia: Guards triple-check badges at each entrance, codebreakers eye each other suspiciously. The provost marshal conducts badge inspections in all restricted areas. Some propose solutions like issuing color-coded cords for the badges or requiring employees to remove the badges from their coats at the entrance gate. Others take matters into their own hands; a civilian in the Machine Branch steals his coworkers' unattended badges and turns them into Headquarters until he's told to stop.

The focus on security breeds distrust and dissatisfaction among the employees, so the leadership backs off. Resignations, absenteeism, and low morale are already a problem. Since VE-Day, people have been resigning from Arlington Hall in droves. Sweethearts return from abroad, and codebreakers rush to the altar. To cajole workers to stay, the Agency secures vacation facilities at the Orkney Springs Hotel in the picturesque Shenandoah Valley. They propose picnics, order art supplies, and stress the importance of communication between supervisors and personnel. In the Machine Division, where clerks work IBM keypunch and tabulator machines day in and day out, supervisors grant frequent leave without pay to prevent personnel from resigning. This policy leads to more absences, with employees skipping out one or two days a week without leave. A job relations program, a poster campaign, even a pay raise fail to stem the tide. The division chief worries that cracking down will increase the problem—so again, they back off.

No official reprimands. No suspensions.

No one gets shot.

Martha's one-day suspension for tearing up secret trash is out of proportion with the Agency's cautious approach to disciplining its white workers. Black women in government agencies often report harsher treatment.

White workers fall on the opposite side of the disciplinary spectrum. The Agency strives to keep them happy. Reports show a sticky web of egos and expectations—Army men resent the women and civilians; civilian men feel disrespected by officers. University women snub the high school graduates; men complain female bosses won't train them. WACs complain their male Army supervisors treat them "like small school children." Complaints about pay grades, weather, supervisors, training, transportation, housing—the litany is endless. Everyone thinks they have it the worst. The Agency fears discontent boiling over into labor disputes and mass resignations. Government workers can unionize. Better to relax security and appease them than risk a walkout. They even make clearance exceptions for employees with "doubtful backgrounds."

The Agency is right to be nervous: most employees don't stick around long. On average, cryptanalysts serve for a year and a half, specialists for five months, clerks for seven. No amount of perks or patriotism can make them stay. They come and go through a revolving door of entitlement.

There's a reason the WACs could move around unseen. Despite rumors of blindfolds and firing squads, no one's really worried about security. Division Chief Frank Rowlett recalls, "The basic reason for requiring the secrecy oath . . . was to keep people from spilling their guts out after the war was over." The Agency doesn't want a repeat of former MI8 chief Herbert O. Yardley's *The American Black Chamber*. Back in 1931, the tell-all book described the Agency's inner workings, secretive sources, and questionable methods. Now they are more careful not to let classified details slip out. However, aside from "making noise," the codebreakers are not a security threat.

They're honest, patriotic, white Americans—and that's enough. To these intelligence experts, saboteurs are easy to spot. Years later, Rowlett explains their strategy: "The Japanese would be identified by color. I mean, there was a race element, which people now say to ignore, but there are times when you don't ignore the difference in people's skin color. The German was a little more complicated question but somehow or other we got through without any bad luck." When security threatens to disgruntle white people, the Agency prefers to trust their gut—even if it means opening their doors to Nazis. They rely on getting "lucky." Filling the ranks with people who look like them is a talisman against espionage. Anyone who doesn't look like them is suspect.

Martha's suspension doesn't shake her resolve: She's as committed to the job as ever. While white codebreakers leave for greener pastures, Martha receives an emblem from the War Department for six months of faithful civilian service. A blue bar with a red-white-and-blue star insignia that she can pin on her left lapel over her ID badge—which is never out of place.

SERIOUS EXPLOITATION

Germany surrenders unconditionally to the Allies on May 8, 1945, but the war isn't over yet.

As Allied victories mount and Japan shows signs of weakening, the

Agency needs as much Japanese shipping intelligence as it can get. One of those codes is called JAH. Sometimes called LA or "L," it's a diplomatic trade code. The Japanese use it for utility, not secrecy. For content they "merely wish to keep from post office officials." It was one of the Agency's first codebreaking efforts, and Cryptanalytic Division Chief Frank Rowlett recalls that breaking it wasn't "too much of a job." Many at the Hall consider its intelligence value minimal because its security is low. In fact, JAH has incredible value: As analysts are starting to learn, high-level intelligence doesn't always come in high-level packaging. Whether by a lack of more sophisticated codes or human, sensitive information finds its way onto wide-open circuits.

Case in point: JAH. The Japanese use it often, not only for shipping but also for diplomatic cables—sometimes of consequence. Trade routes, ship names, diplomatic exchanges. Who, what, when, where, how—if it's shipping in Asia, it's recorded in JAH.

Exploiting JAH is an international team effort, and the Agency is falling behind. Its constant traffic and relentless tracking demand more personnel than they would like to spare for such a minor, if ubiquitous, code. Meanwhile, Ottawa is cabling for decrypts; Berkley Street wants to compare notes. JAH travels all the major trade routes: Bangkok to Tokyo, Tokyo to Rangoon—a Southeast Asian party line of shipping intelligence.

Rowlett says JAH is simple—and by cryptanalytic standards, this is true. But learning the system takes effort. The code runs on three substitution tables built from three types of letter pairs: vowel–consonant, consonant–vowel, and double letters. Bigrams—two-letter groups— represent Japanese syllables. Tetragrams—two bigrams together—stand for whole words, dates, and proper names in both Japanese and English. Three extra systems—EX, OG, and UJ—handle special spellings, numbers, and alternate codes. Decoders also memorize the frequency table: *I*, *U*, and *A* appear most often, followed by *Y*, *A*, and *C*; *Q* appears only to end a passage in one of the special codes.

The code is solved and rarely changes, so the challenge is speed. Decoders must recall combinations instantly and move quickly through five-letter groups, spotting when a bigram or tetragram is split between two words. Most messages run under one hundred words. For longer ones, the Agency uses "spot decoding," scanning for key words instead of producing full translations. Each message is dated, numbered, and logged. Decoding is only the first step—fast, accurate work is essential to feed the long chain of recordkeeping that follows.

Cryptanalytic Division Chief Frank Rowlett has been watching the Commercial Code Unit. Every so often, he stops by and checks on their progress. He sees their efficiency, their professionalism. Their indexing system makes finding even the rarest codes easy. When he needs a group to exploit the backlog of JAH, he knows whom to call.

Ethel and her translators receive the boxes of intercepts, and they roll up their sleeves and get to work. The JAH chart covers Ethel's desk like a picnic cloth—three feet of stiff yellow graph paper, its dozen hand-inked grids boxed and labeled in neat block letters. Each square holds its own secret: bigrams and tetragrams lined up in rows, substitutions spelled out in tiny print. To anyone outside the Agency, it might look like a crossword puzzle or an unfinished blueprint. To Ethel, it's a map, a tool, and a test all at once.

The messages arrive in five-letter groups, typed in faint purple ink, often smudged or garbled by static. Ethel scans a line, pencil in hand, eyes darting between the paper strip and the chart. Spotting a split bigram—half at the end of one group, half at the start of the next—means the difference between sense and nonsense.

After months of backlog, Ethel's team is here—shoulders hunched over the big yellow sheet, sleeves brushing the worn edges—calling out combinations as they break the coded syllables into words. The work is mechanical, almost soothing—until the clock intrudes, reminding them that each decoded slip is only the start of a long chain of hands, stamps, files, and reports. Speed and precision matter.

In a month, Ethel's team clears the backlog, never falling behind on their own work in the process.

This success leads to more projects for the Commercial Code Unit.

The Special Projects unit hands them several French systems that aren't top priority, but that the Agency still needs to keep an eye on. The unit's analysts work ciphers from Belgium, Haiti, and Luxembourg, some of which haven't been solved yet. These countries are not central players in the war, but they are bellwethers for those that are.

The last new project is Liberian ciphers, which Naomi tackles on her own. She gets three systems. One diplomatic enciphered code, partly solved but still unreadable. A commercial code for confidential communiques, and a polyalphabetic diplomatic cipher with thirty-one alphabets. It's a daunting task, but she's up to it.

Why is Liberia important? Rubber. Liberia is the biggest source of natural latex under Allied control, and it needs to stay that way. Japan controls the rest in Southeast Asia (JAH). Harvey Firestone, tire magnate, leases one thousand acres of Liberian land for his rubber plantations. Dark-skinned men and boys scrape bark from the sides of slim rubber trees, tap the cuts with a metal spout, and catch the milky latex in buckets. Thousands of trees—thousands of buckets of latex—every day. More dark-skinned men in Firestone's factories turn the latex into gas masks, fuel tanks, and pneumatic tires. Firestone's been accused of using forced labor, but that's not the point. The United States has built an airfield and infrastructure of roads and water towers in Liberia. They send Black troops to Liberia, one of their few postings abroad. They fly anti-submarine patrols, provide air defense in the North African theater, transport supplies to the South Atlantic. Liberia's more important than it seems.

The Agency publishes most of Naomi's decrypts, and the bulletin goes Agency-wide. If things are happening in Liberia, the Agency needs to know about it. If the Liberian government decides to play hardball and strike a deal with Hitler, if the Axis powers are planning an attack on the airfield, if the Liberian frontier army revolts, if the Liberian and the Italian diplomat have an affair—the United States could be in trouble.

Manufacturing one Sherman tank requires one ton of rubber.

One battleship—seventy-five tons.

Lose the latex, lose the war.

5

VICTORY AND DEFEAT

AUGUST 1945–OCTOBER 1946

Ethel Just crosses A Building's concrete sea, passes the checkpoint, and heads down to Arlington Hall's entry gate. The stream of workers leaving for the day is just a trickle. Only last week, the site teamed with exuberant youths, and on August 6, the country erupted in celebration. Everyone at Arlington Hall and across America knew they'd won the greatest victory of their time.

That reverie doesn't last long at Arlington Hall. After victory comes … nothing. Codebreakers have been resigning for months—only aggressive hiring kept up with the turnover. Since VJ Day, the staff has plummeted to six thousand and keeps dropping. The cheerful WACs head off to college, family, or new careers. Military men transfer to new assignments. Civilians bolt for the private sector. The Agency's Japanese and German operations shut down, taking two whole branches of staff, equipment, and progress with them. The General Cryptanalytic Branch—what's left of it—consolidates and waits to see how the world takes shape.

At the beginning of the war, when Ethel was the associate dean of women at Virginia Union College, she plunged into civic organizing. Running the Girl Reserves at the Phyllis Wheatley YWCA. Speaking at their annual celebration. She encouraged veteran organizers like herself to always look toward the future: "One must be young in ideas today, although you might not be young in years." Then fifty-six, Ethel spoke about the Young Women's Christian Association as "the Guardian of Tomorrow." They must remember the grandmothers who came before them and paved the way, and they can't do it alone: "We must heed the civil liberties program of the national YWCA," she urged.

That statement is more controversial than it sounds. Like most women's organizations, the YWCA bars Black women from membership. Determined not to be kept from the suffrage movement and the advancement of women's rights, Black women have formed their own groups, beginning with the National Association of Colored Women, founded by Mary Church Terrell, in 1896. Fourteen years later, in 1910, Ethel sat in Mary's drawing room at 326 T Street alongside Lucy Diggs Slowe and fifteen other Black educational luminaries to charter the College Alumnae Club, the first association for Black women with college degrees. Back then, Ethel was Ethel Highwarden, a young professor of German at Howard University, beloved by students for her enthusiasm and interest in their work.

Now sixty, Ethel maintains that enthusiasm but keeps a lower profile. Since joining the Agency, her public appearances have stopped; if she keeps up with her advocacy work, she doesn't talk about it. New generations run those clubs now, as they should. Besides, she has a different mission—and its chief requirement is silence.

On the drive back to 412 T Street, detached from the people and things around her, Ethel might draw grids in her mind. In those small boxes she pencils in digraphs and trigraphs, reversals and substitutions. Codebreaking has a beautiful rhythm, variation within repetition, just like the concertos of Johannes Brahms that she loves so much. Without the day's demands, the exercise is like a *Wiegenlied*, a lullaby, that melts worries into mist.

Ethel drives down Lee Boulevard, named for the Southern General Robert E. Lee, and passes Arlington House, Robert E. Lee's family estate.

In Arlington, the legacy of slavery hasn't faded. When people say the Agency has a Southern culture, this is what they mean. Its hierarchy, its assumptions, its rules.

Segregationists don't demand separate facilities just because of Black people's skin color; it's because of their blood. To them, "Black blood" is a contaminant. If mixed with "European" or "Anglo-Saxon blood," it will lead to the deterioration of the white race. Integration is the first step toward miscegenation. To segregationists, miscegenation—sexual relations that create an offspring between a white and a Black person—is a crime and a sin.

This might seem contrary to Christian values, but for segregationists, it's baked in. They believe God made Black people morally and intellectually inferior to white people. Racism is nature's hierarchy.

These beliefs are behind the "one-drop rule." The reason Black women in the South cannot ride in ladies' cars or sleeping berths on a train, even when traveling great distances. Drinking fountains, swimming pools, bathrooms, restaurants are all risk zones for racial contamination. Sitting next to a contaminated person on the bus, breathing the same air, jackets, maybe even knees, touching—segregationists recoil at the thought.

Ethel drives because she can. Because she sees how patterns— whether in ciphers or policies—signal what's coming next.

Word travels fast at Arlington Hall. Conversations from the boardroom quickly filter down to the staff—sometimes faster than official memos. Lately, the buzz is about mass resignations—especially in one place: the Machine Branch. The branch has a reputation: clattering, cramped, unbearably hot. Discipline and morale break down. The branch's forgiveness policy for absenteeism isn't working. But they're in a bind. Cracking down risks sparking more resignations. If the past is any guide, they'll need more than their poster campaign.

Replacing the WACs as clerks and stenographers is another needle to thread. The Agency's first priority is not to upset the workforce by replacing WACs with civilians all at once: "Such transfers should be accomplished slowly, so as not to inconvenience or impede operations in the Branches."

It's not clear how the civilian workforce will differ from the WACs doing "basic" clerical work; typists and stenographers are usually trained in their roles before they're hired.

The last problem is how to manage the shrinking budget. The Supply Branch is having a difficult time keeping up with demands: They sent the Machine Branch faulty fans—and it's made conditions even more unbearable. The Supply Branch chief suggests substituting "inexpensive items for expensive ones" to cut down on overall costs.

To most, it's just administrative chatter. But Ethel knows this language. She's heard it before—tighten the belt, find efficiencies, repurpose equipment and labor. It means something else when it comes on the heels of victory. During the First World War, urgency compelled the government to hire Black women for office work. They lost these positions, and hundreds of other qualified candidates were turned away. In a few cases, they were hired for the lowest-paying jobs—even when higher-paying ones were available. Postwar downsizing, tightening the belt—the opportunities Black women have worked so hard for may be snatched away yet again.

As Ethel pulls onto T Street, with its stately homes and genteel residents, she knows she'll have to keep her eyes open in the days ahead.

POSTWAR PROMISES DEFERRED

After the war, Black men and women come home expecting more from their country: better jobs, better schools, better housing, civil rights. They fought for democracy abroad, but at home, America clings to segregation. The contradiction is too obvious. The self-proclaimed leader of the free world cannot deny basic rights to its own citizens, and yet official and unofficial segregation, police brutality, and systemic injustice remain business as usual.

The postwar economy is booming. Patriotic pride soars as people cash in on new opportunities: The GI Bill provides veterans with education, a strong dollar means increased spending power, war bonds mean savings in the bank, and homeownership is on the horizon. These gains are fewer and further between for Black Americans. Their wartime sacrifices don't outweigh America's commitment to white supremacy. Jim Crow laws, restrictive housing covenants, and low-wage job funnels get worse as white communities begin to fear Black encroachment. The war shook up demographics. Soldiers in need of housing forced campuses and formerly all-white towns to integrate. As neighborhoods grow more diverse, white residents panic. Their leaders preach that segregation offers "separate but equal" peace. For these people, even a hint of integration can unravel society. It challenges the basis of all their beliefs.

With straight faces, political and business leaders insist segregation is not discrimination but concern for Black people's safety. "Achieving racial harmony" and avoiding "unnecessary friction" become catchphrases, meaning that if white people riot or engage in acts of violence, the presence of Black people is at fault.

Things are particularly bad in DC, where the backlash against wartime progress is instant. Downtown businesses, like Lansburgh's Department Store, that started serving Black customers during the war revert to segregation when white customers complain. The city's Board of Recreation votes to reinforce segregation of public facilities rather than repeal it. Segregationists in Congress shut down the Fair Employment Practices Committee. Mississippi Senator Theodore Bilbo, chair of the Senate District Committee, vows to cheering crowds back home that he will keep Washington a segregated city.

Their weapon is housing. About a third of the 670,000 residents in Washington, DC, are Black while the rest are white. As more people arrive, redlining intensifies. Black migrants are restricted to the city while white newcomers move to the suburbs.

Suburbanization drains resources from DC, as veterans use their GI Bill benefits to buy homes outside the city, avoiding neighborhoods that might lower property values. Redlining ensures that even one Black family in a suburb can cause property values to plummet. As a result, real estate companies consolidate Black families in city neighborhoods with fewer opportunities and resources.

The federal GI Bill, theoretically racially neutral, is implemented in ways that exclude Black Americans. Despite qualifying for housing loans, Black veterans are routinely denied mortgages. Of the thirty thousand homes built in DC during the 1940s, only two hundred were available to Black families. Discriminatory practices also limit Black veterans' job training and career progress. While a few rural suburbs like Sandy Springs, Maryland, see a Black population, the city itself sees growing segregation, especially in housing. With more Black families moving in, investment dries up. By 1946, 12 percent of Black homes lack running water, and 16 percent lack electricity.

Racist policies extend to schools too. DC schools spend 27 percent less per Black student than white student—$126.52 versus $160.21—leading to overcrowded, underfunded Black schools. Discriminatory policies prevent Black children from enrolling in white schools, which lose most of their students during the white exodus to the suburbs. To cope, the city splits the school day into shifts, meaning Black students get only 4.5 hours of education per day—well below the city's six-hour minimum.

Around the country, other cities follow suit, walking back progress instead of following through. The Ku Klux Klan, which closed its doors during the war, revives in Atlanta, and soon enclaves spring up all over the country, branding themselves as anti-communist. A bill creating a permanent Fair Employment Practices Committee, established by executive order during the war, is filibustered by Southern Democrats in the Senate and dies. Things aren't just bad, they're the *opposite* of how they should be. Laws can't stop segregation when the lawbreakers aren't punished. Segregationists refuse to play with a fair deck. They keep stacking all the cards, keeping all the chips on their side.

America's inequality is a favorite target for Soviet propaganda, especially when it happens in DC. Black activists argue that the nation's racial hypocrisy—particularly the racism in Washington—undermines America's moral authority. Articles in Washington's *Afro American* claim that America's strongest defense against communism is civil rights.

Enforcing anti-lynching and antipoll tax laws, ending Jim Crow travel restrictions, and passing fair employment legislation will prove to the Russians that America is serious about democracy.

Black women's organizations lead the charge in unifying civil rights efforts across the country. Religious, cultural, academic, and political associations band together to promote not just Black civil rights, but rights for all women to participate in the country's governance and the rights of all children to receive an education. The National Non-Partisan Council works with the NAACP to draft legislation integrating government offices, like the State Department. The College Alumnae Club continues to provide scholarships and promote education among Black women, even as employment opportunities diminish. The YWCA opens libraries, sponsors speakers and cultural events, and continues to train Black women to work in the USO and Hostess Houses overseas. Sororities like Zeta Phi Beta join forces with Black women's clubs and the National Association for Colored Women to support—and fund—national civil rights projects.

Meanwhile, the Southern Christian Leadership Conference leads efforts to combat discrimination against returning soldiers. During the war, Southern communities feared the presence of educated Black men in the military, who demanded better treatment than those accustomed to Southern racism. Riots, lynching, murder, battery—all these soldiers suffered in the United States at the hands of their white countrymen. That violence against Black soldiers during the war leaves many unwilling to accept postwar discrimination. They won't go down without a fight.

The "Negro Problem" is a focal point in the media and policy discussions, as it has been throughout history whenever Black Americans push for greater rights. For white racists, the problem lies in finding Black people a proper place in society—not alongside white Americans as equals. Civil rights advocates argue that Black Americans have always deserved equal rights under the Constitution, and now they have given too much through service, sacrifice, and activism to be left on the sidelines of America's prosperity or pushed to society's margins.

POSTWAR TRANSITION

Stacks of cables rustle as a breeze from the open window catches the edges. Ethel adjusts her reading glasses, skims another telegram, and sets it in the "decode" pile. Around her, the hum of typewriters and faint clatter of heels echo in a room that feels both familiar and hollow.

The air is thicker now—less charged but more anxious.

Amid the Agency's restructuring, the Commercial Code Unit is caught in a liminal space. Now located in the Army Security Agency (ASA), its designator is AS-93K, but Ethel still calls it the Commercial Code Unit. The work feels the same. Still part of the Cryptanalysis Branch, still sifting through and breaking commercial codes—but things are changing.

The stacks of intercepts get taller every day. Unregulated trade surges as countries scramble to put their economies and businesses back together. The unit is busier than ever—but the urgency that lit the room from within is gone. They still oversee every piece of foreign trade traffic that passes through the United States, but the purpose is fuzzy.

The Agency is shifting beneath Ethel's feet. Everyone feels it. China and Russia are the new obsessions. Balkan and Slavic languages flood the training bulletins. ASA Pacific strengthens its stations, establishes a new chain of command: All intercepts go straight to the Pentagon. From now on, every signal that flies over those waters is mission critical. At Arlington Hall, B Building echoes with the scraping of wheels as decryption machines are hauled into storage. Crates of German and Japanese intercepts are locked away like a bad memory. The Axis powers are vanquished—but a new enemy is on the horizon. The war is over, but the next one is brewing.

Around Ethel, chairs sit empty. Resignations pile up—one after another.

Martha is first. She packs up her desk with brisk, decisive movements. After Martha's suspension, she was reprimanded for being absent without leave to see her brother off before his deployment. She lost a day's pay and a promotion. Ethel suffered her own suspension in the 1930s—after a six-year legal battle with the DC public school system for an infraction just as minor as Martha's. When Ethel challenged the action, the superintendent called her "impertinent." Ethel knows exactly why Martha is leaving. The Agency is no place for a Black woman who speaks up for herself.

Naomi—brilliant, methodical Naomi—is next to go. Promoted just months before, she's the only other Black woman besides Ethel to become a Research Analyst, P-1. Clearly, the Agency wants her to stay, but Naomi has other plans. She leaves the secretive installation and picks up where she left off—Purdue. Teaching credits. Program complete, she sets off for the Dunbar School in Metropolis, Illinois. Her specialty is high school science, but she'll likely teach grade school and middle school too. Black teachers have to do more with less—and Naomi is up for the challenge.

Charismatic Audrey is transferred to Intercept Control—but she's demoted to typist. In her new role, Audrey will be transcribing intercepts instead of translating them. They may get another French specialist, but to Ethel it's unlikely. The Commercial Code Unit is thinning out. Their wartime victories—breaking critical trade ciphers, tracking diplomatic shifts, scanning tens of thousands of lines of coded traffic—are already fading from memory.

Then comes Operation Shamrock.

An operation so secret even most Agency staff don't know it exists. Ethel hears the whispers. The Office of Censorship that supplied the unit's cables during the war is defunct, but the Agency still needs those intercepts. Private telegrams from RCA, Western Union, ITT. A gold mine of diplomatic trade traffic. Illegality brushed aside. "Necessary for national security."

The Agency is siphoning foreign telegrams, copying them in secret, running them through hand-picked processors. This is exactly the kind of work Ethel and her team are built for. They were trained for this under fire. They know the codebooks, the indicators, the jargon, the chaos. The Agency didn't want to admit it, but during the war, the Black codebreakers held their own.

The Agency pressures these cable companies to keep the pipeline of private traffic open. Every department wants a piece of Shamrock. The FBI, the State Department. There are more demands than hands, more cables than clerks. And fewer people every month.

Without the Office of Censorship's clerical army to handle the traffic, the Agency has to build its own—and they use the women from the Commercial Code Unit. Not to solve and analyze the codes, but to scan, select, and transcribe it for other branches. Over half of the unit's staff is whisked away to form Shamrock—a top secret clerical operation.

The Commercial Code Unit could be at the center of Shamrock. They exploited the same traffic during the war with excellent results. Instead, the Soviet branches take over.

The unit is pushed to the sidelines. They become invisible, even as the Agency builds its postwar empire on the infrastructure these women maintained.

Ethel doesn't voice her frustration. She doesn't have to. Bill tries to keep morale up, but a knowing silence settles in. It resounds in each rejected transfer request. In clipped memos citing "resource constraints."

By July 1946, only ten codebreakers remain in the unit. The desks feel farther apart. Without the friendly, familiar faces—Martha, Audrey, Naomi, all the decoders and processors who helped win the war—the unit feels incomplete. Bill is still here. For now.

They fall into new workflows, new routines. The work is slower, lonelier, but it still matters. Low-level panic courses through the Agency. Even shorthanded, they're marching into an unknown future, forging a peace that looks a lot like war. With no clear mission, the codebreakers of the Commercial Code Unit do what they've always done—bust through codes and burn through backlogs.

Then the final insult: Ethel's position is reallocated. A P-1 Research Analyst no more—the first Black woman to earn that title is also the last.

They offer her a grade 4 clerical role.

She takes it.

At sixty-one, Ethel is not about to start over. As an answer to why she's accepting the post, on her reapplication form, she writes in clear block letters, "NO DESIRE TO SEVER CONNECTION WITH ASA." She's earned this job a dozen times over, and she'll earn it again if she must. A steady income. Retirement security. That's what matters. She's a master of reinvention—and this is her second World War.

THE IRON CURTAIN

On March 5, 1946, Winston Churchill steps onto the stage at a small-town college in Fulton, Missouri, and delivers a speech that changes history. He's there as a favor to President Truman, who invites him to speak at his alma mater, Westminster College.

At the podium, Churchill paints a stark new reality. "From Stettin in the Baltic to Trieste in the Adriatic, an iron curtain has descended across the Continent." He is talking about the Soviet Union, the new world giant that has amassed a startling portion of territory on the Eurasian continent.

The war is barely over, but Churchill is already warning about a new conflict—a shadowy struggle between East and West with an enemy the United States neither knows nor understands. Churchill doesn't speak for Britain anymore—after winning the war, he lost the election—but he is a voice of authority. Stalin has gone from an uneasy wartime ally to the face of a growing threat. Churchill's call for a "special relationship" between Britain and the US makes the path ahead clear: The democracies need to stick together.

Ethel is more than conversant in the principles of communism—and the danger of conflating fear and identity. The College Alumnae Club has a standing lecture series on world politics. Even if Ethel isn't on the roster anymore, she knows the parallels, the warning signs of mass paranoia. In her master's thesis, she wrote about "the black peril" and "the rising tide of color" that alarmists believe is threatening white supremacy. Alarmists who twist equality into encroachment and inclusion into infiltration. The backlash is swift—and violent. Based in fear. Not logic.

Arlington Hall is a ghost town behind the gate. White buildings and telephone poles stand sentinel, awaiting orders. Couriers crisscross an empty campus. The Machine Branch has more tabulating machines than people.

The Cryptanalytic Branch runs with a skeleton crew and just enough maintenance to keep the lights on. What work remains falls on the shoulders of whoever hasn't resigned. That often means the typists—especially the all-Black units formed after the war. These women, many veterans of the Commercial Code Unit, now process high-volume traffic on impossible deadlines. It's grueling, thankless work.

In the new all-Black units, Black men become supervisors. The Agency awards Bill Coffee a Meritorious Civilian Service Award, and he's put in charge of a new typing unit. Herman Phynes takes over as head civilian in the Commercial Code Unit. Without a white officer overseeing the groups, Herman and Bill become the first Black men to head professional units at the Agency. There's a sinister message behind this progress: Black leadership emerges from shrinking spaces, not stable ones.

Getting reliable intelligence on the Soviet Union is crucial to charting a way forward—but it's nearly impossible. The Hall doesn't have the money or the manpower to make it work, and the target is tougher and less familiar than before—ruthless, meticulous, with unknown capabilities.

Russian intelligence comes from two sources: the Washington-Ladd Field line in Alaska—a Lend-Lease gift to the Soviets during the war—and Shamrock. Spy teleprinters in a dark corner of A Building download and copy each telegraph that travels over the Alaskan line. These intercepts reveal a startling alliance: Stalin is selling Lend-Lease machinery to China. China was an ally during the war—they too received Lend-Lease aid. But another alliance is taking shape. The United States doesn't know how yet, but they're part of Stalin's plan.

With Shamrock, the Agency scarfs up low-level diplomatic codes and trade, finding intel that fills crucial gaps. The Iron Curtain speech forged a tighter bond between the US and Great Britain—a "special relationship" to pool their resources against Stalin.

Codebreakers at Bletchley Park—now part of the Government Communications Headquarters (GCHQ)—already have a Soviet operation underway, and the Agency climbs on board. The collaboration is called Operation Bourbon—a combined effort against Soviet ciphers. They've each made some progress, but not nearly enough.

The British are working on Russian plaintext telegrams. They've proved valuable, but the US hasn't bothered: Their sights are set on high-level traffic. Plaintext comes from the Soviet civil telegraph network, which is open to the public. No one would send an important message over an open line. Enciphered or not, there's too much risk. The United States doesn't have manpower to wade through haystacks just to find a few needles. They need to know Soviet intentions in Europe, and Stalin's generals will hardly send that through the Central Telegraph.

While the Agency is looking overseas, Soviet spy networks gain precious ground in the United States. The FBI doesn't share its data: It's part of an intelligence turf war that keeps the US agencies at one another's throats. They hoard resources instead of pooling them. Each wants to prove they cracked the code or got the intelligence first. As a result, neither the president nor the Agency knows the full scale of the threat.

Unfortunately, the greatest threat is in the Agency's own living room. William "Bill" Weisband, a former Army language expert, has been at the Agency since 1943. In his late thirties with a receding hairline and an easy, outgoing nature, he seems harmless. He chats with anyone he sees—and before the person realizes it, they're friends. A Ukrainian American, Weisband is fluent in Russian and aids the analysts working the Russian problem. As a linguistic advisor, he has full access to decrypted Soviet communications—even the sensitive stuff coming out of Venona, the Russian section's top secret project.

Weisband is an NKVD spy. Codename "Link." On paper, he's a naturalized American born to Russian émigré parents in Egypt. He's passed all the Agency's background checks. His Top Secret Codeword clearance at Arlington Hall gets him past any guard, any door. In the halls of B Building, he lingers by desks, asks innocent-sounding questions, and secretly reports it all back to Stalin.

And then there's Amtorg. Since its days peddling furs and caviar, the Soviet trading company has grown to seven hundred employees—all of them spies—spread over nine floors and seventy-five thousand square feet of real estate in the heart of Manhattan. Couriers, handlers, captains, contacts, informants—every link in the Soviet spy chain connects there. Each contact has their own connections, and there's no telling where the branches end. Amtorg is the center of the KGB spiderweb, with a whole operation for reproducing stolen plans, memos, blueprints. Microfilm. Forgeries. Shamrock times a thousand. Amtorg still does millions of dollars of business each year with major US companies—Ford, RCA, General Electric. The FBI buzzes around Amtorg but never gets close enough to sting.

Ethel has never met Weisband, but it's easy to see where offices are filling up as others empty out: They need Russian linguists and translators. Hiring native speakers is tricky, so the Agency retrains everyone it can. Japanese experts take an intensive four-week course and emerge as Russian specialists. Analysts and translators from all branches are scooped into the Russian problem. Branch chiefs besiege Personnel with requests for anyone with a strong language background.

Not only is Ethel bilingual in German, she also taught high school Spanish and Latin for years. Personnel has her résumé on file—BA in German literature from Ohio State in 1906, MA in English from Boston University in 1936, summer programs at the University of Pennsylvania and Harvard College. Decades of teaching, education, and translation.

Ethel's name is never called. Her file is never pulled.

6

SCARED NEW WORLD
DECEMBER 1946–NOVEMBER 1947

Ethel is in charge of the new trainee—cryptanalytic clerk Alberta James, grade 3. Tall, sharp-browed, with wavy hair and fair skin, Alberta is Black by "one drop." She could pass for white, but she doesn't. She marks "Negro" on her forms, but the Personnel Office overrides her, marking "*W*" on her paperwork.

It's surprising for the unit to get a new hire. The postwar economy slowed—then reversed. The cost of living is up 28 percent, and inflation rises as the United States pumps dollars into Europe. Ethel has only herself to support—her children are living away or married. Old friends from Howard and colleagues from Virginia keep her busy, but she hasn't returned to public life. The government is more paranoid about loyalty than ever. Everyone who's stayed with the Agency has signed an affidavit vowing not to strike against the government. Federal employees can unionize, but the Agency can't take that risk. With union activity growing across the country—and fear of communism rising alongside it—dissatisfied workers pose a threat. The Agency is struggling to keep its workforce—let alone keep it happy—and political foment is the last thing it needs.

Only one thing matters: Does Stalin have the bomb? That question fills every operation, every decision. And the clock is ticking. President Truman is demanding intelligence. He needs insight on what to do next.

The worst thing for the United States is not being able to act. Doing something, even the wrong thing, is preferable to inaction. The Agency knows this—and as one source of intelligence after another falls short, they have to change their game plan.

Ethel doesn't talk about her past, but she watches Alberta closely: how carefully she checks the substitution tables, how methodically she completes each task before beginning the next. Ethel mentors young women like Alberta at the YWCA—so full of purpose but aware of the walls ahead. Black women are trained to be meticulous in their work; they know the world doubts them, that their performance can make or break opportunities for everyone like them. Alberta trained as a teacher at Miner Teachers College, and it's not clear how long she'll stay.

Maybe Naomi writes to Ethel now and then, maybe not. She has left Metropolis for Chicago for a biomedical internship. She's stunned by the rich culture and opportunities in Chicago. Like DC, Chicago experienced a Second Great Migration with the war, with thousands of Black families moving northward to escape the worsening Jim Crow South. Bronzeville and the South Side are Chicago's "Black Metropolis," where Naomi and other newcomers escape the restrictive housing covenants that circumscribe white neighborhoods. Like the LeDroit Park community in DC, these neighborhoods boast their own amenities and services—mostly. But these small areas can't sustain the rapid growth happening in the city.

Chicago's population nearly doubles from 278,000 to over 500,000. Housing and social services strain and then crack under the pressure, leaving people without safe housing and basic necessities. Whites use public housing developments like the Ida B. Wells and Robert Taylor Homes to reinforce segregation: They point to them as evidence that Black people don't need to move to their neighborhoods, drawing red lines tighter. The city passes Urban Renewal legislation, giving them power to seize derelict properties for "rehabilitation." The effort displaces tens of thousands of

Black Chicagoans, forcing them into quickly deteriorating public housing.

The same thing happens across the country in Philadelphia, New York, St. Louis, Los Angeles, Oakland. Black families are barred from the suburbs. Squeezed into housing projects. City neighborhoods are overcrowded. Public funding is cut and services privatized. Resources disappear.

But Black Americans have labor—and organization.

Chicago's Black workers fill jobs and strengthen unions. In the Congress of Industrial Organizations (CIO), they fight for real jobs and fair pay. The integrated union—one of the few—draws leaders from the Communist Party USA. They have close ties with Moscow—for global solidarity.

Naomi keeps her activism in the church. She's keenly aware of world politics, but right now, civil rights are more important than foreign conflicts. Before leaving Metropolis, as part of a church youth convention, Naomi gave a talk on "What the Young Negro Wants." No doubt, she focuses on one theme: opportunity. For education, employment, inclusion in civic life. A voice. A vote.

The Double V.

Or the Triple V, for Black women.

Changes aren't taking place in only Chicago's Black communities. The dust from the bombs hasn't settled. Tests continue—on islands far from the public eye—but physicists are split between war and peace.

The atomic science community is struggling to de-weaponize nuclear research, with varying degrees of success. The Chicago Met Lab, once home to the Manhattan Project, becomes Argonne National Laboratory. Run by the Atomic Energy Commission (AEC), it develops nuclear reactors and radiation treatments. Biomedical labs like Michael Reese test these new life-saving technologies: radiation therapy, isotope tracers, diagnostic imaging. Once at the forefront of codebreaking, Naomi is now on the front lines of biotech research.

But it's not all good news. Nuclear technology moves too fast.

Researchers, the government, the public—no one understands its implications. Even in the aftermath of Hiroshima and Nagasaki, the United States defends its decision to drop the bombs—despite protest from the scientists who built them.

The Soviet Union claims it is on the side of peace, disarmament. They reject the US plan for international arms control and propose their own: "The Russians tell the Americans, raise your nuclear secrecy curtain and we will raise our iron one enough to allow you to visit periodically our mines and our plants." The United States rejects this plan. Stalin must throw open the curtain—release real production figures and test site locations.

Behind the Iron Curtain, they have one mission—build the bomb. They're not there yet—but they're close. "Task #1," Lavrentyi Beria calls it. Beria leads Russia's secret police *and* nuclear program, which keeps US atomic secrets flowing into Moscow. The Kurchatov Institute leads the science, and on Christmas Day, December 25, 1946, the F-1 reactor goes critical. Sustained nuclear fission is no longer America's alone. The Soviets aimed for—and achieved—the same pace as the Manhattan Project: Zero to fission in under three years.

The West says regulation—the Soviets, disarmament. With so little intelligence, the United States doesn't know whether Stalin is bluffing. Is he daring the US to disarm first, only to launch a surprise attack? Stalin's words in a *Guardian* interview are cryptic. When asked if he has the bomb, he tells the journalist: "Atomic bombs are intended for intimidating weak nerves . . . But a monopoly on the bomb cannot last long."

Does Stalin mean he has it, is close to having it, or that soon all atomic weapons will be prohibited?

There is no clear answer, no data from which to draw conclusions.

The United States decides not to take chances, and the AEC expands nuclear weapons production. The Americans now have about thirteen nuclear bombs—of the Fat Man and Little Boy designs dropped on Hiroshima and Nagasaki. Los Alamos and Sandia Labs focus on making more compact and efficient models. The MK-3—an improved version of Fat Man—enters production. The fledgling stockpile grows—casings, detonators, and warheads rolling off the assembly line.

"SOMEBODY HAD TO DO IT"

With three years of French, Alberta could fill Audrey's role—but the unit hasn't been doing much translating. Instead of decoding traffic, most of the time they're sorting it. Ethel's title is still "Translator," but the work has changed. They're still officially the Commercial Code Unit, but clerical tasks have crept in—and taken over. The Agency reports that "a lack of personnel" makes analyzing new commercial traffic impossible. The personnel do exist: They've just been erased. Stuck in a back office. Converted to clerks. How long will it be before Ethel's title changes again—until she's downgraded another step? She's ready for anything, but the prospects aren't ideal.

The Agency calls on the Machine Branch to work the commercial traffic. IBM decoding—another labor-intensive task—reveals secrets about foreign financial, scientific, and technical activity. It's a rich mine for shipping, communications, even data on key players. It does the same thing the Black codebreakers do—only faster. Ethel's always been healthy. At sixty-one, she's outlived the Black life expectancy of fifty-four and is nearing the white one. She gave birth to her three children at home, as was common for Black women denied hospital care. Her mother was long-lived, passing in 1935, just before her seventy-fifth birthday. If IBM cards are the future, Ethel will take her place at the machine. She's never run from a challenge, but there's no telling how long she'll hold out.

Clerical work is shifted onto the Black codebreakers because the white codebreakers want out. A constant complaint in the Agency is the need for a better division of labor between intelligence and clerical staff. In wartime, everyone did everything. Translators filed and analysts typed.

The Agency shaped itself to meet wartime needs, whatever was needed for the mission. But scanning, sorting, filing, copying, and indexing never end. Government work is paperwork—even supersecret intelligence work is mostly recordkeeping. After the war, intelligence personnel begin to get angry that they are still responsible for mundane tasks.

During the war, cryptanalysts stayed an average of one and a half years—clerks for seven months—but those numbers are dropping. Pay and morale are low. "Need to know" secrecy keeps codebreakers and clerical staff from understanding how their daily work contributes to the larger mission. With heightened secrecy around missions like Bourbon, Venona, and Shamrock, the disconnect between workers and their contribution gets worse. Not even Audrey knows she's doing "Shamrock." She's just transcribing messages.

As the first chill of the Cold War sets in, UN meetings conclude without peace deals. Tension among world leaders is high. The press feeds a rattled public, and the administration wobbles on shaky ground. A deluge of diplomatic chatter creates a flood of intelligence work. Only speedy decryption, translation, and distribution can keep American representatives fully informed. At the Agency, intransigence among analysts who resent doing clerical weight is poorly timed.

The brunt of this information storm falls on typists like Audrey and the other codebreakers who transferred to Shamrock. They had no idea what was in store. Being a typist might sound easy, but it's one of the most thankless jobs at the Agency. The work is high-volume: Every branch chief wants their copies yesterday. In a world of vanishing opportunities for Black women, it's where most of the Commercial Code Unit was transferred, and where most new hires end up.

Audrey is feeling the weight of this role. Codebreaking was collaborative, full of challenges. There were victories to celebrate, a sense of accomplishment. But now Audrey and a room full of other women are chained to their desks, performing rote tasks under strict discipline for low pay. Audrey's hit the promotion ceiling: A grade 4 clerk, she may get pay increases, but she'll never advance to grade 5. That's the starting grade for supervisors, and that role will be filled by a white woman or a Black man. With the wartime experiment of hiring Black codebreakers over, the Agency has resumed its traditional hierarchy: white military men heading departments, white civilian men doing high-level research, and white women doing clerical and mid-level work. Black men run the all-Black units or get stuck in the mail room and quit. Black women get whatever is left over.

One day, Audrey has to leave early, and the next day, she comes to work one hour late. The penalty? Three days' suspension. There's no record of what happened—whether she had a medical or personal emergency—but the reason doesn't matter. In a workplace bending over backward to accommodate the lateness and absenteeism of its white workers, a high-performing Black woman loses three days of pay for a five-hour misstep.

Audrey knows she's worth more than this. She's on track for law school, ready to start a family. A bright future lies ahead. A week later, she resigns. The Agency can bully someone else.

Shamrock continues to secretly duplicate copies of domestic commercial traffic sent to the Agency by RCA, ITT, and Western Union. As the messages become more crucial to intelligence, more and more departments require copies, which strains the already burdened workforce. The teletype operation has special difficulty keeping up with demand: Producing one good copy of these messages, as was required last year, is no longer enough. Then, Shamrock was a photographing operation, taking photos of the copied telegrams rather than printing them. The process was arduous but straightforward. Now, when the machines malfunction, the teletype operators must throw out failed copies and service the machines under strict time constraints to get multiple good copies as required.

Part of this burden eases when RCA converts its commercial circuits from cable to wireless teletype, which means the companies can now send reperforated tapes containing many messages instead of sending printed tapes that require the operators to type out the messages onto sheet paper one at a time.

"Reperforated" means that the cable company's staff reencode the message, which comes into the cable company's office on a long string of Morse-encoded perforated tape, after running it through the teletype printer that translates the Morse code into regular text. The printed messages are snipped off the tape and sent to the recipient, either a private citizen or a governmental department.

The technological advance marks another change in Black workers' roles. Because the teletype printers translate Morse code into plaintext, Shamrock becomes mainly a machine operation. The staff's job is to operate and fix jams in the printers as needed. It's happening all over the Agency. As many operations as possible now use teletype printers. The technology is so cutting-edge that the Agency even installs one in the presidential plane.

White workers continue to beg their way out of these grade 2 and 3 machine-processing roles, but it's the single greatest need for producing Soviet intelligence. Shamrock, the Machine Division, and Russian plaintext all need typists and machine processors.

In 1947 the Agency makes a decision. No policy, no memos. Just a silent, systematic hiring of Black women as key punchers, card punchers, teletypists. Dozens of them. They have no leverage. They can't demand raises or transfers. And they've signed anti-strike agreements.

No one wants to do this work, but as former unit chief Benson Buffham says, "Somebody had to do it."

GLOBAL AND DOMESTIC PARANOIA

The Cold War's new world order ushers in both global and domestic paranoia, as the United States navigates its shifting alliances. Inside Arlington Hall, the Russian Section's Venona project discovers that a Soviet spy has infiltrated the War Department's General Staff. The decrypted messages are from 1944, which means that the spy's ring has been active for a while. The FBI is already investigating Soviet agents whom Elizabeth Bentley, "the Blond Spy Queen," identified the previous year, but the FBI can't use wiretapped evidence in court. Venona's discovery remains hidden for now, and neither the government nor the public knows just how deeply the US atomic program has been compromised.

The United States has its own double agents, but they are not nearly as effective as Stalin's. The FBI turns one such agent, Hollywood producer Boris Morros, codename FROST, into an informant. Morros reports the activities of the almost defunct Soble spy ring and sends low-level misinformation back to Moscow.

The FBI's spy trials raise public fears of Soviet infiltration—real and imagined—and these mix with lingering fears from the previous war. In March 1947, Eleanor Roosevelt and the Society for the Prevention of World War III convene in New York City and argue for a "harsh peace" with Germany instead of helping them rebuild as the US intends to do with the rest of Europe. Though Hitler is dead, a strong Nazi Germany could rise again, this time with atomic weapons.

The Society includes prominent members of the political and scientific communities, but the movement does not gain traction. Germany is too big to fail, and too important as the United States' easternmost defense front against Soviet encroachment into Europe. West Berlin, inconveniently located in Soviet-controlled East Germany, is an asset the Allies can't afford to lose. The Allies have a wartime pact with Stalin that allows them to transport supplies in and out of West Berlin, and destroying Germany's economy poses great danger to the people and occupying forces who rely on this aid.

With proxy territories like East and West Berlin representing Soviet and US power, Truman realizes that the Cold War will not only be a standoff with Russia. The rest of the world is involved, whether they want to be or not. Ideology—democracy versus communism—is still at the heart of the conflict as each side tries to strengthen their global presence.

On March 12, 1947, Truman gives a speech pledging US support to any country resisting communism. The war has not damaged the United States as it has its European allies, so in current and imminent Soviet attempts to overthrow governments weakened by fascism, the US can intervene without the United Nations' agreement. This speech becomes known as the Truman Doctrine, and it forms the modern view of the US as the world's sole defender of democracy. Truman intends the speech to arouse public support for intervention in strategically located Greece and Turkey. Because the US has its own economic troubles, no one is eager to spend tax dollars on foreign aid.

To strengthen his commitment to democracy and stem growing fears of Soviet infiltration inside the government, on March 21, Truman issues Executive Order 9835, establishing the Loyalty Program, which requires federal employees to sign oaths and undergo loyalty screenings for suspected communist ties.

RUSSIAN AT THE PENTAGON

Government loyalty goes in only one direction. While the Agency drowns Ethel in busywork, her LeDroit Park Civic Association honors Oliver Cowan, a young policeman who fights for integration in the community. "If you let children associate when they are small," he says, "they will love one another the rest of their lives." Ethel knows the value of an integrated upbringing. In 1890, Ripley, Ohio, was home to a German immigrant community of Quakers, who lived side by side with the town's Black residents. Ethel grew up speaking German among classmates, friends, and neighbors. More than fifty years later, the idea sounds radical in America. A new kind of fear grips the country, one that Ethel couldn't have predicted. In 1900, when she attended an integrated high school in Columbus, Ohio, Marie Curie had just coined the term "radioactive" to describe uranium's strange behavior. Albert Einstein hadn't yet discovered relativity. It was a different universe.

It must be difficult to see the country sliding backward, but Ethel knows change doesn't happen on its own. She's not on the frontlines of civic activism now, but she'll keep supporting those who are.

Meanwhile, the Agency is flying blind.

Unlike the British—who've been tracking Soviet Lend-Lease sales to communists in China since the war—the United States has almost no reliable intelligence on the Soviet Union. The Agency needs new sources of SIGINT and a workforce fluent in Russian, loyal beyond question. But it doesn't have the funding. Or the personnel. Or the time.

So they try something desperate.

The director of intelligence greenlights a part-time pilot project to translate Russian plaintext traffic intercepted from the Soviet civil telegraph network. It's so secret they don't even run it out of Arlington Hall. Instead, they bury it inside the Pentagon.

At first, it's chaos. A few Russian linguists are given stacks of intercepts and told to translate anything "with intelligence value." With no prioritization system, they pick telegrams that are easiest to read—never mind where they came from or what they contain. Most yield fragments. But some tell stories.

The messages come from the Soviet economic ministries. Production quotas. Shipments. Banking arrangements. Each snippet provides a glimpse of how the Soviet economy works—details the Kremlin strives to keep hidden.

British intelligence knows the value of this material. American liaison Oliver Kirby, back from Bletchley Park, brings in Jack Gurin—a Russian native speaker and former Japanese linguist—to salvage the effort. Gurin sees the potential immediately. To him, plaintext isn't a waste of time—it's a *gold mine*.

In the basement of Arlington Hall's cafeteria, Army and Navy technicians jury-rig new machines to speed up plaintext scanning. With the right tools, one person can review hundreds of messages a day. But the problem is nobody wants to do that.

Processing plaintext means feeding punch tape into radioprinters that convert signals into Cyrillic text. It's loud, repetitive, and exhausting. Tapes get stuck, machines jam. One by one, the white clerical staff bail out. They request transfers. Take sick leave. Anything to get away from the Flex machines.

Without the processing staff, the project stalls.

Supervisors scoff at the whole idea. They tell Gurin, "If it were important, the Russians would encipher it." The traditionalists dismiss plaintext as background noise; they hold it in "contempt." But Gurin keeps fighting for the only source of Russian intelligence they have. Not only is it better than nothing—it's a window into a new world. Gurin recalls, "We didn't know anything about the Soviet economy, it was all kept very secret."

To organize the chaos, Gurin splits up the work by economic ministry. His main linguists head sections devoted to different sectors of Soviet production. Olin Adams heads the main section on atomic energy and nonferrous metallurgy. Pat O'Sullivan takes the aviation ministries. Heavy industry, transportation, and Soviet production are major areas of research. New personnel arrive, and suddenly, plaintext is a full-fledged operation.

In May 1947, the Plaintext Group is reborn—first at the Pentagon, then in a wing of B Building. By November, the team has grown: forty linguists, fifteen processing clerks. The clerks are Black, transferred from the Census Bureau and segregated from the white staff. David Bryant, a Navy veteran and former statistical clerk, leads the group of fourteen women. They're stationed in the "Flex room," a corner of A Building's basement named for the clattering teletype machines they run.

Their task is the same one the white clerks rejected: Load the tape. Press the button. Fix the jams. Monitor the output. Print three hundred messages a day.

They do it—without recognition or complaint, under pressure.

The intercepts pour in—one hundred thousand Soviet plaintext messages every month. The Flex room scans, separates, and prints them. They produce 4,500 pages of intercepts per day.

And with that, the Plaintext Group finally delivers.

By the end of the year, Russian plaintext has a codename: Task I, just like the bomb it aims to destroy.

The Agency has something it's never had before: a consistent, accurate stream of intelligence from behind the Iron Curtain. For the first time, the United States knows what Stalin is building, and how fast he's building it.

They have numbers. Names. Nuclear data.

And they have it thanks to the Flex room staff.

COUNTDOWN TO DOOMSDAY

The Agency's plaintext breakthrough is monumental. But it's not enough.

While they translate the gold mine of telegrams, Lavrentyi Beria—head of the Soviet secret police—is mining something far more dangerous.

Soviet extraction teams descend on northern Korea in search of radioactive thorium and uranium. The coming war won't be won on intelligence alone: rare elements, wire, timber, steel—resources the Soviets can't afford to lose. They will be tracking these shipments thoroughly.

Stalin strains production to its breaking point: In East Germany, prisoners in Soviet-run mines produce more than 150 tons of uranium—double last year's output. Another 130 tons come from Central Asia.

Meanwhile, in the southern Ural Mountains, Gulag laborers complete Chelyabinsk-65, the Soviets' first secret nuclear city. It doesn't officially exist—or appear on maps. Its inhabitants are struck from the census. They can't leave its gates.

Hidden behind barbed wire, Chelyabinsk-65 houses the Mayak reactor complex, the Soviets' first plutonium production plant—and the heart of Stalin's nuclear ambitions. It's modeled directly on the United States' Hanford site, thanks to blueprints stolen by Beria's spies from the Manhattan Project.

This is where Stalin's first bomb will be built.

Back in Washington, Truman creates Strategic Air Command (SAC), a new branch of the US Air Force tasked with preparing for nuclear war. While the Atomic Energy Commission manages weapons production, SAC focuses on delivery—securing overseas air bases and refining long-range bombing strategy. The B-29 Superfortress, which destroyed

Hiroshima and Nagasaki, is now standard equipment. Meanwhile, Truman introduces the Marshall Plan to rebuild Western Europe—and position US forces closer to the Soviet border.

But none of this answers the central question:

How close is Stalin to the bomb?

The United States doesn't know what the Soviets have—how many plants, how much uranium. Grain, coal, cigarettes—anything a society needs to function. Soviet embassy reports suggest modest production goals—but the US doesn't trust them. All the Americans know about Russian trade is furs and caviar. They've been giving the Soviets raw materials since the war—but there's no telling what's stored behind the Iron Curtain.

In Chicago, a group of physicists—veterans of the Manhattan Project— see where this is going. They issue a warning to the government and military. They know better than anyone how close the country and the world are to self-annihilation.

On the cover of their magazine, *Bulletin of the Atomic Scientists,* they place a symbol: a stylized clock, white against safety hazard orange, its hands poised at seven minutes to midnight.

They call it the Doomsday Clock.

It's ticking.

PAINTING THE BLACK SCARE RED

Outside the Agency, civil rights activists risk their lives to push for integration. On April 9, 1947, Jackie Robinson debuts for the Brooklyn Dodgers, breaking Major League Baseball's color barrier. He faces violence, racial slurs, and death threats from hostile fans, opponents, and his own teammates. Even his family is threatened, but the Dodgers' manager makes Robinson promise not to retaliate. Later that month, the Journey of Reconciliation, led by the Congress of Racial Equality, tests compliance with the Supreme Court's 1946 ruling against segregation in interstate bus travel (*Morgan v. Virginia*). Riders face arrests and violence in the South.

Each advance faces a backlash. Mary Church Terrell integrated the American Association of University Women (AAUW) in 1905, but after merging with the Southern Association of College Women, the organization blocks Terrell's membership. At this crucial point in history, it's a common story. White women seek equality with men, but their racial solidarity with white men trumps their gender solidarity with Black women. White women are the swing state of opportunity in a race- and gender-divided world—and they almost always vote one way. At times, white women's institutions accept white-passing women, but when their race is discovered, they are expelled.

Terrell's legal appeals are denied. As the postwar women's rights movement gains momentum, Black women are locked out of the country's most powerful advocacy group for women's education.

Terrell doesn't give up hope. She's been crusading for fifty years and is not about to give up. The AAUW is part of a bigger problem. "I believe something must be done by the United States Government to force the States that violate the 14th and 15th Amendments of the Constitution," she tells the *Baltimore Afro-American*. "If this were done, the colored people in those states could protect themselves by their vote." Southern politicians brand resistance to voting rights and integration as anti-communist. "It would be laughable if it were not such a tragedy to hear everyone called a communist who believes in giving the colored man the right of citizenship and privileges of which he is entitled." She finds DC more prejudiced now than ever: "I can remember when I had no trouble whatsoever going to the moves and getting served in the drug stores."

Terrell is right: America is becoming more hostile to equal rights. The House Un-American Activities Committee (HUAC) sharpens its investigations into "subversive" Black labor unions and civil rights groups. With the FBI, they focus on highly visible figures like W. E. B. Du Bois, the cofounder of the NAACP, to send a message. Paul Robeson, an actor, singer, and activist who publicly denounces HUAC and defends the Soviet

Union's record on racial equality, draws government scrutiny, and is put on Hollywood's blacklist. The Civil Rights Congress, a civil rights group founded in Detroit, is labeled as "communist influenced."

Before the Cold War, communism was seen as a political threat but not a moral evil. The Truman Doctrine equates communism with everything that opposes American values. Labeling civil rights groups "communist" is the same as labeling them "un-American." Early on, Black interest in communism divorced itself from world revolution and focused on organizing labor. The US's Communist Party is a hub for spies, but HUAC knows that Black Americans have nothing to do with that side of the party. But they know they can catch two birds with one stone: quell civil rights and Black labor activism *and* unmask traitors. HUAC uses the "subversive" label to put anyone under suspicion—especially those already deemed troublesome—well before grand jury testimony reveals who the spies are.

W. E. B. Du Bois isn't accused of passing secrets to Stalin. He's targeted for calling out American abuses of human rights. He submits a paper to the UN titled "An Appeal to the World!" describing decades of human rights violations under US law. The paper never makes it to the floor. The reason? The UN doesn't intervene in a country's "domestic jurisdiction." The United States is too powerful an ally—and too formidable an enemy. Black Americans will have to fight their battle without international support.

Du Bois's paper fuels social discord that's already at a fever pitch, but Truman sees a way to capitalize on it. 1948 is an election year, and the most divisive and critical issue in the country is civil rights. At least strategically, Truman is on board.

He's already set up a committee to investigate civil rights violations. Its report, titled "To Secure These Rights," recommends anti-lynching laws, voting protections, and broad desegregation. Many such laws exist but are not enforced, such as Executive Order 8820, which forbids segregation in the federal government. Roosevelt issued an executive order to desegregate the armed forces in 1940—but the military ignores it.

Southern lawmakers believe segregation is the American way of life. Changing that threatens the values on which the country is based. Equating civil rights with communism doesn't have to make sense. It gives segregationists a rallying point. They are patriots protecting the country from a dangerous foreign enemy.

Days before Ethel turns sixty-two, she's promoted back to grade 5. The same grade she started with. Things are changing, and it's not clear where Ethel fits in. There are more Black workers at Arlington Hall, but they're not in B Building. Maybe Ethel has heard rumors of a new unit somewhere in the basement. The "plantation." Some of the Commercial Code staff have been transferred out and are most likely there. The little bit of trade traffic they're analyzing has moved to the Machine Division. The IBM conversion process isn't the modern revolution they thought it would be. It's slow and clunky—it can only analyze a fraction of the traffic—but the Agency still prefers it to having the Black codebreakers remain in professional roles. Ethel's a born teacher. She doesn't mind helping Alberta learn the ropes. Coined by Mary Church Terrell, the motto of Black women activists is "lifting as we climb." For every advancement a Black woman makes, she carries the whole community with her—her own generation and the next. But even true believers like Ethel must get tired. The ladder is high, and there's still so far to climb.

7

ESCALATION

DECEMBER 1947–JULY 1948

As the Agency deepens its postwar mission, Ethel and the Commercial Code Unit fade from sight. Despite their talent, they are the Agency's past—not its future. A vestige of a bygone era, a glimmer of optimism snuffed out. They work hard, tackle new projects when they can, but they're slated for obsolescence.

The future is automation.

Machines require labor, and the Agency makes a plan. Any Black person who steps into the Personnel Office, regardless of their credentials, is going "down in the hole." It's not circulated in a memo or logged in a meeting summary, but it's clear. Machine operators, tabulators, key punchers are grades 2 and 3. They have the highest rate of turnover; keeping the Machine Division staffed has been a constant problem. Workers are late or AWOL, and the Agency needs that to stop. Instead of trying to appease its workers, they hire Black people into those positions. They no longer need to care about their comfort or well-being. They can crack down on discipline. No promotions, no transfers. No time off. "Of course, that puts a fear into you," former Machine Processing Division (MPRO) employee Shirley McConnell recalls. "You can't lose this job; it's all you have."

This is work on "the plantation." The nickname isn't a joke. "The way they talked to you at that time was just so demeaning . . . You could see that it was like keeping you in your place."

In December 1947, Geneva Trust Arthur is the first Black woman to arrive in the Machine Processing Division. Data conversion via punch cards is the heart of MPRO's codebreaking process, and Geneva is assigned to key punch, a typewriter connected to a desk-sized machine that perforates IBM cards with tiny rectangular holes. Soviet traffic keeps coming, and some of it can only be decrypted by the machines of the second floor of A Building. The MPRO processes more than five thousand messages a month—more than twice the amount they did the previous year—but they have far fewer employees than they did during the war. The mammoth codebreaking machines aren't movable, so Geneva and her cohort work alongside the white staff of card punchers, tabulators, and other equipment operators in the Agency's first racially integrated operation.

Geneva stands at the whirring, clacking machine all day, transcribing enciphered messages into a format the machines can read. The IBM cards are 3″ × 8″ pieces of stiff cardboard that fit eighty characters lengthwise in twelve rows, so a page-long telegram requires a stack of twenty cards. Since the holes can't be unpunched, there's no room for error. If she makes a typo, she must throw out the card and begin a new one. Once the cards are correctly punched, Geneva batches them for routing or stacks them in decks to be processed by the tabulators, who operate the deciphering machines. Tabulators stand at their floor-to-ceiling machines all day, feeding them cards and rewiring the switchboards to change operations. It's strenuous and noisy. The windows are paneled over for security.

Geneva has to stand too: "They thought you worked better if you stood, and you weren't permitted to sit on stools." The bosses keep the stools at the workstations for appearances' sake, but the workers can't use them. Without air-conditioning, it's stifling. Standing for eight hours, minus lunch and two breaks, is painful.

Each card puncher and tabulator processes tens of thousands of cards per day, almost without a break. Reproducers, sorters, and collators comprise the division's other data analyzers, and each rapid analytic machine requires a lot of punched cards and human labor. Overall, the division's five thousand monthly messages require five million cards and more than two hundred staff members working round-the-clock shifts.

Geneva's encoding job comes with heavy lifting. The IBM punch cards arrive in sixty-pound cartons, five boxes of two thousand cards each, that a delivery man stacks in a corner near the supply door. Geneva and the other card punch operators have to leave their machines, pick up the boxes of cards, which can weigh up to twenty pounds, and carry them back to their desks. All in cute pumps and calf-length skirts.

As more listening stations sniff out Soviet frequencies, messages pour in from Russia, Yugoslavia, and the Balkans. Geneva goes through five or six boxes of IBM cards per day. Hired at the lowest end of the pay scale—communications clerk grade 2—she and the others endure repetitive, strenuous work in a pressurized environment. At the end of the day, she takes an hour-long segregated bus ride back across the Potomac River to Northeast DC.

More and more, Black women like Geneva and Shirley find themselves in MPRO, working as tabulators and card punchers at the same low grade. The white women and men gradually transfer into better-paying jobs, and the office becomes less integrated, with Black workers and white supervisors.

BIG DATA: CLERKS WANTED

The Machine Processing Division is only one piece of the new operation that is going to break Soviet codes by brute force. The Russian Plaintext Project will use mountains of their data to extract Soviet intelligence, and it will rely on Geneva's lightning-fast clerical labor. Jack Gurin convinces the Agency to invest in plaintext on the idea that small bits of data analyzed in aggregate can yield valuable information. In this case, they're looking at millions of commercial receipts to get intel on the Soviet atomic program.

This is the concept of "big data," which is central to modern technological analysis. Big data is characterized by its volume, velocity, and variety. Plaintext volume is up 500 percent from the previous year. The stream of traffic coming from a continuous collection source (TASS), the speed at which it is processed (clerks), and the variety of messages (every Soviet trade agency) reveal the Russian plaintext operation to be big data analysis before such a concept exists.

Data processing is the bread and butter of this process, and the Black cryptologists hold the knife. They are the CPU driving a massive data processing operation that yields the only hard intelligence on the Soviet atomic program. All areas of the Soviet economy contribute to the big picture—and it's up to the linguists and analysts in B Building to connect the dots.

Cryptanalysis uses the "hunt and peck" method of selecting individual enciphered messages that are difficult to crack. During the war, the Allies built complex machines to perform innumerable calculations on a relatively small data set of messages. No one thought to reverse the process and apply a relatively small number of processes to an immense data set. Prejudice against low-level sources and low-level work prevented the Agency from imagining this as an option.

The Black cryptologists who aren't working the machines are assigned to manual processing, and that means performing keyword searches. So far, David Bryant and the women in the Flex room have kept pace, but the volume of plaintext is increasing, and scanning it is a priority. Keyword searches are usually a cursory phase of a much larger process, but they're the heart of plaintext. Cryptanalysis focuses on numerical operations, not words. Translated words are the end product, not the beginning. Keyword scans weed out unnecessary traffic so analysts can home in on the messages that matter. The idea that the simple act of a word search can form the basis for an intelligence operation never enters the Agency's mind. But it's all they can do with this plaintext. Word search technology is decades away—the only search engines the Agency has are people.

The Flex room clerks now process more than 150,000 messages a month, using their ability to read Baudot code and the accompanying Russian text. They scan based on a list of three thousand Russian keywords with their English equivalents, technical terms that signal a message contains intelligence. The clerks sort traffic according to the messages' address codes, stamp them with serial numbers, and route them to B Building for analysis. Scanning each message must take under two minutes because the Black clerks have daily quotas.

When the project started, the Task I linguists couldn't scan fast enough to keep plaintext intelligence flowing. The Flex room clerks have a quota of scanning three hundred messages per day—and consequences for failure—ensuring that their numbers stay high. They are hired at the lowest levels, grades 2 and 3, despite most having college degrees, which merit a 4 or 5. The Task I analysts can't keep up with the volume of traffic the unit sends their way despite having more than forty people on staff. Thirty percent of the messages go into a backlog that's never cleared. The rate of intelligence production slows. The Agency doesn't lighten the clerks' workload though—they just let the scanned traffic pile up, leaving valuable material unread.

Despite its shaky start, Task I's first project is a success. With all that material from the Flex room, the analysts compile a report on Soviet nonferrous metallurgy that earns a letter of appreciation from the director of intelligence. Nonferrous metallurgy includes radioactive isotopes. Finally, the US has real data on the Soviet atomic program.

The letter of appreciation commends the Task I group on its teamwork. Part of Bourbon—the US-UK Russian intelligence project—plaintext is a joint effort between agencies, including the Army and Navy. Even though they can barely stand one another, they work together on this, and it pays off.

The Agency's annual report extols Task I's processing and intelligence results. They recognize the 1.8 million messages handled by the Flex room throughout the year and note how well the program is run. Getting the right messages to the right analysts is tricky: The clerks separate them into seventy categories that are routed to eighteen different sections in the B Building based on subject area, date, time of intercept, frequency, intercept station, and circuit of origin. Printouts are nicely batched and organized when they reach the analysts, significantly cutting down their workload.

SOVIET SECRET CITY #2

Unfortunately, one report doesn't tell the whole story. A second secret city, Arzamas-16, is the Soviets' first nuclear weapons design center—and it is up and running. The All-Union Scientific Research Institute of Experimental Physics carries out its deadly mission beneath the white columns and gilded onion domes of Sarov Monastery, empty since the Bolsheviks shot the monks in 1923. Now tens of thousands of researchers, builders, factory workers, and prison camp laborers swarm the town of Sarov. A fence patrolled by Red Army guards ensures no one gets in or out. Wiped off of all unclassified maps, Arzamas-16 does not exist—its residents are ghosts. Only government planes land in the small airport, and the forests behind the monastery wall now hide explosions of compressed plutonium. The *Katyusha* rocket-launcher factory from World War II is already there—how convenient!—and more factories and nuclear design labs spring up practically overnight.

The denizens call it Los Arzamas because it's built on the blueprints for the US's secret atomic city, Los Alamos. Smuggled out of the Manhattan Project by KGB spy Klaus Fuchs, those plans are not so secret. A bespectacled math whiz, young, polite, Fuchs is a British physicist—implosion expert, to be exact. He's back in the UK, still at large, researching implosion for plutonium bombs. Not even the British spymasters know that the head of their Theoretical Physics Division at the Atomic Energy Research Establishment is funneling the West's latest research to Stalin.

The Soviets are not as far behind as the Americans think.

EARLY WARNING

Even with the new hires in MPRO, the division can't keep up with demand. The goal is real-time processing, or as close to real time as possible. An Agency report warns,

> War in the future will come with devastating suddenness. Only by signal intelligence successfully conducted in peacetime will we know the secret thoughts, actions, and machinations of a predatory and ruthless enemy.

SIGINT's greatest strength is that it can be done from afar. That means time to prepare—for an attack, an offensive, or evacuation. The earlier the warning, the quicker the alarm travels and the more hope people have of finding safety. The United States doesn't have that yet. It doesn't even know the basics. If the Soviets fly a pack of bombers armed with warheads over the US, the American people are sitting ducks.

Most of the Agency's Soviet intel is old news. All CIA attempts to gather human intelligence by placing spies in the Soviet republics have failed. Most CIA intel now relies on Soviet defectors who volunteer their knowledge and FBI interrogations. CIA analysts gather intelligence from Russian scientific publications, when they can find them, and tap into the embassy rumor mill for tidbits on Soviet movements abroad. These sources can provide real-time updates on what the Soviets are up to, but they are sporadic and rely on chance.

The second Soviet intelligence source is the Target Intelligence Committee (TICOM), a secret program that seized Nazi intel during the war. TICOM documents reveal German intelligence on the Russian military, economy, and cipher systems, but some of it is more than twenty years old. Interrogating Nazi scientists helps us estimate the Soviets' scientific progress, but the Russians have their own Nazi scientists now, conducting top secret research behind the Iron Curtain.

Allied SIGINT is the United States' final intelligence source. It's the most productive, with the US Navy, the British, Canadian intelligence, and Arlington Hall coordinating efforts to crack Soviet codes. Operations on Central and Eastern Europe, Russian Air Force and military, traffic analysis, and weather round out the Soviet problem attack.

In the United States, SIGINT works across agencies. As its code-breaking successes mount, Venona pieces correspondences together, helping the FBI uncover the identities of the spies working in rings across the country. Most of the messages are several years old, but the FBI uses the partial decrypts to confirm its ongoing investigations, and it gives them an edge.

The man known for breaking Venona is Meredith Gardner, one of the Agency's top linguists. He doesn't do it alone. Gardner is one of a large team of codebreakers, most of them women, whose groundwork on the unbreakable system launches him to cryptanalytic fame. Gardner also has help from Bill Weisband, the Russian linguistic advisor. Weisband watches Gardner decrypt the message containing names of the Manhattan Project scientists, and he helps Jack's group translate garbled radio intercepts. He works on machine ciphers, as well. As soon as Venona discovers the Manhattan Project compromise, Weisband speeds a message to the Kremlin, informing Stalin that the Americans have found a way in. The NKVD make a plan: Change the codes, tighten security, and prevent another break. For Stalin, the Venona decrypts are old news, but they could be the start of something bigger.

DEFENSE VS. OFFENSE

Venona has gotten the United States some major breakthroughs on ciphers thought to be unbreakable. But it's counterintelligence: defense, not offense.

Intelligence is offense. Learning secrets by spying on the enemy gives your country an advantage. Counterintelligence is defense—keeping the enemy from spying on you protects your country.

The Agency needs to play offense, not defense. Venona is reactive—the conversations in those telegrams happened years ago. The spies are still out there, but the damage has been done. The FBI can only try to contain it and give the Agency information that sheds new light on old data. Through Venona, the FBI corroborates witness testimony, verifies otherwise undocumented accusations, and targets suspects for questioning, but the operation is counterintelligence. Signals intelligence is offensive by design. Thieves of the airwaves, the Agency breaks into networks that don't belong to them. The more positive intelligence they can gather on the Soviets, the better they can make decisions based on solid evidence.

LONGFELLOW

The Soviets constantly upgrade their cipher machines, which use settings based on onetime pads to print enciphered messages. The British helped the United States break the Soviet cipher machine "Coleridge," and now the Americans are working on "Longfellow," nicknamed after the American poet Henry Wadsworth Longfellow, who wrote "Paul Revere's Ride." Revere hanging a lantern in the Old North Church—*One if by land, and two if by sea*—was the colonists' warning to prepare them for Britain's attack. The United States still needs to sound the alarm for an impending attack—only now it's the Soviets, an enemy on whom they can't spy. The Agency can read the Coleridge messages, and they're close to reading Longfellow's, but reconstructing a Soviet cipher machine from scratch takes time.

The question remains: Does Stalin have the bomb, and if so, will he use it? With intelligence estimates as reliable as a crystal ball, the short answer is—they don't know.

TO SECURE THESE RIGHTS

Soviet spies have free rein in America, but Black Americans do not. In late 1947, the President's Committee on Civil Rights submits a report calling for better protection of Americans' four essential rights: personal safety and security, citizenship and its privileges, freedom of conscience and expression, and equality and equal opportunity. "In the time that it takes to read this report," it begins, "1,000 Americans will be born . . . Their skins will range in color from black to white. A few will be born to riches, more to average comfort, and too many to poverty. All of them will be Americans." The majority of Americans are white, Anglo-Saxon Protestants, and though immigration has been curtailed, one out of every four Americans is a "foreign-born white" or a child born to foreign white parents. One out of every five white Americans speaks a native language other than English.

A person's degree of nonwhiteness determines their "degree of apartness" in America. European immigrants are "minority groups" in relation to WASPS but "part of the white majority in relation to the Negro minority." Color and physical traits more than language, national origin, or religion mark people as other here: "Groups whose color makes them more easily identified are set apart from the 'dominant majority' much more than are the Caucasian minorities. The Negroes are by far the largest of these groups." The problems Chinese and Japanese immigrants face "are greatly intensified by physical characteristics which no amount of acceptance of western ways could change." In this racially indoctrinated setting, whiteness ensures acceptance, as evidenced by dozens of Soviet spy nests in secret American facilities.

Whiteness also can ensure immunity, as it does in lynchings. In the South, state and local law enforcement participate in the crimes and impede investigations. Witnesses have a "convenient 'loss of memory'; grand juries refuse to indict; trial juries acquit in the face of overwhelming proof of guilt." When lynchers go unpunished, Black Americans "expect other forms of violence" and live under constant threat. The phenomenon is not unique: "The almost complete immunity from punishment enjoyed by lynchers is merely a striking form of the broad and general immunity from punishment enjoyed by whites in many communities." Police brutality is "disturbingly high," sheriffs violate the Thirteenth Amendment by indenturing prisoners to local officials and business owners to work for free under threat of re-imprisonment. More than one hundred thousand Japanese Americans interned during the war have yet to receive compensation for property and business loss or any recognition of their violated rights.

For these and hundreds of other violations, the committee calls on the Supreme Court to become the guardian of civil rights and empower Congress to override unjust state laws. To apply Chief Justice John Marshall's "liberal construction" of the Constitution and interpret federal power broadly as it concerns the protection of civil rights. They recommend sweeping civil rights reforms, including the complete and immediate end to segregation. They warn that US civil rights are a global issue: Now more than ever, the world's opinion of America's democracy matters. It is the government's duty to secure these rights.

On January 7, 1948, Truman makes his State of the Union Address to Congress. Based on the committee's report, he proposes a program to secure civil rights, adequate health care, and equal opportunities at home and to achieve world peace and economic security abroad. The United States will gain the latter by aiding Europe's economic recovery—not a popular idea, since inflation, food, and housing prices are sky-high. But it's a worse idea to leave war-torn Europe weakened and ripe for Soviet takeover. On February 2, Truman follows this with a Special Message to Congress on Civil Rights that proposes nearly all the committee's recommendations, including permanent Presidential and Joint Congressional Commissions on Civil Rights; stronger federal laws safeguarding people and their property; federal protection against lynching, voter intimidation, unequal housing and employment practices; and an end to Jim Crow practices in Washington, DC. No longer should Black passengers have to hear "State line!" and move to the back of busses and trains when they enter DC territory. No longer should they be barred from restaurants, hotels, hospitals, and schools in America's capital. Hawaii and Alaska should become states, and Japanese Americans should finally have their evacuation claims settled.

These are strong words from an unpopular president in a divided nation. Franklin D. Roosevelt's unexpected death less than three months into his fourth term catapulted the new vice president, Harry S. Truman, into the president's chair on April 12, 1945. Truman's campaign for the 1948 presidential election is not going well, and things get worse on February 10, when a former State Department aide, Alger Hiss, is accused of being a Soviet spy. HUAC seizes the opportunity to discredit Truman and give the Republicans a PR win, as a new wave of anti-communist investigations begins.

STRANGE NEW CODES

The Commercial Code Unit still solves codes by hand. Unlike the IBM Division, their room is quiet. The only sounds are scratching pencils, ruffling papers, shoes clicking to and from the file cabinet, a chair scraping the floor.

Despite the calm, there's excitement. Since the war's end, commercial code traffic has exploded. Now, not only has the volume of traffic increased, the type of traffic has changed too. Every day, the Agency intercepts more unfamiliar codes and ciphers. Without wartime restrictions, businesses, governments, and even individuals can create and modify codes as they please. Ethel has already expanded her skillset; now she encounters any of the three hundred known codes and more. On a typical day she sees more collaboration, more passing sheets back and forth, more whispering and comparing notes. Out come the heavy codebooks and long index files. She conducts frequency distribution studies, looking for patterns in the code that might indicate the original language. Ethel helps Alberta and the others learn the strange language of the new codes.

The brevity of commercial telegrams doesn't give her much to go on. Military telegrams average around two hundred letters, but commercial messages can be much shorter. Sometimes it's only a note to say a shipment has been delivered on time. Trying to reconstruct a key with only a single message to go on might be impossible, but it gives Ethel something to reach for. Knowing the system's type can give her a way in: Is it a substitution or transposition cipher? A cipher or a code? An enciphered code? Russian export companies still use international commercial circuits. Do these strange codes signal secret business deals between Russia and its satellites, or even China? Even with Task I covering the Soviet economy, any clue to Soviet activity helps build the bigger picture. Ethel's job can be discouraging at the best of times, with hours spent devising tables and grinding through theories for no results. Now it's just the challenge and distraction Ethel needs. Outside, there's a war on civil rights. Despite Truman's promises, lynchings and police brutality continue.

Ethel ramps up production to keep pace with the new codes pouring in, but a backlog develops. When employee review time rolls around, something strange happens. For the first time, the unit keeps production records on its output. They're evaluated on quantity as well as quality. The personnel shortage doesn't change the leadership's expectations of the codebreakers' productivity. In fact, their expectations rise. This reflects the moment's intelligence needs, but it also reflects the Black workers' shrinking relevance. Without racial quotas, the Army no longer has to hire Black codebreakers—and it doesn't plan to integrate anytime soon.

Despite the backlog, no one else is hired into the unit. With all eyes trained on the Soviet problem, breaking commercial codes isn't a priority at the moment, and neither is hiring Black cryptologists. Risking the loss of valuable intelligence, the Agency files the strange new commercial traffic away. Alberta's position is changed to an Excepted Appointment, which means she cannot apply for competitive jobs in the Agency; another opportunity becomes a ceiling. Maybe Ethel doesn't notice, but her morale and energy slacken. When she receives her annual evaluation, for the first time since her hiring, instead of "Excellent," she rates as "Very good." The difference may seem small, but to Ethel, it's seismic. Her attention to detail, accuracy, and cooperativeness are still outstanding, but her industry and output are merely "adequate." Is she slowing down? She might be, but she has no intention of leaving. The ground of the Agency is shifting under her feet, but she'll hang on as long as she can.

A few months later, Ethel receives her annual pay increase, which brings her salary to $3,476.40. Would she be making more if she hadn't lost her analyst status? There's no way to know—each pay grade has multiple steps, different rates of increase. It's not a bad wage; the median income for a white urban-dwelling person is $3,300. For Black urban dwellers, it's $1,800. For rural Black folks, it's $900.

SOVIETS 13, ALLIES 1

The only foothold the United States has in Moscow is its embassy. This is both good and bad news. It is good news because it gives the US an opportunity, however scant, to observe and interact with Soviet officials and thereby glean intelligence. It is bad news because it means US intelligence systems, those they use to communicate with Washington, CIA, the Agency, and military and diplomatic entities worldwide are in the heart of the hornet's nest. If the US is full of NKVD spies, Moscow swarms with them. All foreigners in Moscow are tightly policed, especially those on official business. Their homes are bugged, and their phones are tapped. Their Russian "assistants" and translators are all agents of the secret police.

The embassy houses a cryptographic communications center operated jointly by the military and naval attaches' offices, and it contains all the embassy's information about State, Army, and Navy cryptosystems. One of the center's employees is a young code clerk, Sergeant James McMillan Jr., who is just about to finish his two-year assignment and return to the United States. Code clerks can pose high security risks because they handle all encrypted communications that go in and out of government offices. They encipher outgoing messages and decipher incoming ones. They have access to every key used to communicate with diplomatic and military stations at home and abroad. An employee in the military attaché's office, McMillan doesn't work with naval communications, but the naval office's key is in his safe. It just so happens that on the eve of his departure, McMillan falls in love with a Russian spy. The woman is Galina Dunaeva, daughter of an NKVD general and the wife of another

American sergeant formerly at the embassy, John Biconish, now stationed in the US.

It doesn't take much to turn McMillan. In May 1948, Soviet spy Sergei Kondrashev offers McMillan a large sum of money and a Moscow apartment to defect, and he does, taking hundreds of classified documents and top secret knowledge with him.

The McMillan compromise is a May Day present for Stalin. The Agency's year-end summary of the event reads like the world's worst grocery list: "Systems compromised included a SIGROD system . . . held by most Attaches in Europe and the Middle East and by major Army installations in that area. On hand and subject to copying by Sergeant McMillan was material effective until July 1, 1948. Three one-time tape systems were compromised, including one link each with Washington, Headquarters; Headquarters, European Command; and Headquarters US Air Force, Europe. Two onetime pad systems were in his purview, one with Tehran and an 'air-gram' pad with Washington. Further, a SIGROD Emergency Key Phrase, which enables communication in cases of extreme emergency, has been memorized by Sergeant McMillan." This is only one of twelve major intelligence losses the United States suffers to global communism this year. Perhaps the worst happens during the "Bogotazo," a siege in Bogota, Colombia, where protesters against "Yankee imperialism" siege the city in what the CIA calls South American Pearl Harbor. Amid the chaos, an open safe is discovered in the US military attaché's office. All its codes, ciphers, and intelligence missing.

The Soviets win a thirteenth victory for global communism on February 25 when Czechoslovakia's Communist Party stages a coup and takes control of the government, snuffing out the last democracy in Eastern Europe. Even though Soviet troops don't intervene, the fear of Soviet reprisal if the country takes aid from Western Europe spurs an internal takeover. The Soviet Bloc is now complete, creating a bulwark and buffer zone between Russia and Western Europe, should the imperialist powers decide to attack. It also gives the Soviets a key resource in their quest for the atom bomb. The Czech uranium mines are second only to

East Germany in the region for their wealth of radioactive ore. Stalin dispatches German POWs from the Gulag, and they get to work in Jáchymov, a spa town turned forced-labor mining camp. Only one Western presence in Eastern Europe remains that can endanger Stalin's total control in the region: West Berlin.

Berlin's unfortunate location two hundred miles inside Soviet-controlled East Germany, christened the German Democratic Republic, or GDR, means that the United States, Great Britain, and France must run supply routes from the city through Soviet territory and back to the West. Germany's shattered economy prevents West Berlin from securing food, fuel, and other essentials without outside aid. The Marshall Plan, Truman's postwar economic revitalization package for the Allies (minus the Soviets), pumps investments into Western Europe so that they can share the burden of supporting Berlin without the US completely footing the bill. The prospect of a stronger Berlin piques Soviet fears about Western incursion into Eastern Europe, and Stalin decides to take the last piece on the Cold War chess board.

On June 24, 1948, Soviet occupying forces block land, rail, and water supply routes in East Germany to West Berlin, breaking the city's only link to the outside world. They also cut off West Berlin's electricity, which runs on a grid separate from both West Germany and the GDR. The city is rubble. If West Berlin's 2.5 million residents do not get aid from the Allies, they will starve. Stalin is no stranger to weaponized famine; the Soviet-engineered grain shortage in 1932, known as Holodomor, starved millions of Ukrainians to bring them to heel under Soviet rule. The blockade creates the first major crisis of the Cold War, as the one-time frenemies—the Soviet Union and the United States—and new postwar world powers face off in a battle of wills that will characterize the rest of the twentieth century.

The Allies' response to the blockade is an era-defining moment. Stalin hopes to force a zugzwang, making the outnumbered Allies fight to regain control of West Berlin, or flee. Instead, the Allies decide to keep the Cold War cold and invoke the Potsdam Agreement, which gives them access to GDR airspace. On the morning of June 25, they organize the Berlin Airlift, an aerial convoy that brings life-saving supplies to the stranded city. Lieutenant General Curtis E. LeMay of the newly minted US Air Force coordinates the international operation that marshals British, US, and French airpower with Canada, New Zealand, Australia, and South Africa providing operational backup. RAF and US Air Force planes wait, lined up on the runway of Tempelhof Airport, to unload their goods in the city. As soon as a plane unloads, it takes off to procure a new shipment and circle back. Planes land every forty-five seconds, unloading thousands of tons of food and coal to keep the city alive until Stalin withdraws the blockade almost a year later in May 1949. The effort is a major victory for the Allies, but it deepens the rift between the Soviet Union and the West.

THE PLAINTEXT PLANTATION

Bernice Mills is a teacher from DC, but at the Agency, her typical night shift starts at midnight. In the city, the heat doesn't let up after the sun goes down. As a member of the Campbell AME Church's Missionary Society, Bernice knows the story of Jonah—the prophet who tried to flee from God. As punishment, a great fish swallowed him up. Bernice spreads the Good News, but she's suffering the same fate. Her office in A Building's basement is hot, sticky, and damp, like the belly of a whale.

Bernice is one of a new cohort of Black workers who scan and sort Soviet telegrams by hand in the Traffic Processing Branch. Every day is a race. The unit processes more than 150,000 messages per month. With each worker's 300-messages-per-day quota, the cryptologists can spend only one and a half minutes scanning a message to see if it contains any of the 3,000 Russian keywords they've learned during their training.

Depending on who trained them, the traffic processors have varying levels of Russian. Some have a working knowledge of the language. Others have memorized the alphabet and learned to read the dictionary. To most Americans, the Cyrillic alphabet itself is a code. Just try to pronounce ЗДРАВСТВУЙТЕ!, the Russian word for "hello." МИНИСТЕРСТВО ("ministry"), ЯДЕРНЫЙ ("nuclear"), and ПРОМЫШЛЕНОСТЬ ("industry") are some of the terms the unit has to recognize by sight. Looking for the Head of the Mining Department? Just ask for НАЧАЛЬНИК ГОРНОПРОМЫШЛЕНОВОГО УПРАВЛЕНИЯ. If you need the Machine Works, keep an eye out for МАШИНОСТРОИТЕЛЬНЫЙ ЗАВОД. The average word in Russian plaintext is 6.4 letters, but the cryptologists are looking for technical, industrial, and economic terms, which can be much longer. They might get an easy one like ФЛОТ ("Navy"), but they can just as easily get РЕНТГЕНОВСКИЕ АППАРАТЫ ("X-ray equipment").

Bernice meets the day-shift people filing out just as she and the other night-shifters file in. On this schedule, she'll miss the Scout Parents meetings that she and her husband run for Boy Scout Troop 512 and Girl Scout Troop 137. She'll even miss the Halloween party. Work comes first, when it must.

Bernice finds a free space at one of the long tables lining the walls, where the clerks scan, print, stamp, and microfilm Russian plaintext telegrams. Bernice is a scanner, so her table is piled high with paper tapes. Blinking under the fluorescent lights, she might wonder how such a huge space can feel airless. The cracked radiators spew heat. The walls are solid brick. A Building's basement is an aboveground foundation, built mostly without windows for wartime expediency. Only Black people work down here: the mail sorting room, receiving area, daily records office, traffic processing, and MPRO are all-Black operations.

The sharp odors of the unkempt space prickle Bernice's nose as she scans her first tape:

To: Nagorni, Council of People's Commissars, Central Administration for Petroleum Supply.

"It is necessary to ship to the factory light wire for the preparation of hooks, with shank diameter of 3-4-5-6-7 mm, a minimum of 70 kg. of each size. Ship one tone of each size 4 and 5 mm. Welding wire (?) 100 kgs. Of fluid _____ flux (?)."

Bernice is not reading this in English, or even in Russian. She's reading a string of holes punched in a long paper strip that represent Russian words in Cyrillic. The five-bit telegraphic code, Baudot-Murray, is what Russians use to send their telegrams—and it's the form in which the Agency intercepts them. The holes are meant to be read by machines, not people. The paper strip, or tape, is about an inch wide, and each letter is a combination of five 1s and 0s. In Baudot code, the Russian letter "A" is (000–11), or three unpunched holes and two punched holes:

A tiny row of holes runs vertically between the third and fourth dots to keep the tape on track as it feeds through the encoding and printing device.

Bernice's telegram is 350 characters, including spaces. About ten characters fit onto an inch of tape, so the message she's reading is thirty-five inches, or about three feet long.

With a quota of three hundred messages per day, Bernice has one and a half minutes to parse this message out, translate the dots into Russian words, note if any are on her list, and decide whether to keep the tape or send it to the incinerator. This isn't technically codebreaking. Signal codes like Morse and Baudot are one-to-one substitutions with the letters they represent. They transmit words in plaintext—most of the time. As a person scanning machine-encoded plaintext, Bernice is doing a cross between signals intelligence work and data processing.

The telegram is from "Prokhorov at Nalchik." "Prokhorov" is a pretty common last name. Bernice may not know that "Nalchik" is a spa town in the foothills of the Caucasus Mountains. She knows the Cyrillic alphabet and has a list of three thousand Russian terms in seventy different categories. The Agency offers all levels of instruction in Russian, but they do not allow Black hires to take these courses during training. Instead, Bernice compiled Russian dictionaries, learning the language by rote. She knows thousands of Russian words but not how they fit together.

The sender's part of the message doesn't contain much information, so Bernice looks at the addressee: "To: Nagorni, Council of People's Commissars, Central Administration for Petroleum Supply." Okay! Now she's getting somewhere. Nagorni isn't a name; it's a district in Moscow, not to be confused with the Siberian town of the same name. Even if Bernice doesn't know that, she probably has НАРОДНЫЙ КОМИССАР ("People's Commissar"), ЦЕНТРАЛЬНАЯ АДМИНИСТРАЦИЯ ("Central Administration"), and НЕФТЬ ("Petroleum") on her keyword and address lists. The words' endings are different, but she gets the gist.

From the addressee's line, Bernice can categorize this message as "Fuel and Power" since it deals with the petroleum supply. But to be sure, she needs to look at the next two feet of tape to make sure she doesn't miss anything. She makes out "factory . . . wire . . . 70 kg . . . welding wire (?) . . . 100 kg . . ." She sees some numbers (3, 4, 5, etc.) but is not sure what they relate to. The end of the message is unclear; if the transmission signal is poor, the holes aren't completely punched, and the tape is difficult to read. Based on this info, Bernice could route the message to "Construction" because it references factory and wire. No doubt she wishes she knew more, but this is the first of three hundred messages she has to complete during her shift. Now for the decision: Keep or burn? If she keeps it, where does it go? Fuel and Power? Construction? Time's up! On to the next tape.

Teaching traffic scanners the language would make their work easier and more efficient, but the Agency doesn't give them that option. With the rising demand for Russian linguists and translators, the Training School now offers intensive two-week Russian language courses and a six-week course that meet for forty hours per week. The Russian and Bulgarian sections now contain five hundred codebreakers, all of whom need to know at least some of the language. Adding Bernice and twenty other clerks to that roster would not strain resources, but the Agency considers it a waste to train low-level employees.

Anymore, "low-level" means Black. A retired analyst observes, "It's hard for me to believe, but I know it's true intellectually. It's true. It happened that the Agency . . . failed to take advantage of all of the resources by not letting people work up to their potential and their capability. The Agency hurt itself because there were good people with degrees, with knowledge, with talent who were put in menial jobs."

This is only one of Bernice's jobs. In the evenings, before her night shift, she teaches Black veterans at Hilltop Radio Electronics, a vocational school on U Street.

STOCKPILE

The intelligence from the Traffic Processing Branch is put to work on the war-torn streets of Berlin. The Allied strategy in occupied Germany isn't all peaceful. At the beginning of the Berlin airlift, along with its supply planes, the United States deploys B-29 Superfortress bombers, which are capable of carrying atomic weapons, just in case. The US still doesn't know Stalin's nuclear capabilities, and though the Americans don't plan to start a nuclear war, they have to be ready in case Stalin does. In addition to solidifying political and financial control in East Germany, controlling West Berlin would expand Stalin's uranium mines, which have already doubled their output. Meantime, the Americans conduct Operation Sandstone, three nuclear weapons tests, thousands of miles away at the Pacific Proving Grounds on Enewetak Atoll. With one and a half times the nuclear yield of the Fat Man dropped on Hiroshima, the new Mark 4 bomb renders the old models obsolete. Its design is so streamlined that it can be mass produced, opening a chasm of military and diplomatic possibilities.

On July 21, military and civilian leaders of the US's atomic program gather at the White House. Packed in Truman's office, they argue about how best to proceed. "We have been spending 98% of all the money for atomic energy for weapons. Now if we aren't going to use them, that doesn't make any sense," Secretary of the Army Kenneth C. Royall submits. This doesn't help to settle matters. The AEC officials think the military people are "damn fools," and the officers think the AEC people are "damn crooks." With the 1948 election looming, Truman can't openly support an aggressive nuclear weapons policy, but he can't ignore the Soviet threat either. Publicly, he commits to keeping the country's atomic energy program under civilian control, but secretly, he greenlights ramped-up production and stockpiling of nuclear weapons at Sandia.

While the Allies are airlifting food to Berlin, the Elektrokhimpribor Combine in the phantom city of Sverdlovsk-45 produces highly enriched uranium. Chelyabinsk-40, the Soviets' first plutonium production reactor, comes online and starts producing plutonium warheads.

The era of escalation begins.

8

BLACK FRIDAY

AUGUST–NOVEMBER 1948

Because the Black cryptologists' signals work isn't technically code-breaking, history consistently downgrades their contribution to Cold War intelligence. Even publications like Carol B. Davis's *Candle in the Dark: COMINT and Soviet Industrial Secrets*, which praise the Traffic Processing group's work, manage to downplay their expertise. When describing the tape scanning process performed by linguists, Davis writes:

> Linguists thus had to cope frequently with corrupt, sometimes very corrupt, text and voice. This might involve the occasional missing or incorrect letter(s) or, in the worst case, the corruption of significant portions of the text, making recovery difficult or impossible. Linguists had to examine the traffic carefully, always keeping in mind that they might have to supply elements of the text in order to determine the correct words, terms, and names. This skill was an integral part of the linguists' familiarity with the specific target or targets.

"Linguists" here refers to the white professionals in the B Building side of the plaintext operation rather than its clerical staff. The linguists have Russian language training, working aids, and experienced senior colleagues to consult.

The same skill comes across differently when Davis describes the Black workforce: "The scanners were able to read the punched tape, selecting what should be printed out." This summary seriously understates the skills required to perform the task, as the long description of the linguists' work attests. Davis adds, "Their burn bags were checked periodically to ensure that they were not rejecting valid items." By all accounts this is true—the scanners had limited knowledge of Russian—but emphasizing their need for oversight implies a lack of ability rather than a lack of training. *Candle in the Dark* details the traffic coordination process, but like *The Invisible Cryptologists*, it stresses the physical rather than the intellectual and psychological aspects of the Black cryptologists' work.

Cryptology is a zero-sum game when it comes to assessing value. If plaintext scanning isn't as difficult as cryptanalysis, it doesn't merit mention. Matthew Aid's *The Secret Sentry* minimizes the whole plaintext operation, at once admitting its importance but diminishing its impact: "AFSA was deriving intelligence from low-level plaintext intercepts, and even that effort was not doing very well." Aid notes that the program "only" produces intel on foreign trade, consumer goods, gold production, petroleum, shipbuilding, military and civilian aircraft, and civil defense. This is inaccurate based on the many available primary and secondary sources. No other intelligence source at this time comes close to providing this breadth of information. Only operations like military traffic and weather analysis, which are also considered low-level, provide tactical intelligence on Soviet defense. Aid admits that traditional cryptanalysis is "unproductive" at this time but insists that the Agency makes a mistake by pouring its resources into plaintext.

Equating low-level systems with low-level people is a habit of both the Agency and its historians. "Low level" and "high level" are trade speak for different grades of cryptanalytic systems based on the relative difficulty of their solutions. "High" and "low" can also describe priorities. A high-level target is one that everyone agrees gets top priority in their intelligence operation. Too often, that language translates into judgments about the people who work on said systems. At the Agency, analysts are viewed as "living on Mount Olympus" while people at the lower grades are considered "lower creatures." Historians who carry this bias forward reinforce dangerous beliefs, as this high-low paradigm reflects the racial and gender biases of the time.

CODE 1 AND CODE 2

At the Agency, categorizing people as "high" and "low" translates into a racialized personnel code. Personnel officers file employees into two categories based on their race. "Code 1" for white, and "Code 2" for Black. To bypass Black employees for transfers, promotions, or training, all they have to do is pull from the Code 1 file and let the Code 2 file collect dust. It's one of the many unspoken rules that keep Black employees in menial roles, not just at the Agency, but across the federal government.

Not all white supervisors agree with this system. Jack Gurin needs clerks for the plaintext program, typists to transcribe analysis reports. But as the Agency's need for clerks grows, so does its need for a strict racial hierarchy. Gurin's taken all the clerical personnel the Agency has, but he still needs more. One day, in the Personnel Office, an administrator shuts him down.

"I've given you all the people I can lay my hands on," the personnel officer says. "The only other people I can give you are code two."

Gurin asks what this means, and the officer tells him "Code 2" means Black.

Gurin can't believe what he's hearing and responds, "What in the hell's wrong with that?"

The personnel officer agrees to provide the Code 2 employees but warns Gurin that he will face backlash from his staff.

Gurin runs the idea by his white typists. There are a hundred of them—surely several Black people won't be a problem.

Sure enough, a "very dignified, good-looking Alabama lady" objects. She "cannot sit next to a colored person at work." Some of the others agree.

Gurin does the opposite of what most people at the Agency would do at this time. He moves the desks of the problematic white people and transfers five new Black hires into the office: one man, who "made himself in charge," and four women. Milton Zaslow, Gurin's colleague, oversees the movement of the disgruntled racists. Milt is astounded—in a good way—by Gurin's inclusion of Black clerks in the unit. He recalls that it "made the difference between success and failure" in the plaintext operation.

Bernice is interested in the wider world. She's planning a program on African culture for Giddings High School in Southeast. The embassies of Liberia, Nigeria, Great Britain, France, Ethiopia, and Egypt are involved, as are the National Council of Negro Women and the All-African Student Union. Exhibits of art imported from Africa and from the Founders Library at Howard University will be on display. But no one's offering Bernice an overseas assignment. Despite the value they add, the Traffic Processing Branch is a dead end for the folks who end up there. The Agency recognizes that constraining intelligent people to menial tasks demoralizes them. The workers have "low morale," but their supervisors never take steps to address the cause. Former traffic processor James "Jim" Pryde recalls,

> We couldn't analyze the traffic, all we could do was look at the addresses and determine whether or not it was a tape that should go someplace else . . . There were advances within [Traffic Processing], but at that time, there were no advancements out.

Though some tasks like scanning require analysis and quick thinking, others like printing and stamping do not. Looking back, Pryde, who eventually became a missile defense expert and high-level executive at the Agency, notes, "At the time we were fairly used to being separated, but now I think it's terrible . . . It didn't matter what your education level was or experience or whatever. If you were brown, [the plantation] is where you went."

In 1948, Pryde is a veteran and radio operator with a photographic memory. He reads Morse code. The Agency keeps him in the mail room for years before acknowledging his ability to contribute. They withhold training from Pryde, Bernice, and the rest of the Black cryptologists. In an institution that trains every one of its hires, they create an underskilled Black workforce to prevent them from leaving. Pryde notes that this was intentional: "For training, you had to have some hope of going some place else . . . Some job boards were 'white only,' some boards were 'Colored.'"

EXECUTIVE ORDER 9881

Outside the Agency, the country is moving forward. As part of Truman's civil rights campaign, he issues Executive Orders 9880 and 9881 to desegregate the military and mandate fair employment in federal government.

Their timing in mid-1948 isn't a coincidence. The Selective Service Act recently passed, and Black activists warn that Black soldiers will not fight another war in a Jim Crow military. They've already done that—and many paid with their lives. The least their country can do is ensure their fair treatment.

Executive Order 9981 states: "There shall be equality of treatment and opportunity for all persons in the armed forces without regard to race, color, religion, or national origin." In 1941, Roosevelt's order 8802 stated, "There shall be no discrimination in the employment of workers in defense industries and in Government, because of race, creed, color, or national origin." The executive orders are practically the same, but Roosevelt's order didn't succeed because the military ignored it.

Can Truman enforce these orders? Will things be any different now?

American society hails Truman as making a great step forward, forgetting they've been down this road before. But 1941 feels like a lifetime ago. The United States is a different country now, and the world is a different place.

At Arlington Hall, Truman's executive orders don't mean much. When change does happen, Black men benefit more than Black women. In 1948, the Agency hires its first Black engineers in Research and Development but maintains the racial order by hiring them at lower grades than their white coworkers. The office is integrated, but the hierarchy remains.

Veteran and electrician Charles Matthews, a graduate of the Hilltop Radio Electronics Institute, has to hound the Agency for a job.

> I was hired as an engineering technician, Grade 9 (subprofessional). To my knowledge the Agency didn't recruit, but I and two others decided to apply. I was so anxious to get a job, I kept bugging them, and I was the first to get hired.

Fellow Hilltop graduates Carroll Robinson and Mitchell Brown come on board, but none of the positions are ideal.

> "It was a good start," Matthews says, "but whites that were hired as engineering technicians with comparable experiences and sometimes less training were always hired at a higher grade than we were."

The Agency sets such low grades for Black employment that any exception seems like progress:

> Even though you were hired at a grade lower than your white counterparts, it was still a job . . . Most of the Blacks in the Agency were in the custodial force or were messengers. Even with a college education, that was the extent of employment. The best jobs for blacks at that time were with the post office.

Even with a shortage of technological experts, the Agency would rather keep Black hires low-level than risk them outpacing their white colleagues. The Army has a policy that no Black officer in a mixed command may rank higher than a white officer, and no Black officer shall ever command white troops. The same thinking seems to apply at the Agency even though most positions are civilian.

BLACK FRIDAY

In August 1948, the United States is confident that the Soviet Union is still years away from building the bomb. Furs and caviar, that's all the Soviets have, or so the Americans believe. The belief comes from outdated intelligence about just how embedded the Soviets' spy network really is. The Americans have clues, but nothing close to the whole picture. Their assumptions are dangerously flawed.

The dominoes Bill Weisband set in motion the past year by reporting Venona's progress topple faster, cascading in long lines, curling around corners, crisscrossing paths, tripping up ramps, until they reach their goal and Stalin does something no one expects.

On August 25, the Soviet Union cuts off all encrypted radio and cable communications. The Intelligence Community calls it "Black Friday," the day the Soviet Union goes dark. Now high-level secrets pass only over Kremlin landlines whose security the Agency can't crack. The Soviets pulled the same trick on the Nazis during the war—a prelude to Operation Bagration, one of the most devastating offensives in military history.

The war is not so distant. The US remembers what happened after the Soviets went dark. The Agency scrambles for answers: Are they compromised? Is the timing a coincidence? No more traffic comes through on Coleridge and Longfellow—all their work on those systems is lost. The US and UK can't agree on what Black Friday means. The British rule out the possibility of an attack, but the Americans aren't so sure. All their SIGINT dries up. Like the Nazis, they are sitting ducks.

No one suspects Weisband—not even a little bit—but the Agency fears it has a mole.

Meanwhile, the Soviets accelerate uranium enrichment at Krasnoyarsk-26 and plutonium production at Chelyabinsk-40. Behind the Iron Curtain, the USSR rapidly assembles its first nuclear weapon, RDS-1, while the Intelligence Community bickers over why the enemy went silent. They keep knowledge of Black Friday in-house. Truman doesn't need to know, but the threat of nuclear war hangs over every decision.

TASS

With no more high-level sources left, the Agency turns to the only thing it does have—Russian radio telecom. The Soviets' public telegraph agency (TASS) carries unencoded telegrams, radio broadcasts, and phone calls, although these can be tough to catch. Despite its lack of security, TASS carries traffic that should, by protocol, be encrypted. Just as a Soviet code clerk might print an extra copy or two of a onetime encryption pad, an overworked foreman in Irkutsk might radio HQ for updated production quotas on heavy armored vehicles without using standard encryption. Another might use the wrong channel to report on aircraft assembly in the far-off port city of Taganrog.

The Agency has always been skeptical of plaintext. If the content is important, the sender will encrypt it, they reason. They've spent most of their time and resources on solving mind-bogglingly difficult ciphers and codes and enciphered codes. If the message is already in plaintext, there's not much to do. No one wants to pick through Happy Birthday grams to find one nugget of usable Soviet intelligence. It's high-investment, low-reward. Better to stick with what the Agency knows.

Producing intelligence from plaintext disrupts the Agency's hierarchy. For plaintext to work, the wrong people have to be in charge. Linguists, translators, and traffic analysts don't provide intelligence to the CIA; they provide raw material, which the CIA turns into intelligence. The Agency is supposed to process SIGINT, not produce it. Successful cryptanalysis reveals text for someone else to analyze. With nothing to reveal, cryptanalysis never comes into play.

No matter how much the Agency brainiacs and CIA Ivy Leaguers dislike the idea of working on plaintext, after Black Friday they don't have a choice. Progress on Russian naval traffic grinds to a halt. British success on other systems dries up. With a collective groan, the United States and its allies turn all frequencies to Radio Moskva, and byte after byte of precious data streams into Arlington Hall. Every Soviet bureau and directorate uses TASS. Controlled by the Ministry of Communications, it is the "central information organ of the USSR," providing more than a glimpse behind the Iron Curtain.

Plaintext may not deliver the Soviet atomic program on a platter, but it provides a panoply of facts from which shrewd policy can be made. A weekly CIA intelligence summary from November details the escalating situation in East Germany based on industrial and economic data:

> Deteriorating economic conditions in the Soviet Zone of Germany may further increase the USSR's problem of controlling the dissatisfied populace. Despite the warnings of German Communist leaders concerning the adverse effect of these deteriorating conditions upon the German people, the USSR has taken little constructive action. Meanwhile, Soviet efforts to increase food crops have not improved the food ration, and Soviet methods of collection have antagonized farm elements [and] industrial production within the Soviet Zone has not reached levels which can satisfy domestic requirements. The importation of supplies from western zones has been reduced by interzonal traffic restrictions, and efforts to promote trade with the Satellites have proved unsuccessful, largely because of Soviet unwillingness to part with acceptable Soviet Zone commodities in exchange for coal and raw materials.

With its focus on agriculture, industry, transport, and trade, this report likely includes plaintext intelligence. Its fact-based statements provide solid basis for predictions. If eighteen million cold, hungry, overtaxed East Germans revolt against the Red Army, World War III could erupt. This report circulates to sixty-eight top-level policymakers, including the president, secretary of state, Joint Chiefs of Staff, and the directors of the FBI, Armed Forces, and Atomic Energy Commission. They'll need all the traffic the Black cryptologists can process to make their next move count.

JONAH AND THE WHALE

From the morning of August 26, it feels like the fate of democracy rides on cryptologists winnowing data in the basement of A Building. Night after night, Bernice descends into the belly of the whale, but now something is different. It's always chaotic, noisy, exhausting—but there's a new urgency. She doesn't know why—none of them do. They're not updated on the unfolding situation. The white officers guarding the door give nothing away. The cryptologists feel the pressure build, like the whale is getting ready to vomit them onto land. But it doesn't. Bernice scrambles, all hands and eyes, unrolling cables like streamers at her station. Knocking elbows with the woman on either side of her. Processing more data than any translator can translate, more than any B Building analyst can analyze. Bernice's shift feels like three days and three nights. The traffic is endless. Her contribution, invisible. In this unit, she won't crack the war-winning code or solve the unsolvable cipher. The codebreakers' work is a symphony of stamina, of mental acrobatics and flow state concentration to keep up the repetitive work at a breakneck pace.

Like Jonah, Bernice has to deliver a message, but it's from a collective voice, not a singular one. Stalin's blockade is squeezing East and West Berlin, and his scientists are racing to build the bomb. Bernice's vigilance turns fragments into clear warnings, a message not shouted from the mountaintop but delivered in clean files in neat stacks. Stamped by hands covered in ink, sorted by thumbs sliced with paper cuts, typed by blistered fingers.

Bernice is only part of the process. The analysts in B Building must rise to the challenge, clear the backlog, analyze and contextualize the data, deliver the finished reports.

The question is—will they?

The Pentagon needs daily updates on Soviet air defense. With co-ordinated air transport from London, information on Russian flights in Europe is available within a few hours of being scheduled. No other agency produces real-time intel at this rate. Britain and the United States continue to lament the "shortage of competent linguists" who can process the mountains of plaintext at the volume needed to keep up with collection, ignoring that in refusing to train the Black cryptologists, the Agency ties one hand behind its back. The Russian plaintext operation in B Building is nearing two hundred people, but they need more.

Meanwhile, Bernice and the processing unit fight on in A Building, knowing they have little chance for advancement.

With the switch to plaintext, the Agency faces an identity crisis. They're used to relying on cryptanalysis—using those big brains to make tiny breakthroughs. Even if it takes years and yields little, it's worth it. Rather than seeing plaintext and cryptanalysis as two sides of the same mission, the Agency sees them as opposites. Incompatible. In competition. The war began a "revolution" in cryptanalysis, but now it's stalled. Plaintext is a "new and unusual" project. For the CIA, the "Golden Age" of Russian plaintext is the "Dark Ages" of COMINT. For the Army and Navy, the late 1940s is a "period of damaging retrenchment," as they embark on the Soviet problem with "little experience, less money, and no expertise."

For others, plaintext is a "candle [in] the darkness of the early Cold War." It rises "like a phoenix" out of the ashes of Black Friday. Plaintext is a battle between good and evil, hope and despair.

Racism is the "dark side" of plaintext. In the post–Black Friday world, segregation isn't just a social or political evil—it's an operational one. Several sources call attention to this injustice, but none correlate it with the era's intelligence failings. "Change or die" is SIGINT's directive, but failure to adapt puts the Agency in danger of going out of business. It resists opening "new doors" and creating the new working models the changing moment demands. Instead, it falls back on that most American work model—the slave plantation. The only thing the processing unit lacks is strong Russian-language training. As Gurin says, they all have college degrees; "they all have some kind of brains."

Though the traffic unit processes more than two million messages this year, and the plaintext group publishes 748 reports (more than two a day), no phoenix rises from the fire of failure raging at Arlington Hall. A backlog of unprocessed printouts builds as B Building's analysts fail to keep pace, and the calls to action from A Building go unheard.

PUBLIC DISTRUST

Meanwhile, by mid-1948, Venona is deep into decrypting Soviet espionage, confirming at least three spies through the FBI—and more keep surfacing. The dam bursts when defected spy Elizabeth Bentley names Harry Dexter White, a former senior Treasury official, as spying for the Soviets during World War II. This is her second interrogation: She's been outing spies since 1945 when she realized her own position in the spy ring was shaky. In her HUAC testimony, she names a slew of communist operatives, including Whittaker Chambers, who in turn implicates Alger Hiss and others. Before exposure, many of these agents succeed in stealing vital intelligence, including Treasury, State Department, and scientific documents.

There's a secretive feel to these cases that unsettles the public. Bentley's testimony raises questions about how the FBI uncovers these spies, but Venona is too classified to disclose. By law, information gained by wiretapping isn't admissible in court, and the Agency doesn't want to reveal that they've broken Soviet ciphers even if they're nearly ten years old. Leaking codenames risks losing potential informants, who might flee to the Soviet Union before testifying. For all these reasons, the FBI can't use Venona to publicly corroborate Bentley's or anyone else's testimony. That means no arrests can be made unless someone pleads guilty before HUAC, and no one wants to do that. All the FBI can do is watch and wait. Tail their suspects and take notes. In the meantime, agents like Weisband funnel intelligence to the Kremlin with alarming speed.

Hard evidence. It's what the government needs most to allay fears about communist spies, but outside of a few testimonies it proves elusive. The Red Scare consumes American public life, as people begin to question whom they can trust. Are Bentley's accusations true? If so, why can't the government reveal its sources? Henry Dexter White is not a communist, which is scarier than if they'd found stockpiles of propaganda under his bed. Anyone, it seems, could be a spy.

Thomas Dewey, the Republican presidential nominee, uses this momentum to blast the Democrats as soft on communism at home and abroad. During the war, their New Deal government was crawling with spies: How can Americans trust them now, when the fate of the world is at stake? What if a Red has their finger on the button? The moral panic reaches fever pitch as HUAC becomes both courtroom and stage on which dissenters are interrogated, condemned, and banned. Conservative lawmakers capitalize on the moment to push their one-note agenda. Attorney General Tom Clark issues the "Attorney General's List of Subversive Organizations," naming groups like the Civil Rights Congress and Black and communist-led labor organizations. The Mundt-Nixon Bill requires communist organizations to register with the federal government. It's an obvious trap: register and risk prosecution, or don't and face legal consequences anyway. HUAC targets anyone who advocates for civil rights, like New York City Councilman Benjamin Davis, who is charged under the Smith Act for conspiring to overthrow the government. Anti-communism is the weapon of social control du jour, and sadly, it works. Solidarity falters as individuals try to avoid losing their jobs and organizations their credibility.

Truman denies the charges against his government, but no one's convinced. Communism isn't just a "red herring," as he claims. Rats quickly abandon a sinking ship, and the Southern lawmakers secede to form a third party, the Dixiecrats, based on upholding segregation under the guise of states' rights. Their presidential nominee, Strom Thurmond, is disturbingly popular. He claims that both mainstream candidates, Truman and Dewey, threaten to steer America into "the rocks of totalitarianism," where states have no say under an oppressive federal government. In Strom's rhetoric, in pushing for federal civil rights legislation that supersedes state laws, the federal government is fast becoming a Soviet model of centralized control.

Suddenly, the United States is a far-right sandwich with Black people in the middle. If HUAC, the Dixiecrats, and the turncoat communists aren't bad enough, the Republicans' Lily-White Movement terrorizes Black voters in the South to dissuade them from party membership. The country is a web of contradictions. On July 31, *The Chicago Defender* runs two headlines. "President Truman Wipes Out Segregation in Armed Forces" and "Posse, Bent on Lynching, Searches Woods for Prey." Black South Carolinians register for the Democratic Party in droves after a federal judge orders Strom and the Dixiecrats to grant Black voters full party membership. Truman's New Deal platform sounds promising, but with stakes this high, promises aren't enough.

DEWEY DEFEATS TRUMAN

All year, Dewey is ahead in the polls, and by October, the presidential race is the closest it's been, with 50 percent supporting Dewey to Truman's 45 percent. McCarthyism looks poised to plunge the country into a deeper, darker, redder scare. Strom only polls at 2 percent, but in such a close race, that 2 percent can make or break the election.

On November 3, 1948, Americans wake to a miracle. Harry S. Truman has pulled off the greatest presidential comeback in history. In Missouri, a Secret Service agent wakes the president at 4 a.m. with the news. By afternoon, forty thousand people crowd the town square in Independence, Missouri, to celebrate their hometown hero. Truman wins without the majority vote but pulls together enough support from Roosevelt's New Deal coalition of Black, Jewish, Midwestern, and white liberal voters. Farmers back Truman for continuing their subsidies despite a sinking economy. Labor stands with Truman against the Republicans' anti-union witch hunt. Despite the Dixiecrat rebellion, Truman carries a few Southern states. His upset caps a Democratic sweep. They regain control of Congress, and Truman proves the pundits wrong. In the most iconic photo of his career, Truman grinningly displays the *Chicago Daily Tribune* headline that prematurely announced his defeat.

How does he pull off such a win? All through the election year, Truman has something in his pocket the United States sorely needs: accurate, actionable intelligence. Back in November 1947, veteran White House Counsel Clark Clifford drew Truman a road map to victory. Clifford's careful, detailed estimate of the coming year's events positions Truman to lead the national debate, and thus the vote, in 1948. Clifford predicts that Dewey will be the Republican nominee and that he'll be "resourceful, intelligent, and highly dangerous." Despite its rancor, the South won't revolt. It is staunchly Democratic, *and in formulating policy, it can be safely ignored.* Instead, Truman should focus on supporting agricultural communities in the West and South and securing young, independent voters as early as possible, who Clifford claims will make or break the election.

Not every estimate hits the bull's-eye, but even when Clifford gets it wrong, he gets it right. He correctly foresees that breakaway Democrats will raise a strong third-party candidate. Clifford predicts a Marxist rather than a States' Rights rival, but the strategy is the same: Secure the labor vote to prevent undecided progressive and minority voters from drifting toward the Republicans. Dewey is already drafting antidiscrimination laws in his home state of New York, so Truman must work harder to prove Democrats can deliver on the civil rights and economic opportunities promised during the war. Even though the election is a nailbiter, Clifford's well-crafted intelligence estimate helps Truman to victory.

The Intelligence Community can learn from this election. Clifford has the advantage of observing his target firsthand, which the Agency does not. But the Agency makes several mistakes he avoids. Clifford never underestimates Truman's opponents. He carefully considers Dewey's and the third-party candidate's strengths and resources in forming a plan of attack. He takes a proactive rather than reactive stance in the conflict and gets an early start so as not to be caught off guard. Most important, he does not rely on outdated assumptions when deciding how to win. Minority and fringe voters are just as important to Truman's campaign as influential mainstream ones.

9

FOREARMED BUT NOT FOREWARNED

JANUARY–AUGUST 1949

Snow skitters over the parking lot as Ethel walks toward the gate. Wind whips through the branches, and she holds her coat close. Another morning at the Agency, where everything is the same, yet different. They're preparing for change—new directives, talk of restructuring. Supervisors with armfuls of paper rotate in and out. From the administrative office, it feels distant. Change swirls around Ethel but doesn't whisk her up in its current. Her role is uncertain, her future opaque as the white sky.

When the annual reviews arrive, Ethel holds her breath. Once again, the rating, scripted in black ink: "Very Good." As ever, she is accurate, cooperative, and dependable. But now, not only has her industry fallen, her attention to detail and "skill in the application of techniques" have slipped. Imperceptible adjustments, day by day, have led her into unfamiliar territory. There's no road back, and only uncertainty lies ahead.

Ethel isn't the only one weathering disappointment. In the pale dawn of 1949, the glow of Truman's come-from-behind win is fading. In Washington, Black activists' optimism turns to anxiety as the president's bold civil rights plan stalls in Congress. "To Secure These Rights" sits untouched: Southern Democrats dig in their heels and Northern liberals lose their nerve. It's a hostile climate, and everyone's trying to keep the target off their backs. In the Democratic Party, it's every politician for themselves.

Civil rights are the first barrel thrown from their sinking ship—heavy cargo that splashes and gurgles beneath the waves of a fomenting public. The president who dared to desegregate comes about, sailing with the wind instead of against it. In this new reality, the vision of freedom is a black flag—a political liability.

The whole political order shifts. Voters for justice feel betrayed. Voters for law and order exalt. Segregationists put on their battle armor ready for all-out war with the federal government. To them, state sovereignty is still under attack. The Double V is put back in its box, slid under the bed for another time—for another war. The New Deal coalition is dead, and with it dies the trust of Black Americans who voted for change. The era that was supposed to rise like a phoenix from the ashes of postwar turmoil turns out to be just ash.

Meanwhile, the Red Scare gaslights an increasingly spiraling public imagination. States build "little HUACs," committees designed to sniff out communist influence in schools, unions, civil rights groups, even churches. Every demand for loyalty oaths, every threat of investigation sends the message that dissent is dangerous. Subversive—and punishable. There's no stopping the anti-communist machine—they will find you, communist or not.

To prove it is serious, HUAC makes a lesson of Paul Robeson, a Black singer and actor who rose to prominence during the Harlem Renaissance. Robeson sees the Soviet Union as a society that, in contrast to Jim Crow America, treats all people equally. At home, while the wave of anti-communism builds, Robeson speaks out in support of the Soviet Union, advocating for peace and an end to the Cold War. The Soviet propaganda mill embraces this image and deploys it strategically, hoping to win influence in the Global South and among oppressed peoples worldwide.

Robeson becomes a vocal advocate not only for civil rights in the United States but for socialism, believing it offers a path to racial equality.

Robeson never officially joins the Communist Party USA, but his open support of communism is more than enough fuel for HUAC—in a time when communism is a political liability, Robeson encourages Black Americans to consider its promise of justice and solidarity. Not surprisingly, this stance quickly isolates him in the United States. While his international reputation grows—especially in the Soviet Union, where he becomes a beloved performer and a symbol of Black excellence—his reputation at home begins to fray.

In the summer of 1949, Robeson travels to Paris to speak at the Soviet-sponsored World Peace Conference, and his speech is covered by the Associated Press. Robeson speaks about uniting labor, forging racial solidarity, and achieving peace with the Soviet Union. A journalist on hand dispatches a heavily distorted speech to the United States in which Robeson allegedly compares the US government to Hitler, claims that Black Americans will not fight in a war against the Soviet Union, and advocates for a socialist revolution. American news outlets run with the story, reprinting the inflammatory remarks without checking their authenticity.

Robeson returns to a country seething with anger—overnight he becomes "the Most Dangerous Man in the World." An outraged public denounces him as subversive and anti-American. For anti-Black, antisemitic, and anti-communist parties, he is the perfect target. A few months later, Robeson has a benefit concert for the Civil Rights Congress, which is CPUSA affiliated, in Peekskill, New York, but before it begins, it erupts in violence. What begins as a protest turns into a mob made up of white veterans from the American Legion and white local protesters. The concertgoers and Robeson supporters are veterans and union workers—Black, white, and Jewish. The two groups face off, shouting and threatening each other, and soon the mob attacks, shouting racist, antisemitic, and anti-communist slurs. They lynch Robeson's effigy and burn a cross on a hillside. A Navy veteran is stabbed and no one knows who did it, which fuels greater violence. The local sheriff calls for backup, but it never comes. More than 140 people are injured.

The event crystallizes the racial and Cold War paranoia of the moment. Cultural infiltration is always based on an evil-intentioned, racialized "other." Because the Soviets are white and because their spies are seemingly respectable white Americans, in the civil rights world, the evil face of communism becomes Robeson, an outspoken Black man. Another prime target are Jews, prominent in Hollywood and in labor unions, giving white supremacists an easy outlet for their antisemitism. These racialized others are important to those trying to separate the "good" Americans from the bad "Commies"—the subversive anti-Americans. If the anti-Americans look just like the "good" Americans, what are Americans to do? Full-on existential crisis for white supremacists and their fellow travelers. Seeing a spy in the mirror triggers uncomfortable self-reflection, so they find a reassuring scapegoat.

Robeson's targeting in particular is also a result of the white mediocrity ceiling, in which Black people cannot be more talented, more intelligent, or more successful than any white person. At six three, Robeson is literally a towering figure. A star in every way—scholar, athlete, world-famous singer, and actor. Academic scholarship to Rutgers. In baseball an excellent catcher, shortstop, runner, hitter. Basketball—a prime defender. Ran track, solid at tennis. A "football genius," a "veritable superman"—a freshman college walk-on star. Affable, charismatic. And, until the Red Scare, universally loved. So much Black excellence comes with a high price—a lifetime of practice downplaying his success so as not to anger jealous whites. The advice from his father, who was born enslaved: "Do nothing to give them cause to fear you." So much control in the face of hate also comes with a price, and being treated like a human being in the Soviet Union for the first time in his life—like a friend and compatriot and not a threat—makes Robeson unafraid to speak out against the evil that causes so many to suffer in silence.

The riot draws public sympathy for Robeson, but the press

overwhelmingly blames Robeson for provoking the protesters with his anti-American speech at the Paris World Peace Conference. Fearing similar violence, cities cancel eighty of Robeson's upcoming concert dates. A few months later, the government revokes Robeson's passport, silencing his international voice and placing him in financial hardship.

HUAC's high-profile espionage grand jury trials in Washington, DC, feed the country's reckless paranoia, stoke public fear, and erode the government's credibility. The most sensational case is Alger Hiss. Three years after he was first accused, he's on trial for his alleged involvement in a Soviet spy ring in the 1930s. As a former member of Roosevelt's New Deal government, Hiss proves how deeply embedded Soviet spies have been in the United States—and how long they've gotten away with it. The trial captivates the nation with dramatic revelations like the "Pumpkin Papers"—leaked federal microfilms and handwritten documents hidden by Hiss's accuser, Whittaker Chambers, in a hollowed-out pumpkin on Whittaker's farm. Hiss's first grand jury trial ends in a hung jury, but his second presents enough evidence to fuel suspicions of communist infiltration in the highest levels of government.

At the same time, Judith Coplon, a current Justice Department employee, is arrested for passing classified documents to the Soviet Union. She is accused of two counts of espionage—one for copying Justice Department security reports on Soviet espionage, and the other for stealing FBI investigative reports on the same. Coplon is *still* a political analyst in the Justice Department's Foreign Agents Registration Section while she is on trial, a position that gives her privileged access to the records of all people connected with public or private foreign agencies. The evidence against her is overwhelming, but the trial exposes the FBI's illegal surveillance methods, including warrantless wiretapping, arrest, and search. The FBI argues that they were tailing Coplon at the time of her arrest and witnessed her exchange with a known Soviet agent, so their actions are justified. The case wears on, more names and accusations drop—there are so many spies! People who seem to have nothing to gain by betraying their country, and yet they do. Even as the FBI's tactics come under scrutiny, Bureau chief J. Edgar Hoover expands his surveillance operations, keeping in close contact with Venona, which provides choice leads, codenames, and other treasures.

"REAL CHEAP"

Ordinary citizens, activists, and political dissenters are on the FBI's radar, so Shamrock makes copies of their correspondence too. A project once aimed at discovering assassins and foreign agents gradually extends to surveilling citizens who might "subvert national security." If Americans are sending messages abroad, they are fair game. The trend erodes the difference between "foreign" and "domestic" intelligence so that the Agency, FBI, CIA, and Department of Defense, which also gets the Shamrock take, can spy on whomever they want.

The companies providing the telegrams are the same ones who did so during the war—RCA and Western Union. They realize they are in a legally gray area and ask to get out. Instead, the secretary of defense assures them that it's fine. Their arrangement is legal and endorsed by the president. They'll be immune from any criminal charges that may result from their participation—not that anything criminal will happen. The companies don't know what the telegrams are used for, and they don't want to know. They proceed, accepting that it's "in the highest interests of national security."

Shamrock shifts stacks of intercepts to Bernice and the traffic processing team. Like most businesses, Soviet trading groups send their messages through commercial carriers.

The unenciphered ones go straight to Task I.

The page-printed copies are a nice change from the Vint Hill tapes with their endless dots and hanging chads. Bernice can read the original Russian text, pick out keywords, and quickly route the messages to their next stop. The Shamrock intercepts come prescreened—none ever touch the burn bag.

Bernice doesn't know where these pages come from; that somewhere in Arlington Hall, an office of women like her—Black, college educated, and hungry for advancement—work behind typewriters and teletype machines, churning out clean, polished copies for analysts to devour.

It's sanctioned by the highest levels of government—but Shamrock has a dark side. It's grown beyond foreign intelligence gathering to target civil rights activists, artists, and actors—voices of influence the government wants to silence. Figures like Paul Robeson are under watch—and they're being forced offstage.

Behind the Agency, the FBI is pulling the strings, using Shamrock's intercepts to shape public opinion, to muzzle dissent without the need for open trials or evidence. Suspicion alone is enough to end careers, blacklist writers and directors. Sow fear and doubt. The film industry, still recovering from the antitrust battles that shattered Hollywood's old studio system, is on the brink of a new Golden Age. But HUAC and its allies want to silence as many influential—especially Jewish—voices before the new era.

Making drop copies is such a central part of the FBI's domestic surveillance program that they have their own drop copy operation called Drop Copy Operation. No need for codenames. Like Russian plaintext, Shamrock and the FBI operation are massive data collection projects. They require large clerical workforces to do the processing, and that means the Agency is hiring more Black women at low grades to do the work.

For the Agency, Shamrock is a bargain. Frank Rowlett recalls, "It was a cheap way of getting intercept—real cheap." Fast and secure. The photographed messages give analysts a sneak peek into the enemy's code room: Is the message printed by machine or handwritten? Did the encoder scratch something out, change the length of a column, alter the indicator? Copies circulate beyond the Agency into Pentagon boardrooms.

Shamrock is top secret logistical data processing—not analysis. It's how the copies are made and where they go that makes Shamrock. The personnel are *low-level employees* in Intercept Control, the messenger center, the photography lab. That's why it's "cheap." History conflates the analysts who decrypt Shamrock messages with the operation itself, but "Operation Shamrock" refers to the collection, copying, and distribution of messages. By Black women.

A NEW AGENCY

The Armed Forces Security Agency (AFSA) launches in mid-1949 with high hopes of consolidating the country's leading military intelligence into a single superagency—but it quickly becomes a self-annihilating disappointment. AFSA's goal is to unify the cryptologic work of the Army, Navy, and Air Force under a single command to streamline the intelligence-gathering process and keep pace with the Cold War's rapidly evolving world. Instead, AFSA does the opposite. Each military branch refuses to subordinate itself to the organization. They require AFSA's director to change his title to "Coordinator." He can make suggestions—but can't give orders. And no one has to listen.

Since the war's end, the Agency has preached "efficiency and economy." AFSA delivers neither. The Army, Navy, and Air Force guard their intelligence like contraband, refusing to share with one another. Rival branches duplicate each other's work, bleeding time and money while the Cold War heats up.

Bernice sees the signs, but not the whole picture. She's not alone: Analysts are kept in the dark—not by accident but by design. Top-level requests for cooperation go unread. More than five hundred people walk out in less than a year. Masses of data go unanalyzed, game-changing leads stay locked in storage, gathering dust.

Whole lines of inquiry go cold for reasons no one explains: It's just the way things are. The hands in the traffic rooms keep moving, even if they don't know whose orders they're following. Bernice knows not to ask questions—the changes are way above her pay grade. She may not expect things to get better, but she surely doesn't want them to get worse.

Unfortunately, the men at the top are happy to let AFSA go up in flames. When the joint staff do work together, they disagree. Arguments over interpretation stall intelligence reports, leaving policymakers little to go on. Departments give half answers and conflicting briefs, and no one is held accountable.

The branches don't even want to share space. Arlington Hall is still AFSA's official headquarters, but the Navy clings to its own station on Nebraska Avenue, and the Air Force bolts entirely—leaving only a token presence behind enemy—meaning Army—lines. Petty rivalries grind cooperation to a halt: Without oversight, each branch shapes its own policies, its own priorities, its own reality.

Even the structure is a trap. AFSA answers to the Department of Defense and the Joint Chiefs, not the Intelligence Community. Its directors have no authority to force coordination. Civilian agencies on the United States Communications Intelligence Board—the CIA, State Department, even Britain and Canada—have opposed military control from the start, and they treat AFSA's proposals as dead on arrival. As the fledgling agency flounders, it becomes little more than a stack of subcommittees that spend most of their time arguing and angling for control.

AFSA proves disastrous at a moment when the United States needs sharp, united intelligence. The country is scared. Stakes are high as trials uncover the extent of Soviet espionage in the US. The world's power balance is shifting—communist rebels in China are close to vanquishing the nationalists (whom the US supports). The outcome of China's civil war will determine a whole new intelligence strategy. American leaders are more desperate than ever for insight into Stalin's intentions. Instead of delivering timely, focused intelligence, the jokers at AFSA jostle for control of their little kingdom and miss the big picture.

ANALYSTS TO AFTERTHOUGHTS

AFSA's dysfunction trickles down to the cryptologic floor. Reorganized branches merge or split. A new pay grade system appears. Duplicate units are shuffled or shut down.

It happens in Ethel's corner of the Agency. The Commercial Code

Unit—once a steady source of wartime intelligence—no longer has a purpose. Most commercial traffic now runs through MPRO or the Traffic Processing Branch, which feed it to the Task I analysts. The remaining workload is slim, and nobody at the top is making a case to keep the Black cryptanalysts on staff. The progressive spirit of earlier times is gone, and despite Truman's order, segregation at the Agency hasn't budged. The few integrated offices that exist are the exception rather than the norm.

AFSA keeps the unit together, but it's folded into an administrative office, under the Cryptanalytic Division's assistant chief. Now it's called General Processing. Everything's become vaguer. For now, their pay and titles stay the same, but the work is different. More clerical, less analytic. More status reports than translations. The unit is one step deeper into clerkification, that steady stripping away of their technical roles until they're part of the mass of the Agency's low-level clerks. Ethel doesn't say whether she's heard of the "plantation," where so many Black employees now work, but she knows enough to suspect it's real. And that anyone can wind up there.

AFSA plans to audit its personnel and decide if changes need to be made. Washington's directed the new agency to "consolidate"—to do the most work with the fewest people. Fresh eyes will be on the Black cryptologists' work, and that could mean another change.

Meanwhile, Bernice feels the pressure in the Traffic Processing Branch—not just because the cracked radiators make it boiling hot. She's barely been there a year, and already the Black Friday backlog feels endless. The workspace is cramped, the air stale, and the floor littered with papers. Janitors don't come down there—the clerks are expected to clean the office themselves. The lists of keywords she's supposed to watch for change without warning. Nobody explains why. One day it's new Soviet trade terms, the next it's a cluster of names she's never heard.

The Traffic Processing Branch is already working overtime to clear the backlog caused by Black Friday. The conditions are terrible, the pay is low. The other half of their division—the Traffic Distribution and Exchange Branch—is fielding traffic from all over the world. They handle everything that isn't Russian plaintext, performing much the same process as the Traffic Processing Branch. Together, these branches comprise the Traffic Division, and they process all the Agency's cryptologic content, day in and day out. Distribution and Exchange is also in the basement—on the "plantation"—so every message the Agency collects is sorted by an underground operation of underpaid Black workers. And AFSA's dysfunction makes their bad situation even worse.

Bernice's branch pays for the Agency's lack of direction. The Traffic Division is overworked, understaffed, and left in the dark about the data they're processing. Bernice doesn't know where the messages go once they leave her hands, and she's not sure she wants to. She can't talk about her work, not even with her friends at lunch. The longer she's here, the more invisible she feels. She's not one to feel defeated, but she is tired.

During the war, the Agency tried to shield its workers from this feeling. Memos urged supervisors to make staff feel valued, reminding them that the mission can't be properly performed "without the enthusiastic support of every member." Leaders were told to think beyond the workday, to ask if their people were happy—"Not only at work, but at play." To help them with "housing, transportation, and innumerable items" that could improve morale.

They know what unrelenting, thankless work does to a person's spirit. But the postwar Agency isn't making those efforts, at least not for the workers on the plantation. Whatever the memos once promised, Bernice knows that no one is checking on whether she's happy "at work or at play," only whether she's keeping up with the reams of messages in front of her. There's a message in that omission, a reflection of what the Agency believes about its Black employees: They can be counted on to produce what's needed—but they aren't necessarily human.

JOE SAYS HELLO

In late summer 1949, a US reconnaissance plane flies over Alaska, just close enough to the Soviet border to peek into Russian airspace. It picks up something strange—a disturbance over Central Asia. What looks like a weather anomaly reveals itself to be much more.

A shock wave.

The Soviets have detonated their first atomic bomb.

It takes everyone by surprise. Task I's been playing Atlas, but one Titan can't win a war against the gods. AFSA, the Department of State, the CIA, the Atomic Energy Commission, and every other intelligence agency rush to pick up the pieces of their colossal failure.

One thing is clear: The balance of power has shifted. The United States is no longer the world's only nuclear power. That monopoly was the only thing keeping the US in the driver's seat of world affairs. Now—anything can happen.

Now the question remains: Will he use it against America?

No intelligence has greater implications for US survival, no link between intelligence and policy is clearer. If accurate, it can dispel fears of a Soviet invasion. A surprise attack. If not—it can amplify them to disastrous proportions. In hindsight, Black Friday makes sense: The Soviets weren't preparing for an attack—they were preparing to introduce Joe-1. To demonstrate their arrival as a nuclear power. Thanks to Bill Weisband, they knew the US had broken their codes in advance and tightened their security to keep Joe-1 a surprise.

There's no American Bill Weisband—no spy inside the Kremlin. Because so few sources of Soviet data exist, every piece is charged with political energy. Any single fact, tape, or report can be a turning point. The CIA can't help; they're not producing HUMINT, and their research is spotty. Not long ago, they estimated the Soviets were still years away from having nuclear technology. Now they must reconsider those estimates—and fast. Without better intelligence, all they can do is dust off their crystal balls and gaze.

Out of existential fear and an abundance of caution, the CIA estimates that in three years, Stalin will have one hundred nuclear bombs. In four or five years—two hundred. Now the Soviets have or can easily produce enough aircraft to deliver nuclear payloads to all US targets, enough to immobilize the country in one quick strike. A decisive attack, it will psychologically destroy the Americans' will to fight. Even if Stalin has only ten bombs—which he will soon if he doesn't already—he can knock the United States out of a war if those bombs are delivered accurately to their targets. If Stalin believes he has the upper hand, nothing can stop him from creating a communist world order.

The Atomic Energy Commission concurs with the assessment, but the Army, Navy, and Air Force disagree—with the CIA as well as with one another. Moreover, the Soviet Union is the main world power calling for nuclear disarmament. Stalin calls it a "peace offensive." The United States has around 170 atomic bombs—mostly the plutonium implosion type like the one dropped on Nagasaki, and a few uranium bombs like the one dropped on Hiroshima. But if both the Soviet Union and the US dismantle their stockpiles, the Soviets' military will be superior. This is what the military sees: The Red Army has recovered from the war and has staggering means of waging conventional warfare. Without a nuclear-capable US, the Soviets can roll through Europe with little opposition. The US military is scattered, underfunded. Its refusal to desegregate has made it politically toxic, and there is limited support for starting World War III. The US has plenty of anti-communist hate but no firepower to back it up.

America isn't the only country making calculations. The NATO countries and the UK—the Western bloc—are running their own numbers. By NATO's calculations, Stalin doesn't need two hundred bombs, or even ten. All he needs is one—aimed squarely at Great Britain. That will disarm the United States indefinitely. Great Britain is a big world power packed onto a tiny island. It's bigger than Mississippi but smaller than Michigan. The US has bases there—now they'd be useless.

There are two options for US-NATO relations from here. In the best-case scenario, NATO demands more aid and equipment from the United States to prepare for a Soviet attack. Since the US cannot provide much more aid than it already does, the worst-case scenario would ensue—Western Europe breaking their alliance with the US and declaring political neutrality. The UK would have no choice but to follow suit, as devastating for them as it might be. Japan, a US ally, would almost certainly declare neutrality. Or an alliance with their Russian neighbors.

Joe-1 has moved the Doomsday Clock ahead, but the *Bulletin*'s scientists temper the rising anxieties with caution: "We do not advise Americans that doomsday is near . . . But we think they have reason to be deeply alarmed and to be prepared for grave decisions."

They assure the American public their bombs are far stronger, far better, than the "Beria bomb" exploded in Siberia. Compared to the US arsenal, it's "amateur handiwork."

But the clock is still ticking.

Three minutes to midnight.

10

THE LAST STATION

MID-1948–APRIL 1950

Rain pelts the windows, blending with the rhythms of adding machines and carriage returns. Iris Price Corley (later Carr) rises from her seat and takes one last look around. The clerical wing holds a sea of typists, recordkeepers, statistical clerks. The women work diligently, divided by an invisible line. Black women on the left, white women on the right. One office, two halves. Implied rivalry.

Six years at the Recorder of Deeds Office is enough.

Belongings packed, she moves quickly down the center walkway, a demilitarized zone, whispering bye to friends as she passes. The boss looks up, and Iris gives a civil nod. She should be in that chair, but it's not her fight anymore.

Iris came to Washington from Austin, Texas, in 1944 to do what she couldn't do in her home state—pay into retirement.

In Texas, Black teachers can't earn state pensions. Iris majored in English and math at Prairie View College, and it was easy to run the numbers. After more than a decade in the classroom, she wouldn't be able to get ahead, no matter how hard she tried. At the end of a twenty-, thirty-, or forty-year career, she'd have no safety net.

Iris pictured herself as an old woman of seventy—still sharp but frail, with no savings to fall back on, nothing to protect her independence.

The image haunts her.

She's done everything she can. Texas doesn't allow Black students to attend its universities, so Iris went to an HBCU. Black students can't earn postgraduate degrees at any school in the state—white or Black—so Iris drove 1,700 miles every summer for three years to New York City to get her master's degree from Columbia University's Teachers College. She taught in Austin for over a decade—math, physical education, English, grade school, high school. Wherever she was needed. Whatever she could get. She helped her father build a State Teachers' Association and supervised schools across the county. When the war broke out, she ran a motor corps, trained twenty women, learned mechanics and radio communication.

In 1943, when her husband left for Fort Sam Houston, Iris had to make a choice. At thirty, she'd built a life, a career, and a community in Austin. But was it enough? Iris is a steel-willed idealist. She comes from a lineage of teachers, but giving up her future for the struggle didn't sit right. Like everyone else, she deserved to pursue her dreams. Financial independence. Home ownership. American hallmarks of success.

The war sparked visions of a new future—one where she could break through Texas's Black ceiling. Teaching in the South offered little hope of achieving the things she wanted in life. Washington, DC, wasn't the North, but government work offers security. Her husband would join her when he was discharged. By then, she'd be settled, in a career groove, a bridge club. Earning benefits. Building a future.

But that isn't what happened.

Iris's younger sister, Jewel, came to Washington with her. She got a job at the Pentagon but left after only a month. Smart, poised, and elegant, Jewel couldn't take her "ignorant" boss. She didn't go into details, but Iris could guess. She let Jewel go; teaching in Texas would be better than whatever Jewel experienced here.

Iris's husband, Reginald Corley, isn't happy. Like Iris, he has a master's degree; he was a school principal in Texas. Now he's a machine operator in federal accounting. They're not about to make a Black man a supervisor, so he's stuck. He misses his band, the Royal Aces. A saxophonist, he played all of Austin's major events.

To make ends meet, the Corleys have a lodger. William Payne, a veteran like Reginald. Works as a mail carrier. Not ideal for a couple trying to restart their lives.

Iris has her bridge club. And she wins. Trounces the competition with her partner and future husband, Dewey Carr. She plays the masters' circuit, collects trophies. But it's not enough.

With her marriage and career uncertain, Iris looks ahead—but she can't see very far. It seems like there are no jobs in government for an educated Black woman with a strategic, analytical mind. With organizing skills and leadership experience. With a background in high frequency radio communications.

THE TWO KOREAS

Just across the Tumen River on Korea's mountainous northeastern edge lies Siberia—the white bear of the Soviet Far East. For Stalin, this narrow border is a buffer and a bridge: a barrier against Japanese expansion and a secret post for Soviet command in East Asia. While the war against the Axis rages, the Soviets quietly set up camp in Khabarovsk to train young, exiled guerrilla fighters—communist rebels from China and Korea—with their leader, Kim Il Sung. Kim has been fighting with his Chinese and Korean comrades against the Japanese, but now they join the Red Army, forming the Eighty-Eighth Separate Rifle Brigade, and Kim becomes a captain. By 1945, Kim has the right blend of credentials—anti-Japanese fervor, loyalty to Moscow, and a useful degree of political pliability. When the war is over, he becomes the Kremlin's main man in Korea.

After Japan surrenders, Korea is suddenly back on the map. For thirty-five years, the peninsula suspended between China and Japan has been under Japanese imperial rule. The brutal occupation decimates Korean culture—resistance earns forced labor and worse. Starvation controls a strong but weary people. Now, with the war over and the occupiers routed, the country is a prize no one was planning to claim.

The United States lands in Korea not because of a grand tactical vision, but because of a hasty decision made in the war's final days. Soviet troops are moving down from the north, crossing into Korean territory. To keep them from taking over the peninsula—and its strategic Pacific access—two young US officers in Washington negotiate a symbolic border with the Soviets that divides the country into north and south. Using a National Geographic map, they choose a point thirty-eight degrees north of the Equator that slices through the country—the thirty-eighth parallel. North of that, the Soviets will accept Japan's surrender; south of it, the Americans will. The deal is done quickly, without Korean input and no thought for the long-term. But that's how we end up occupying southern Korea.

The rushed setup never recovers. General John R. Hodge, who's in charge of the transition, would rather be on the battlefield. Korea, to him, is a "hornets' nest." To US troops, it's worse than war-torn Japan. The outposts are poor and mountainous. Rough roads, scarce amenities. It's not a blank slate: Seoul's population is more than one million. There are railroads, street cars, automobiles. One US soldier writes, "The streets are paved and kept cleaner than in some of the towns in the States."

Political tensions are rising: Korea wants independence. They're ambivalent about Hodge, who disbands local governments and reinstates the wealthy democrats, former Japanese collaborators. To maintain order, Hodge keeps the Japanese colonial police in place. It's a bad move, stoking resentment and deepening distrust. Support for the US shrinks, and communist sympathies grow stronger.

Meanwhile, in the north, the Soviets are giving Koreans exactly what they want—revenge against Japan. They take land from Japanese collaborators and redistribute it to peasants, earning the people's support. They nationalize industry and centralize the economy, mirroring the Soviet apparatus. Education promotes socialism—the will of the people to fight their imperial oppressors—and Soviet-backed police maintain stability while training local forces. The north's young leader, Kim Il Sung, has fought bravely to defeat the Japanese, and he returns from Russia a hero. The Soviets consolidate his power, nurturing his cult of personality and suppressing rivals.

Two very different countries emerge—one headed in Pyongyang with a strong communist vision and a national spirit, the other in Seoul with tenuous democratic ties to the United States and no real sense of closure from the war. It doesn't take long for the rift to widen and opposition to form. The problem is that there are still communists in the south and non-communists in the north. Families unwittingly separated by random political acts find themselves on the wrong sides of a closed border. Homes, businesses, communities, dreams—all broken like a bored child's toys. The US is looking past the Korean people to see what the Soviets are doing in the north. Hodge is carrying out a plan—Baker 40—the US occupation of southern Korea, but it's not his plan, and he doesn't like it. Hodge wants a speedy resolution to stem the growing chaos.

But why draw a line? As the ill-fated division unfolds, *The Korea Times* publishes an editorial that reveals a disturbing parallel:

> Joyful and grateful as we are, it is very difficult for us to understand why Korea has been divided in two . . . Why a Dixie Line in Korea? Korea has always been racially and culturally homogeneous.

The American instinct to draw a line between North and South changes the fate of millions, imposing a foreign model of antagonism on an undivided nation. North and South can work together: In Korea, the North has all the resources—coal, dams, fertilizer, and timber. Everything needed to sustain an agricultural society. Without them, when winter comes, the South will perish. Surely the United States and the Soviet Union can help North and South build an alliance. Different parts of the same whole needn't be enemies: They can maintain their individual characters yet work together—right?

In 1948, the two Koreas declare independence—each claiming sovereignty over the peninsula. The Republic of Korea (ROK), backed by the United States, rises in the south. The Democratic People's Republic of Korea (DPRK), with Soviet support, rules the north with an iron fist. It's a powder keg, and everyone knows it. Both occupiers agree to withdraw their armies and let the countries govern themselves. But the Agency's intercept station picks up trouble: Contrary to ground reports, Red Army troops in North Korea don't deactivate. Traffic analysis shows that they hole up in a new headquarters in Pyongyang.

The North-South battleground Americans take for granted is, for Koreans, a "punishment" and a "curse." There's something about drawing a line. Iris knows it. You have to pick a side—a choice that can't be taken back. And so it is with Korea. The North and South develop different dialects, different governments, different ideologies, and different beliefs about what it means to be Korean. The "racially and culturally homogeneous" nation now sees the other side as foreign. Like the US North and South, they will be mired in never-ending conflict. Linked ineluctably across the thirty-eighth parallel, each the other's shadow. "Let there be no Dixie Line in the Land of Morning Calm," the editor pleads.

But it's too late.

THE HILLTOP

It's Saturday night between Ninth and Fifteenth on U Street. Streetcars rumble over the sounds of laughter and clicking heels, crowds gather outside the Lincoln Theater, neon marquees buzz above clubs and cafés on Black Broadway.

Fish fries, car horns, smoky ribs, exhaust—the sounds and smells of U Street waft up to the second-story window of the Hilltop Radio Electronics Institute, where Iris Corley sits in a classroom grading papers. The night life beckons, but Iris has work to do. The new school for Black veterans, formed under the GI Bill, needs teachers to train radiomen and electricians. During the day Iris teaches business English, and at night she grades math papers. It pays better than the Recorder of Deeds, but she still pulls overtime. All the teachers do. Bernice Mills and Beulah Giles, two women she works with, have day jobs and teach their classes at night.

Iris likes Hilltop. She's a whiz at math—the work is in her wheel-house. At Hilltop, she can use her skills and values to support veterans entering the workforce. Capitol Radio Electronics Institute, Washington's main technology training school, is off-limits to Black veterans. So they started their own.

The echo of low heels in the corridor announces Bernice and Beulah's arrival.

Iris gathers her papers—she's just finishing up. Soon the room will fill with young men—and some older ones—looking to get better jobs, support their families. If hiring is truly based on skills, then they should have a shot. If it isn't, they have to try anyway.

Bernice knows a bit about Iris. She's seen how fast she grades, how intensely she works. She knows Iris's last job fizzled out and that she's still not where she wants to be. As well as it pays, Hilltop does not offer benefits. Iris is still on the hunt for a job that does.

As they chat in the hall, standing aside as the first few students walk in, Bernice pulls a folder out of her purse. She hands it to Iris.

"You should be working at the Agency where I'm working," she says.

Iris looks at the folder—inside is an application. "Well, I don't know. I haven't ever heard of it."

The other women smile.

"No," Bernice says. "Not many people have heard of it, but I'll take your application in."

Iris decides to think about it.

Outside, the street is alive. Iris looks up to the window and sees the classroom filling with students, Bernice chalking words on the board, Beulah handing out papers.

The trolley clangs as it roars past, bringing Iris back. She straightens her coat, tucks the folder in her bag, and heads down the street toward her stop.

THE OUTPOST

For ASA Pacific, Korea is a miserable post. The Army's postwar SIGINT operation, headquartered in Okinawa and stretched across Japan, China, and the Pacific islands, has one last station on the peninsula.

It might as well be on Mars. The Pacific signal companies are thousands of miles apart. They get more static than intercept, can barely hear their checkpoint's "Roger that." Cut off by distance, water, and unreliable supply chains, morale hits new lows. Since the end of the war, Japan's airwaves have been silent. Communist traffic is rare. Other posts cover Chinese air defense. With no clear mission and barely enough electricity to keep the equipment running, the urgency isn't there. Muggy summers, arctic winters—a surprisingly mountainous terrain that locals navigate with ease. Seoul is bustling, modern, but the countryside is poor and nobody speaks English—not that the Americans have even tried to learn Korean.

After two and a half years, the 111th Signal Service Company is at a breaking point. They've switched out personnel, received fresh supplies, but operating the station is a constant battle. Their diesel generators interfere with their signals. Sloping V antennas stretch hundreds of yards into the rice fields, and locals keep cutting the lines—sometimes out of desperation, sometimes sabotage. Under Hodge, the US military has become an occupying force, and there's no love lost between the Americans and locals.

There is a mission: Russian air and military traffic, funneled through illegal Soviet stations in North Korea. They pick up Russian broadcasts in Japanese, signaling a secret Moscow-Tokyo alliance. There's Chinese traffic too, but they can't be sure of the source, whether it's from North Korea or China, whether it's communist or other governmental.

The intelligence is good, if sparse, but at night, local raiders breach the perimeter again and again—the steel chain links cut and pried open—despite nightly guards and K-9 patrols. Informants report communist plots, and US security troops march into villages to arrest several "ringleaders." Locals deny the rumors, and political tension climbs.

As the US peacekeeping mission winds down, the outpost wants to pack up with them. It's so much trouble for so little payoff. The Soviet threat *feels* remote, even if it's right next door. They don't know what's happening in Pyongyang, and they're not convinced they should care.

By May 1948, the Army suspends operations. Syngman Rhee's government is in place. Conditions are sufficiently stable. The signalmen pack their crypto gear into crates, turn the rest over to the Korean Military Advisory Group, and fly out to Okinawa. For the first time in months, they're smiling.

When the last station in Korea closes down, the United States loses more than an outpost—they lose perspective. Even with the raids, the illegal Soviet–North Korean networks, the lingering Red Army troops in the north, they write the area off as insignificant. Alaska can track Russian air and military traffic, but other than that, no one looks back as the peninsula fades into the distance. A mere fifteen thousand peacekeeping troops and a thin wall of South Korean forces remain—all that's left between the fragile South and the vicious North.

When the last station goes, Korean intelligence goes with it, leaving a vacant perimeter—the last remnants of vigilance—behind.

"SHOULD WE BE WORRIED?"

The Kremlin's conference room is dreary, with yellow walls, heavy brown drapes, and a portrait of Lenin staring down with unsmiling authority. Smoke curls from a dozen pipes and cigarettes, thickening the air. At the polished table, Joseph Stalin sits in enigmatic silence, fidgeting with his pipe, while Andrei Shytkov, his blunt-jawed ambassador to Korea, hovers at his side.

Across from them, Kim Il Sung leans forward, every inch the eager protégé. At just thirty-seven, his round, boyish face hides the steel of a guerrilla commander who has already spent years in the Red Army. His foreign minister, Pak Heon-Yeong, sits watchfully to his right, while a translator waits on his left—not for Kim, whose Russian is flawless, but for his ministers. Kim clasps his hands together, then unclenches them, trying not to betray nerves.

After pleasantries, Kim cuts to the chase. American troops still occupy southern Korea, and their influence is spreading. The North, he insists, is strong on land but exposed at sea. They need Stalin's help to strengthen their naval forces.

Stalin does not look up. He toys with his pipe and asks, almost lazily, how many Americans remain. Kim estimates twenty thousand. Shytkov corrects him—fifteen to twenty. Stalin nods, then asks whether the South even has an army. Kim admits they do: sixty thousand men, but no police force to speak of.

At last, Stalin looks at Kim, a smirk tugging at his lips.

"Should we be worried?" he asks. The words are polite, but the challenge is clear. Kim has potential as an ally, but the Americans aren't to be toyed with. If Stalin is going to help start a war, he needs to be sure he can win.

He's really asking Kim, *Are you afraid?*

Kim's chin lifts. He isn't afraid, but he does need assistance. After a silence, Stalin asks bluntly, who is stronger: Kim or the Americans?

Another silence. This time, Kim's foreign minister fills the gap: "The northern army is stronger, Comrade Stalin." Kim breathes a little easier, but the old man gives nothing away.

Two nights later, the mood is transformed. Kim is a guest of honor at a Kremlin gala. In the ballroom, chandeliers blaze and marble floors gleam as dignitaries swarm to garner favor. Kim is flattered, feted, and treated as Stalin's chosen protégé. But beneath the glitter, he is restless. He catches Stalin aside, lowering his voice despite the ballroom's roar. "The South despises its American oppressors," he insists. "Guerrilla fighters are already in the field. The people are ready to rise!"

Stalin lets him speak, his expression fatherly, patient. Then he shakes his head. Kim must not advance. Not yet. The South Korean army is larger than he thinks, and an attack would invite US intervention. Moscow still has an agreement over the thirty-eighth parallel that they can't risk breaking. The northerns' dream of reunification will have to wait. For now. If the Americans plan aggression, they'll strike. When they do, North Korea will be the defender—not the aggressor. Then the world will understand and offer their support.

Stalin's advice carries a warning: His blessing is contingent and easily revoked.

With Kim rendered silent, maybe the United States is right about North Korea being a small pawn firmly under Stalin's thumb.

"WELL, LOOKY HERE!"

Iris did let Bernice take her application in, and now she is pulling on a rubber apron in a warehouse-like basement full of people, paper, and machines. The air is heavy with gear oil and sweat. As she ties the strings behind her back, a rat scurries by.

So this is "the Agency."

She looks down the length of the wing; just as cavernous as the Recorder of Deeds Office, but here, all the workers are Black. Long tables run along each wall. Neatly dressed women sit in front of automatic typing machines. They feed in telegram tapes; the typewriter prints messages in Russian.

"Well, looky here!"

A gruff, mock playful voice makes Iris turn. Her supervisor saunters over. His eyes aren't joking. There's an edge.

"I got a college graduate working for me."

He appraises her. Iris avoids the unpleasant grin, smooths the apron over her skirt.

The man sidles up to a machine. It's an ink stamper, smudged and hulking. The lever is sticky. He waves her over. "Come on, let me see how you look with your hands dirty." He leans in unpleasantly. "I'll give you a job so you can get your hands dirty."

Iris is repulsed but unfazed. She didn't think professionals in Washington would be like this. She expected . . . a certain caliber of people. Educated, organized. This was stupidity—chaos.

She steps up to the machine, regards the stack of papers in the inbox. The work surface, the lever, all dirty. They should be wearing gloves for this. She tests the lever—it whines as she pulls it down. The stamp lands with a thud. She returns the lever. It leaves a dark stain on her hand.

"Oh, you don't mind that?"

"I think I know how to get them clean if they get dirty."

Her teacher's tone puts him off, and he slinks away. Iris feels sorry for him. She doesn't know whether he has a degree, but he's not . . . intelligent.

He's still a level above her, and that makes her fume.

After her interview, she took a battery of tests, all math based—and aced them. During her clearance period, she compiled Russian dictionaries. In a few months, she had a working knowledge of the language. Her hiring grade? 3. Communications clerk. With her credentials, she should be a 7.

If there's a ladder, Iris will climb it. Even if she has to start at the bottom.

Plus, she has benefits.

She moves to the machine, pulls out another paper, and gets to work.

Operations Building A sits behind barbed wire on the National Security Agency's Arlington, Virginia, campus. The "plantation" or "snake pit" was located in the building's basement. *Photo taken in 1989, courtesy of the Library of Congress, Prints & Photographs Division, HABS VA, 7-ARL,12V--1.*

Due to the "one-drop rule," white-passing people like Alberta James McCray were considered Black. Alberta was quickly transferred to a white unit when the Agency reorganized in 1950. *Federal employee ID photos courtesy of the National Archives and Records Administration.*

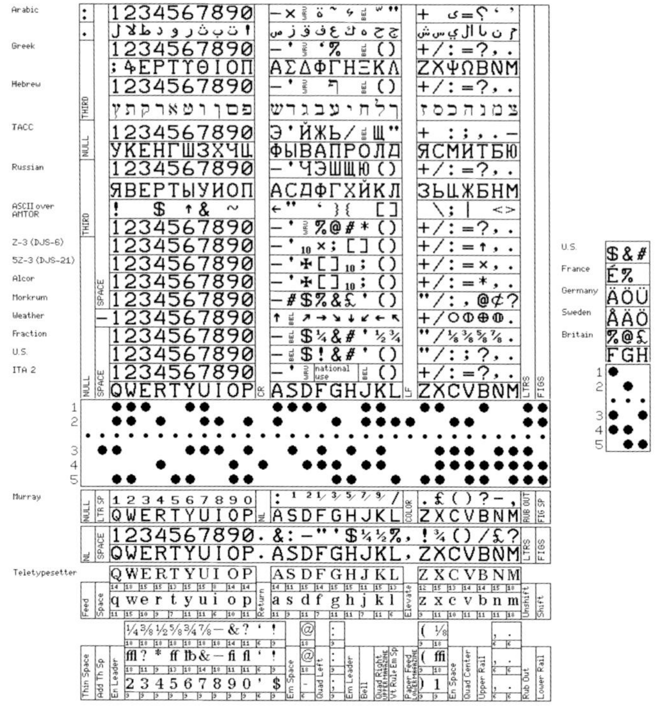

Baudot telegraphic code key. *Image courtesy of John J. G. Savard.*

During World War II, white codebreakers processed, decoded, and transcribed Baudot intercepts (note the code key on the wall). After the war, white workers largely refused to do this essential but tedious work. *Photo c. 1942, courtesy of the National Security Agency, Center for Cryptologic History.*

William "Bill" Coffee (*right*) receives the Meritorious Civilian Service Award for leading the Commercial Code Unit during the war. General W. Preston Corderman presented Coffee with the award on April 3, 1946. *Photo courtesy of the National Security Agency, Center for Cryptologic History.*

This posed photo shows the Commercial Code Unit at work. Bill Coffee, the unit's leader, stands in the center toward the back. Ethel Just sits in the fourth desk of the left row. Raquel Flagler and Audrey Fox sit in the first and third desks of the center row, respectively. The rest of the codebreakers in the photo have yet to be identified. *Photo c. 1944, courtesy of the National Security Agency, Center for Cryptologic History.*

A photo of Ethel Just (*right*) with a colleague at Virginia Union University in 1941. *Photo originally published in the* Baltimore Afro-American, *courtesy of the AFRO American Newspapers' archives / Afro Charities.*

Ethel Just (*second row, left*) in a photo of Virginia Union University's faculty in 1942. *Photo courtesy of Virginia Union University Archives and Special Collections.*

Iris Carr (*right*) and her sister, Jewel Ross, competitive bridge players, at the twenty-fourth annual American Bridge Association tournament in 1957 at the Fort Pitt Hotel, Pittsburgh, Pennsylvania. *Photo by Charles "Teenie" Harris, courtesy of Getty Images, © Carnegie Museum of Art, Pittsburgh.*

Iris Carr receives an NSA Career Service Professionalization Program Resource Manager certificate from Deputy Director Louis Tordella just before her retirement in 1971. *Photo originally published in* The Invisible Cryptologists: African Americans, WWII to 1956.

Martha McWatt's ID photos for the Agency, 1944. *Photos courtesy of the National Archives and Records Administration.*

Minnie Kenny early in her career. *Photo 1960s, originally published in* The Invisible Cryptologists: African Americans, WWII to 1956.

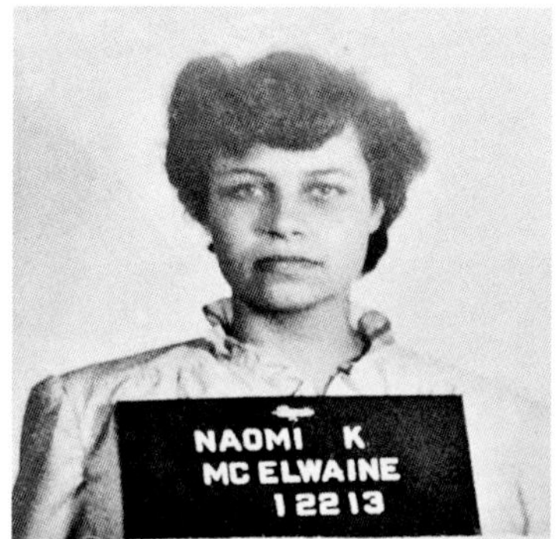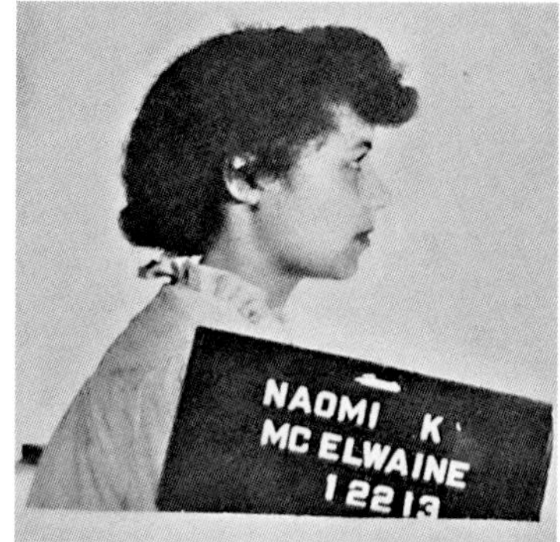

Naomi McElwaine's ID photos for the Agency, 1944. *Photos courtesy of the National Archives and Records Administration.*

TRAINING SCHOOL—REPORT CARD *

McElwaine,	Naomi	K.	SP-5 (Ana.)
(Last Name)	(First Name)	(Middle Name)	(Civil Service Rating)
1930	N. Hampshire N.W.	Washington,	D.C.	1 July 44
(Number)	(Street)	(City)	(State)	

Week	Course	Grade	Absent	Late	Teacher	Week	Course	Grade	Absent	Late	Teacher
FIRST	Crypt.	I	O	O	Kolb	**THIRD**	Code	G	O	O	McAvin
	English	I	O	O	Enlow		9 Messages	G	O	O	McAvin
	Post Reg.	I	O	O	Kolb		Code Analysis				
	Mil. Cust.	I	O	O	Enlow						
SECOND	Crypt.	G	O	O	McAvin	**FOURTH**	B II Unit 1	A	O	O	Yeakel
	Army Org.	VG	O	O	Hayward		B II Unit 11	A-	O	O	Beardwood
	Sig.Com.	G	O	O	Hogan		B II Unit 111	A-	O	O	Beardwood
	War Outline	G	O	O	Corley						
	Geography	VG	O	O	Olsen						

Explanation of grades:
S—Satisfactory   I—Incomplete
U—Unsatisfactory   D—Dropped
Official: _______________ (Adm. Officer)

*When trainee is assigned and leaves school he shall take this Report Card and present it to the Branch Personnel Officer.

1696

Naomi McElwaine's report card from her cryptologic training, 1944. *Photo courtesy of the National Archives and Records Administration.*

An unnamed employee processes tapes in the only existing photo of the all-Black Russian Plaintext Traffic Processing Division. *Photo c. 1953, originally published in* The Invisible Cryptologists: African Americans, WWII to 1956.

The federal government hired thousands of Black women as typists and punch card operators, such as in this Veterans Administration office in Washington, DC. The National Security Agency had similar offices though no photo records of them exist. *Photo 1949, courtesy of Getty Images.*

11

THE FORGOTTEN WAR

MAY 1950–1951

Task I is the Agency's lifeline, and it is drowning in its own success. Only when the backlog becomes unmanageable do they finally bring in someone who should have been there all along. Ethel Just, sixty-five years old, with decades of language experience and five solid years at the Agency, has a glowing personnel file that never quite translated into opportunity. Until now. Today, she is the first Black woman invited to join a major intelligence project.

Her promotion comes with a new badge and top secret clearance. It also comes with a new title: research analyst specialist, higher than her post as a clerk-translator, but one rung below the analyst position she held in her first year.

On Ethel's first day in the wing, a guard stops her. She's a new face, and perhaps not a welcome one. Ethel straightens her back and adjusts her lapel to show her ID badge—earned, not borrowed or stolen. She doesn't wait for a sign to proceed—she knows she belongs.

Inside is a factory of chaos. Young analysts shuffle between desks carrying folders, ties or ponytails askew, their jackets draped on chairs. On one side, translators hunch over Russian industrial reports, scribbling notes in pencil before sending their drafts down the line. On the other, analysts cluster in small groups, arguing over production numbers, energy outputs, the implications of a coal shipment rerouted from one oblast to another. A huddled group of women gesture at graphs, voices low but urgent. The din is relentless, but beneath the chaos is purpose. Frank Rowlett, once a skeptic, visits often. Gurin asks if he can help him. "I just like coming down here," Rowlett says. "There's such a live atmosphere, what with people working and printing stuff out." He's right—the air crackles with energy. Task I is the heart of American knowledge about Stalin's war machine.

Ethel is shown to an empty desk, its surface already buried under folders. She's one of 167 workers staffing the division. She doesn't know who pushed her name forward, but Frank Rowlett has insisted that Gurin keep the pipeline full of talent. Like the other analyst specialists, she's slotted into one of the ministry sections. Finance or Foreign Trade would fit; coming from the commercial unit, she already knows Russian banking and exports. But she's likely put where brains and bodies are needed most—on Olin Adams's atomic energy team, tracking production, research, and ore extraction. That's where the backlog is worst and the stakes are highest. Stalin's bomb has gone off. The West can't afford to miss signs of what's next.

On a nearby desk is a shipping manifest in Russian, numbers arranged in neat columns, abbreviations Ethel doesn't recognize. It could be a half ton of uranium ore transported from one plant to another or production totals from a smelting facility. Trivial alone, these data sheets accumulate into stories: Stalin's plans written in the ink of his bureaucrats. The data feed two series of reports—the intelligence products of Task I. The Russian Plain Language Analysis Reports (RUPLAR), thick dossiers that explain how each ministry operates and where it fits in the schema of weapons production. The other is the Russian Plain Language Analysis Item (RUPLAI), shorter, sharper supplements added when a message merits its own analysis. Plaintext is cumulative, and RUPLAI update previous intelligence in the light of new findings. An uptick in transmissions across industries like weapons production, oil, coal, and state reserves could indicate mobilization. Shipment of goods from civilian producers to the Soviet Army, like petroleum; the locations of munitions production sites, and the sizes and locations of supply depots. Transportation capacities. Vehicle production. All potential signs. Stalin exerts supreme control over economic production, and even the smallest factories must keep their "masters" in Moscow informed of their progress if they want to stay in operation.

Around Ethel, analysts pore over fact sheets, scribble notes in the margins, stack them with handwritten summaries stapled to untranslated telegrams. Typists in the next wing hammer these drafts into their final form, producing polished intelligence that reaches the CIA and State Department. They can't keep up with the sheer volume of reporting and reorganize their branches to manage the influx. Ethel sees their representatives, men who visit Gurin and consult with top linguists like Juliana Mickwitz and Olin. Soon, the CIA men are a fixture in the office. The State Department rotates in its own staff while an agent from the Pentagon hovers nearby. Even the grumbling Navy posts an envoy. Everyone wants a slice of plaintext.

Ethel doesn't see her old colleagues from the Commercial Code Unit, nor the clerks from the basement "plantation" whose hands move mountains of raw traffic. They stay hidden in A Building. She knows word of her promotion has reached them—she can feel the weight of their hope and disappointment. They know she should have moved up long ago. But that didn't happen. Now that it has, it feels more like a warning than a triumph: Even the best will wait years for a seat at the table, if they're even invited in the first place.

For Ethel, it's both. She has fought too long for this seat not to savor it. For the first time in years, she is where she was meant to be—at the heart of the work, in the fight, making a difference. But she is only one analyst out of hundreds. One Black woman in an agency still blind to its failures.

NO RED FLAGS

The Soviet Union isn't working alone. In May 1950, the CIA submits its assessment of North Korea: A tightly controlled Soviet satellite, it won't take initiative of its own. Even though its military is stronger than the South's, and it's positioned to pursue its "main external aim"—the takeover of South Korea.

Despite the steady rise in propaganda, infiltration, sabotage, and guerrilla attacks against the South, the CIA doesn't believe war is imminent. The North is massing troops, tanks, and heavy artillery along the thirty-eighth parallel. Civilians are being evacuated—but this is hardly cause for alarm. North Korea's goal is to eliminate the Republic of Korea—to form one country under communist rule—but is this a *real* problem? Maybe at some point in the far, far future, but for now—no Red flags.

For once, the Agency agrees. They have a bigger problem. An explosive one. South Korea has been clamoring for aid—for the Americans to finish what they started. The United States acquiesces but warns that this is their last effort. The Korean aid bill barely passes. The US sends South Korea $100 million ($50 million less than requested) and hopes the problem goes away.

Behind the scenes, Stalin's plans have changed. After the successful detonation of Joe-1, the United States is no longer the world's only nuclear power, and Stalin has more leverage than before. He won't cross the thirty-eighth parallel, but he can support North Korea's campaign. He revises his advice to Kim: Instead of waiting for the Americans to attack, North Korea will go on the offensive. They'll have support, training, and equipment from the Soviet Union, but no troops. China—the newest communist power—has pledged its armies and support. The Americans didn't intervene to stop a communist victory in China, and they won't lift a finger when Kim rolls his tanks into Seoul.

For the United States, conflicts in East Asia aren't the focus. America's priority is Task I. Somehow they don't see the two as related. As Ethel settles into her workflow, the Joint Chiefs demand everything Task I can dig up on Stalin's nuclear project—weapons systems, aircraft, guided missiles, tanks—anything that hints at mobilization. After Ethel, more new hires pour into plaintext, but even so they're drowning. Less than half of the 150,000 tapes sent from Traffic Processing are analyzed each month. The rest—some of the most critical intelligence they have—sits in backlog while leaders clamor for insight.

And yet, the solution is right next door.

In A Building, Bernice Mills and a hundred Black workers—many with Russian-language skills—are stuck doing low-level processing work. The idea of bringing them into B Building never comes up. Security is one reason. They've finally caught Bill Weisband, but spies are still hidden in Arlington Hall. They should have asked more questions about Weisband from the get-go: Why was he strolling into restricted areas? How did he afford those lavish parties on a linguist's budget? Turns out his background was false—and no one checked. They don't convict Weisband—that would be terrible PR. He disappears, and no one tells his colleagues why he's gone.

Meanwhile, dozens of squeaky-clean Black workers on the traffic side of Task I could greatly help on the analysis side—but ingrained racism makes the idea of bringing them in unthinkable. Ethel's promotion was a miracle that should have been the norm, but the traffic processors' exclusion isn't up for debate. At the Agency, it's the natural order of things. The Commercial Code Unit proved that Black cryptanalysts could perform, but AFSA would rather fail spectacularly than give up its CPU—its carefully cultivated cast of data processors.

KOREA

At 4 a.m. on June 25, 1950, the 105th North Korean Army Tank Division rolls into Seoul with 180 Soviet tanks. They massacre the South Korean Army. The United States has no prior warning. Except that they do.

They just ignore it.

Because they can't agree on whether the signals they catch are from

China or North Korea. Because, against orders, they downgrade North Korean intelligence to low-priority. Because the analysts watch T-34 tanks line up behind the thirty-eighth parallel and do nothing. AFSA's stomach-churning rivalries and their refusal to prioritize these warnings—what few there are—means they go unheeded. The Agency thinks Korea is a low-stakes outpost—that China and the Soviet Union won't risk confrontation with the United States.

They are wrong.

The US sends unprepared troops into foreign terrain against an enemy they don't know or understand. In the Battle of Chosin Reservoir, General Douglas MacArthur pushes too far north and provokes a massive intervention by the Chinese People's Volunteer Army. With no avenues for retreat, American soldiers freeze, starve, and die in the Taebaek mountains, surrounded by thousands of well-trained enemy troops that no one expected.

For the American public, the war is a gut punch. Just five years after celebrating victory against the Axis powers, Americans are asked to rally again—but this time the cause is murky, the goal unclear, and the enemy is everywhere. China, a former ally, is now a communist power, and Korea—little known and barely reported on before the invasion—is the new front line on a battlefield where Stalin and Mao Zedong are pulling the strings.

As casualties mount, confidence in Truman erodes. Approval ratings plummet. Newsreels show American boys dying in the frozen hills with no clear path to victory, and families start asking why they're even there. What is this war really about? Why isn't America winning? It barely registers that this is the United States' first war fought with integrated Armed Forces. In practice, most units are still segregated—all-white or all-Black. More Black women than ever serve as nurses and support personnel, but their conditions are no better. Black soldiers still face terrible racism and violence. The war effort is failing so badly that Truman fires General MacArthur, who wants to extend the battleground into China. The dismissal fuels growing suspicions that the US's foreign policy—its alliances, intelligence agencies, its military and Cold War strategies—might all be wrong.

The war also cements a new reality: The Cold War is not going to be cold. It is already being fought on foreign battlefields, in frozen hills, and behind the intelligence agencies' closed doors. In State Department board rooms. In the Pentagon. This war is about choice—using the tools, judgment, and experience at the country's disposal to decide whether to take a risk or play it safe. Right now, no option feels safe, no path clear. Every choice America's leaders make pushes them one step closer to—or further away from—Doomsday.

JOE-2

Meanwhile, Stalin expands his nuclear arsenal. In mid-1950, the Korean War spirals from containment to catastrophe, and the United States is caught in yet another disaster it didn't foresee. Instead of offering informed solutions, the Intelligence Community argues about which branch—Army, Navy, Air Force, CIA, and so forth—dropped the ball. Each attempt at a new policy—security enhancements or sharing information across agencies—is either ignored or botched by a team that refuses to work together. Meanwhile, Stalin is sprinting ahead, watching the US drown in a conflict it helped create.

When Stalin worked out his deal with China to back up Kim's troops, he was thinking two steps ahead. Now, while the United States digs itself deeper into war, sacrificing troops and resources it can't spare in the first place, Korea is no longer Stalin's problem. The Soviet-backed invasion is handed off to Mao Zedong, and China floods the peninsula with more than one hundred thousand troops. The Soviet Union recedes from the battlefield and lets China take on the political and military burden. For Stalin, it's the perfect arrangement. With the front lines stabilized, Stalin redirects his focus—and resources—to the arms race.

Under Lavrentyi Beria and the NKVD, Soviet nuclear research accelerates. Factories churn out plutonium. Bomb designs evolve from crude copies of the American Fat Man into more efficient, more deadly devices. The second Soviet bomb test—Joe-2—comes in 1951, revealing clear improvements in efficiency and design. At the same time, a new team, led by the young physicist Andrei Sakharov, begins work on a hydrogen bomb. Their design—the so-called Layer Cake—marks the next quantum leap in Soviet capability.

With none of the US intelligence agencies cooperating, Soviet espionage continues largely undetected. Despite a wave of FBI investigations, arrests, and defections, leaks from US and British atomic labs still trickle into the Kremlin. It's the height of McCarthyism—HUAC isn't just chasing fake communist "subversives." Real spies have been caught red-handed—yet the FBI, CIA, and AFSA refuse to join hands. Venona feeds corroborating tidbits to the FBI, but neither of them shares their findings with the CIA.

It's one more example of the Soviets capitalizing on American failures. US commanders can barely get supplies to the Korean front, but the Soviets' Tu-4 bombers—reverse-engineered American B-29s—are already being modified for atomic delivery. Pilots train on remote runways, warheads are readied for deployment, and Soviet generals begin shaping a doctrine that anticipates nuclear war. US morale in Korea is collapsing, and even this late in the war, signals intelligence offers no help. When the North Koreans invaded, the SIGINT specialists left in the US-run Korean Advisory Council destroyed all their crypto equipment with thermite— burning it down to useless hunks of metal. But they didn't even get *that* right: Soon they realize enough rotors remain intact for the enemy to reconstruct their machines and solve their codes. But guess what? North Korea doesn't even care. They leave the half-melted rotors in the scrap pile where they lie—they're getting all the US intel they need from the Soviets. With no new intel of their own, strategic planners in Washington stagger through meetings, fall back on old assumptions, and are caught flat-footed by every new move from Pyongyang and Beijing. Also—critically—with their focus in Asia, the US has less time and fewer resources to devote to Western operations like Berlin.

The calculus is infallible: Let the Americans freeze on the battlefields of Asia while the Soviets build the future and shore up their resources. By the time Washington catches its breath, Stalin will have more bombs, better delivery systems, and a thermonuclear device in the works. The Soviets are setting the pace, no longer trying to catch up. Building the foundation for nuclear parity—and soon, superiority. Without firing a shot, Stalin is preparing to win the next war.

ETHEL'S GOODBYE

Ethel doesn't get to enjoy B Building for long. After a few months on the new project, her health falters. At first, she takes a few sick days, hoping to recover. Then, the absences stretch into weeks. As summer turns to fall, Ethel remains on extended leave. She won't be back. On February 8, 1951, she retires on disability, two weeks before her sixty-sixth birthday. Her final position is Research Analyst Specialist, GS-5, $3,725. A shamefully low grade for six years of exceptional service.

Missed chances echo in the wake of her departure. Her short-lived tenure in Task I is a testament to what might have been, a reminder that the Agency had years to integrate her unit into its central operations. Instead, they waited until a crisis forced their hand, sacrificing talent and effectiveness in the process. She was the first member of the Commercial Code Unit to transfer into a major operation.

She is also the last.

The others—her wartime colleagues—remain tucked away in clerical corners, their titles shrinking as their workloads grow. Even Herman Phynes, once a P-2 analyst, is now a supervisor "down in the hole." The war promised possibility, but peace delivered confinement.

Back on T Street, Ethel resumes her old routines. She tends her garden when her strength allows, reads on her porch, keeps in touch with her grown children. This year, her oldest, Margaret, is a Visiting Fulbright Professor in the humanities at the universities of Lyon and Grenoble Alpe in France.

The world outside Ethel's door is not the same one she left when she joined the Agency in 1944. Washington's Black neighborhoods are restless. Veterans who were promised home loans on the GI Bill crowd their families into aging rowhouses. Once fashionable and pristine, LeDroit Park is giving way to low-income housing, as domestic workers, handymen, bookies, and clerks strive to find safe, affordable spaces in a city of vanishing possibilities. On U Street, jazz clubs still excite, but the joy they bring is short-lived. A minor chord reverberates as the prosperity hinted at in wartime passes most Black residents by.

Black Washington, like her, has been asked to wait. She signed multiple loyalty oaths, as have others—on paper and in blood. Loyalty that costs Black lives, men killed in combat, or lynched on home soil. Black women who pick up the pieces, whose labor wins others credit. Who lift as they climb. The Cold War pours money into the military and the Agency she served, but little of that bounty filters into the lives of those who live in its shadow.

What does the future hold? Ethel can't quite see it. Change is coming, if not for her, then for the young people walking past her window on their way to campus. The school year has begun.

For all her skill and service, she left the Agency as she entered it: underestimated, underpaid, her potential only partly recognized. She has photos and yearbooks from her teaching career. Performance pamphlets, commencement programs, course catalogs. Folders of newspaper clippings that chronicle her years as a young academic and civic leader. A bound copy of her master's thesis received the same year Margaret received hers. From the same university.

There's no trace of Ethel's six years at the Agency—no trace of her at Arlington Hall, and no trace of it here. She could take nothing with her: no personnel papers, not even her ID badge. All returned or burned.

Yet in the room she briefly occupied in B Building, there might be the sound of a Black woman's pencil scratching across paper, of her heels clicking down the hall with delicate precision.

By the time Ethel leaves, Task I has begun hiring Black men in professional roles. David Bryant, one of the original traffic processors from the Flex room, is taking Russian-language courses to become a translator-analyst. He's the first traffic processor the Agency promotes. A supervisor, he's also one of few men in the group.

He'll fill the opening Ethel leaves behind.

12

A NEW GENERATION

1951–1953

Iris Corley has gotten off the ink stamping machine and into the supervisor's office, where she's promoted to statistical clerk, grade 4. She and Bernice work the adding machines and keep track of the branch's productivity. The quota system is serious: Clerks who don't consistently hit their numbers are "counseled," which means they get written up. Iris doesn't want to risk getting moved back to the scanning floor, and she realizes that she can advance by picking up extra work. Her supervisor never gets his weekly reports in on time (he's a 7)—so Iris comes in on her lunch break and off time to complete them for him.

But they need Iris on tapes. Scanning plaintext is more important than ever, and Iris has some of the best Russian skills in the branch. She has a Russian dictionary and knows more than just the terms on the keyword sheet. Her research makes the job more interesting. Russian plaintext has a "need to know" policy, and people in the processing branch don't "need to know" what happens to the tapes after they leave A Building. By putting clues together, Iris has picked up on the system. She knows they're analyzing the messages in B Building. Taking all the bits and pieces of information and stringing them together. She's been doing that herself; as she reads each tape, she mentally catalogs it, building her own plaintext database in her head. She encourages her younger coworkers to do the same; the work might be boring, but it's important, and it makes a difference.

Iris's coworkers have no idea why she is so diligent. For most, the Agency is just a job, and not a great one. They're all overqualified, stuck doing grunt work. Iris doesn't mind the conditions or the monotony. If the work is worthwhile, Iris is going to do her best.

But here's the thing. Those tapes they're scanning don't just come from intercept and Shamrock. Some of them come from the trash, delivered to the unit in the black bags that the Agency steals from garbage cans. They don't say where they come from, and they don't clean the tapes, don't separate them out—they just deliver the *whole trash bag* containing discarded plaintext tapes and regular refuse to the Traffic Processing Branch. They must come from a Russian source because they're not encoded like intercept—they're the final product. Russian-language telegrams that a person or agency has received, read, and thrown away. The Agency is desperate for intelligence, but the analysts aren't putting their hands in those trash bags themselves. "This stuff was nasty," Iris recalls. "I know why they gave it to us." Day after day, Iris and the other scanners root through trash bags to provide data that B Building's analysts can't even process.

"SEPARATE THEM AT ALL COSTS"

The Agency continues to debate the classifications of "high-level" and "low-level" intelligence. What can they do to: (1) stop persistent leaks, (2) protect against new ones, and (3) make the most of the sources they have? The first idea is to greatly increase security for the "really top-level, really sensitive COMINT" and greatly increase the usefulness of "lower-level, less sensitive COMINT." The solution? Separate them. Separate them at all costs. This means handling them differently "so that the high-level, sensitive COMINT will not be imperiled by association with low-level COMINT."

Likewise, if low-level intel has the same high level of security as the "really top-level" stuff, it won't be able to circulate as widely and therefore won't be as useful as it might be. The writer of this proposal, a Navy captain, really wants to drive this point home: "Unless you *separate* them, *you will not accomplish this purpose*" (original emphasis). The thing is, he admits the current system doesn't even do a good job of this: Both the products of high-level cryptanalysis and low-level traffic analysis are disseminated to an equally broad group. He also admits that the designations "high" and "low" are already in dispute: There can be "easy" cryptanalysis and "difficult" traffic analysis, which makes the high/low categories irrelevant or too complicated to matter.

The proposal, which is both antagonistic and vague, doesn't provide any solutions. The COMINT segregation for which it advocates falls flat when the writer admits the current categories of high and low no longer hold. A rebuttal addresses this, pointing out that if a low-level system like plaintext were given a correspondingly low amount of security, the source would quickly be ruined: If the enemy learns we're getting certain information from plaintext, they'll start enciphering it, cutting off that source of intelligence entirely. (Someone writes "Good!" with a big arrow next to this point in the margin.) The point is that the traditional high/low classifications are not providing any guidance on how to handle, secure, or disseminate intelligence in a way that (1) makes it accessible to the people and agencies who need it, and (2) protects it against leaks.

Another year goes by before someone states the real problem. The deputy director of intelligence, J. N. Wegner, scolds the Agency for wanting to "have its cake and eat it too." Large numbers of people are involved in each stage of the plaintext operation, but they refuse to make significant changes to its security policy or the way it is run. Plaintext is already separated into initial and final processing stages. It's in those final stages, where the bits and pieces are drawn together, that security or personnel need to change. Wegner continues:

> If workers cannot use a product as required for the best results, perhaps some change can be made in the workers, their work, or the materials they use. This is an approach to the plaintext problem which may not yet have been adequately investigated.

The staff aren't getting the most out of the data provided to them—either in the volume of their processing or in the collating of their intelligence. Adding non-COMINT sources like records, profiles, and statistics is vital to plaintext reporting, but that means communicating with support units, which doesn't always happen. A change in the workers could imply changing who they are, how many there are, what roles they are assigned, how they are trained, or what level of clearance they have. Changing the work might suggest a different division of tasks, a different organizational structure, different production requirements, or a difference in how the final intelligence product is presented. Changing the materials they use could refer to anything from the drop copies and tapes produced by the Traffic Processing Branch to the working aids the Agency provides, to the collateral information required to round out a plaintext report.

The memo's mention of "the workers, the work, or the materials they use," doesn't necessarily imply a proposed change to the A Building–B Building separation of the project's two halves, or a proposed change in the function, personnel, or training of the Traffic Processing Branch relative to the Plaintext Analysis Branch. But it might. It implies some change to how things are done in the plaintext project that the rest of the Agency does not want to consider.

The rest of AFSA ignores Wegner's suggestion—it skates too close to the heart of the problem. A couple of months later, Wegner circulates a memo reminding the Agency that it spends half a billion dollars a year on plaintext and that its potential value is "incalculable." Does anything change in the end? Not really. The analysis side changes the way they write their reports to obscure the fact that the intelligence comes from Russian plaintext traffic. Changes that shake up established working norms in the Russian Plaintext Project are never proposed again.

THE MESSAGE

One day Iris sees it. The message every codebreaker hopes they find. The One. That can turn the tide, change the course of history.

Out of the trash bag. A shipment with an address—ДВЕСТИ ТАНКОВ. Iris doesn't need her word sheet to know it means two hundred TANKS. She has the date, the address, all the shipment info. She knows where they're going and when. Kim Il Sung rolled into Seoul with nearly two hundred Soviet tanks. Where are these going? The war in Korea is still raging. Are these tanks coming in to finish the job? Or maybe they're going to Berlin? While the United States' back is turned, embroiled in a losing battle.

Wherever they're going, the message is an early warning. Accurate, timely, actionable. The kind of intelligence we're always trying to get but never quite manage to. A peek into the enemy's plans and preparations. *They sent a note about two hundred tanks in plaintext.* What else did they send?

Iris scrawls the translation on her index card, puts it in the outbox, and reaches for the next tape. She wants to put the pieces together. What if the next message is two hundred BOMBS? Or what if it's a plan? Kim Il Sung pays for his tanks in gold, in lead, in cotton. He sends coded telegrams to Stalin—reporting a shipment of over two thousand tons of lead (more than agreed on). Five thousand more are on the way. Does the Agency have these tapes? Is anyone in plaintext talking to cryptanalysis—putting these pieces together—that if Kim's shipping Stalin lead, Stalin is shipping Kim two hundred tanks?

Iris just keeps reaching for these tapes, trying to find the next one—no amount of nasty is going to stop her from finding what comes next. She knows what they're doing in the next section, that they're putting the pieces together, so why shouldn't she? She can do it—she's been doing it. If she can just find the next one . . . She wants to help *so much*. To prove she can do it. For herself. For the Agency.

But what if that tape is in someone else's burn bag? Carelessly tossed out. What if it's in B Building already, copied onto a nice clean white index card in a backlog that no one will read? Or at the bottom of one of these heavy black trash bags piled in the corner?

Iris never finds the next tape. Or maybe she does.

Do they put it together in B Building?

No one will ever know.

DOWN IN THE HOLE

Despite broader integration at the Agency, the folks on the plantation are no closer to freedom than they were when they were hired. Transfers are still rare. Those who do make it out are mostly men. For women, promotions stay within the unit, never out.

One of the women promoted is Iris. She moves off the Traffic Processing floor into the branch's personnel office. She advocates fair employment and draws her boss's attention to cases of discrimination. She is a trusted, talented worker who is devoted to the Agency, and her superiors recognize this. But just like her plaintext efforts that go unrecognized, her advocacy can't prevent prevailing inequalities. Not long after her promotion, the Agency audits the Traffic Division and downgrades everyone to grade 2. The lowest pay grade the Agency used for its employees. No matter if they're a 3, 4, or even 5, they are back to where they began—or worse.

A few things do change for the Russian plaintext operation in the early 1950s. The first is that the Soviet-encrypted traffic that disappeared on Black Friday comes back online in 1952. It's still a bear for the analysts, but resources that were diverted to plaintext now come back to strengthen Russian cryptanalytic operations. After the long intelligence blackout, partner agencies are eager to get those Russian decrypts. As a result, the 350-person growth projected for the plaintext project (not including traffic processing) doesn't happen. Even though the volume of traffic remains high, there are fewer linguists, translators, and analysts to analyze it. Backlogs grow, and the time between intercept and reports goes from several weeks to several months—in some cases, more than a year. Plaintext remains a high priority, and the Agency addresses this by getting some analysts on loan from the CIA.

The Traffic Processing Branch endures the worst of these cutbacks. After the downgrading, the cryptologists' low pay is even lower, but their quotas remain the same.

The ever-growing backlog remains the same. The dirty ink stamping and nasty trash diving remain. The thundering, ear-splitting teleprinters remain. Segregation remains. The only attempt the Agency makes to raise morale in the Traffic Division is to pipe music into the wing. A personnel memo notes, "Since this is considered an area of low personnel morale as a result of recent downgrading and the monotonous work, it is believed the music will be well received." The plan never comes to fruition: There would be no way to hear the music over the ear-splitting clatter of a hundred teletype machines. Many of the clerks have no choice but to stay. With a saturated private section that prioritizes white hires, where else can they go?

The Agency knows that government employment, with its benefits and security, is more attractive to lower-level employees than it is to high-level specialists, who can command higher salaries at other agencies or in private industry. They take full advantage of Black workers' lack of options.

> This imposed a definite hardship on those employees, who, because of loyalty to the Agency, continued to perform the duties for which they could receive no credit or corresponding pay.

The employees' lack of advancement takes an emotional toll. It is discouraging, and these people leave for jobs at other agencies—CIA, Navy,

State Department. They acknowledge that the longer one stays in the technical side of the intelligence field, the fewer career options they have due to the specialized skills involved. Here again, they are talking about their professional male employees who might suffer income loss due to a change in circumstances. At the same time, they boast that they have no problem hiring enough staff at the lower grades because "in those grades, Government service is more attractive." They know these people can't leave, and by stashing them in A Building's basement, they make sure the data processing staff has nowhere else to go.

Because the Agency has been making requests for additional personnel funding for its top-level people since the war, they've long acknowledged the negative effect that short- and long-term underemployment creates. They care so much about their white staff's emotional well-being. This means they know exactly what they are doing to the people in A Building's basement—they just don't care.

THE PLANTATION EXPANDS

Instead of moving toward integration, the Agency doubles down on segregation. Data processing is more critical than ever, and in a frantic grab for workers, the Agency creates two new hiring policies that are the death knell for Black career advancement in these divisions.

The first is that the Personnel Office will hire all grade 2–4 applicants from outside of Washington, DC, without an interview or prior approval by their prospective supervisors. This means that the Personnel Office has full control over placement, and with their Code 1–Code 2 policy, there's only one place Black hires are going.

The second policy is that interviewees will not be told about the salary for the positions they're applying for. Only after they're approved will the salary be revealed and no matter their credentials, they'll be brought in at the lowest step in their grade. This might not be bad for white hires, who have a chance of moving up the ladder or transferring to other government jobs, but it locks most Black hires into low-paying roles they'll never get out of. The Personnel Office has an understanding that any Black person the Agency hires is going "down in the hole." The "plantation," the "snake pit," "little Africa," the "black hole of Calcutta." All the data processing offices—Traffic Division, Machine Processing, Key Punch, and Tabulation are known to be all-Black, and no one questions it.

"DON'T CALL ME TOOTS!"

Minnie Kenny has been at the Agency for only a few months when she learns what it means to be down in the hole. At first, it's just a phrase she overhears in passing—in the cafeteria line, at the end of a hallway, carried on a laugh that doesn't sound entirely amused. Slowly, she pieces it together. "The hole" means the basement, the "plantation," where the Black clerical staff work long hours in the Traffic Processing Branch. Their world is one of endless intercepts, flickering fluorescent lights, and no recognition. Minnie doesn't learn this through official channels; there are no "official channels" that explain the "hole" or plantation. Whatever name they call it, the division exists on paper as AFSA 213, a bureaucratic designation that hides a visceral reality. A natural at collecting intelligence, Minnie keeps her ears open—in the cafeteria, in the morning and evening badge check lines—letting fragments of conversation drift her way until she forms a picture.

Soon Minnie edges closer to a few of the women from Traffic Processing, enough to exchange greetings and small talk. But it rarely goes deeper. Their statuses at the Agency are too different; the implications are palpable. They can't chat about their assignments. They can't gripe about promotions or pay. They can't even share the same frustrations outside of general topics like DC's changeable weather. The traffic processors must know the rumor turned legend about how Minnie got her job—the coincidence of a class ring that saved her from entering their ranks. So many of the processors have the same—or better—qualifications. There must be a tinge of resentment.

The rumors, the divide, keep them wary and distant.

So Minnie finds her friendships elsewhere. The man running the snack stand outside of B Building knows her name and is always ready with a smile and a pack of peanuts or a soda. With him, Minnie doesn't have to worry about hidden hierarchies or workplace politics. Their talk is casual—about the weather, about baseball, about nothing that matters. And that, Minnie finds, is a relief. Inside the Agency, every word carries weight, but at the snack stand, she can just be herself.

Minnie's daily routine is her grind as a communications clerk, making sense of boxes of backlogged traffic in the Southeast Asian department in B Building. She works in an integrated office, but not everyone is comfortable with her being there. Not only is Minnie Black, she's from the North and doesn't take abuse from white people.

People in the office take turns getting coffee. They collect all the cups on a big wooden tray, fill them up, and take them around to everyone. Minnie isn't a coffee drinker, so she doesn't participate. One day, a woman comes over to Minnie's workstation (she has a table, not a desk) and plunks the coffee tray down on the papers Minnie is working on.

"No, I don't drink coffee so I'm not going to get coffee," Minnie replies. She moves the tray off her papers, but the woman puts it back down on Minnie's papers. She looks at her and says, "You will get coffee, *toots*!"

That word "toots" makes Minnie mad.

"I will *not* get coffee, *toots*!" she replies.

"Don't you dare call me toots!" the woman yells.

Minnie stands up, grabs the woman, and the next thing she knows, they are fighting on the ground. Minnie pins her, and they fight until the other workers pull them apart.

Minnie walks out, sure that she's lost her job.

When she gets home and tells her father what happened, he says, "You're going back, and I'm going with you."

Minnie's father is a ward leader in Philly with high political connections in Washington. He taps his friends from Congress and lets them know that people at the Agency are abusing Minnie. They "clean it up," and Minnie gets her job back. From then on, the white people in her office realize they can't mess with her, and it scares them a little. They're used to having power over Black people, not respecting them as equals.

Minnie is part of a new generation of Black codebreakers at the Agency. They are integrated throughout the workforce, still hired in lower-grade roles, but they have the opportunity to advance. Not all the white staff are happy with the arrangement. Minnie is one of four Black communications clerks, grade 4, who are hired to work "upstairs" in B Building. They're dispersed throughout the wing, not clumped together or segregated. Minnie is a stand-out talent, and she advances quickly—first to a 5, then 7, 9— until she's a division chief.

On the one hand, Minnie's ascent is a triumph. A chance encounter saves her from the hole. She works upstairs decrypting traffic right away and arrives at a time when just enough has changed at the Agency so that someone with her talents can get promoted. On the other hand, she faces constant uphill battles. Her very presence makes her coworkers angry. Her race already marks her as out of place, but her poise, defiance, and her refusal to show white people deference makes her a threat. When Minnie comes back to the office, people treat her strangely—they're kind of afraid. She's supposed to submit, but they learn quickly she's not like that. Minnie is from Philadelphia, where she's used to being treated as an equal.

Minnie gets her job back because her father has connections. Only white people at the highest levels at the Agency usually have this kind of pull, but Minnie is different. This too brings her challenges. If she attends a high-society function, people don't understand why she's there or how she fits in: "I didn't come through the garden door, I came in the front door." The burden of having to explain or justify your presence wherever you go is heavy. It's not just a kind of social friction one experiences, but a deeply held isolation. Minnie's not the type to make herself small for others' comfort—but their expectation that she will and their rejection when she doesn't are likely the source of stress, even if she's familiar with those dynamics.

Another factor that makes Minnie hard to place for some people is her skin tone. Most of the Black women at the Agency are light-skinned. But Minnie is dark. In Black social circles, she suffers colorism because in Black society, light skin is traditionally seen as desirable. This is especially true for women. Light skin signals proximity to whiteness. Many of the Commercial Code Unit members are light-skinned women, some are white-passing or listed as "mulatto"—mixed race. As Minnie notes, Washington's Black society has its own politics:

On the black side, it was more who you knew and what you had to offer. If you had something that someone from the "Tans" wanted, you were accepted by them and if you had something that the "Lights" wanted you were accepted by them. But if you didn't, you know, "Blackie Step Back."

These dynamics exist among the Agency's Black employees too. The Traffic and Machine Divisions have a tight-knit social circle. They have parties, gatherings—but they don't invite Minnie. Their colorism and the "upstairs-downstairs" dynamic between them make socializing a bad fit. Someone like Minnie faces many levels of discrimination—the politics of belonging don't always break down along easy racial lines. Every group has the power to exclude, and sometimes that manifests in unexpected ways. White supremacy is the origin of colorism. Historically, Black people who had a white parent or ancestor were judged to be more intelligent, cultivated, and better overall than dark-skinned Black people. In the 1800s, people chose light-skinned spouses and encouraged their children to stay out of the sun. Light skin became a marker of both class and privilege in a white-privileging society.

As Minnie settles into the East Asian Division, the Agency is called to account for its many failures. The Korean War is at a low point, and for the faltering Agency, it's the last straw. Truman forms a committee headed by New York attorney George A. Brownell to investigate what exactly is going on in AFSA. In 1952, the committee determines that the entities that make up AFSA (Army, Navy, Air Force, and the Joint Chiefs) have been withholding information, duplicating work, and wasting resources. Their poor cooperation and decision-making means that very little has gotten done.

On the committee's recommendation, the White House disbands AFSA and establishes the National Security Agency. It retains the Agency's original personnel while the Army, Navy, and Air Force all return to their own spheres. The new charter gives NSA exclusive control over communications intelligence and security. They answer to the secretary of defense. No more endless committees and meetings. Hopefully, they'll actually get something done.

FORT MEADE

After reorganizing, the Agency hunts for new headquarters. On one hand, they're expanding. On the other, they need a location secure from a nuclear attack. The Joint Chiefs recommend a move to a military base, close—but not too close—to a major city, with a network of resources and a "reasonably equable climate." The first pick is Fort Knox in Kentucky, but the relocation is too far. Employees threaten to quit. Next they consider Fort Meade, just south of Baltimore, Maryland. Both states are segregated. Black employees will have nowhere to live, eat, or shop. No childcare or doctors. No access to public spaces. The only Black housing near Fort Meade is in run-down, segregated neighborhoods. Analyst Richard Watts is asked to scout the area and returns his assessment: "These are not the kinds of houses that Blacks around the [executive] level want . . . Nobody wants houses looking like that."

The Agency sets up the "Meade Mobile" to provide information about the new location but never addresses the lack of adequate housing for Black employees.

Minnie feels the burden of this change. With the time, money, and energy she spends navigating a hostile landscape, she has little left for herself.

She powered through a year of night school to earn her language training, but she hasn't finished her college degree. When Minnie describes segregation at Fort Meade in her interview, her tough-as-nails mask slips. "Many of our white coworkers were ex-military. They did not have degrees." She pauses. "But they could move out here, they could go to work, come home, and go to college . . . The Blacks had this long commute. By the time they got home, they were tired. You see, there was this—" Minnie stutters, then stops. When she recovers, she only says, "It was a burden."

The move coincides with a high point of racial tension. In 1953, protests and police brutality surround the desegregation in Washington schools. Minnie's seen it firsthand, as she marches up and down US 40 with the other protesters. "People were getting their arms broken, their heads knocked in and everything. So it wasn't that it was unknown." The Meade Mobile doesn't address it. Not the violence, the lack of services, or the housing.

The conflict isn't just ideological. Fort Meade's racial climate opens the door to a hostile element. The Agency recruits from its new backyard, and a flood of hires pour in from Glen Burnie High School in nearby Pasadena. Ex-military. No degrees. "Red Necks," Minnie says. "Pure and simple. They came in, they got the jobs, they moved up." They slot themselves into the old boys' club and multiply. Crushing tender shoots of progress.

Soon, "Glen Burnie conflicts" erupt—a personnel race war that mirrors the world outside. Black employees reach their limit and resign. Milton Zaslow, chief of B Group and Minnie's boss, sees what's happening. Racism is just part of the problem: "You had to send people overseas, to Europe, to the Far East." Glen Burnie hires drive to Fort Meade on the back roads; some have never seen the Baltimore-Washington Parkway. Minnie is used to playing charades at lunch with her coworkers—in Greek. When she speaks with a Glen Burnie recruit, she has to simplify her English so they can understand.

In an organization based on language expertise, cultivating narrow worldviews and weak language skills is a recipe for disaster. After the

Korean War and the recommendations of the Brownell Committee, the Agency has to muster what credibility remains. This doesn't help. But it saves money.

In the Far East Group, Minnie works on recovering systems in Chinese, Burmese, and a raft of other languages. She doesn't have time to slow-walk clerks through the Latin alphabet. Another cost-benefit analysis: Make nice with the Glen Burnies. She's decrypting Communist Chinese chatter over North Korean networks as the world shifts in the wake of the new nation. She has mentors watching her progress, crafting her path forward. Minnie's never held her fire, but one complaint to the wrong person on the wrong day could ruin everything. Ms. Kenny is "arrogant." "Insolent." The Glen Burnie recruits probably don't know these words, but some version of *The Black lady was mean to me* could end Minnie's career before it starts.

13

THE DIGITAL PLANTATION

1953–1980

Shirley McConnell has worked in the Machine Division for three years. A young mother of three and a Washington native, she's a tabulator in the population section. Shirley has been taught that a career in government is the best choice for Black people like her. It offers benefits and stable employment. Upward mobility. In high school, even a career in teaching was out of the question; her father made her attend Cardozo, the only Black business school in DC. Now Shirley works a split shift at Arlington Hall, six weeks of nights and twelve weeks of days.

On one of her night shifts, she sees something strange. Her coworkers notice it too. Lights on the upper floors of A Building. No one should be there, but the white employees who work the day shift are still in the building. Night after night. Week after week. Shirley and her colleagues watch them leaving.

Eventually they find out why. The white workers are enrolled in computer training. Their shift ends at 4 p.m., and they attend class until 8. Dozens of Machine Division employees who already have years of experience in the field are never told about the training. It's the dawn of the computer age, and the Agency needs a technical workforce. They train white people as programmers to head up the units when the time comes. The Machine Division is downsizing, and the operators are transferring to other areas. They're tested but don't qualify as programmers, according to Personnel. Most go into clerical fields, and this is what happens with Shirley. She tests to become a programmer but doesn't make the grade. At least she isn't let go, which is what happened at her previous job. Her father was right: Government work is secure.

SLOW THAW

The Agency is preparing for a new era. Behind the Iron Curtain, change is afoot.

On March 5, 1953, Joseph Stalin dies after days of silence in his private dacha. A day goes by—the Russian people hear nothing. When TASS finally announces Stalin's death, thousands of Muscovites surge toward the Kremlin. People perish in the crush, trampled by a crowd mad with grief. In homes and factories, people wail, lost without their leader. For nearly three decades, Stalin ruled the Soviet Union through secrecy, terror, and absolute control. But to many Russians, he was their savior, caught in an unjust system and beset by foreign enemies—just like they were.

When Stalin dies, the kettle of the Cold War lets out its steam. The pressure, the urgency dissipate, and everyone takes a breath. The Americans, who built their Cold War worldview around the brutal logic of Stalinism, aren't sure what comes next. In the Agency, there's a push for aerial and satellite surveillance, more requests for analysts fluent in Russian. And, of course, more programmers. Everyone is trying to get a clearer picture of what's really happening inside the Kremlin now that Stalin's shadow has lifted. Under Stalin, the Soviet Union operated like a fortress—nothing unwanted got in or out. With the bulwark gone, US intelligence must parse the behavior of competing Soviet factions, guess at internal power dynamics, and adapt to a regime that suddenly seems more flexible—and yet more opaque.

Diplomatically, Stalin's death opens a crack in the wall. The Soviets signal interest in ending the Korean War, which grinds to an armistice in July 1953. There's renewed talk of "peaceful coexistence" between North and South. American officials note the Soviets' shift in tone—less bombastic, even circumspect—but no one trusts it. The nuclear arms race has its own momentum, and neither side is slowing down.

In 1953, the United States tests its first hydrogen bomb. The Soviets follow with their own H-bomb test later that year, stunning analysts with how fast they've caught up. Stalin's death doesn't slow the race but accelerates it. The USSR, under its new leader, Nikita Khrushchev, wants to project strength without sparking direct confrontation. Nuclear capability is the key to that power. Meanwhile, Beria is executed, Malenkov is pushed aside, and Khrushchev begins consolidating power. He talks of de-Stalinization but tightens internal control in his own way. Soviet espionage efforts shift too: less focused on ideological recruitment, more professionalized, more brazen. Even so, American counterintelligence is caught off guard. While the US hopes the regime might liberalize, the KGB is expanding its reach. Outside the Agency, the US is making its own transition to a post-Stalinist world.

Stalin's death does not slow down the KGB spy game. White Americans' trust in those who look like them makes Soviet espionage shockingly easy—even after years of McCarthyism, spy trials, an arms race, and an anti-communist war. No codenames, cover stories, or fake passports needed: White Soviet operatives slide right into American life and conduct their espionage out in the open. They walk into libraries, bookstores, engineering conferences, and military-surplus shops, gathering maps, aerial photographs, technical manuals—any publicly available material with hidden (or obvious) intelligence value.

Meanwhile, Black Americans still face suspicion, and domestic surveillance draws a tighter net around civil rights activists. Anti-communism can justify anything. In a country that equates whiteness with belonging, racial identity—not citizenship—determines who Americans can trust. People of color are hounded like subversives while white foreign agents are given carte blanche.

Most spy operations are costly and dangerous—and they fail. In the United States, Soviet agents bypass all that by carrying legal IDs and exploiting America's obsession with race. Soviet "tourists" acquire the holy grail of nuclear intelligence—aerial imaging—by visiting airports and buying maps. It's one of the most difficult kinds of intelligence to come by, and the most useful. Both superpowers guard their airspace fiercely. From high-altitude balloons to dangerous "ferret" flights along Soviet borders, US attempts to gain aerial intelligence yield little success. The Soviets snap up aerial surveys of Minneapolis–Saint Paul, Dallas, Tulsa—and the military bases around them.

From the point of view of a KGB spy, the United States offers near total access. An open society, true to its democratic ideals. Soviet engineers attend dozens of industry conventions each year—electronics, aerospace, plastics, machining—where they help themselves to thousands of pounds of conference proceedings, leaving their haul at the coat check before returning for more.

Since Stalin's death, the United States has been eager to accept overtures of friendship. The Soviet Union is more open to foreigners, and new Soviet leader Nikita Khrushchev wastes no time in denouncing Stalinism. He brands the "thaw" as drawing back the Iron Curtain and melting the ice that has hardened US-Soviet relations. Despite Soviet openness, American spies don't fare much better than they did under Stalinism. Every hotel room in Moscow is bugged, and every guide or translator is a KGB agent.

All this espionage has consequences. For the first time, the United States is in a tech race *that it's losing*. The CIA estimates a "bomber gap," believing the Soviet Union has more planes to deliver nuclear payloads. When the Russians launch Sputnik in 1957, the first satellite to orbit the Earth, a new race begins. The polished metal ball elegantly announces Soviet dominance. Currently, the US plans to launch its first satellite in 1980.

Where is the intelligence on this? Behind every Soviet advancement lies a stack of American blueprints, but the Americans don't even know what the Soviets are building. The Space Race is on, and the implications are chilling: If the USSR can launch a satellite into space, it can deliver a nuclear warhead anywhere on Earth.

The age of ballistic missiles has arrived—and the Soviets got there first.

WORD SPOTTING

Shirley doesn't like doing clerical work, but she is dependable and good at her job. After nearly a year, her supervisor confides that Shirley did qualify to be a programmer. "When you became liked," she recalls, "you found out that you really didn't belong in the clerical field. You should be in the technical field." She tests again, and this time, she's assigned to be a radar technician.

Her aptitude is uncanny. With a keen sense of hearing, she can tell whether the radar signal is on a ship or bouncing off of one. She's poised to work with the Navy on signals analysis, but after training, she hits a wall. "Over here, people can move you into another avenue with an excuse, then your whole career changes." And it's not for the better. Before Shirley knows it, she's back in the Machine Division, on the plantation, preparing data for computer processing.

All along, the Agency has been trying to get Black people to do what machines are built for—the repetitive operations of data processing. Information processing—translation, data sifting, indexing, data conversion, and filing for storage and retrieval—all must be completed before intelligence can be turned into a finished product. "If human beings had infinite resources of memory, mental energy, and time, there could be no such thing as too much intelligence data." In trying to get people to work like machines, the Agency works them like slaves. They do produce too much intelligence, but human processing has limits. Trying to push human processors past their limits is bound to fail. Scanners produce thousands of telegrams per day, but without analytic support, the project falls apart. There's no feedback or calibration between the two halves of the Russian Plaintext Project.

This is a job for technology, not people. And new projects are in the works.

One concept is the *word spotter*—"a device that will automatically record the presence of preselected words in teletypewriter text." Turns out, the keyword search that scanners perform every day is incredibly hard to program.

In the 1950s, general computing does not exist: "Special purpose computers" perform specific tasks, but each new program requires a new machine to run it.

The word-spotting computer is designed to scan punched tapes or magnetic tape at a maximum of fifty thousand preprogrammed words per minute. An extremely technical ten-page description follows complete with diagrams, charts, and equations. It is so opaque that the publication's editor has to insert plain-language footnotes, and even those are rather challenging for the nonspecialist to follow. The Agency has always been obsessed with data processing—since the war, its needs have been characterized by analyzing, sorting, storing, and indexing massive quantities of data. Its focus, then, has been on developing processing systems that are "logical and transformational" rather than "computational."

The Agency developed "Key Word in Context" programs that used punch cards to input and store data as early as the 1930s, when the first IBM punch card machines came into use. Though the Agency further developed these machines for cryptanalytic use, refining and expanding information processing remained a parallel goal on its own research track. Special attachments to card and tape machines, like the Baudot tape readers attached to teletype machines, which the Agency designed for the Russian plaintext operation, represented early efforts in this direction.

In 1951, when plaintext processing became more urgent and personnel shortages were at their height, AFSA floated several ideas for increasing the speed of traffic processing while reducing the number of people required for the task. These included "higher-speed printers" for creating page copy to cut down on the tape-to-page-processing time; "high speed reading of chadless tape," which was not unlike what the Traffic Processing Branch was already doing, except that many of the tapes contained chads (incompletely punched holes), slowing down and complicating the scanning process; and "machine scanning of messages, which was beyond the reach of available technology at the time."

All these efforts speak to the Agency's desire to turn the people processing their data into machines, or at least use them *as* machines, prioritizing repetitive tasks at the highest possible speeds and quantities instead of training the cryptographic clerks to have a broader skill set, allowing them to process data like the human analysts in B Building. Those human analysts had a much lower bar for the quantity of work they produced, and this directly impacted the speed at which plaintext intelligence made it into the hands of those who needed it to make decisions and direct intelligence needs. Even the fusion analysis they were doing, which compiled data from a number of sources to contextualize the plaintext intel, which didn't require traditional cryptanalysis, was given more operational freedom than the information-processing stages. The almost maniacal insistence on keeping the lower-level operations separate from the high-level ones made both sides of the project worse when they had every opportunity to make it better.

Failure to fix security issues leads to another massive leak, this time to the Dutch, who are working with the Russians. As in Weisband's case, background checks ignore clear red flags in the associations of analyst Joseph Sidney Petersen Jr., who has been working at the Agency since 1941—and on the Russian problem since 1946. When they begin investigating Petersen in 1953, they realize the evidence has been there all along, but "the responsible official discouraged his subordinate from reporting it." It's not known exactly what Petersen leaked, but the material is "catholic" in scope, suggesting that almost everything at the Agency is now in the hands of the Dutch—and thus the Soviets.

Egos and politics keep security measures shaky. Security wants to crack down, but civilian department heads balk at what they see as a grab for control. The military doesn't want to police its own; the rising stakes don't seem to make a difference. Pearl Harbor, Joe-1, Joe-2, Korea. Every compromise creates a whirlwind of proposals for change that die down as operations return to normal.

The level of security needed to prevent such leaks would infringe too greatly on the personal freedoms of white employees. In the end, they refuse to submit to the level of policing that Black Americans deal with every day. The restriction of knowledge, information, movement, and privacy is what security requires. They decide their comfort is worth the risk. That comfort comes at a cost.

SOAPFLAKES

By the late 1950s, the flood of Russian plaintext is overwhelming. The Agency is drowning in nearly thirty tons of paper tape every month—1.5 million messages, more than any team of clerks could possibly handle. Hand-sorting and tabulating, even with IBM machines, is like bailing water out of a boat with a Dixie cup.

Enter "Soapflakes." Designed by Linus Frederick "Fred" Ruffing—a linguist-scanner turned programmer—the system is the Agency's first real leap into automation. On the surface, it's a simple keyword search engine. In practice, it's a revolution. Soapflakes scans Russian plaintext tapes. It sorts and formats them, then pulls out messages containing keywords. It can shift tasks on demand, drawing from a "dictionary" of two to three thousand terms—whatever the analysts need at the moment. It effectively does what the Russian plaintext scanners do by hand, only much faster.

The breakthrough doesn't happen in isolation. Ruffing builds Soapflakes with the scanning unit—a group of about one hundred women, many of them Black workers from the old Traffic Processing Division. They know the terms of Soviet plaintext communications better than anyone, and they help shape the keyword lists that form the backbone of the program. At first, skeptics sneer: How could women who don't even know Russian contribute to such a project? But when the system upgrades from IBM 704s to the more powerful 7094, the problems vanish. Soapflakes works like a dream.

For the Agency, it's nothing short of a miracle. Further ahead than any commercial or industrial technology. Just a few years earlier, automated word spotting was still a theory. Now Soapflakes is tearing through intercepts in close to real time. It doesn't translate the Russian—it doesn't need to. Its job is speed, and speed is what the Cold War demands. An arms race of data. Analysts can no longer do their work without it. The keyword engine is a turning point, the moment Cold War cryptology crosses from human-powered processing into the age of computing. It solves the problems of scale and speed, answering the Agency's desperate need to process its increasing stream of intelligence.

And yet, there's a paradox. Soapflakes owes its existence to the painstaking labor of the Russian plaintext scanners. For years, these women have combed through endless reels of tape by hand, memorizing patterns, catching keywords, flagging what matters. Their expertise makes the system possible. But once Soapflakes proves itself, they're no longer needed. By 1959, the scanning unit shuts down, leaving one hundred women jobless.

It's a bittersweet victory. Automation frees these workers from monotonous, low-paying jobs the Agency never valued. But it also erases their story. Soapflakes, hailed as a technological triumph, buries the fact that a group of underpaid Black women helped build its foundation. The Agency moves on to faster, smarter machines like "Harvest," projects that will push computing still further. But it leaves behind the human hands that got it there, raising questions about who benefits from technology and who gets discarded in its wake.

The Russian problem is still the Agency's main focus, encompassing most of its resources and personnel. Somewhere in that apparatus is a place for the Russian plaintext scanners—especially since linguist-scanners are employed a little higher up the food chain. They do similar work to traditional scanners, but they have more specialized training and work in close contact with analysts. There are no doubt many linguist-scanners working on Russian plaintext. With the advent of Soapflakes, plaintext doesn't go away—people still have to read the tons of traffic that Soapflakes discards. Plaintext 2.0 brings new opportunities to the modernizing workforce, but not to those who know the project best.

In the wake of automation, a new class of clerical worker emerges: the "communicator." By the early 1960s, Soapflakes is one of three text-processing systems, all of which need technical staff to run them. Communicators manage the flow of data—feeding tapes and punch cards into the machines, monitoring outputs, troubleshooting errors, and ensuring the smooth transmission of messages through newly mechanized channels. Unlike the early scanners, communicators work in temperature-controlled rooms, which the computers need to function. The job is cleaner, more technical, and imbued with a sense of modernity, but it remains a low-level role: Communicators are still clerks in grades 2–5 with little chance of upward mobility. They rank far below the cryptanalysts, and "unbelievable enmity" between the groups hampers collaboration.

Like the key punchers and tabulators, communicators manage the first stage of data processing. With Soapflakes, all the intercepts analysts request can be processed and on their desks the next morning. This work still requires human labor, and the same hierarchies prevail as in decades past. Soapflakes and programs like it signal progress and exclusion. While the Agency's technology moves forward, its most experienced Black workers—those who built the foundation on which these innovations are based—find themselves jobless or shuffled into new low-level roles.

A watershed in data processing, Soapflakes rarely features in the Agency's computing histories. An interview with Cecil Phillips, one of its original programmers, describes the project in detail, as does a declassified study from 1986. Other mentions are vaguer. One source reports that Soapflakes is "believed to be" the Agency's first keyword scanning system. This makes Soapflakes sound more like legend than fact. *It Wasn't*

All Magic, a broad study of early computing, notes that by the late 1950s, the Agency operated more than twenty special-purpose data processing computers. The unnamed machines converted analog signals to digital data using magnetic tapes. They edited intercepts, and "even [scanned] the messages for keywords," saving "thousands of hours of analyst time." Soapflakes is the only such system operating at this time, and the time it saves does not belong to analysts. It belongs to hundreds of clerks, many of whom were Black women. Even in the days of hand processing, these workers' contributions were erased. Technology buries them a step further.

Despite being the only reason the Agency gets a second chance at high-tech innovation, much like its workers, Russian plaintext gets short shrift in most histories of the period. They prefer to dwell on cryptanalysis, even when there isn't much to say. Most histories skip from Abner to Harvest—the Agency's first general processing computer—lingering on the Nomad debacle (see Appendix 1) and scooting past plaintext entirely. Thanks to these omissions, plaintext seems to disappear when the computer age begins—but this is hardly the case.

In 1953, a scientific advisory board to the National Security Council announces the great successes of Russian plaintext amid enfeebled cryptanalysis. The board recommends more resources for plaintext, including machines for data processing and voice intercept. "But," the history adds, "the recognition of . . . noncryptanalytic functions" should not be accompanied by "cryptanalytic defeatism." Echoing wartime propaganda, the text positions Russian plaintext as a subversive element that has the power to undermine the foundation of intelligence. It's not an either-or proposition: Both functions contribute to early attacks on Russian communication systems. Whereas success in cryptanalysis defined the World War II era, in the early Cold War, the success of Russian plaintext overshadowed all other efforts, including cryptanalysis. However, such comments reveal that the Agency would rather highlight its Soviet-era failures in cryptanalysis rather than celebrate its successes in Russian plaintext.

THE DIGITAL PLANTATION

Once more, Shirley tests her way off of the plantation. She becomes a data tech, maintaining a digital library of radar components. She should be operating—not cataloging—them, analyzing intercepted radar signals, but that opportunity is gone. After a few more years, she goes too. Shirley works at the Agency for nearly ten years and ends up not much further than when she began. As her father promised, she always had a job—but she didn't have a career. "It was difficult," she recalls. "There should have been more opportunities for me to excel at the things I knew." After the Agency moved to Fort Meade, hiring became a hardship. Still they neither hired nor promoted more than a handful of Black workers.

The master-slave analogy has long described computer architecture. One machine or program issues commands while the subordinate units follow them. In engineering, master-slave terminology originated in the early 1900s and arrived in computing around 1964. Even before then, human-led data processing followed this paradigm of control. In the United States, subordinating labor in this way harkens back to the slave plantations that dominated the American South and the system of legal enslavement that dehumanized its Black subjects. At the Agency, the plantation model is more than a metaphor. It represents a racialized hierarchy of skill and intelligence that elevates white employees and ties Black employees to manual, lower-skilled jobs. As the Black codebreakers and technicians like Shirley prove, the paradigm has little to do with actual intelligence, experience, or skill and everything to do with the persistent, outdated belief in white supremacy.

One of the critiques of computing's master-slave model, aside from its objectionable name, is the fact that commands aren't always unilateral. Often, they're shaped by feedback from the subordinate elements, or the command structure is multidirectional from the beginning. The collapse of a clear command hierarchy makes the terms irrelevant. This ambiguity of function mirrors cryptanalysis, which requires both manual and intellectual labor. From its inception, the Agency drew a hard line between these classes of work, which is why most cryptanalysts considered the clerical side of codebreaking beneath them. In their minds, they were the masters—not the slaves. In a segregated, male-dominated era, the "slaves" are defined by their race and gender.

The Agency has always seen itself as a grand plantation for the production of knowledge instead of tobacco or grain. In the late 1950s, the Agency puts this concept to work as it researches its first general-purpose computer, Harvest. Working with IBM, they embark on two studies— one for the computer's high-speed memory, "Silo," and one for its central processing unit, "Plantation." Plantation is meant to solve the large-scale data processing problem and fix the flaws that sidelined Nomad. With more than $1.5 million in Agency funds, IBM sets up a secret laboratory in its Mohansic research facility, and the Plantation think tank crafts the "perfect machine"—one with mass processing capabilities and the iterative functions that power cryptanalysis. An automated tape machine— "Tractor"—eliminates the need for "messy" human intervention in selecting and mounting data. In cryptanalysis, Plantation is the "slave," an automated super clerk that carries the programmer-analyst-master's commands at a greater speed and scale than a legion of traffic processors. It needs only maintenance and a power source, and it works without dreams or desire. The old plantation's clerks couldn't operate this way, no matter how much the Agency cracked its whip.

Not all the old ways are gone. In 1964, the Agency still needs a "small army" to encode hard-copy data for digital processing. Key punchers manually encode IBM cards on the same devices they've used since World War II, with only a handful of updates. Data conversion is still the most time- and resource-intensive side of computer processing. Data clerks encode data streams several times per job. This division is MPRO—the Machine Processing Division that expanded with Russian plaintext in the early 1950s. The IBM Branch that was rife with absenteeism during World War II until they replaced the white workers with Black women.

One of the units "down in the hole," a piece of the plantation that hasn't become obsolete. Novella Carr, who began her career as a key puncher in 1951, is still here, as are Maebelle Holmes and Dorothy Amis, all of whom attest that throughout their twenty- and thirty-year careers, the Machine Division's clerical staff remained majority Black, aside from the white supervisors. Maebelle recalls how quickly her white colleagues advanced—"They would go to lunch with the bosses and would move right on up." The Black women linger, trapped in a Jane Crow nightmare. "You didn't get transferred," Novella recalls. "You just stayed. Supervisors would change, and they would reorganize, but you just stayed."

The Agency's advancements look clean on the surface, but the digital plantation is still "the hole" for the women who work there. Fingers punching keypads still stiffen, backs hauling boxes of punch cards ache. Women with college degrees and sharp minds are still chained to monotonous tasks. They remain the backbone of a burgeoning industry while the white world of technology surges around them.

SOFT POWER

As Iris moves higher in Personnel, she helps women like Novella, Dorothy, and Maebelle, who have college degrees and are highly overqualified for their dead-end jobs. As a personnel advisor, Iris builds her reputation by establishing trust with her employers. She builds relationships, not networks, with those in authority who know and value her work. Her belief in the Agency's mission speaks for itself—she works nights, holidays, and weekends. Does the jobs of those above and below her. No one doubts her dedication or skills. She doesn't climb the ladder for her own sake: Her advancement makes the Agency better, and her promotion helps other Black workers. Her success is their success—it's a philosophy she lives by.

Iris doesn't have a high-ranking title. Rather, her authority comes from making herself indispensable. When she presents a candidate for promotion or transfer, her competence reflects positively on them. This is soft power: the ability to influence without coercion. Long before the term originates, Iris understands its core concept, that "credibility is the scarcest resource." Like Minnie, to maintain that credibility, Iris sets clear boundaries. Just as Minnie meets requests to take on extra work with a quick "What's in it for me?," Iris's extra work hours advance her cause. By solving problems on her own, by coaching staff on how to handle conflicts, she becomes the Personnel Office's first line of defense. Later, if she brings an issue to her boss, he can be sure she's exhausted all other options. First as a personnel advisor to the chief of the Traffic Division and later in the Office of Collection, Iris crafts a role as head counsel— the neck that turns the head of state. She works with leaders like Oliver Kirby and Lou Tordella, both of whom head the Traffic Division before taking on leading roles in the Agency. Building these relationships gives Iris her own channels to go through when issues arise. In an interview, she sums up her strategy: "I happened to know some people in authority who were right minded, that I could talk to and they would see to it getting straightened out."

In the 1960s, racism and sexism abound. In one case, she pulls a brilliant young woman, Alice Alleyne, out from under a tyrannical boss, risking her own position to make the transfer. Alice could have remained a clerk forever, but Iris refuses to let that happen. The Agency is a dangerous place for Black women. Polygraph examiners force them to answer sexually demeaning questions. If they're promoted over a white peer, the doctor can have them dismissed for being "mentally unstable." Iris can't change every abuse of power, but she raises awareness and makes it harder to get away with.

Iris makes tough calls too. When a young secretary at the Naval Security Station begs to be transferred, Iris says no. The woman, Miss Blackwell, is smart and capable. Iris's top candidate for the job. Miss Blackwell's skill is no match for the Navy's deeply entrenched hostility to nonwhites. Her boss doesn't want a Black secretary; he tries to send her back. Her colleagues avoid her like she has the plague. Every day Miss Blackwell cries—sits alone, isolated, at lunch.

Iris tells her to endure it. "Take a book. Eat alone. Let them see you're just as competent as they are." Miss Blackwell needs to prove that a Black secretary is just as good as any other: "You've got to let people know that your skin coloring has nothing to do with your capabilities in the office." Iris knows it's torture, but Miss Blackwell's pain serves a higher cause. She stays. Eventually, she is promoted, but the emotional cost is high.

Iris believes she'll appreciate the experience someday.

Her placements serve a purpose. She is loyal to the mission first, not the individual. She believes the Agency can be better—and she isn't above sacrificing others to realize that ideal. It's a dark approach, but Iris wants to challenge the system, and she puts herself on the line too.

In 1963, Iris is up for her own promotion in Personnel Management. Her committee, all senior-level white men, begin by asking her why she needs a promotion when she drives a better car than they do. She replies: "Well, I hope I NEVER need a promotion, because I thought in government you get equal pay for equal work. If I don't deserve it, I don't get it. If I work for it, I'm entitled to it." She tells them she'll be fine if they deny her. Her husband buys the groceries in their house.

She walks out of the interview—and gets the promotion.

Before retiring in 1971, Iris faces her greatest challenge. She recommends a young Black MBA for a top personnel job. Harvard-educated with glowing recommendations, he stands out in a competitive field. The director, Otis Wilson, selects his application out of the top three, but the man's interview only lasts a few minutes.

Wilson's explanation isn't subtle: "Any person that gets this job in my office is going to be White, Anglo-Saxon and Protestant."

Iris doesn't flinch. "You poor thing. Don't you know I could have you fired for saying that to me?" The Agency still uses "Code 1" and "Code 2" in its personnel files, but some things have changed. She doesn't turn him in but tells him firmly, "You can't talk to me like that."

Somehow, before Iris retires, Otis Wilson becomes her dear friend. Wilson changes his politics—becomes a Democrat. Asks Iris how to vote. He takes Iris to the George Washington University Club, which doesn't admit "Negroes"—but he makes them make an exception. Iris doesn't say whether Wilson's hiring practices change, but she seems satisfied with her influence.

Iris doesn't only find like-minded bosses, she makes them.

MINNIE'S MINI

In the East Asian Division, another master of soft power is hard at work. As computing develops the same elitist hierarchy that plagues cryptanalysis, Minnie strategizes a way to make herself heard. Her department needs computers, but the gatekeeping is fierce. In 1972, if an analyst wants to use a computer program, they have to sit down with programmers, develop an application, and run it through the central network. The process is slow. Bureaucratic. Impractical.

Minnie dreams of operational freedom. A system that works as fast and creatively as her mind does. But Minnie can't get anything done at the Agency by storming the gates. To move forward, she has to change the terrain.

So she founds a monthly magazine—*Dragon Seeds*—for the East Asian Division (B Group), but she makes it sound like an ancient book of spells. In the December 1973 edition, her editor's note reads: "There is fantasy, irony, and a bite of reality in the name [*Dragon Seeds*]. It speaks of the East, and like the East, it suggests much, says little." The magazine features articles written by the division's analysts on current topics in their field, like developments in Chinese communications and SIGINT missions in Vietnam. There are humorous poems about the Training School and an advice column called "Ask the Dragon Lady." Some pieces discuss personnel issues like budget cuts, job stress, and low pay. Frustrated with the backward hiring structure, the division's personnel manager writes: "We spend enormous energy considering whether people fit the [assignment] structure instead of whether the [assignment] structure fits the people." The Agency's personnel policies are a "myth world . . . prodigious in their complete divorce from operational needs."

The main topic this month is computers. "Are You Using Computers?"

one writer asks. Another is more straightforward: "B Needs Its Own Computer." This is exactly what Minnie wants to see. People voicing concerns as a first step to action. She knows the key to sparking change without rustling feathers is plausible deniability. *Dragon Seeds* is a Trojan horse for disruption. In the forum, Minnie's voice is one of many. She's not a troublemaker—she's part of a collective voice for change. And the collective of the B Group wants computers.

Her contribution is "Minnie's Mini," a playfully written account of her quest to find—and then make—a desktop, or "mini" computer. It's unheard of, and by most tech measures of the time, impossible. Most articles in *Dragon Seeds* are a dozen pages long, but in less than a page, Minnie revolutionizes computing. When power outages in Central Control brought her team's work to a halt, she came up with an idea: "I began dreaming of desk-top terminals for [cryptanalytic] applications." Minnie is a fierce intellect, just as capable of scholarly discourse as her colleagues—but she keeps her tone light: "Can't you imagine a user-controlled system of mini-computers, say, one master and three slaves with an interchangeable hierarchy (to eliminate service interruptions when there's a malfunction), and a terminal on each analyst's desk? Why you'd hardly need cross-section paper and pencils!"

Minnie Kenny proposes desktop computing for cryptanalysis years before the Agency even considers the idea. With teenage wonderment, she describes fault-tolerant networks with user interfaces and real-time problem-solving that will become the norm decades later. R&D is intrigued by her idea, and lures her into the Albrecht study, a task force investigating computing solutions for her group. They promise her a prototype of the system she describes—but they never deliver.

So, Minnie makes one on her lunch break. "One day I stumbled across several idle CRT [monitors]. I was nosing around in [C Group] at the time. I HAD to have them. Hooked up to one of the general processors, they'd make an adequate substitute for my dream system." She loses out again. "I could pirate the terminals but I couldn't 'bootleg' the hook-ups." Minnie isn't trained as a computer engineer, but that doesn't stop her from becoming one. The playful tone disguises the magnitude of her foresight. Not only does Albrecht not deliver her system—they can't even conceptualize it. In the study, as a research intern, Minnie breaks down her group's stickiest cryptanalytic problems: diagnosing unknown cipher systems, recovering parameters, and decryption—and proposes how to translate those functions into programming. Instead of the minicomputer system they promised, the R&D team creates a large data storage system with a punch card terminal, printer, and paper tape input . . . basically the status quo of multipart processing systems that take up entire rooms instead of a single desk.

Five years later, Minnie's "mini" still isn't realized. In 1978, an article in the Agency's magazine *Cryptolog* proposes the same idea: a personal computer "scratch pad" for real-time analysis. Wisely, the editors republish Minnie's article from 1973 alongside it, but her "desktop scopes with programmable keyboards and split-screen and scrolling capabilities" remain a fantasy.

Its resistance to small, personalized computers puts the Agency at risk of falling behind in a field it once led. It's no longer the Soviet Union with which the Agency's technology competes. China has already developed minicomputers, machine translation, and integrated circuits. They're on the fast track to supercomputing, farther ahead than most of the outside world realizes. Minnie realizes it. She's been a Chinese communications expert for more than a decade, monitoring high-level secret networks. She knows more about the state of communications technology in China than most people at the Agency. Though she's now the chief of the Language and Linguistics Division—NSA's "ivory tower"—not for nothing does she still push for updated computer systems in B Group. After the Vietnam War, the Agency fails to acknowledge the urgency of breaking China's notoriously difficult codes. Then an assistant director of Production, executive Milton Zaslow calls the failure "a kind of tragedy," one in a series of missed opportunities to make real progress.

Meanwhile, huge investments in Harvest and other systems of the 1960s failed to bring the Agency "into a new age of heroic cryptanalysis."

The period remained a desert of Soviet intelligence though they "seemed to be" gathering valuable information through traffic analysis and plain-text. In 1976, they buy the first commercial computer, CRAY 1, but their own designs continue to fail.

Tasked with innovating the system, Milton Zaslow recalls the Agency's penchant for "big computers." They count their computers by the acreage cover, not by their numbers. "What we overlooked however was that there was a new day dawning, which was the day of small computers." In 1978, Zaslow gets around the problem by buying six of the "cheapest" Radio Shack computers and giving them to analysts on the sly. No special software, no input attachments. They just play around and see what happens. Zaslow wants to prove that desktop computers are not only useful but vital to cryptanalysis. Though most analysts and programmers resent being in the same building with such low-level technology, six months later Zaslow's gambit proves a success. He retires in 1980 after reshaping the computer culture, but Minnie's network of "minis," much like their creator, are still far ahead of their time.

AFTER THE AGENCY

The stories in this book span decades, but they still don't tell the whole story. After the early Cold War years, the cryptologists' lives branched out in all directions. Some stayed with the Agency for their entire careers and redefined the system that excluded them. Others moved on to new adventures and continued their success—and their advocacy—in different venues.

After leaving Metropolis, Naomi McElwaine never went back to teaching. She stayed in the biotech field in Chicago and became a blood vessel specialist at the Chicago Heart Association's artery bank. In 1959, she married a physician, Robert Smalls, and they had a happy life together with a warm extended family. According to her nephew, Marlon McElwaine, each year, she and her husband traveled to Africa to teach doctors how to administer anesthetics. A lifelong student, she continued to study after her internship and earned multiple degrees. She never mentioned her codebreaking work to her family. They learned that she was involved in secret activity after she passed away in 2016, when they found a letter from President Bill Clinton thanking her for her service among her belongings.

Naomi broke away from the traditional career path set for Black women in the twentieth century. Becoming a codebreaker was just one example of how she gracefully pioneered her way onto the forefront. By concentrating her coursework in physiology and histology, Naomi turned a home economics and teaching degree into the perfect credential for a biomedical specialist. Women had to maneuver around systems designed to keep them in place, especially when it came to careers.

Martha McWatt Haynes stayed in Charleston, West Virginia. She became a civic leader, fundraising for nonprofits like the Junior Women's League and the Business and Professional Women's Club. Whether cancer awareness, eyeglasses for children, or a piano for a local school, her volunteer work brought necessary resources to her community. Martha continued her own love of learning through social groups like the Book Lovers Club, which held literary events. She passed away in West Virginia in 2002.

In 1951, Alberta James McCray left the Agency and moved to Charleston, South Carolina, to begin a thirty-year career as an English teacher. Outside the classroom she indulged her love of reading, bridge, and travel. Alberta was also an advocate, a member of the Links, Incorporated, a nonprofit serving Black women around the world. Alberta passed away in Charleston, South Carolina, in 2013.

After three years at the Agency, Audrey Fox Anderson returned to New York City, eventually earning a law degree from Fordham University. Her legal career defied every convention: In 1955, she opened a private practice as a criminal defense lawyer in New York City and later moved to Honolulu, where she took on cases in state and federal court, from workers' comp to wills, real estate to corporate formation. Audrey ran for State Senate in 1974 and 1984, becoming a pillar of professional and civic life in Hawaii.

Audrey made lasting contributions on a much bigger stage than the NSA. She was admired not only for her legal skill but also for her perceptive, self-assured, and principled presence as a Black woman. "She asserted a control in her life through choice and perseverance," Ayin Adams notes in *African Americans in Hawai'i: The Search for Identity*. Being invisible at an Agency that doled out arbitrary punishments showed Audrey the future she *didn't* want for herself—or the country. As a criminal defense attorney, she believed that punishment should fit the crime, and she made sure the people she represented had the chance to be innocent until proven guilty, not guilty by virtue of their skin color. As a candidate, she urged people to use democracy's tools for change: "Apathy is a deadly disease—VOTE!" She passed away in 2010.

Ethel Highwarden Just retired on disability in 1950, after months of unpaid sick leave. Clearly, she hoped to return to work on the Russian Plaintext Problem, but she was too ill. Some sources list Ethel as working as the dean of women at South Carolina State College, Orangeburg, in 1951, but the university has no record of her employment.

Even in Ethel's waning years, she was a star. At Freedmen's Hospital in 1951, the activist Pauli Murray happened to recognize Ethel, a fellow patient. They weren't acquainted, but that didn't matter. Everyone in Black Washington knew Ethel. Murray leaned over to her aunts, who were visiting, and whispered that Ethel Just was one of "Washington's 400." The procession of elderly friends who visited her—matrons from "the old established families of tradition."

Ethel represented the Black upper class. She could trace her heritage back to a signer of the Declaration of Independence, but more important, she exemplified the ruthless pursuit of education, tireless work ethic, unfailing community service, and unshakable principles that women of her status were called to maintain. Internalized racism, classism, colorism, and other biases troubled the relationship between the upper class and ordinary Black Americans, but the upper class shone with an aura of unlikely success in a world bent on destroying Black vitality. Leaders of a bygone era, Ethel's generation forged a model of achievement that became more and more accessible as the movements they founded gathered steam. Their lives were far from glamorous, but the perception that they were gave Black people a homegrown high society—an alternative to the hostile world of white wealth.

Ethel Just passed away after a long struggle with illness in 1959. True to her oath, she never disclosed her codebreaking work, and her time at

Arlington Hall remained a secret. Her family only knew that for about five years, Ethel worked as a translator in the War Department.

Ethel's codebreaking legacy lies in reclaiming her "firsts." Minnie Kenny and her cohort are credited with being the first Black people hired "upstairs," but that honor belongs to Ethel. In 1950, Ethel is the first Black person placed on a major postwar intelligence operation.

Her achievements didn't lead to change; she broke the color barrier, but not the system that upheld it. Her legacy doesn't lie in how far she opened the door for others, but in how early she walked through it, and what it cost her to do it alone. Ethel Just was a forerunner, even if no one saw it, and it would be years until another Black woman came close to that kind of assignment.

A cipher that remains unbroken. A precedent written in near-invisible ink.

Ethel didn't build a lineage, but she proved one was possible.

A bolder legacy as a teacher and activist lived on through Ethel's daughter Margaret Just Butcher. If Ethel was a star, Margaret was a supernova. She fought for equality in the DC school system and achieved even greater heights as an international educator, congressional advisor, and civic advocate. Margaret studied in Naples, graduated from Emerson College, earned her PhD from Boston University, and attended the Sorbonne in Paris—all by age thirty-five. A humanities professor who spoke French, Italian, German, and Arabic, Margaret served as a Visiting Fulbright Professor in France, becoming the director of the English Language Training Institute in Casablanca and the assistant cultural affairs officer at the US embassy in Paris. Margaret replaced Mary McLeod Bethune on the National Civil Defense Advisory Council, consulted for the NAACP, and was elected the District of Columbia's delegate to the Democratic Party's national convention. Twice.

Ethel suffered some things in silence so Margaret wouldn't have to. She forwent personal aspirations to build a world where her daughter could realize hers.

Bill Coffee spent his career with the Agency. In the postwar years, he managed a number of Black typing units. He headed a group that did transcription work during the early Cold War, and in the 1960s, he oversaw an office in the Soviet Division that produced and distributed intelligence reports on Red Army Ground Forces.

Many of those who stayed at the Agency developed tight-knit communities. Bill met his wife, Norma Wooten, at the Agency, and they married in 1955. Black men in Washington organized social clubs, and Bill was a member of a men's club for "local gentlemen of merit and distinction." Like the women's groups, the men hosted social events and promoted career advancement. Several of the club's members, including David Bryant and Clarence Toomer, worked for the Agency.

Bill retired in 1972, after a thirty-year career. He passed away in 1989.

After Iris retired in 1971, she returned to Dallas, Texas, to reunite with her sister, Jewel. Iris remained active in her alumni organizations and took care of Jewel through a long illness later in life. Jewel passed away in 2007, and Iris passed several months later in 2008.

After retiring from her forty-three-year career in 1999, Minnie Kenny remained an active advocate for women and people of color, chairing a number of professional organizations. Minnie passed away in Columbia, Maryland, in 2005.

THE RED CARNATION

To excel as a Black woman in such a system requires what is now called soft power. Minnie and Iris had success and influence in the Agency, but they had to strategize their way to that success and wield that influence indirectly.

Minnie Kenny's career was extraordinary—but not just for the titles she held. She rose from cryptanalytic prodigy to become the Agency's director of the Language and Linguistics Division, later serving as staff language advisor to the NSA director and assistant director of training at the National Cryptologic School. A gifted linguist and systems thinker, she chaired multiple high-level panels—on language careers, training, and external education—and helped shape national policy on cryptologic linguistics. She became known, half-jokingly, as "Mama Language."

Her work had teeth. In 1982, Congress passed the Foreign Language Incentive Program based in part on testimony Minnie prepared. She pushed for HBCU recruiting and expanded internship and early career programs to promote access in an overwhelmingly white field. In 1987, she helped sponsor legislation with Rep. Louis Stokes to create the Undergraduate Training Program (UTP), offering full scholarships, paid work, and postgraduate positions to talented minority students. The CIA and DIA later adopted similar models.

In her last post, as director of the Office for Equal Employment Opportunity, she elevated the EEO's organizational status to the director level—ensuring it would never again be buried in the bureaucracy.

For this work, Minnie earned nearly every major civilian honor: the Meritorious and Exceptional Civilian Service Awards, the Intelligence Community's Distinguished Service Award, and recognition from Presidents Ronald Reagan and George Bush Sr. But Minnie didn't push boundaries for accolades. She led to change the systems that had tried to push her out—and to create space for those coming up behind her.

Still, there were moments Minnie couldn't control—when her brilliance was reframed as a symbol, her success as a favor. "You know, Minnie has been a beneficiary of people who feel that we haven't been fair to others," Milton Zaslow says, years later, in a reflection on her early career. "She's competent. She's very competent . . . She was a very respectable analyst, absolutely."

Minnie was tokenized, but she used that tokenism as a tool for change. Being the "first" or the "only" often came with a penalty: Her success proved the system was working, not that it needed to evolve. Her presence was used to avoid promoting others. Her success looked like it came at a qualified white man's expense. Becker notes that the Agency's white women leaders—Juanita Moody, Ann Caracristi, and

Polly Budenbach—were called "the three fakes" by some employees. He emphasizes their isolation: "Other than those three, it was a totally white male-dominated system. So you had your recruitment, your personnel, administration from top to bottom in the hands of whites." The white women's merit can never make up for their lack of masculinity. They'll always be usurpers.

Helen Eagleson, a Black mathematician and cryptographer, held a management position in 1952, the same year Minnie was hired. Minnie knew the Agency would never tolerate three Black women directors, so she'd have to do the work of two.

Even the recognition—the awards and titles—came with caveats.

If Minnie were the first—and she often was—she used every bit of access, platform, and title they gave her to make sure she wouldn't be the last. The Agency was a white man's world, and holding soft power meant using that bias to her advantage: She had to create something that couldn't be seen as filched—as "fake." Her contribution had to be something that didn't already exist.

She saw analysts who could build systems, run programs, lead departments—but who couldn't mentor. Couldn't listen or connect. She had risen through sheer force of intellect and self-restraint. But she didn't want the next generation to have to do the same.

So in 1985 she proposed an award—the Red Carnation.

Not for technical skill, but for something less tangible and even more valuable. The qualities that had kept her afloat through decades of resistance: empathy, honesty, generosity, trust. For people who led by example, who could communicate. Inspire.

The hierarchy "balked." No doubt scoffed; said it was sentimental, not rigorous.

Instead of fighting, Minnie sat back and waited. When the squawking died down, she pushed the award through.

Minnie had calculated and won: The men's resistance proved she wasn't taking something they thought was theirs. They revealed how badly the Red Carnation—and Minnie herself—were needed.

Within a few years, the Red Carnation became one of the most respected honors in the building. Minnie had given people permission to recognize what the system never had. To be rewarded for how they stood out from the status quo rather than how well they fell in line.

Minnie never said that she created the Red Carnation for people like her. Like her daughter. Who would have to lead from the margins before they were allowed in the center. Who could hold anger without letting it consume them. Who didn't move through life with a chip on their shoulder, but carried thousands of pebbles—some smooth, some jagged. The weight of calculations guiding every step.

Minnie believed Black employees had two jobs: the job they did and the job of mapping where they wanted to go. "You have to know the formal and informal politics operating in the workplace," she said. "Know about the jobs above, below, and around you. Plot a path to where you want to go and work on getting there even if you have to get training on your own."

The white men thought promotions were made in boardrooms, after they'd submitted a candidate's name for a position, discussed their merits, and agreed on their selection. They had no idea what the people around them were doing to get the minimum recognition they deserved, or what they had to do to get their name on that piece of paper in the first place.

THE ETHICS OF INTELLIGENCE

The Commercial Code Unit has a strange legacy in its relation to Operation Shamrock. The cable companies' fears about the program's illegality were founded: In 1975, after thirty years of secret domestic surveillance, Operation Shamrock came under scrutiny by the US Senate for violating citizens' right to privacy. It was one of half a dozen illegal surveillance operations set up by the intelligence agencies: The CIA's notorious MKULTRA, with its mind control and LSD experiments; HTLINGUAL, which intercepted mail sent between the US and the Soviet Union; Operation CHAOS, a domestic spy program targeting antiwar and civil rights activists; the FBI's COINTELPRO (Counter

Intelligence Program) that infiltrated the Black Panthers and other "subversive" groups; and NSA's Project MINARET, Shamrock's sister program that created a watchlist of American journalists, activists, and civil rights leaders and tracked their communications without warrants.

The Senate's Church Committee investigated all these programs, uncovering decades of misconduct and revelations that shocked—and scared—the public. The investigation led to reforms like the Foreign Intelligence Surveillance Act in 1978, which limited domestic surveillance and established more mechanisms for transparency and oversight.

The programs raise questions about the ethics of labor and informed consent. MKULTRA was in clear violation of these principles: It performed experiments on unwitting subjects—including prisoners, psychiatric patients, and civilians—who were subjected to dangerous substances and traumatizing experiences without prior consent. Shamrock's violations are murkier. The operation relied on the coerced cooperation of commercial entities and the labor of clerical workers, most of them Black women, who processed the traffic without knowing the project's legal or ethical implications. Benson Buffham speculates that there was a "rationale" for putting the Black women on the project but stops short of saying what it was.

Shamrock's high-ranking officials faced scrutiny, but the women who performed the work were neither named nor punished. Their role raises questions about the moral complexity of intelligence labor: What does it mean to serve a mission you don't fully understand? What responsibility do institutions bear for the ethical burden their workplaces impose on their lowest-paid employees? There are no clear answers, but in an age of data harvesting and ever-expanding surveillance, the questions remain important.

Those whose careers suffered under segregation have also left their mark. No matter how unjust the Agency's policies, how demeaning its conditions, the folks in the Traffic Division and the other offices down in the hole refused to be erased. They created programs that brought the Agency together, like the Credit Union and the Miss NSA contest, programs that everyone could participate in and enjoy. Of her first years in the Agency, Minnie notes, "In the early days, we had joyous things happening. You had jazz concerts, you had art shows and I mean real art shows, . . . you had all these things but most of that came out of what was going on in this [Black] society." At this time, Agency social events like the NSA Dance and NSA Boat Ride were still off-limits for Black employees.

The cryptologists' lives were filled with joy and love inside and outside its gates—morning carpools, lunches on the lawn, and evening walks in the park were some of the ways the cryptologists made Arlington Hall Station feel like home even if it wasn't meant for them. Their "society" was a bulwark against the discrimination around them, but instead of walling themselves off, they used their solidarity to make the Agency a more welcoming place. When they clocked out, work stayed on the plantation. Each day, they went home to live their lives, untethered from the Agency, until the next shift.

For most of the cryptologists, the working conditions were the cost of being Black in America. Lynching and denying opportunities to Black people were still the law, de facto if not de jure. That cost was too high in a country that prides itself on justice and freedom. In the 1950s, most of the country, including the South, was working to abolish segregation and move toward equality. The Agency had the opportunity to do so, but it didn't. Instead, it chose to profit from its Black employees' stolen labor. The word "agency" means having the power to act, exert influence, or effect change. At a critical moment in history, Arlington Hall used its agency to engineer an unequal system that would take decades to dismantle.

LIFE BEFORE THE AGENCY

This section takes a deeper look at the lives of several cryptologists who had careers before joining the Agency. The book focuses on the codebreakers' experiences during their service, but the stories of how they found their way to Arlington Hall are important for understanding their journeys and the times in which they lived. The stories of codebreakers like Naomi, Martha, and Minnie, who joined the Agency just after college, have already been told. Older codebreakers, like Bill, Ethel, and Iris, have deep pasts that tell not only their stories but reveal Black American life in the nineteenth and twentieth centuries.

These stories are the product of research into public and government records, university collections, biographies, newspaper archives, and genealogy resources. As portraits of personalities, families, aspirations, and ideals, they attest to the lie of white supremacy that ruled American psychology during the early twentieth century. They show the monumental obstacles that the codebreakers and all Black Americans faced and celebrate their tireless efforts to overcome them. Their example inspired their communities and set high bars of achievement for future generations. Their relentless excellence in the face of genocidal racism challenged their country—and the Agency—to live up to the ideals they professed to hold.

WILLIAM "BILL" DANIEL COFFEE
(1917–1989)

William Daniel Coffee is born in Abingdon, Virginia, to Walter and Lura Coffee on November 2, 1917. From an early age, Bill is ambitious. He goes to King's Mountain Training School and later plans to attend college. His father, Walter, supports the family as a cook in a private household, but after his unexpected death, the family falls on hard times. Bill's mother, Lura, and his older sister, Lucinda, work as maids. With his younger sister, Sue, still in middle school, Bill has to help his family survive. School will have to wait. Bill finds work as a house cleaner and farmhand, but the jobs have no future. They are typical of the jobs Black people must work in the Jim Crow South.

But there are other options. The Civilian Conservation Corps is part of President Roosevelt's New Deal plan for economic recovery. Men aged eighteen to twenty-five can sign up and be placed on a civic building project designed to improve public spaces—cities, parks, and nature preserves—build affordable housing, and help workers acquire trade skills. The program is open to men of all races, but the Corps is segregated. As elsewhere, Black men are given the lowest-paid and most dangerous jobs.

On October 15, 1935, Bill enlists in the Civilian Conservation Corps. He's eighteen and a sophomore in high school; his draft card lists him as five foot four, 132 pounds, with a dark complexion. Corps members are paid for their work, and Bill arranges to have $25 out of every paycheck sent to his mother. After completing his service, he hopes to continue his education.

Bill's training begins at Fort George G. Meade in Maryland, the future home of the NSA. In the 1930s, Fort Meade is the starting point for all Corps enrollees. They undergo basic training, learn to operate in regimented units. The CCC is supposed to be integrated, but this soon changes. White people become so incensed that Black men are working in or near their communities that they protest and riot. As a result, 150 Black

Corps camps are built on remote federal lands; they'll do the essential, if deadly, work of clearing forests and keep Black workers out of sight.

Bill's first duty assignment is in Williamsburg, Virginia. He's hired as a laborer, but the work is piecemeal. He squeezes in a few months of waiting tables in Abingdon's Barter Theatre and studies English at Knoxville College in Tennessee but doesn't have time to finish his degree. He's honorably discharged from this duty assignment after a year and a half, at the end of March 1937. In general, Corps assignments are project-specific. Civilians train in a profession for about a year, and then they transition to the private workforce. This isn't how it works for most Black men. When they aren't given manual labor, their camps are hidden from the public, doing work that doesn't easily translate into a profession.

Most Black camps work in forestry. When Bill reapplies in late 1937, he's placed in Company 1390, an all-Black group stationed at Camp Gallion in Virginia's Prince Edward State Forest. Even deep in the woods, far from white eyes, Bill's company isn't welcome: In the 1930s, Virginia bars Black Americans from visiting its state parks. However, Camp Gallion is the only place Virginia will allow Company 1390 to work. They've been working since 1933 to convert the dense, uncleared forest into an expansive park on Virginia's Twin Lakes. They thin hundreds of acres of forest, build dozens of lookout towers, and carve out hundreds of miles of forest-fire lanes, truck trails, and bridges. They fight forest fires, often without the right equipment. The company plants thousands of trees and builds recreational facilities to create a beautiful natural refuge that they will be allowed to visit only in 1949, when it becomes the Prince Edward State Park for Negroes.

Bill is eighteen, the minimum age to join the CCC. As the youngest in the group, he is assigned to "kitchen police," or kitchen help. Washing dishes, peeling vegetables, sweeping floors. It's a common assignment for junior enlistees so that senior members have more opportunities to learn skilled work. Bill is ambitious and wants to develop well-rounded skills, even if he doesn't get the best assignments. The Corps includes an education program to help enlistees finish school, and Bill takes full advantage.

He studies journalism, table-waiting, first aid, and drama. He boxes and sings in the glee club. To gain more work experience, he volunteers to be a forester's orderly, providing field support on construction and clearing projects.

Not far away, the Public Works Administration in Washington, DC, is building its first housing project—Langston Terrace, a 274-unit complex designed to curb DC's affordable housing shortage. The project employs Black laborers, tradesmen, and engineers who learned their skills through the CCC. Despite the Depression, DC continues to grow. By the late 1930s, its population is close to six hundred thousand, and its Black population has grown by 40 percent. The Supreme Court building, the Federal Trade Commission building, and the Department of Agriculture headquarters are all federally funded building projects built by skilled labor under the New Deal.

Company 1390 does dangerous work. Constructing towers, fighting fires, and using equipment like chainsaws in adverse conditions are just some of the hazards that made forestry a risky assignment. The company braves black bears, snakes, and bobcats. Falling trees and "widowmakers"—dead branches that can fall at any moment, crushing bones and spines—are constant threats. Hauling heavy loads over rocky, slippery terrain means every assignment could end in catastrophe.

And it does.

On September 3, 1938, Bill is rushed to the Army hospital with two broken legs. His right leg is shattered, the bones in the lower half of the leg crushed, and his left fibula is snapped. The doctor determines that Bill did not sustain these injuries in connection with his Corps work, nor were they due to misconduct. Whatever happened, the Army is determined not to take credit.

That injury ends Bill's time in the Corps and his chances of learning a trade. He is transferred to Freedmen's Hospital in Washington, DC, where he spends seven months. He is discharged on disability in March 1939, having earned the professional qualification of "laborer."

When the draft begins, Bill signs up but isn't eligible. For the next two years, he works various jobs, including waiter and hospital orderly, but he never gets back to school. Eventually, he finds his way to the Arlington Hall Junior College for Women. When the Army buys the property in 1942, Bill fills out a federal employment application and is hired as a junior janitor at the Agency.

ETHEL HIGHWARDEN JUST
(1885–1959)

Ethel William Highwarden is born in Ripley, Ohio, in 1885. Since its founding by freedmen in 1812, the town has been a crossroads into freedom. Perched on the northern bend of the Ohio River, it faces Kentucky, a former slave state. Ripley's white residents are abolitionists—Quakers—and along with their Black neighbors, they were the first stop on the Underground Railroad for thousands of freedom seekers headed north to Canada.

Ethel spends her early years in a bilingual world: Ripley's white residents are German immigrants, and the Black and white communities live side by side. In school instruction and daily life, German is as common as English, and Ethel grows up among Black and white friends.

Coming from generations of free people, Ethel has a different experience than most Black Americans. Her mother, Bell Johnson, is a teacher and store owner. Her father, William Highwarden, runs a freight line that travels between Cincinnati and Portsmouth. Both parents graduated from Oberlin, a school known for admitting Black students. They are two of the first. The family believes in progress—education, enterprise, the power of hard work. And for a time, that is enough.

But the world is changing. Cities grow more segregated. The privileges her family enjoys—education, integration, autonomy—become precarious, uncertain.

Still, Bell is determined that Ethel should not be left behind. When William dies in the 1890s, Ethel moves with her mother to Columbus. She attends an integrated high school and graduates from Ohio University in

1906, the first Black person to do so. Her degree is in German and education, with coursework in English and Spanish.

Ethel is petite, with a lighter complexion and long black hair. In a high-necked white blouse with a tall belt cinched around her waist, she is the perfect Victorian young woman. Bell instills a high-mindedness in Ethel that might pass for snobbery, but that formality of manner is a bulwark against the contempt and ridicule that await Black women in America. Bell has lived it—she wants Ethel to be prepared.

They move to Washington, DC, which opens a world of opportunity and tightens the strap of segregation. Ethel teaches German at Howard University, one of two faculty in the Modern Languages Department. She's a demanding but enthusiastic teacher. Her first-year students will read no less than two hundred pages of German prose, learn sight translation, and master the classic Joynes-Meissner Grammar. Second year adds syntax, poetry, and drama: Vilmar's *Die Nibelungen*; *Walther und Hildegund*; Lessing's *Minna von Barnhelm*; Goethe's *Herman und Dorothea*; and Storm's *Immensee*.

By the time Ethel and her mother come to DC, white neighborhood commissions keep Black families out to protect their property values. Ethel and Bell live in LeDroit Park, an upper-class Black neighborhood near Howard. Outside the enclave, restaurants, shops, hospitals, and transportation are off-limits. Black neighborhoods have their own theaters, restaurants, beauty shops, and tailors, but the city pulses with animosity. No public space is safe. As the city grows, Blacks are pushed further toward the margins.

Ethel envisions a life of scholarship and service, and when she meets a young professor named Ernest Just, that doesn't change. But when they marry in 1912, his career takes precedence. Ethel tucks away her dream of a European honeymoon while Ernest pursues his PhD at the University of Chicago. In the summer, he conducts research with his mentor, Frank Lillie, at the Marine Biology Laboratory, in Woods Hole, Massachusetts. Ethel and Ernest's first daughter, Margaret, is born, but as time goes on, their relationship becomes strained. He is always away, and full-time motherhood is not what she envisioned. The more time Ernest spends with his white colleagues, the more fractious and eccentric he becomes. By 1922, they have two more children: a son, Highwarden, and a daughter, Maribel. Ethel raises the children, runs their stylish townhouse on T Street, and translates Ernest's papers into German. But it's not enough: He wants an admirer, a wife who can assist him in the lab. Ethel is dutiful but not submissive. She has a full civic and social life—three children to raise, an education to pursue. As if in protest, Ernest has affairs—with his research assistant, his benefactor's secretary, possibly his colleague's wife—women many years his junior.

Ernest's behavior is jeopardizing his position at Howard, so Ethel goes back to work, substitute teaching in DC's public schools. In 1930, she's suspended for "failure to report for duty and insubordination" and is denied a position. After a three-year court battle, the judge finds that Ethel was past the forty-five-year-old age limit when the position became available and was therefore ineligible in the first place. It's a bizarre math, but the suspension is upheld.

Readers of the *Washington Afro American* have different views about the decision. One draws attention to the white superintendent referring to Ethel as "impertinent" for appealing her suspension, noting that impertinent means "offending propriety, especially in the treatment of elders or superiors." The reader links this descriptor with other terms like "presumptuous," "insolent," and "sassy," which are used to describe Black people who refuse to subordinate themselves, whereas uncooperative white people are simply described as "rude," "uncivil," or "domineering." They believe the insult is endemic to society's desire to keep Black people "in their proper place," and they applaud Ethel for standing her ground.

Another reader is less sympathetic. They believe Ethel deserved to lose her case because she set a "bad example" by hiring a white lawyer to defend her in the District Court of Appeals: "Should a Negro teacher seeking appointment in our schools pass up several of our own capable lawyers, who could have rendered her the same service and go uptown and hire herself a high-priced white lawyer?" The reader argues that Black students are already discouraged about their chances for success, and that Ethel's actions are an "uncalled for example of patriotism." Meaning, perhaps, that she disregarded racial differences as an equal under the law. Ethel's actions are seen as political statements, whether she intends them to be or not. It is a burden white people rarely bear, as their actions are considered a matter of personal choice, and not a decision made for the collective good.

Meanwhile, Ernest spends most of his time in Europe, living with his new German lover and research assistant, Hedwig Schnetzler. In Paris and Italy, they go to the theater, take strolls in the park, lie in the grass near the lake, and talk passionately about literature and science. They work on Ernest's book, *The Biology of the Cell Surface*, which Hedwig partly authors.

Hedwig is just like Ethel—German-speaking, well-read, exuberant about the arts—but Ethel can't be white. Everything about being Black in America causes trauma and shame for Ernest. The more successful he becomes, the more hated he is by his white peers.

Ethel has no time for this. She walks the same tightrope of professional rejection but does so with dignity, without infidelity or complaint. She gave up her career so Ernest could pursue his, and he's abandoned her and the children. Ethel is sought after in her own right, but for much of her life she is also Mrs. Ernest Everett Just, the wife of the noted biologist. This label might seem to erase her, but just as Ethel is a feather in Ernest's cap for being a beautiful, gracious, and educated Black woman, he is a feather in hers. Being the wife of an accomplished Black scholar accords Ethel immense respect; Black women are considered the moral leaders of the race, and that role is important to Ethel. Her steadiness as a wife, mother, and civic organizer despite her husband's behavior is part of what grants her standing.

No matter how hurt she is by Ernest's behavior, she maintains a strong front and continues creating opportunities for herself, her children, and others. A "popular Washington matron," she "charms" at dinners, receives flowers for volunteer work. When Ernest is home, they visit friends like

Alain Locke. She keeps up appearances but maintains her boundaries. Once, at Ernest's urging, she brought the children on one of his summer research trips to Woods Hole. Everyone shunned her—like she had a disease. Ethel will not submit to that humiliation again. If a white colleague stops by their home, she refuses to serve them, and Ernest speaks to them on the porch.

In 1934, Ethel enrolls at Boston University to get her master's degree in American literature. She takes Highwarden and Maribel with her; unlike Ernest, she must continue to raise her family while pursuing her personal goals. Her thesis is titled "Negro American Folk-Plays of Paul Green with Special Attention to Their Sociological Value." Green is a white writer from North Carolina known for his depictions of rural life in the deep South. His characters are Black and white, and all come from the lowest socioeconomic levels in society. His play *In Abraham's Bosom* won the Pulitzer Prize in 1927. Ethel sees Green's work as proof that equality between white and Black Americans is achievable outside of progressive enclaves like Ripley. Through literature, the rest of the country can learn about the contribution everyday Black people make to American society as a whole.

In 1936, Ethel's master's degree is one of four graduations in her family. Margaret, her eldest, also graduates from BU with a master's degree. Highwarden finishes Dunbar High School and Maribel graduates from Shaw Junior High. Ethel's thesis is accepted for PhD study, but she is too tired. Tired of fighting the system for the most basic rights. Her disaffection with the school system doesn't keep Ethel from her activities. When war breaks out in Europe in 1939, she chairs the Black YWCA's Girl Reserves, preparing teens for war work and civic engagement. By now, Ernest is gone; he married Hedwig in Europe, had a child, and disappeared. The Nazis have taken over France. The press hounds Ethel for news about her husband, but she has none.

In 1940, Ethel divorces her absent husband, joins the Modern Languages Department at Virginia Union College in Richmond, and blooms. Finally reconnected with her beloved teaching, she becomes the assistant dean of women and the dean of Porter Cottage, a faculty residence. She hosts speaking events, continues her civic work, and quickly becomes a star of Richmond's social scene.

The honeymoon doesn't last. War comes to the United States too, and in September 1943, as students are sucked into the draft, Virginia Union reduces its faculty. Ethel is on her own.

Maybe she sees a recruitment flyer, or maybe a recruiting officer spots her in DC. Either way, she's an easy sell for the Agency. Not only is she a language expert, she has a lifetime of experience keeping secrets.

Ethel doesn't need a correspondence course to learn cryptography.

On February 21, 1944, Ethel fills out a federal employment application, and two days later she reports to Arlington Hall for duty.

IRIS CARR
(1913–2008)

Iris Emma Price is born in 1913 in Taylor, Texas, where more horses than cars pass over its tamped streets. It's a special city; a tough town carved from clay and black soil on the south bend of Mustang Creek in Williamson County, where juniper and mesquite trees dot the hills, and pecan orchards span the plains. Founded on trade, the town is hopeful as the railroad headed west, fearless as the bulldogger who grabs a steer's horns and wrestles it to the ground.

Iris's parents, Reverend Oliver Lewis Price and Louise Crawford, are children of farmers and washwomen. Sometimes, there's a generational leap; parents who cannot read or write make sure their children go to college. Iris's grandparents had those dreams for their children. Louise was born in a one-room log cabin in Alabama, and both she and her husband earned bachelor's degrees from Prairie View College and master's degrees from University of Colorado, Boulder. Oliver, a Baptist minister, is the principal at the Blackshear School, where he and Louise teach. Leader of the local NAACP and Boy Scouts chapters, Oliver passes the fire for education and advocacy on to his children.

That fire is hard to keep burning. Slavery is gone in name, but the antebellum past, like dust storms, blocks the sun of progress and keeps Texas scrambling in the dark. Black blizzards fill the skies like a plague for the state's white primaries, poll taxes, and torture of Black bodies. During the Depression, the New Deal and the Dust Bowl struggle for Texas's soul: One builds, the other sweeps away. The state is poor—electricity and schools are scarce. Afraid of immigrants, Blacks, and Jews obtaining wealth, the new Klan gathers followers and fans out across the state. At the same time, the Federal Writers' Project interviews the formerly enslaved, records their stories—testaments to an era not so long ago. On these very farms, now sharecroppers, once property.

Iris is the middle child, between an older brother, Lewis, and younger sister, Jewel. They are all bright and motivated—not only by their parents, but because they live in a diverse, forward-thinking town. Most of Texas is agrarian, but Taylor looks toward the future: Commerce and interstate travel drive the town's economy. Taylor's freedmen are unionized: The Ex-Slave Union Association of Industry began fighting for fair wages decades before the Pullman porters. Ranchers modernize: The Czechs, Swedes, and other immigrants stop driving cattle to Nebraska on foot and ship it to St. Louis and Chicago on the railroad. Mexican farmers leave their adobe houses on the outskirts to build schools and homes around the Mission Chapel. The International & Great Northern Railroad connects the small town to the wider world. Even before Iris finishes high school, she knows what it means to be going places. She's raised to branch out, test boundaries, and make her own decision. When Taylor yells "all aboard," Iris listens while the rest of Texas lingers on the platform.

Still, she takes a classic career route. In 1932 she graduates from Prairie View Normal and Industrial College with a Bachelor of Science degree— double major in English and math. Double majors aren't common, but Iris doesn't let anyone limit her options.

In 1930s Texas, Black women's paths to advancement are narrow and full of pitfalls. State laws catch Black women in a Jane Crow bind: Race and gender discrimination restrict their options for education. Texas does not allow Black Americans to attend mainstream universities, like the University of Texas, or to earn a degree beyond a bachelor's. Instead, the state gives "segregation scholarships" that pay for Black students' transportation to attend universities out of state. The catch is that they can travel only once every three years. These programs are common in the South: They allow states to fulfill their requirements for "separate but equal" facilities. Rather than gestures of equity, they're tools to maintain white supremacy, loopholes to keep people down while maintaining what passes for fairness under Jim Crow.

Texas and other Southern states have HBCUs, but like their white counterparts in the North, not all admit women. Whether the state pays or not, travel is an obstacle. On trains, Black women must travel in second or third class "Black cars" that are dirty, dangerous, and lacking in facilities. At a time when white women are "the fairer sex" and given accommodations to maintain their privacy and dignity, Black women are treated like animals, with no legal or personal protections, no regard for their feminine needs. Even if a woman drives, few places along the route are safe to eat or rest—if they're not entirely off-limits. The potential for accidents and harassment on the road is great; stopping at gas stations is a risk. *The Green Book* is published in 1936 to guide Black travelers to safe services and lodgings. Before that, women are on their own.

For the moment, Iris remains local. After graduating, she moves to Austin and becomes a teacher. Like many Black teachers, she teaches multiple subjects and grades; third-grade physical education until noon, high school math in the evenings. From the beginning, Iris challenges systems that claim to be based on merit but are actually founded on prejudice. She knows the odds are stacked against her community, and she preaches readiness. Don't sit back and wait for things to change: Go to school, get a degree—get multiple degrees—and do your best, so that when opportunity arrives, you are ready. Iris has a dual mission: to reform the education system and to make sure Black people don't fall short of their potential.

Getting a higher education isn't common for anyone. In the 1930s, most white people in Texas don't have college degrees or high school diplomas. It's one reason segregation is enforced so violently: To keep Black achievement below white mediocrity. They believe Blacks must stay "in their place," and attempts to rise are brutally suppressed. A civil rights forerunner, Booker T. Washington believed that only "severe and constant struggle" would earn Black people the privileges that white Americans got for free. He advocated earning citizenship through enterprise: If Black people enriched the economy, they would be accepted. The plan relies on two assumptions: that white people acknowledge Black achievement, and that the desire to profit is greater than their desire to uphold racism.

Iris knows this, and she plans for it. Her aspirations extend beyond teaching: homeownership, financial security, the American dream. At a time when women aren't supposed to outearn their husbands, Iris wants to succeed on her own terms. Men can find success in business and trades that don't require higher education, but Black women must be teachers. If that fails, what other avenues exist? Iris plans to earn a graduate degree, and for that, she will have to head north. Again, Jane Crow. Some white universities admit women, but very few white women's schools admit Black women. In 1900, W. E. B. Du Bois found that white men's universities accepted Black men, but white women's colleges would not accept Black women. He found their opposition to admitting Black women unyielding.

Iris has fewer options and more obstacles in pursuing them, but she doesn't want life to be easier—she wants it to be fair. She'll work until America makes good on its promise of recognizing merit, regardless of skin color.

Iris isn't all work and no play. At twenty, she's a woman about town. The society pages of the *San Antonio Register* and *Houston Informer* chart her exploits: lawn parties, scenic drives, winter getaways to Galveston, Juneteenth barbeques, and four-course dinners adorned with white roses and green ferns. Bouillon, baked chicken, marshmallow-topped sweet potatoes, chocolate cake, and coffee demitasse—East Texas elegance on full display.

Between work, school, and cross-country travel, Iris meets Reginald Corley, lead saxophonist for the Royal Aces Orchestra. They play all Black Austin's major events. Corley's also the vice principal of the city's public schools. He already has a master's degree, and Iris takes notice.

In 1940, they marry and settle into a cottage on sunny Tillotson Avenue in the redlined district of East Austin. Being Black homeowners is uncommon, especially in the South, but so are they. Young, ambitious, committed to helping their people defy the odds.

They're also committed to serving their country. Corley registers for the draft, and on December 7, 1941, the Japanese attack Pearl Harbor.

Corley's number isn't called—not yet, but Iris heeds the call to arms. "Race Women Organize for Nat'l. Defense," *The Dallas Express* reports in late December. Iris is elected head of the Negro Women's Motor Corps.

Motor corps are civil defense groups that provide transportation, first aid, and other military logistical support. On the home front, these groups are organized by women in the Red Cross. The local Red Cross women help Iris set up her motor corps, but they don't let the Black women join theirs. It doesn't matter. Black women are fighting for the Double V— victory over fascism abroad and victory over racism at home. And a third war, if you count Jane Crow.

Twenty-three women sign up to drill, learn first aid, become auto mechanics, and learn radio communications. Soon, they are delivering supplies to camps, hospitals, and military bases. Despite America's flaws, Iris believes the country can be better. Supporting the war is just another opportunity to fulfill her mission.

When Reginald's number is called in 1943, he reports to Fort Sam Houston, just north of San Antonio. Fort Sam Houston is infamous—the burial ground of seventeen Buffalo Soldiers falsely accused and executed in the Houston race riots of 1917. Now it's a major recruiting center and it holds 1,600 Axis prisoners of war. The country is in a patriotic fervor— parade crowds throng the streets—but war's ugliness is always just below the surface. Despite the dangers of serving in a segregated Army, Reginald is one of the eighty thousand Black Texans who enlist.

Iris is also a realist: Reginald may not come back from the war. It's a reality every woman with a husband, brother, son, father, or boyfriend in the war has to face. He may not go overseas, but plenty of Black soldiers are dying at the hands of their white countrymen. Abroad, even as a service worker, he could be in danger. To be a Black man anywhere is a risk—how much more so among armed white men.

Iris decides that she can help the country *and* herself. If she can't do that in Texas, she'll go someplace where she can: Washington, DC.

She tells her teary-eyed father that she's going "to feather her nest." She's leaving the education empire they've built and all the progress they've made for Black schools behind. Black women are supposed to use their careers to "lift up the race," but Iris decides she can't sacrifice her future for tradition. There are many ways to make an impact.

In Texas, Iris is on the periphery.

She wants to be in the center.

AFTERWORD

I encountered so many stories during my work on this project that it's impossible to recount them all here. Hundreds of Black people worked for the Agency during the postwar years, and most of their names remain unknown. From clerks and custodians to analysts and engineers, these individuals made the field of American intelligence what it is today.

One of my goals at the start of this project was to identify everyone in the ubiquitous Commercial Code Unit photo on the cover of this book. For years, Bill Coffee (standing) was the only name that was known. This task proved more difficult than I thought. I found many names in the archive records, but only a few personnel files contained photos. When I saw these photos, I realized they didn't match any of the people in the picture. The unit's composition fluctuated between 1944 and 1945, but even those who worked in the unit both years aren't pictured. Naomi and Martha aren't in the photo. Neither is Herman Phynes. The only ones I've identified are Ethel Just, who wears a black shirt and sits in the left row second from the back, and Raquel Flagler, who sits front and center in the middle isle. The woman seated two seats behind Raquel may be Audrey Fox Anderson. All the others are waiting to be named.

As disappointed as I was not to end up with a full roster, I am happy to pass the torch to the next set of storytellers who will continue to piece this tapestry together. One of the most exciting things about this project is that there are many layers of history and experience to explore. Reconstructing the Black cryptologists' identities is a project that reaches far beyond this book.

In some cases, I found personnel records that matched or partially matched names listed on the cryptologists' organizational chart, but the records did not list their service. Work at the Agency during World War II was secret, and in some cases, it might not have appeared in federal employees' work histories. Mysterious employment gaps during the summer of 1945 point to possible codebreaker work in some of the files. For instance, on the chart, Margaret Brooks is listed as head of the Commercial Code Unit's decoding section, but there's a gap in her employment file that year. In 1944, she takes maternity leave from the War Production Board and pops up on the record again in 1946, working for the US Census. Her son is born on September 2, 1944. Could she have sneaked back to work to decode secret telegrams for the Agency? This woman's file indicates that she was Black: "Code 2" and "Negro" are added on several hiring forms. She has a degree in French and Spanish from Miner Teachers College. From these details, her employment in the unit seems likely, but without clear evidence, it's hard to prove.

Another example is Alberta James. She resigns from the Bureau of Printing and Engraving on her doctor's advice in May 1945 and pops up working for the War Department in the Adjutant General's Office in 1946. She transfers to the Agency at the end of that year. Is she the "A. James" listed on the June 1945 chart? I'd like to think so, but "A. James" could be anyone. Researching personnel files, I found at least half a dozen "maybes" in which details suggest that the women could have been part of the Commercial Code Unit during a period of strict secrecy when there really was "No Such Agency." Analyzing gaps and coincidences is the first stage of conspiracy theory, so I decided to leave the "maybes" out of the book until more concrete details surface.

The NSA has the personnel files of anyone who worked for the

Agency past 1952 under lock and key, so accessing them requires a Privacy Act request. After the war, Raquel Flagler continued her career with NSA. She began as a cryptographic specialist, but by 1950, like many of the women, she'd been downgraded to clerk. Raquel's file, along with those of Geneva Arthur, Bill Coffee, and others, are queued for processing while the Agency works through their "significant backlog" in requests.

When I first encountered *The Invisible Cryptologists*, reading their story made me angry. The introduction describes the book as "by turns infuriating and inspiring," but I was not prepared for how truly awful and cruel the "down in the hole" setup was. The architecture of segregation—putting the Black people in the basement while the white analysts worked upstairs in the sunlight—reminded me of Jordan Peele's psychological horror film *Us*.

In the film, a family of underground doppelgangers seeks revenge on the people to whom they're psychologically tethered. The doppelgangers are poor, but they have to imitate the aboveground people. So, for instance, when a woman above ground gets plastic surgery, her doppelganger has to carve into her own face with a knife.

The Agency created an underground world of doppelgangers by hiring a workforce of talented Black people with *the same credentials and skills* as their white colleagues to do menial tasks in the basement. In many cases, the Black doppelgangers did the same work as the white linguists and translators but never received credit for it. They are "tethered" because their advancement can shadow but never exceed their white counterparts'. They're relegated to the work their white counterparts refuse to do.

In the 1950s, white women used the phrase "I'm free, white, and twenty-one" to mean they could do whatever they pleased. Originally used to define who could vote—that is, white men of adult age—the phrase implies its opposite. An enslaved or imprisoned Black child.

Someone with complete agency versus someone with no agency. This is the doppelganger paradigm of segregation at work at the Agency. Instead of creating spaces for Blacks and whites to work together, it forced them into opposite roles. For every white woman at the Agency who is free, white, and twenty-one, there is an equally qualified Black woman chained to a teletypewriter or ink stamping machine.

The Black cryptologists' experience drove home that segregation isn't just physical. It has long-term consequences that are rarely addressed. Eugene Becker describes a 1967 investigation into discriminatory practices at the Agency: "The white supervisor would say 'We don't have any problems. We get along well . . . We are like one big family.' Then you would talk to Sarah or Frank or a minority black lady who had trained umpteen supervisors in her career to do the job above her. She was still sitting down there earning her steps through the seven level and she was not happy at all . . . It was striking . . . the level in the gap, in the perception that the white folks have as against the Afro-Americans and other minorities." People broke down in tears telling their stories to Becker after years of holding back. The final report recommended drastic changes, but most were never implemented. Then, the report "suddenly disappeared." Even with the segregated units gone, by ignoring the problem, the Agency kept its Black employees down in the hole. As of writing, the report is still missing.

The Black cryptologists left many legacies. The Cold War cryptologists have many members in the Agency's Cryptologic Hall of Fame. Iris, Minnie, and some others in this book have that distinction. But other than Bill Coffee and Herman Phynes, none of the Commercial Code Unit members have been recognized. It's significant that most of them are women, and their erasure is part of a long history that undervalues women's labor, especially when it concerns nation-building. Their service didn't only help win wars—it shaped the United States government, foreign policy, and surveillance state.

Ethel, Naomi, Martha, and the other women from the Commercial Code Unit are described here for the first time. Some of their names appear in historical publications: Naomi and Ethel are mentioned in *The History of the Signal Security Agency*, Volume 2, along with translators Audrey Fox and Eloise Daniels, whose story remains elusive. *The Invisible Cryptologists* mentions secretary Annie Briggs. The June 1945 organizational chart names recordkeeper Annie Hansford and decoding section head Margaret Brooks.

Analyst Raquel Flagler, decoders Martha McWatt and Martha Bullock, traffic processors Alberta James and Eloise Bullock, custodian Mildon Whitley, and file clerk Ethel Laney were discovered through brute force research—guessing names to match last names and initials from the chart and pairing them with genealogical records and personnel files.

During the war, the Agency also employed Black people in its Communications Security Division (COMSEC). There was a large print shop for making the codes and ciphers the United States used in its official communications, and "several" Black people worked in that operation. This book focuses only on the Agency's Cryptanalytic Division, but there were six major divisions: Security, Cryptanalytic, Cryptographic, Laboratory, Communications, and Research and Development. Each division had subsections that required support activities. The Security Division's print shop had a Photo Plate Section, an Offset Press Section, a Letter Press Section, and a Bindery; Black workers could have staffed any of these sections.

The Cold War cryptologists remain even more obscure—and more numerous. Exact numbers are hard to pin down, but a fair estimate is that in 1951 and 1952, around six hundred of the Agency's six thousand employees were Black women.

Sources provide clues. In 1951 and 1952, there were up to three hundred people in the Traffic Division, which included the Processing and Distribution Branches, and at least that many key punch operators and tabulators, as the codebreaking moved toward automation. Shamrock's typists may have been thirty strong. Navy Intelligence is also reported to have an all-Black traffic unit, but there are no details about their numbers. These figures will become more precise as more records become available.

Regardless of their exact numbers, each group left an important legacy. The World War II Black cryptologists opened the door for Black professionals at the Agency even though their careers suffered from postwar institutional racism. They proved their merit and patriotism though most weren't recognized for it. Most members of the Commercial Code Unit left before the Agency's move to Fort Meade, but some, like Raquel Flagler, Bill Coffee, and Herman Phynes, stayed on, making them the Agency's first Black career hires.

The Cold War cryptologists suffered unjust and unethical conditions, but they sparked a wave of reform at the Agency that continues today. At the height of the arms race and amid the turmoil of social change, the cryptologists who rose in the ranks—and those who stayed buried in them—paved the way for new generations of intelligence workers who had more rights, opportunities, and visibility.

Comparing the World War II and Cold War groups proves that progress isn't linear, and conditions don't always get better with time. They can get worse—much worse—depending on who is in power and what the country values at a given moment. The cryptologists' story is, in part, a cautionary tale about the high stakes of cultural stagnation. Many people in the story, Black and white, are committed to moving the country forward. They actively fight racism, and they look toward the future rather than the past. They're the ones who bring positive results.

Another caution in this tale is the price of institutional hubris. In extolling its achievements, the Agency forgets to appraise its faults. AFSA was a mess, and the rivalries between military branches and intelligence agencies had disastrous consequences, but no account of the postwar period casts a sustained critical eye on what was done wrong and what it cost. Maybe secret organizations prefer to keep their self-criticism in-house, but when their work affects the country, those discussions should be public—even if they're a tad embarrassing.

The cryptologists' story helps us reflect on a difficult past and use the lessons we learn to shape the present and future.

It is our privilege to do so. Their legacy deserves no less.

ACKNOWLEDGMENTS

I would like to thank the National Endowment for the Humanities for awarding me a Public Scholar grant in 2024 for my work on this project and the National Archives Foundation for naming me a Cokie Roberts Commended Scholar in Women's History in 2025. Both awards provided crucial support for writing, travel, and research. I would also like to thank the Authors League Fund for material support when the Department of Government Efficiency (DOGE) terminated my NEH grant, along with fourteen hundred others, in 2025 for representing "radical and wasteful" government spending on Diversity, Equity, and Inclusion (DEI). I thank the Authors Guild for successfully suing DOGE and the NEH, having the grant terminations ruled unlawful, and continuing to pursue their reinstatement. Finally, I thank the legal team of *Bartz v. Anthropic* for protecting my published work and the work of thousands of other authors from piracy by artificial intelligence companies. In these strange times, the importance of human authorship and the First Amendment rights it requires can't be overstated.

This book would not have been possible without the aid of federal employees, who generously shared their expertise and performed their work passionately through uncertain times. Rob Simpson of the National Cryptologic Museum, Dave Hatch and Sandy Hagenhoff of NSA's Center for Cryptologic History, and former historian of the Center for Cryptologic History Betsy Rohaly Smoot were excellent guides in researching intelligence history and weeding through the FOIA declassification process.

Thanks to the folks at NSA's Mandatory Declassification Review office for fulfilling my requests for never-before-seen interviews with the Black cryptologists and their colleagues and to Cara Lebonick at the National Archives in St. Louis for finding dozens of obscure personnel records that added names, faces, and documentation to the cryptologists' stories. Thanks to Sondra Austin and her team at the Civilian Personnel Records Center in Valmeyer, Illinois, for photocopying and mailing hundreds of pages of ancient personnel records in the midst of a presidential administration change when much more urgent requests required your attention. Special thanks to the staff at the National Archives in College Park, Maryland, who assisted on many research requests and patiently guided this novice through the intricacies of archival research.

Other individuals who greatly aided my research include Gregory S. Cooke, the writer, director, and producer of the film *Invisible Warriors*, which chronicles Black women government workers, the "Black Rosies," during World War II; and the librarians and research staff at Purdue University, Virginia Union University, Howard University's Moorland-Springarn Research Center, Arlington Public Library's Center for Local History, the Maryland Center for History and Culture, the *Baltimore Afro-American*'s archives, and Pittsburgh's Carnegie Public Library. Liza Mundy and Steven Dunn were early champions of this project, helping me expand my network of contacts and boosting the book's visibility. Writing can be lonely, and knowing that these world-class writers (and genuinely great people) found the project exciting was incredibly heartening during what was, at times, a daunting and fraught journey.

A special thank-you to my agent, Gillian MacKenzie, who supported this project from the beginning, and to my editor at HarperCollins, Adenike Olanrewaju, who bravely took on an orphaned title and provided useful, astute feedback throughout the writing process. This book wouldn't exist without either of your help. Finally, thank you to my friends and family for brainstorming titles with me and for generally providing moral support.

APPENDIX 1

GLOSSARY

INTRODUCTION

This glossary offers accessible definitions of key cryptologic terms, roles, agencies, and operations that appear in this book. The glossary is narrative and contextualizes these terms' use and significance in the story. Entries are organized alphabetically in each category.

The intelligence terms are adapted from the CIA's *Glossary of Intelligence Terms and Definitions* and William Friedman's textbook *Military Cryptanalytics Part I*. The definitions are both general and geared toward their mid-twentieth-century use. Both texts are great sources for further study. Computer terms are adapted from *History of NSA General-Purpose Electronic Digital Computers*.

While some of the terms are obscure or outdated today, they shaped the daily lives and decisions of those who worked in wartime intelligence. Where possible, these terms are illustrated through the experiences of characters like Iris Carr and Ethel Just, whose work reflected the broader challenges Black women faced at the Agency as well as the breakthroughs of American codebreaking during and after World War II.

INTELLIGENCE AND ESPIONAGE

Types of Intelligence

Defined by their sources, agencies, and methods of collection.

Communications Intelligence (COMINT)

A subset of SIGINT focused specifically on intercepting and analyzing communications—usually encoded or encrypted messages. This includes voice, Morse code, and encrypted radio or teleprinter traffic. COMINT was at the heart of operations in Arlington Hall. Since their meanings are close, COMINT and SIGINT are sometimes used interchangeably.

Counterintelligence

Activities aimed at protecting a country's intelligence operations from foreign espionage, sabotage, or infiltration. This includes identifying and neutralizing enemy spies, preventing leaks, and ensuring the security of sensitive information. In the United States during the Cold War, counterintelligence efforts were often entangled with fears of domestic subversion and excessive surveillance.

Electronic Intelligence (ELINT)

Another subset of SIGINT, ELINT deals with signals that are not meant for communication, such as radar emissions or weapons systems testing. ELINT is often gathered aerially and helps identify and map enemy defenses, including missile launch sites and air defense systems. ELINT was an important development in early Cold War intelligence.

Human Intelligence (HUMINT)

Intelligence gathered directly from human sources. This can include informants, defectors, diplomats, prisoners, or undercover agents. The CIA and FBI gather HUMINT while the NSA is responsible for SIGINT. HUMINT provides insight into enemy plans and intentions, and is often used to corroborate other kinds of intelligence. It is gained through coercion (interrogation, blackmail), incentive (bribes, gifts), and voluntary confession (defection).

Intelligence

Information used to understand the capabilities, actions, or intentions of foreign powers or adversaries. Intelligence is used to inform military, diplomatic, and national security decisions. It can be collected through a variety of means, including surveillance, interception, and human sources.

Signals Intelligence (SIGINT)

Intelligence derived from the interception of signals, whether between people (communications) or from electronic systems not used for communication, like radar. SIGINT is a broad category that includes COMINT and ELINT. It was central to US codebreaking efforts during and after World War II.

Major Intelligence Operations

Successes in the Agency's codebreaking efforts during and after World War II led to major wartime victories and sophisticated developments in later codebreaking technology.

Magic

The code name for US decrypts of Japanese diplomatic traffic. Though not directly tied to the Black cryptologists' work, this program was central to Arlington Hall's mission and provided valuable intelligence breakthroughs during the war.

Russian Plaintext Project

This focused on the direct analysis of unencrypted Soviet communications—material that wasn't encoded but still revealed valuable information on the Soviet economy, military, and weapons program. Russian plaintext required a massive workforce due to the volume of telegrams the Agency intercepted—reading and processing this intercept was the Traffic Processing Branch's responsibility.

Shamrock

A mass surveillance operation in which the Agency collected copies of all international telegrams sent to and from the United States. Though not known to most at the time, its scale and secrecy later raised major civil liberties concerns.

Ultra

The British counterpart to Magic, focused on German ciphers, particularly the Enigma. Ultra's success was widely studied and admired at Arlington Hall.

Venona

A secret Agency project that decrypted Soviet diplomatic cables from the early 1940s. Venona aided FBI investigations into known and suspected Soviet spies and shed light on the Soviets' extensive intelligence operations in the United States. Venona made minimal progress due to the Soviets' secure communications but provided useful information. The project lasted until the 1980s.

Codes and Ciphers: Key Terms

This section includes technical terms used in codebreaking and cryptanalysis, including processes, types of codes and ciphers, and other vocabulary.

Additive Cipher

A numerical cipher in which numbers are added to the plaintext values. In some cases, code identifiers were also altered using additive values. Analysts learned to reverse engineer additive tables using brute force—exhaustive trial and error—and intuition.

Baudot Code

A five-bit binary code developed in the 1870s by Émile Baudot for use with teleprinters. Unlike Morse, which encodes letters as varying-length sequences of dots and dashes, Baudot assigns a fixed five-bit digit number to each character, using a thirty-two-letter alphabet. It was widely used in military and commercial teletype systems in the early-to-mid-twentieth century and was known as the International Teleprinter Code. Russians used the updated Baudot-Murray code, better suited to the long Cyrillic alphabet. The Black cryptologists learned to read Baudot-Murray code in Russian to select messages for intelligence gathering.

Book Cipher

Used by spies, this method relied on both parties having the same book as a reference. The book could be a popular novel or any text that's agreed upon in advance. Such ciphers are almost impossible for outside parties to break because the choice of the text is random.

Bookbreaking

Bookbreaking is the process of reconstructing a codebook in whole or in part from clues in encoded messages. This is a process that can't be taught: It requires skill, artistry, and perseverance. The Commercial Code Unit were bookbreakers, reverse engineering altered or unknown code systems based on the messages they studied.

Cipher System

The overall method of encryption, including procedures and key changes. In cipher systems, individual letters are enciphered separately. For added security, countries changed their cipher systems regularly, demanding constant cryptanalytic effort. The Soviet Union had notoriously unbreakable ciphers, leading to a lack of US intelligence before and during the Cold War.

Code System

Code systems encode entire words or phrases rather than individual letters, often making them easier to break than ciphers. A coded message can also be enciphered, adding an extra layer of security.

Codebook

Codebooks are keys that can be unique and used for secure communications or be standardized and used for general telegraphic communication. Industries like shipping, trade, and finance had standard codebooks that facilitated domestic and international communication.

Commercial Codes

Commercial codes are widely available code systems used for trade. Rather than providing security, commercial codes are meant to save money by shortening the lengths of telegrams. During World War II, around three hundred commercial codebooks were available globally, but Arlington Hall's Commercial Code Unit discovered that only fifteen of them were used regularly. This discovery, along with their invention of an innovative index system, prevented them from developing a backlog despite handling large volumes of traffic.

Cryptanalysis

The art and science of breaking ciphers. Naomi McElwaine's wartime work exemplified this role—painstakingly reconstructing diplomatic messages by hand. Though unheralded at the time, her work formed part of a broader effort to crack enemy systems without the aid of computers.

Cryptanalyst

Someone who broke ciphers. Ethel Just filled this role, despite being denied the formal title for most of her career due to race and gender discrimination. Cryptanalysts worked in secrecy and were often siloed from one another to protect their secrets.

Cryptography

The creation of secure systems for encoding and enciphering messages. In the Agency, white male officers often held this role formally, but enlisted and civilian women assisted with cipher design and implementation.

Cryptology

The umbrella term for secure communications, including both cryptography (making codes) and cryptanalysis (breaking them). "Cryptologist" is a general term for anyone involved in these activities, whether as clerks, translators, or analysts.

Exploit (a system)

To "exploit" a system means to actively take advantage of a solved or partially solved cipher to gather intelligence from it. Exploitation can involve reading intercepted messages, tracking movements, exposing spies, or learning about enemy plans. Exploiting a system requires both continued access to the traffic and ongoing cryptanalytic work to keep up with any changes or re-encipherments.

High-Level

In cryptanalysis and intelligence, "high-level" refers to communications, targets, or information sources that involve senior military, political, or diplomatic leadership. High-level messages are usually encrypted with complex systems and carry sensitive strategic content—like orders from generals, negotiations between governments, or updates on weapons programs. These messages are rare, difficult to intercept, and often harder to break, but the intelligence they yield is extremely valuable, sometimes changing the course of a war. The ideal goal of cryptanalysis is to break high-level systems to gain high-level intelligence. The people who do this work are also revered as "high-level."

Indicator

A short set of characters (such as "JAH") or numbers included with an encrypted message that provides clues about how the message was encoded or enciphered. An indicator can provide clues like a key, rotor setting, or starting position—allowing the intended recipient to decode it. Sometimes indicators are enciphered, but often they are not. For cryptanalysts, indicators are a critical weakness to study: They can reveal patterns or habits that help solve a cipher.

Intercept

"Intercept" refers to traffic that's been stolen or intercepted, typically without the sender's knowledge. During World War II and the Cold War, US intercept sites collected thousands of such messages daily, forming the raw material for codebreaking and intelligence work.

JAH

Japanese commercial code used frequently during World War II for shipping and trade. Considered easy to break, the low-level system often contained surprisingly valuable intelligence, like Japan's surrender message. Ethel Just and the Commercial Code Unit worked overtime to help clear the JAH backlog while continuing their own commercial code operation.

Listening Station / Intercept Station

A facility—often remote or strategically located—used to monitor and record foreign radio transmissions, phone calls, cable transmissions, or other electromagnetic communications. Operators at these stations often worked in shifts around the clock, collecting massive amounts of signal traffic to be analyzed by cryptanalysts and linguists. Vint Hill Farms was the Agency's main listening station in the United States, but they had fixed and mobile stations throughout the world.

Low-Level

"Low-level" refers to communications or targets involving junior personnel, frontline units, or routine administrative matters. These messages often use plaintext or simpler codes and ciphers. They are sent more frequently and are easier to break. While any single low-level message may seem unimportant, their cumulative analysis can provide a rich picture of troop movements, supply lines, industrial capacity, or preparation for war. Low-level breaks are essential to daily intelligence work and often form the foundation for understanding broader enemy patterns. The Russian plaintext program generated vast amounts of valuable intelligence from low-level communications.

Machine Cryptanalysis

This used tabulating machines and early computing devices to speed up decryption. Early on, while most analysts worked manually, the Agency increasingly relied on machines like IBM card sorters and Bombe-style devices to keep pace with the growing demand for intelligence. This led to computer innovations that were far ahead of their time in the 1950s and onward.

Manual Cryptanalysis

This was done by hand with paper, pencil, and logical deduction. Ethel Just and other women at Arlington Hall used physical charts, frequency counts, and sheer endurance to reveal complex patterns and break ciphers.

Morse Code

A system of encoding text characters as sequences of short and long signals, known as "dots" and "dashes." Invented in the 1830s and widely used in telegraphy, Morse code remained essential through World War II for transmitting messages by radio or wire. Operators learned to recognize the rhythms by ear. Though slower than modern systems, it was reliable under poor transmission conditions and was often used by naval forces communicating at sea.

Onetime Pad

A onetime pad is a key book in which each page can be used once to decrypt a single message. Once used, the page is torn out and destroyed. Onetime pads are thick notebooks—often thousands of pages long. Onetime systems are theoretically unbreakable. The Venona team broke parts of the Soviets' onetime cipher systems because the Soviets accidentally printed multiple copies of these onetime pad pages and used them to encipher multiple messages. This error gave Arlington Hall's analysts enough clues to partially reconstruct the keys.

Plaintext

The readable, unencrypted version of a message—what a person would see or hear before any encryption is applied. In cryptanalysis, the goal is to recover the plaintext from a coded or an encrypted message. For example, if an intercepted message is decrypted correctly, the output is the plaintext.

Solve (a system)

To "solve" a code or cipher system means to figure out how it works—to uncover its structure, logic, and method of encryption. Solving can involve identifying the type of cipher (like a transposition or substitution), reconstructing codebooks, or deducing machine settings. It's the breakthrough moment when a previously unreadable system becomes understandable. Solving a system doesn't always mean every message can be read—but it opens the door to gathering intelligence and achieving future breakthroughs.

Substitution Cipher

When each letter is replaced with a different symbol or letter. Early training often began with substitution ciphers to teach cryptanalytic principles. These were less commonly used in high-level diplomatic codes by the 1940s.

Traffic

"Traffic" refers to the flow of communications or messages, whether or not they have been decoded. Once traffic is intercepted, it undergoes processing that includes selection, sorting, categorizing, stamping with dates and serial numbers, microfilming, and data conversion for machine analysis. Until the late 1950s, this arduous process was done by hand. Most of the Black cryptologists worked in traffic processing during the Cold War, handling every piece of traffic that came into the Agency.

Traffic Analysis

Studying patterns of messages—volume, timing, and origin—rather than content. Traffic analysis was traditionally considered a supplement to cryptanalysis, but during the Cold War, traffic analysis provided valuable intelligence on its own.

Transposition Cipher

A method of scrambling a message's letters rather than substituting other characters for them. Decryption involves rearranging the letters to reveal the original message. Transposition systems were often simpler than additive systems but still required close attention to patterns. Often used in conjunction with another system, like substitution, to add extra security.

Codebreaking Technology

These computers and electronic devices were central to US codebreaking from the 1940s to the 1960s. Many were developed by the Agency for specific cryptanalytic applications. Others, like IBM cards, were used widely in government organizations for data processing.

Abner

The Agency's first computer, completed in 1952. Named after comic strip character Li'l Abner Yokum, who was "a big brute, but not very smart." Abner performed simple cryptologic calculations. Still the most sophisticated computer of its era. One of the first projects the Black engineers worked on at the Agency.

Atlas

First-generation computer developed by Navy Intelligence (CSAW), the Agency, and the computing firm ERA in 1950. Used a plugboard to input simple program instructions. Updated design with a high-speed memory followed in 1954. One of the first projects Black engineers worked on at the Agency.

Harvest

The Agency's first general-purpose computer, developed with IBM in the late 1950s. Harvest served as a major data-processing and codebreaking system that replaced much of the hand processing and analysis performed by clerks in the precomputer era. One of the earliest supercomputers, Harvest handled enormous volumes of classified data.

IBM Cards

Also called punch cards, these were 3¼″ × 7⅜″ rectangular paper cards used to store digital data through patterns of holes. Widely used for codebreaking and data processing in the early twentieth century, they allowed machines to read instructions or data, one card at a time. Many Black women hired at the Agency worked as IBM card encoders.

Key Punch

Machine used to punch holes into IBM cards based on data typed by an operator. Key punch clerks translated intercepted messages, cipher data, or decrypted text into machine-readable form—like modern-day coders.

Microfilm

A photographic technique that reduced large documents to small film images that could be viewed with special readers. It was used during and after World War II to store massive quantities of intercepts, maps, or reports in compact form.

Nomad

Failed attempt to create a large-scale high-speed data processor. Led to other developments, such as Harvest.

Perforated Tapes

Long strips of paper tape with holes punched in specific sequences to encode information. Used in early computing and cryptologic work, tapes were run through machines to process or decode messages, much like punch cards but in a continuous format.

Plantation

The Agency's study contracted with IBM to develop Harvest's central processing system in 1956. Reference to forced labor and racial hierarchy reflected the Agency's use of Black employees to perform arduous, repetitive data processing tasks that white employees deemed beneath them. Also highlights the master-slave dynamic central to computer design. Name eventually changed to "Rancho."

Recordak

A Kodak-developed microfilm camera used to quickly photograph documents for storage or intelligence review. Recordaks were often used to copy decrypted messages, personnel files, or even surveillance materials. The Traffic Processing Branch included a microfilm station to copy translated messages.

Soapflakes
The Agency's first Russian plaintext keyword scanning program. Developed for IBM computer model 704 in 1959. The Russian plaintext scanners helped to build Soapflakes's four-thousand-word dictionary. After Soapflakes, Russian plaintext scanners were no longer needed, and the unit was disbanded.

Tabulator
An electromechanical device that read punch cards and sorted or tabulated data based on the perforation patterns. Tabulators were used to find repetitions and organize intercepted messages—an essential early step in cryptanalysis.

Teleprinters
Similar to teletypewriters, these devices printed incoming messages from remote sources and allowed operators to type and send responses. They were vital for relaying intercepted communications and coordinating across sites. The Agency had "spy" teleprinters that intercepted enemy communications.

Teletypewriters
Machines that sent and received messages over telegraph or telephone lines by converting typed characters into electrical signals. Common in military communications, teletypewriters made rapid, long-distance message exchange possible. The Agency used off-line teletypewriters to translate messages in the Russian Plaintext Project.

Intelligence and Espionage Terms

These are general terms that detail items, roles, and concepts used in the intelligence and espionage worlds with specific reference to intelligence work at Arlington Hall. Some terms used in the intelligence context have different meanings than their dictionary definitions.

Agent
An agent is someone who is recruited to provide information or carry out tasks for an intelligence service, often without being a formal member of the

agency. Similar to spies, agents could be American citizens—like government clerks or engineers—who passed information to Soviet handlers.

Burn Bag

A heavy paper bag used to collect classified paper trash like intercept tapes or codebreaking notes. These bags were closely monitored and were often checked before being destroyed by fire. The "secret trash" Martha tore up was supposed to go into a burn bag, not a regular wastebasket.

Civilian

Person who is not part of the military. Though the Agency was a military organization, most of its codebreakers were civilian women. They lacked military rank but performed the majority of the Agency's intelligence work.

Classification

The system used to label government information based on how sensitive it is and how much damage its exposure could cause to national security. Common categories include Unclassified (not secret), Confidential, Secret, Top Secret, and Top Secret [CODEWORD]. "Classified" doesn't always mean secrets are dramatic—they can include mundane details like supply routes, if they're considered sensitive or mission-critical.

Clerk (Communications, Statistical, Typist)

Document handlers and office staff who support intelligence work behind the scenes. Communications clerks handle message flow; statistical clerks tally data and produce reports; typists format and retype deciphered messages, reports, and memoranda for distribution and storage. Women traditionally fill these roles, which are underrecognized and underpaid though their work keeps the Agency running. Clerks have low security clearance and often don't know the intelligence value or purpose of their work. During the Cold War, most of the Agency's Black female staff were clerks. Even after desegregation, they worked in an isolated, windowless basement, under strict protocols.

Clerk (Cryptographic)

Handled the intake, sorting, and typing of intercepted messages. Cryptographic clerks made up a large segment of the Agency's workforce and did everything from filing and typing to complex analysis. Many Black women, including those in the Traffic Processing Branch, remained in these low-paying roles throughout their careers despite being overqualified.

Codename (Operations)

A random word that indicates a secret operation. Codenames like Bourbon (the Russian problem), Venona, and Operation Shamrock provided a secure language to discuss classified operations without revealing their content.

Codeword

A random word used to signify the highest level of classification. In intelligence documents, codewords are usually written in all caps. Documents labeled "Top Secret [CODEWORD]," like the World War II classification "ULTRA," contain the most sensitive intelligence and are only distributed to a select few.

Consumer / Customer

A consumer or customer is a person or organization that regularly receives intelligence reports from the Agency. They don't pay money—the terms are borrowed from the business world. National organizations like the CIA and FBI are the Agency's consumers, as are the Atomic Energy Council, the State Department, and the Armed Forces intelligence agencies. All consumer intelligence reports—often sixty-five or more—needed to be typed by hand, straining the Agency's clerical staff.

Courier

A person who transports secret messages, documents, or equipment between agents or between an agent and their handler. Couriers were essential for communication in espionage work, especially in the days before secure digital communication.

Cover Name / Codename (Spies)

A false name used to protect a person's real identity. In Soviet operations, agents and informants were typically assigned codenames (e.g., "Liberal" or "Anton") to conceal their activities in written reports and communication. Venona provided key intelligence on the codenames of Soviet spies to corroborate FBI intelligence.

Dead Drop

A secret location where agents can leave or pick up messages, documents, or materials without meeting in person. Dead drops were often disguised as ordinary objects or hidden in public spaces—under a loose brick, inside a hollow tree, etc.

Deep Cover

A long-term false identity adopted by a Soviet agent, often with an entirely fabricated personal history ("legend"). Deep cover agents could live in the United States for years, working seemingly ordinary jobs, all while collecting intelligence or recruiting others. Deep cover spies were especially harmful when they worked in government and/or intelligence agencies, like Judith Coplon and William Weisband.

Double Agent

Someone who pretends to work for one country's intelligence service while actually serving another. In the Cold War context, this usually meant a British, American, or Soviet agent who appeared loyal to one side while secretly working for the other—like Kim Philby.

Drop Copy

A duplicate of a message or transmission made during processing. Before automation, drop copies were handwritten or typed. These copies are often routed to different sections—analysis, cryptanalysis, archiving—for further work. Drop copies are so critical to producing intelligence that the FBI and the Agency have secret typing operations dedicated to making drop copies of their illegally obtained messages.

Front

A business, an organization, or a household that appears legitimate but is actually used to support espionage. Fronts gave Soviet agents a reason to be in the United States, helped launder money, or provided cover for covert meetings and operations. Amtorg was the primary front for Soviet espionage in the United States. As an international trade organization, they had regular contact with major US corporations, which was especially useful in the technical industries, where the engineering intelligence could be gained.

Illegal (Spies)

A Soviet intelligence officer operating without official diplomatic status or protection in a foreign country. Illegals used false identities and forged documents to pose as regular civilians, immigrants, or tourists. Their work was high-risk but sometimes more effective because they attracted less scrutiny.

Informant

A person who provides inside information to an intelligence service, often in exchange for money, protection, or for ideological reasons. Informants may not know they're part of a broader espionage effort—or may rationalize their actions as harmless. This was the case for some Americans who provided the Soviets with nuclear intelligence during World War II.

Legal (Spies)

A Soviet intelligence officer operating under official diplomatic cover (such as working at the embassy or consulate) in another country. They were technically protected by diplomatic immunity, which made it harder for US authorities to arrest or prosecute them—even if they were caught spying.

Machine Operator / Communicator

Staff who operate cryptanalytic machines, teletypewriters, IBM key punch machines, or signal relay equipment. Communicators are computer clerks, a position that develops with technological advances in the late 1950s. Like clerks, machine operators are a large, low-paid workforce mostly comprised of women.

Messenger

An entry-level, often unclassified worker who physically transports classified documents, tapes, or other items within the Agency or to partner organizations. Messengers must follow precise delivery routes and protocols, and they have special security badges that give them access to classified areas. The Agency employed only Black men in these crucial but low-paying positions.

Officer

Commissioned military leaders. Officers ran divisions, branches, and most sections at Arlington Hall. They oversaw general policy, delivered briefings, and sometimes worked alongside analysts. Some were sympathetic to their civilian subordinates' contributions; others enforced rigid hierarchies that privileged military personnel.

Problem

A particular target area—usually a country or region—that is the focus of cryptanalytic efforts. The Russian problem (or Soviet problem) was the Agency's main intelligence focus during the Cold War, while the Japanese problem and the German problem dominated World War II codebreaking efforts.

Security Badge

A physical ID—worn or displayed—granting access to specific buildings, rooms, or classified areas. The color or markings on a badge indicate the level of clearance or department. For Agency workers, badges are color-coded and bear ID photos. They are a valuable means of gaining access that can be easily stolen or forgotten, and this is a recurring problem in the Agency's early years. Badges are also a visual reminder of who belongs where.

Security Clearance

Official authorization allowing a person to access classified information based on a background investigation. In the Agency, clearances determine who can enter certain areas, read particular documents, and work on sensitive tasks. Clearances are graded—such as Confidential, Secret, Top Secret, or Top Secret [CODEWORD]—and reflect the level of trust the Agency places in an individual.

Spy

A general term for someone who secretly gathers information for a foreign power. Spies aim to blend in with their targets to gain trust and avoid detection. Spies can come from any country: They don't have to be born in the country they're spying for. Many Soviet spies were US or British citizens who helped the Soviets for ideological reasons. Others were Russian or Soviet nationals and members of the secret police. Spies can be trained intelligence officers or recruited civilians working in government, industry, or the military.

Spy Ring

A group of interconnected agents and operatives working together to gather and pass along intelligence. Spy rings often included a mix of couriers, informants, and handlers organized around a central figure. Amtorg was a hub for many spy rings operating throughout the United States.

Surveillance

Used in intelligence and counterintelligence, surveillance involves close observation of a subject—a spy, suspected criminal, or a communication network—that is accomplished secretly. Surveillance can be done remotely, through listening stations and electronic transmitting devices like bugs, or in person, by following, or tailing, someone. Surveillance raises ethical concerns when it is conducted on ordinary citizens or used as a form of political intimidation.

Translator

Rendered decrypted texts into English. The Agency provided language training for all its translators, but most had an intermediate knowledge of the language at best. There were few translators at the Agency, like Ethel Just, who were foreign-language experts or native speakers.

HISTORICAL CONTEXT

INTRODUCTION

The events portrayed in this book take place during a rapidly evolving period in history, with many social and political forces influencing events. This glossary covers cultural and political figures, significant historical events, and organizations that appear in this book. The terms are arranged alphabetically in each section. Some terms may seem like common knowledge (World War II, Soviet Union), but the book covers a wide range of topics—from the well-known to the obscure. Since readers will have different levels of familiarity with these topics, I chose to err on the side of clarity. These terms are described with special attention to how they contributed to these events.

POLITICAL AND CULTURAL CONTEXT

The laws, conditions, forces, movements, and events that shaped the world in which the codebreakers lived. These conditions influenced people's beliefs, how they treated one another, and which political actions they supported. Often called "the times," this complex set of political realities influenced—and was influenced by—how government agencies made decisions.

Wars and Conflicts

Berlin Blockade and Airlift (1948–1949)

One of the first major Cold War conflicts. To counter Allied occupation in postwar Germany, the Soviet Union blocked land and rail access to West Berlin, cutting off necessities like food and electricity to its residents. The United States and its allies responded with a massive airlift of supplies that lasted over a year. The event hardened East-West Cold War tensions and contributed to NATO's formation.

Chinese Civil War (1927–1949)

Long period of conflict in the Republic of China between the Nationalist Party—led by Chiang Kai-shek—and the Chinese Communist Party—led by Mao Zedong. The communists won the civil war and created the People's Republic of China in mainland China. Nationalist China was a US ally in World War II, but the People's Republic of China became a strong ally of the Soviet Union and one of the United States' main enemies. The Republic of China, led by the nationalists, became the island nation of Taiwan.

Cold War (1946–1991)

Period of direct and indirect hostilities between the United States and the Soviet Union after World War II. Allied during the war, the US and USSR became enemies due to opposing ideologies and desire for nuclear dominance. The Cold War forced many countries to align with a superpower, leading to proxy wars like Korea and Vietnam. Domestically, it created paranoia about communist infiltration, moral corruption, and nuclear war. The Cold War ended with the Soviet Union's dissolution in 1991.

Korean War (1950–1953)

Proxy war between communist North Korea and democratic South Korea. It began with North Korea's invasion of South Korea in June 1950 and took US intelligence by surprise, leading to poor preparation and an extended, bloody conflict. The war ended in a stalemate, creating ongoing military antagonism between North and South Korea. Known as the "Forgotten War" because it marks a shameful point in US history.

World War II (1939–1945)

Global conflict between the Allied powers—the United States, Britain, the Soviet Union, France, and China—and the Axis powers—Germany, Japan, and Italy. Reshaped international alliances and accelerated technological development, especially in nuclear weapons research. It ended after the US dropped nuclear bombs on Hiroshima and Nagasaki, marking the first and only use of nuclear weapons in a war. It also led to a mass migration of Black Americans to DC and the formation of the NSA and the CIA, and the building of the Pentagon.

Cold War and Civil Rights

Arms Race

Cold War competition between the United States and the USSR to develop more powerful and numerous nuclear weapons. It began in earnest after the Soviet Union's successful test of an atomic bomb in 1949 and escalated through the 1950s and beyond with the advent of hydrogen bombs, ICBMs, and submarine-launched weapons.

Civil Rights Movement

The civil rights movement (the term is traditionally not capitalized) was a decades-long struggle to end racial segregation and discrimination against Black Americans and other ethnic minorities. Its goal was ensuring full legal and social equality under constitutional, federal, and state law. While not always framed as a security issue, the movement was closely monitored by the FBI, which viewed demands for racial justice as a threat.

Civil Service Reform

Postwar efforts to make government employment fairer and more professional. These reforms helped Black federal employees and others secure more equitable roles, though discrimination remained.

Desegregation

Process of ending legally enforced racial separation, especially in public schools, transportation, and other public facilities. In the World War II era, desegregation and antidiscrimination laws were often ignored or resisted.

White communities and institutions fought desegregation laws well into the Cold War.

Integration

Process of creating inclusive environments where people of different races share equal access and participation. Southern states opposed integration—using violence and intimidation—into the late twentieth century. While the US military was officially desegregated in 1948, it remained racially divided well into the 1950s, including at the Agency.

Internment Camps

Large containment facilities meant to hold populations suspected of wrongdoing but not formally charged with a crime. After Pearl Harbor, more than 120,000 Japanese Americans—most of them US citizens—were forcibly removed from their homes and detained in internment camps by executive order. Families lost homes, jobs, and property, often permanently. The government has never adequately compensated families for these losses. In contrast, white Americans of German and Italian descent were rarely, if ever, subjected to such measures.

Iron Curtain

A metaphor popularized by Winston Churchill in 1946 to describe the division between the democratic West and the communist Soviet Union. Quickly entered mainstream political language as a metaphor for the Soviet Union's strength and secrecy. For the Intelligence Community, the Iron Curtain represented Stalin's impenetrable communication security, which led to a dearth of Soviet intelligence in the United States.

"Iron Curtain" Speech

Delivered by former British prime minister Winston Churchill at Westminster College in Fulton, Missouri, on March 5, 1946. Officially titled "The Sinews of Peace," the speech warned that "an iron curtain has descended across the Continent" and urged Anglo-American unity against Soviet influence.

Jane Crow

A term coined by civil rights activist Pauli Murray in the 1940s, "Jane Crow" describes the dual systems of discrimination that Black women faced due to both their race and gender. While "Jim Crow" laws enforced racial segregation and white supremacy across the South, "Jane Crow" captured the special compounded barriers Black women encountered—in law, education, employment, and social life—that were often invisible or dismissed within both the mainstream feminist and civil rights movements. Murray's concept emphasized that Black women's experiences could not be understood by looking at racism or sexism in isolation and needed to be defined in their own terms. Murray's writings on Jane Crow anticipated the framework later known as "intersectionality," articulating a reality long felt by those on the margins of both struggles.

Jim Crow

Southern lawmakers created Jim Crow during the post–Civil War Reconstruction to keep Black Americans in a state of poverty and terror. In the 1921 Tulsa Race Massacre, for example, a white mob razed an entire Black business district, killing up to three hundred people, because they thought a Black man had harmed a white woman. Unconcealed beneath the moral outrage was the desire to destroy Black wealth and keep Black people in their place. This theme pervades the cryptologists' story, as the Agency does everything it can to keep them in subordinate roles doing menial work.

McCarthyism

Anti-communist movement of the early 1950s associated with Republican Senator Joseph McCarthy's aggressive HUAC campaign. His hallmark was publicly accusing left-wing individuals of disloyalty without sufficient evidence. He fell out of favor with the government and was censured in 1954 for his excessive tactics.

Peekskill Riot (1949)

On August 27 and September 4, 1949, white mobs assaulted concertgoers at Paul Robeson's performances in Peekskill, New York. Police allowed the violence, which was motivated by anti-Black racism and antisemitism. Robeson was targeted after false reports claimed he said Black Americans wouldn't fight in a war against the Soviet Union.

Red Scare

Period of heightened fear of communism in the United States that began after World War II. Many individuals with leftist leanings or ties to civil rights activism found themselves under suspicion despite little evidence. Federal employees, including those at the Agency, were required to sign loyalty oaths in 1946–1947.

Segregation

Legally enforced racial separation that shaped many aspects of life for Black Americans at this time. Washington, DC, and Arlington, Virginia, both enforced segregation, leaving the Black codebreakers with few resources in and outside of Arlington Hall. Their story shows that segregation had emotional and psychological costs rather than just being a form of spatial restriction, as it's often portrayed.

Segregation in the Armed Forces

Until 1948, the US Armed Forces enforced strict segregation, which had negative consequences for its Black personnel. Most Black men served in support roles, and Black battalions were almost always placed under white command as part of white divisions. A Black officer could never command white troops, and in a mixed company, a Black officer could never outrank a white one. Violence against Black soldiers was common—and sometimes fatal. Reform took place after the war, but racial discrimination remained.

HISTORICAL FIGURES

This section offers brief references for prominent historical figures mentioned in the text. US presidents, military and intelligence leaders, civil rights activists, and influential global leaders whose decisions shaped the context in which the codebreakers lived. Some of the spies in this section, like William Weisband, were never formally tried or convicted for their espionage activities. Some figures, like Dwight Eisenhower, Harry Gold, and Julius and Ethel Rosenberg, do not appear in the book but add important context to its events.

A. Philip Randolph (1889–1979)

Labor leader and civil rights activist. Organized the Brotherhood of Sleeping Car Porters and planned the 1941 March on Washington, which led to Executive Order 8802 banning racial discrimination in defense industries.

Alger Hiss (1904–1996)

Former US State Department official accused of being a Soviet spy by ex-communist Whittaker Chambers. Convicted in 1950 of perjury (not espionage), his case became a political flashpoint and fueled McCarthyism.

Dwight D. Eisenhower (1890–1969)

Supreme Allied Commander during World War II and later thirty-fourth president of the United States (1953–1961). Moderate Republican who served two terms and won landslide victories in both elections. Focused on nuclear deterrence and the containment of global communism.

Eleanor Roosevelt (1884–1962)

First Lady of the United States (1933–1945), diplomat, and human rights advocate. Championed civil rights, women's rights, and the formation of the United Nations.

Elizabeth Bentley (1908–1963)

Nicknamed the "Blond Spy Queen," Bentley was a member of the Communist Party USA and one of the first major Soviet spies to become an FBI informant. She became a media sensation for exposing two major spy rings and testifying before HUAC in 1948, fueling Red Scare fears.

Franklin D. Roosevelt (1882–1945)

Thirty-second president of the United States (1933–1945). Democrat whose "New Deal" policies led the country through the Great Depression and most of World War II. Roosevelt died in office just before the end of the war, making Vice President Harry S. Truman president.

George C. Marshall (1880–1959)

Army Chief of Staff during World War II, later secretary of state and secretary of defense. Architect of the Marshall Plan. Opposed desegregation of the Armed Forces.

Harry Gold (1910–1972)

Courier for Soviet espionage networks in the United States. Played a key role in passing information from Klaus Fuchs to Soviet handlers. His confession helped break open the Rosenberg case.

Harry S. Truman (1884–1972)

Thirty-third president of the United States (1945–1953). Democrat who oversaw the end of World War II and the early Cold War years. He continued Roosevelt's project of civil rights advocacy, but this changed due to political pressure during the Red Scare. Truman's administration was plagued by spy scandals, which led to the public's loss of trust. Chose not to run for reelection in 1952 due to low popularity ratings.

J. Edgar Hoover (1895–1972)

Director of the FBI from 1924 to 1972. Central figure in Cold War surveillance, domestic intelligence, and political repression.

James McMillan Jr.

US Army code clerk at the US embassy in Moscow who defected to the Soviet Union in 1948. McMillan fell in love with a Soviet spy and was turned by the KGB. He stole American cryptographic material from the embassy's Code Center, handing the Soviets the keys to US intelligence. By defecting, McMillan avoided prosecution for his espionage.

John R. Hodge (1893–1963)

US Army general who oversaw the occupation of southern Korea after World War II and helped establish the US-backed government in South Korea. His administration was often criticized for its heavy handling of political dissent and repressive tactics.

Joseph Stalin (1878–1953)

Leader of the Soviet Union from 1924 until his death in 1953. A central figure in Cold War tensions, he supported North Korea's statehood plans, leading to the Korean War. Stalinist Russia was characterized by extreme repression, secrecy, and military power.

Judith Coplon (1921–2011)

Department of Justice employee convicted of passing classified documents to Soviet agents in 1949. Although her convictions were later overturned on procedural grounds, her case inflamed fears about communist infiltration in Washington.

Julius (1918–1953) and Ethel (1915–1953) Rosenberg

American citizens executed for conspiracy to commit espionage for the Soviet Union. They were accused of passing atomic secrets; their trial and execution were highly controversial and are still debated.

Kim Il Sung (1912–1994)

Founder and leader of North Korea (1948–1994). Fought in the Red Army during World War II and was backed by the Soviet Union. A prominent figure in Cold War politics, Kim created a cult of personality in North Korea that endures today.

Kim Philby (1912–1988)

British intelligence officer and Soviet double agent. Member of the "Cambridge Five" spy ring. His betrayal compromised major Western operations and worsened mistrust among allies. Defected to the USSR in 1963.

Klaus Fuchs (1911–1988)

German-born physicist who worked on the Manhattan Project and passed atomic secrets to the Soviet Union. Arrested in 1950 in the UK and served nine years in prison before moving to East Germany.

Lavrentyi Beria (1899–1953)

Head of the Soviet secret police (NKVD), later the Ministry of State Security. Oversaw internal repression and Soviet espionage abroad. Played a key role in the USSR's atomic program by managing intelligence-gathering on US and British nuclear research. Executed in 1953 after Stalin's death.

Lucy Diggs Slowe (1885–1937)

A Black civil rights activist, educator, and tennis champion, Lucy Diggs Slowe was the first dean of women at Howard University and the first Black woman to hold such a post at any US college. She cofounded Alpha Kappa Alpha, the first Black sorority, and was a chartering founder of the College Alumnae Club alongside Mary Church Terrell, Ethel Just, and others. As an activist, Slowe fought for the intellectual and personal independence of Black women students. Slowe is recognized as an important figure in LGBTQ+ history: She lived with her partner of twenty-five years, Mary Burrill, a fellow educator, though they kept their relationship secret at the time.

Mao Zedong (1893–1976)

Founding leader of the People's Republic of China (1949–1976). His victory in the Chinese Civil War reshaped the global Cold War landscape and heightened US fears of communist expansion in Asia, especially during and after the Korean War.

Mary Church Terrell (1863–1954)

Suffragist, writer, and educator, Terrell was one of the most prominent Black activists of the early twentieth century. She founded the National Association of Colored Women with the motto "lifting as we climb" in 1896 and co-founded the College Alumnae Club in 1910, the first society for Black women with college degrees. Born to formerly enslaved parents in Memphis, Tennessee, Terrell fought for Black women's inclusion in the suffrage movement and was one of the first Black women to earn a college degree. Her 1940 memoir *A Colored Woman in a White World* charts her as still picketing segregated restaurants in Washington, DC, into her eighties, demanding equal rights with unrelenting clarity and grace.

Mary McLeod Bethune (1875–1955)

Political strategist, philanthropist, and educator, Bethune was one of the most influential Black leaders of the early twentieth century. She founded the Daytona Literary and Industrial School for Training Negro Girls in 1904 (later Bethune-Cookman College) and the National Council of Negro Women in 1935. A key advisor in President Franklin D. Roosevelt's Black Cabinet, Bethune fought for New Deal programs to include Black Americans. Her work with Eleanor Roosevelt focused on increasing opportunities for Black women, which she saw as integral to the success of the civil rights movement. Bethune famously declared: "The true worth of a race must be measured by the character of its womanhood."

Paul Robeson (1898–1976)

A prominent Black singer, actor, and socialist advocate, Robeson was outspoken against racism and US Cold War policies. As a staunch supporter of the Soviet Union, he was targeted by the FBI and HUAC during the Red Scare. The Peekskill Riot of 1949, which took place at two of Robeson's concerts in Peekskill, New York, was a flashpoint during the anti-communist era.

Pauli Murray (1910–1985)

Legal scholar, writer, and civil rights activist, the Rev. Dr. Pauli Murray was an early defender of Black women's rights. Her writings on "Jane Crow" and the intersections of race and gender discrimination laid the groundwork for *Brown v. Board of Education* and influenced justices like Thurgood Marshall and Ruth Bader Ginsburg. Cofounder of the National Organization for Women, the first female graduate of Howard's law school, and the first Black woman ordained as an Episcopal priest, Murray broke many boundaries. She is recognized as an LGBTQ+ figure, as she changed her name from Anna Pauline to the gender-neutral name "Pauli," lived as a man, and rejected traditional gender identity. Her memoirs *Proud Shoes* and *Song in a Weary Throat* are revered classics of twentieth-century literature.

Syngman Rhee (1875–1965)

First president of South Korea (1948–1960), Rhee was a US-educated Korean nationalist and staunch anti-communist. His presidency was supported by the United States but marked by authoritarianism, political violence, and fierce opposition to North Korea.

W. E. B. Du Bois (1868–1963)

Scholar, civil rights activist, and cofounder of the NAACP. Du Bois was a vocal critic of segregation and US foreign policy during the Cold War. Presented the Civil Rights Congress's petition *We Charge Genocide* to the United Nations, contending the US government was guilty of Black genocide. Decried as a communist.

Whittaker Chambers (1901–1961)

Former Soviet courier turned anti-communist witness. His testimony against Alger Hiss galvanized the Red Scare and laid the groundwork for McCarthyism. A complex figure whose personal transformation mirrored the era's ideological battles.

William Weisband (1908–1967)

Russian-born US Army linguist and Soviet agent who compromised the top secret Venona Project by leaking information to the Soviets. Codename "LINK." Weisband was never prosecuted due to concerns about revealing

Venona. After failing to testify against CPUSA to a grand jury, he was convicted of contempt and allowed to live out his life as an insurance broker. He died of a heart attack in 1967.

Winston Churchill (1874–1965)

Prime Minister of Britain during World War II and again in the early 1950s. In 1946, he delivered the famous "Iron Curtain" speech in Fulton, Missouri, warning that Soviet domination was descending across Eastern Europe. Churchill's rhetoric helped define early Cold War discourse and justified increased Western coordination.

ORGANIZATIONS AND AGENCIES

This section outlines the military, intelligence, and political organizations referenced throughout the book. These entities played crucial roles in shaping Cold War policies, surveillance networks, and the lives of both government employees and political dissidents. Some entries clarify institutional changes over time and include major sites of operation.

US Agencies and Organizations

Air Force

Became an independent branch from the Army in 1947. Focused on strategic bombing, reconnaissance, and early warning systems. Led massive bombing campaign against North Korea, ultimately weakening their forces. Collaborated with SIGINT units to develop advanced aerial surveillance during the Cold War.

American Federation of Government Employees (AFGE)

A more moderate federal workers' union that coexisted with CPUSA-linked unions in the 1940s. Survived the loyalty purge era and remains active today. While there's no evidence that Agency employees participated in labor unions, many were required to sign anti-strike oaths.

Arlington Hall Station

A former girls' finishing school converted into a top-secret Army codebreaking center during World War II. Located in Arlington, Virginia, it served as a hub for decrypting enemy messages, including Japanese Army codes and later Soviet traffic (as part of the Venona Project). Postwar, it became a central site for the Army Security Agency and early NSA.

Armed Forces

Three major branches of the US military and their subsidiary organizations. The US Armed Forces commander in chief is the US president, and the secretary of defense is its main advisor. During and after World War II, the Army, Navy, and Air Force have an adversarial relationship, and this leads to costly intelligence failures and war.

Armed Forces Security Agency (AFSA)

NSA's immediate predecessor (1949–1952), which initiated racial integration at the Agency. Comprised of Army, Navy, and Air Force intelligence services but meant to function as a single organization. Leadership conflicts, poor funding, and limited authority led to major intelligence failures, including the Korean War. An investigation into its practices led to the creation of the more powerful NSA in 1952.

Army (Post–World War II)

Largest ground force military branch. Continued to play a dominant role in postwar occupations (Germany, Korea), Europe (the Marshall Plan), and intelligence gathering. Arlington Hall was originally under Army command as part of the Second Signal Service Battalion.

Army Security Agency (ASA)

Postwar cryptologic agency established in 1945. Switched focus to collecting Soviet intelligence to meet Cold War demands. ASA lost most of its personnel after the war and was plagued by shortages during its short existence. To increase intelligence production, ASA begins hiring college-educated Black women in 1947 to staff low-paying clerical roles.

Atomic Energy Commission (AEC)

Intended to remove nuclear development from military control, AEC managed civilian and military atomic research after World War II. While it strove for peaceful application of nuclear technology, it often failed to enact clear ethical policies and practices, leading to dangerous radiation experiments and unrestricted weapons development.

Black Chamber (The Cipher Bureau)

The Cipher Bureau, commonly known as the Black Chamber, was the US's first peacetime cryptanalytic organization following the dissolution of the Army's intelligence branch (MI8) after World War I. The Black Chamber posed as a commercial code company in New York City and became controversial when its former chief, Herbert O. Yardley, published *The American Black Chamber*, a tell-all book about the agency's operations. Shut down in 1929 due to questionable intelligence gathering practices.

Central Intelligence Agency (CIA)

Established in 1947 by the National Security Act, the CIA absorbed the OSS and expanded into covert operations, propaganda, and foreign intelligence. The CIA's early years were fraught with failures and shaky intelligence estimates, leading to exaggerated beliefs about the Soviet Union's nuclear capabilities. It became a central player in Cold War policy, including in Korea, China, and Eastern Europe, and partnered with the Agency on projects such as Russian plaintext. Maintained an adversarial relationship with the Agency, which weakened both agencies' intelligence operations.

Communist Party USA (CPUSA)

Legal political party with thousands of members in the 1930s and '40s, including many Black Americans and union activists. Played active role in unionizing Black workers who were excluded from white unions during the Depression. Provided cover for Soviet spies and FBI informants. After World War II, CPUSA came under severe scrutiny and lost influence, as anti-communist sentiment surged during the Red Scare.

Congress of Industrial Organizations (CIO)

Labor federation that supported industrial unionism and initially welcomed Black workers and CPUSA leaders. Due to political pressure, CIO expelled several left-wing unions during the Red Scare.

Federal Bureau of Investigation (FBI)

Handled domestic counterintelligence and loyalty investigations during the Cold War. Under J. Edgar Hoover, the FBI surveilled civil rights leaders, union organizers, suspected communists, and federal employees as a form of intimidation. During the Red Scare, the FBI interrogated many suspected of being Soviet spies, and these interrogations led to public trials and convictions that fueled national panic.

Fort George G. Meade

Maryland headquarters of the National Security Agency since its creation in 1952. Many operations, like Russian plaintext, remained at Arlington Hall until the mid-1950s. The new location allowed for expansion—to around thirty thousand personnel—and provided acres of underground space for ultra-high-speed computer facilities.

House Un-American Activities Committee (HUAC)

A congressional committee tasked with identifying "un-American" and "subversive" activity. Although not technically law enforcement, HUAC's investigations contributed to widespread purges and job losses for anyone with suspected communist ties. Fueled by racism and antisemitism, HUAC targeted Hollywood, civil rights groups, and labor unions.

National Security Agency (NSA)

Formed in 1952 to centralize all US communications intelligence (COMINT) and communications security (COMSEC) operations. Absorbed AFSA's military cryptologic activities and became a civilian agency. Massive organization characterized by extreme secrecy, technological advancement, and exhaustive collection. Dubbed "No Such Agency," the NSA remained largely unknown to the public until 1975 when the government investigated its surveillance practices, like Operation Shamrock.

Navy

Maintained global reach and naval intelligence capabilities. Operated COMINT stations worldwide, including Pacific listening posts that targeted Soviet and Chinese traffic during the Cold War. Intelligence collaborations between Navy Intelligence (CSAW) and the Agency yielded great results, but their adversarial relationship led to duplication of research and organizational disputes.

Office of Strategic Services (OSS)

The US wartime human intelligence (HUMINT) agency during World War II, predecessor to the CIA. The OSS ran espionage and resistance support missions, primarily in Europe and Asia, with mixed success. Dissolved in 1945, but many of its personnel helped form the early CIA.

The Pentagon

Headquarters of the US Department of Defense, completed in 1943. Located in Arlington, Virginia, the Pentagon became the nerve center for postwar military operations, including cryptologic coordination with Arlington Hall and other outposts.

Signal Intelligence Service (SIS)

First US Army intelligence service after the Black Chamber. Precursor to the Army's Signal Security Service (SSS) and Signal Security Agency (SSA). Responsible for all cryptologic work during the 1930s and early World War II years. In 1942, the SIS moved from its headquarters in the Munitions Building in Washington, DC, to Arlington Hall Station, a former girls' school in Northern Virginia. SIS's extreme secrecy remained a core characteristic of the Agency.

Signal Security Agency (SSA)

Formed in 1943 to consolidate Army cryptologic operations. Like its predecessors, SSA was part of the Army's Second Signal Service Battalion, a military service organization. Massive hiring campaigns expanded SSA from three thousand to ten thousand personnel by the end of the war.

United Public Workers of America (UPWA)

A labor union for government employees affiliated with the Congress of Industrial Organizations (CIO). UPWA organized many federal workers, including Black clerical and technical staff, which led to the government requiring anti-strike oaths and loyalty oaths from its workers beginning in 1946. Later labeled subversive and expelled from the CIO during the Red Scare.

Vint Hill Farms Station

A secret Army signals intelligence (SIGINT) station in rural Virginia. Used for intercepting enemy radio transmissions during World War II and the early Cold War. Its remote location helped minimize radio interference, and it was instrumental in collecting Japanese and German military communications.

Washington, District of Columbia (DC)

Formally the District of Columbia, Washington, DC, is a federal district and the capital of the United States. It is located between Maryland and Virginia, both former slave states. Washington, DC, remained segregated into the mid-twentieth century, embedding structural racism in US institutions. Amid segregation, Black DC was a cultural center that left a lasting legacy in the city. Mass migration during World War II made Washington, DC, majority Black by the 1950s, a demographic that lasted until 2011.

Women's Army Corps (WAC)

Women's branch of the US Army established in 1942 and converted to active duty in 1943. Racially segregated. White WACs made up most of Arlington Hall's codebreaking and clerical staff during the war. No Black WACs served at Arlington Hall, though some worked as code clerks at military facilities around the country.

Global Democratic Organizations

Government Code and Cypher School (GC&CS)

Britain's wartime cryptanalytic center, headquartered at Bletchley Park. Collaborated with Arlington Hall and shared intelligence via the UKUSA (BRUSA) Agreement.

Government Communications Headquarters (GCHQ)

Successor to GC&CS, formalized in 1946. Focused on postwar SIGINT and allied collaboration with the United States.

MI5 (Security Service)

Domestic counterintelligence agency, roughly equivalent to the FBI. Tasked with rooting out internal threats, including suspected communist spies.

MI6 (Secret Intelligence Service)

British foreign intelligence agency, akin to the CIA. Employed double agents like Kim Philby (before his defection to the USSR).

North Atlantic Treaty Organization (NATO)

Established in 1949 as a military alliance among the United States, Canada, and Western European nations to counter Soviet expansion. The Soviet Union responded with its own alliance—the Warsaw Pact—deepening the Cold War divide.

Republic of Korea (ROK)

South Korea's official name, founded in 1948 under President Syngman Rhee. Supported by the United States in efforts to build a pro-Western state. Despite uncertain beginnings, South Korea became a major economic power and producer of technical goods. It remains an important US ally in the Pacific region.

United Nations (UN)

Founded in 1945 to maintain international peace and cooperation. After North Korea invaded South Korea in 1950, the UN authorized military intervention under US leadership, forming the United Nations Command.

Soviet and Communist Organizations

Amtorg (American Trading Corporation)

Soviet commercial representative established in New York City in 1924 to facilitate trade between the United States and the Soviet Union. Until 1933, Amtorg acted as the Soviet Union's embassy in the United States. Until the mid-1950s, Amtorg housed major Soviet spy rings operating in the US. Amtorg's telegraphic traffic was one of the Agency's main sources of Soviet intelligence.

Chinese Communist Party (CCP)

Founded in 1921, the Chinese Communist Party came to power in 1949 after defeating the Nationalists. It has remained the ruling party of the People's Republic of China ever since. The CCP shaped China's domestic and foreign policies, aligning with the Soviet bloc during the early Cold War. Along with post-Soviet Russia, China remains one of the United States' greatest adversaries.

Democratic People's Republic of Korea (DPRK)
The official name of North Korea, established in 1948 with Kim Il Sung as its leader. Backed by the Soviet Union and later China. Suffered heavy casualties and infrastructure damage during the Korean War, becoming one of the world's most bombed countries.

GRU (Main Intelligence Directorate)
The Red Army's military intelligence agency, separate from the KGB. Operated many clandestine operations during the Cold War, particularly in the United States, Korea, Eastern Europe, and Southeast Asia.

KGB (Committee for State Security)
Established in 1954, the KGB was the successor to the NKVD. It carried out both domestic surveillance and global espionage, including recruitment of agents like Kim Philby and handling Soviet-aligned defectors.

NKVD (People's Commissariat for Internal Affairs)
Soviet intelligence and secret police agency during World War II. Responsible for internal repression and foreign espionage. Predecessor to the KGB, the NKVD ran many early Soviet spy networks in the United States and Europe.

People's Republic of China (PRC)
The People's Republic of China replaced the Republic of China in 1949 after the communists' victory in China's civil war. Led by Mao Zedong, the PRC became a major communist power in the Cold War, supported by strong alliances with the Soviet Union and North Korea. Communist China's involvement in the Korean War turned the tide in favor of North Korea, making it a costly war for the United States and its allies.

Soviet Bloc
Also known as the Eastern Bloc and the Communist Bloc, these are the countries that aligned with the Soviet Union in Eastern Europe, Asia, and Africa during the Cold War. Their alliance created a global balance of power between

the democratic West and the communist East, but it also contributed to proxy wars and escalating military tension worldwide.

Thirty-Eighth Parallel
The pre–Korean War boundary between Soviet-occupied North Korea and US-occupied South Korea. Likened to the American Dixie Line in its division between North and South. It became the de facto dividing line in the Korean War. After the war, it expanded into the heavily guarded Demilitarized Zone (DMZ).

Union of Soviet Socialist Republics (USSR / Soviet Union)
Communist superpower and America's primary rival in the Cold War. A vast multiethnic state spanning Eastern Europe, Russia, and Central Asia. It was formed by the Bolshevik Revolution in 1917 and ruled by the Communist Party until 1991. Under Stalin, the USSR consolidated power over Eastern Europe and backed revolutionary movements worldwide.

Warsaw Pact (1955–1991)
Post-Stalinist military alliance of Soviet Bloc countries, formed in response to NATO. Formalized the Soviet Union's hold over Central and Eastern Europe and provided a structure for military domination, such as the 1968 invasion of Czechoslovakia after their liberal reforms, known as the "Prague Spring."

NUCLEAR ARMS AND ATOMIC RESEARCH

US and Soviet atomic weapons, research, and production sites. These countries' arms race for nuclear superiority defined twentieth-century politics and culture.

Arzamas-16 (Sarov)
First top-secret Soviet atomic research city to support nuclear weapons design and testing. Built by Gulag slave labor on the grounds of a former monastery in 1946. Housed laboratories and weapons production facilities hidden from the public; Soviet secret cities did not appear on maps, and their residents officially did not exist.

Atomic Bomb

A weapon that uses nuclear fission to unleash massive explosive power. The first atomic bombs were developed by the United States during World War II under the Manhattan Project and were dropped on Hiroshima and Nagasaki in August 1945. Often referred to colloquially as "nuclear bombs" later on, but technically distinct from hydrogen bombs, which involve nuclear fusion.

Chelyabinsk-65 (Ozersk)

First Soviet closed city devoted to plutonium production. Built in 1947 by slave labor from Gulag prison camps, it housed the Mayak plant and was one of ten main secret cities (also called *atomgrads*) that supported the Soviet nuclear program.

Joe-1 (1949)

American code name for the Soviet Union's first successful atomic bomb test, RDS-1, conducted on August 29, 1949. Based heavily on US bomb designs stolen through espionage. The test shocked the US Intelligence Community and accelerated the nuclear arms race.

Joe-2 (1951)

American code name for the Soviet Union's second successful atomic bomb test, RDS-2, conducted on September 24, 1951, at the Semipalatinsk test site in Kazakhstan. Joe-2 improved upon Joe-1, showing that the Soviet Union was catching up to the United States in nuclear weapons research.

Kurchatov Institute (USSR)

Soviet counterpart to the Manhattan Project. Led by physicist Igor Kurchatov, this institute oversaw development of the first Soviet bomb, Joe-1. Like all major Soviet institutions, the Kurchatov Institute was closely tied to state intelligence services and the Russian military.

Little Boy and Fat Man

The two atomic bombs used by the United States against Japan. Little Boy was dropped on Hiroshima (August 6, 1945) and used enriched uranium. Fat Man was dropped on Nagasaki (August 9, 1945) and used plutonium. Their detonation led to Japan's surrender and the end of World War II.

Los Alamos Laboratory (New Mexico)

Main design and assembly site for the Manhattan Project. Scientists here developed the physics behind both uranium and plutonium bombs. Remained central to US nuclear research throughout the Cold War.

Manhattan Project

Secret US research program (1942–1946) that developed the first atomic bombs. Coordinated work across multiple sites, including Los Alamos, Oak Ridge, and Hanford, and employed more than 130,000 people. Led by General Leslie Groves and physicist J. Robert Oppenheimer. Embedded Soviet spies stole critical research, giving the Soviets a head start on their nuclear research program.

Sandia Laboratory (New Mexico)

Initially part of Los Alamos, Sandia became an independent center for testing, engineering, and maintaining US nuclear weapons systems. Still in operation as Sandia National Laboratories.

NOTES

Introduction

xxii *a letter to the workers of America:* Adapted from Vladimir I. Lenin, *Lenin's Collected Works,* 62–75.

xxiii *"If Hitler invaded hell":* Winston S. Churchill, *The Grand Alliance,* 370.

Note on Terms

xxxii *and keep them in their place:* Elizabeth Stordeur Pryor, "The Etymology of Nigger: Resistance, Language, and the Politics of Freedom in the Antebellum North," *Journal of the Early Republic* 36, no. 2, Summer 2016, 203–6.

Chapter 1: Change of Plans

1 *her home department of Home Economics:* Naomi Kate McElwaine, Official Transcript, Purdue University, 1944 (hereafter Official Transcript).

1 *thirty-five minutes or more:* "An American Legacy with Boilermaker Roots," *Purdue University News Archive Online,* 13 October 2021.

2 *"pure white Caucasian":* "New Research Leads to West Lafayette Apology for Past Racial Covenants," *Based in Lafayette, Indiana,* 2024.

2 *live-in servants:* "West Lafayette," *Sundown Towns Database.* History and Social Justice Website, Tougaloo University, n.d.

3 *many can't participate in student clubs:* "Town Girls Discuss Formation of Club at Initial Meeting," *Purdue Exponent,* 19 December 1941, 1.

3 *a town that excludes her:* John Norberg, "African Americans Apply to Purdue's

Residence Halls 1944–1947," *Ever True: 150 Years of Giant Leaps at Purdue University*, Purdue Libraries and School of Information Studies News Online, 4 February 2021.

3 *Black students exist "on the edge" of student life:* Azreen Rehman, "The Black History of Purdue University," *The Odyssey Online*, 24 January 2019.

4 *a festive gathering beyond exams and headlines:* "Cosmopolitan Club," *Debris*, 1942, 285.

5 *Only in integrated spaces like the Memorial Union:* Norberg.

5 *a show of patriotism and a harbinger of war:* "Ornaments, Fir Trees Festoon Union as First Signs of Christmas Hit Campus," *Purdue Exponent*, 7 December 1941, 1.

5 *lights glowing in the common room until curfew:* "Women's Residence Halls," *Debris*, 1943, 334.

6 *protection for the families who resided there:* "From Freedman's Village to Queen City," Arlington Virginia Library Website, 31 January 2018.

6 *Arlington County refuses to provide plumbing, running water, sidewalks, streetlights, or electricity:* Anne Hollmuller, "'Right Out Our Front Door': The Construction of the Pentagon Destroyed a Black Neighborhood in Arlington," *Boundary Stones*, 23 March 2018, updated 9 April 2024.

7 *who are paid less and assigned the dirtiest, most dangerous jobs:* "African Americans in the 'Forgotten Theater' of World War II," *Folklife Today*, Library of Congress Website, 29 July 2019.

7 *President Franklin D. Roosevelt signs Executive Order 8802 demanding nondiscrimination in federal buildings:* Alfred Goldberg, *The Pentagon: The First Fifty Years*, 61.

7 *for a reasonable period of time at no cost to them:* Goldberg, 34.

8 *"you could smell it for blocks":* Jeannette Williams, *The Invisible Cryptologists*, 11.

8 *circumstantial at best, at worst fabricated:* "Dies Committee Uncovers Nazi Propaganda Network in US," *Purdue Exponent*, 3 December 1941, 3.

8 *everything the Red Army needs to win a war:* "Lend-Lease Shipments, World War II," *Quantities of Lend-Lease Shipments: A Summary of Important Items Furnished Foreign Governments*, 31 December 1946, 8.

9 *From here, she'll go to the Lincoln School: Lafayette Journal and Courier*, various articles.

9 *another reminder in the* Exponent *this morning:* "Notices," *Purdue Exponent*, 7 December 1941, 4.

10 *All military personnel must report to work tomorrow in uniform:* "Pearl Harbor Radio Broadcasts—December 7, 1941," namnoiz, *YouTube*, 7 December 2012.

10 *The Signal Corps recruits radar technicians to locate enemy aircraft:* Seanan Lee, "Boilermakers at War: The Involvement of Purdue University in the Second World War," *Purdue Historian* 2021, 2; Thomas R. Johnson, "Purdue University in the War," *Purdue Alumnus*, 1 October 1942, 5–7.

10 *writes down names, takes notes:* Johnson, 12.

11 *She completed her training as a Red Cross Gray Lady in October:* "News of the Colored People: Officers Chosen," *Lafayette Journal and Courier*, 1 November 1941, 8; "140 Years of Service: Women an Important Part of American Red Cross History," American Red Cross, 10 June 2021.

11 *Lafayette's "colored" wards and hospitals:* "The Heritage of Racism and Medicine in Indianapolis," *Invisible Indiana*, 9 August 2020.

11 *ripping through barracks like Hitler's buzz saw:* "A Storied History: Purdue University and the Military," Purdue University Press Website, 4 December 2024.

11 *the aims of cosmopolitanism:* "Cosmopolitan Club to Hold Convention on Campus Sunday," *Purdue Exponent*, 12 December 1941, 1.

12 *visitors are greeted by a circular pool and fountain:* "Arlington Hall Station Photographs: Written and Descriptive Data," *Historic American Buildings Survey*, 3–6.

12 *Black handymen repair: The History of the Signal Security Agency* (hereafter *SSA History*), Vol. 1, 136.

13 *Japan's strategic war plans: SSA History*, Vol. 1, 90–92.

13 *A party of Signal Corps officers chances upon this spectacle: SSA History*, Vol. 1, 124.

14 *holding secret codebreaking courses on college campuses:* Liza Mundy, *Code Girls*, 7–9.

14 *an old log cabin called the Tea House:* "Arlington Hall Station Photographs," *Historic American Buildings Survey*, 2–4.

14 *they must lay a concrete floor: SSA History*, Vol. 1, 124, 127.

15 *they maintain Virginia's status quo:* Frank Rowlett, *Oral History Interview 1976–01*, 128.

15 *"assist with details that take much of the engineer's time":* "Radio Corporation to Train Cadettes in Engineering," *Purdue Exponent*, 22 January 1943, 1; Gretchen Sherry and Ann Hathaway, "Cadettes on Campus," *Purdue Engineer*, 1 September 1943, 244–247.

16 *more military contracts than it can handle:* Dorothy Cochrane, "Meet the Curtiss-Wright Aeronautical Engineering Cadettes," National Air and Space Museum Website, 6 March 2013; "Rosie the Engineer: RCA Cadettes," *Lockheed Martin News*.

16   *the delicate surgery of crafting cathodes and wiring transistors:* Brenda L. Holmes, "RCA Bloomington Boom: RCA Delivers for Nearly 50 Years," *BizVoice: Magazine of the Indiana Chamber of Commerce,* January–February 2020, 61.

16   *they're treated like the help:* "World War II," *Encyclopedia of Indianapolis,* 5.

17   *until the recruiter handed her the contract:* Elizabeth Penney, Elizabeth Penney Interview, 11.

17   *steps onto the production line at RCA:* McElwaine, Official Transcript.

17   *she gives a talk on India's caste system for the International Relations Club:* "Naomi McElwaine Will Speak to Club in Union Tonight," *Purdue Exponent,* 13 April 1943, 1.

17   *it's the Rosies' job to make that happen:* Steven Heller, "RCA Victor's Victory Lap," *Print,* 10 May 2016.

17   *RCA's "soldiers of production":* 24th Annual Report, 9.

18   *until management builds a separate "colored" bathroom:* "World War II," *Encyclopedia of Indianapolis,* 5; Gregory S. Cooke, *Invisible Warriors,* 2020, 0:20:11.

18   *The six hundred thousand Black women who work alongside them are rarely acknowledged:* For a literature review of Black female representation in war propaganda, see Aura Wharton-Beck, "Interrupted Labour by Another Name: Resistance," *Feminist Review,* 2022, 10–23.

18   *"you felt like you were in a foreign country":* Cooke, 0:04:41.

19   *"dangerous machinery in dangerous working conditions around predatory bosses":* Cooke, 0:24:16–0:24:24, 0:09:47–0:10:03.

19   *"We were people":* Cooke, 0:07:54, 0:24:45.

Chapter 2: Trade Secrets

21   *"you just picked up what was going on":* Regene Nissan, Interview, Bletchley Park Website, n.d., 2.

23   *enough workspace to fit fifty codebreakers and typists:* Details about Britain's Commercial Code Section are based on Brigadier Telford Taylor's telegraphed reports to Colonel Corderman at Arlington Hall: #4876 on 25 May 1943, and #4877 on 27 May 1943, from the American Embassy in London; Nissan.

24   *The quaint attraction Speakers' Corner is a defense base for German air raids:* Nissan, 5–9.

24   *flaunting his skill as a classical pianist:* David V. Gioe and Nicholas Reynolds, "Capturing Wartime History to Forge Postwar Intelligence Liaison," *Journal of Intelligence History,* 2024.

25 *The section tracks suspect German contraband deals like blips on a radar screen:* Francis Harry Hinsley et al., *British Intelligence in the Second World War: Its Influence on Strategy and Operations,* Vol. 1, 240.

26 *they don't need the Americans' machines:* Nissan, 6–7.

27 *especially from the German buying corporation:* William J. Donovan, Coordinator of Information, to Franklin D. Roosevelt, President, New York, December 24, 1941; Office of Strategic Services—Reports, December 22, 1941–January 15, 1942, 105; Box 163; Subject Files 1933–1945; President's Secretary's File (Franklin D. Roosevelt Administration), 1933–1945; Franklin D. Roosevelt Library, Hyde Park, NY.

27 *Sofindus-Hisrowak is busting the British blockade of Germany's foreign trade:* Hinsley, 223–225.

27 *but there's so much more:* David P. Mowry, *The Cryptology of the German Intelligence Service,* 2.

27 *"Maybe twenty":* Taylor, 27 May 1943.

28 *its staff reassigned to more important projects:* SSA History, Vol. 2, 229–230.

28 *beckoning them with the promise of grade 5:* SSA History, Vol. 1, 175–176.

29 *"constant and concentrated attention":* SSA History, Vol. 1, 176.

29 *"willing to enter such an organization":* SSA History, Vol. 1, 205.

29 *a hiring push aims to double the workforce:* SSA History, Vol. 1, 481.

30 *the Agency likely has its eye on these recruits:* "Wright Field Girls Will Start War Classes in Radio Today" and "RCA Cadettes Start Careers; Face 44 Weeks of Training," *Purdue Exponent,* 4 May 1943, 1.

30 *the intriguing proposition of doing "secret work":* Comments made to author, Zoom conference, 10 July 2025.

30 *Not everyone can keep a secret:* Marlon McElwaine, phone conversation with the author, 13 August 2025.

30 *pressuring the Army to increase Black enlistment with little success:* John A. Davis and Cornelius L. Golightly, "Negro Employment in the Federal Government," *Phylon (1940–1956),* 1945, 343.

30 *peaking at 10.46 percent in July:* Bell I. Wiley, *The Training of Negro Troops,* 6.

31 *personnel officers could easily discard most Black applications:* Davis and Golightly, 338.

31 *Black "and gainfully employed":* Williams, 12.

31 *As a branch of the Signal Corps, the Agency must meet this requirement:* Williams, 12–13. There are no exact numbers provided for the total number of Black personnel needed in the Agency overall; these one hundred hires make up 12.5

percent of the Cryptanalytic Branch, but the Agency has seven branches at this time and 3,500 staff overall.

32   *"You're my personnel officer to see that I get the right ones":* Williams, 12.

34   *she can say the job is in "communications":* Comments made to the author, Zoom conference, 10 July 2025.

Chapter 3: Breaking Code

38   *and make a pit stop at the Military Intelligence Service on the way:* SSA History, Vol. 2, 232.

39   *decoding, transcribing, and keeping the complex file system up-to-date:* Williams, 16; *SSA History,* Vol. 2, 231–232.

39   *Some books, like the ABC Telegraphic Code, use letters instead of numbers:* Steven M. Bellovin, "Compression, Correction, Confidentiality, and Comprehension: A Modern Look at Telegraphic Codes," *Cryptologia,* 2020, 4.

39   *codebreakers always have to look out for slipups:* Bellovin, 23.

39   *fifteen copies for distribution:* David Kahn, *The Codebreakers,* 516.

40   *They reconstruct six more permutation tables:* Rowlett, 394–395.

40   *They compare the patterns to previous frequency studies:* SSA History, Vol. 2, 231–232.

41   *placed with the service staff "for reasons of policy":* Williams, 16.

43   *"it is all part of a big picture":* Samuel P. Collins, "Introduction, 'The Office of Censorship at War,'" in *Lecture Series "This Is Our War" Delivered at Arlington Hall Station in the Autumn of 1943,* 89.

43   *"What does not concern the war does not concern censorship":* Byron Price, "The Office of Censorship at War," in *Lecture Series "This Is Our War" Delivered at Arlington Hall Station in the Autumn of 1943,* 93.

43   *"It takes a lot of people to win a big war":* Price, 94.

44   *"In no case have we ever objected":* Price, 104.

45   *Black people didn't want to fight in a Jim Crow military:* Negro Press Report, October 12, 1942, 6; Negro Press Report, October 26, 1942, 2–4; Negro Press; Press Items, Re: Negro Newspapers 1944–1946; Box 266, Subversives; Assistant Secretary of Defense (Legislative & Public Affairs) Office of Public Information, Analysis Branch; Records of the Office of the Secretary of Defense 1921–2008, Record Group 330; National Archives at College Park, College Park, MD (hereafter National Archives at College Park).

45   *Even Dr. Seuss stokes racist hate:* "Racism in Anti-Japanese Propaganda," *Anti-*

Japanese Propaganda Informational Sheet, Naval History and Heritage Command, Hampton Roads Naval Museum, Norfolk, VA.

46 *Propaganda is "the direct manipulation of social suggestion":* Lynette Finch, "Psychological Propaganda: The War of Ideas on Ideas During the First Half of the Twentieth Century," *Armed Forces & Society*, 368.

47 *"And any one of us has it in our power to wreck it":* Price, 109.

48 *"their capacity is greater than the position they are now in":* David J. Sherman, "Ann's War: One Woman's Journey to Codebreaking Victory over Japan," *Cryptologic Quarterly*, 2017, 47.

48 *"it's like doing crossword puzzles every day":* Sherman, 45.

48 *Others save up their ration coupons and buy gasoline:* Sherman, 45.

49 *"I'm afraid our consciences are going to trouble us":* Joseph C. Grew, "The Japanese, Our Enemy," in *Lecture Series "This Is Our War" Delivered at Arlington Hall Station in the Autumn of 1943*, 131.

49 *Too caught up in labor strikes and luxuries:* Grew, 132.

50 *They are precision instruments: SSA History*, Vol. 2, 232–233.

50 *"or they crush us":* David Holloway, *Stalin and the Bomb: The Soviet Union and Atomic Energy, 1939–1956*, vii.

51 *The rest belong to diplomats, NKVD agents, and Red Army and Navy Intelligence (GRU):* Robert Louis Benson and Michael Warner, eds., *Venona: Soviet Espionage and the American Response 1939–1957*, 1–6.

Chapter 4: Security Breach

52 *Even food deliveries are camouflaged:* Information on SIS's security practices in this section are from *SSA History*, Vol. 1, 144–150f.

52 *They ask a reference for three other names:* Rowlett, *Oral History Interview 1976–01*, 363.

53 *child welfare major from the University of Minnesota:* Biographical information about Martha McWatt comes from the *St. Paul Recorder*, Minneapolis, Minnesota, 1938–1944, and her NSA personnel records, unless otherwise noted.

54 *secret arms deals with Mussolini and Hitler before the war:* Francisco César Alves Ferraz and Henry Granville Widener, "Brazil-U.S. Relations: Brazil in World War II," Library of Congress Website, 1 May 2024.

54 *you'll be shot by firing squad:* Comments made to author, Zoom conference, 10 July 2025.

54 *wrapping up a Red Cross War Bond drive: SSA History*, Vol. 1, 233.

54 *their codebreaking adventures would make a great story:* SSA History, Vol. 1, 150j.

55 *or being a gentleman:* Melba McCarthy, *Oral History Interview 1999–32*, 18.

55 *"Your country is now facing its greatest crisis":* Letter from G. E. Darling, Separations Officer, to Martha McWatt, 3 April 1945; Martha McWatt, Official Personnel Folders—Department of the Army; Records of the U.S. Civil Service Commission, Record Group 146 (hereafter Record Group 146); National Archives, St. Louis, MO (hereafter National Archives at St. Louis).

56 *two young women walk out of a hotel in downtown Washington:* Description of the event that follows is from *SSA History*, Vol. 1, 150e–f.

59 *"to give aid and comfort to the enemy":* "Hush Hush? Pish Tosh! Secret War Documents Prove About as Hard to Get as a Cold," *Washington Post*, 29 May 1945, quoted in *SSA History*, Vol. 1, 204.

59 *codebreakers eye each other suspiciously:* Perry Molstad, "Operating Services Division Minutes of Meeting Held 13 June 1945," William F. Friedman Collection of Official Papers, National Security Agency Website (hereafter Friedman Documents, NSA Website).

60 *Black women in government agencies often report harsher treatment:* Cooke, 0:25:29.

60 *"like small school children":* Earle F. Cook, "Operating Services Division Executive Committee Minutes of Meeting Held 13 December 1944," Friedman Documents, NSA Website.

60 *Everyone thinks they have it the worst:* Mundy, 231–239.

60 *clearance exceptions for employees with "doubtful backgrounds":* Earle F. Cook, "Operating Services Division Executive Committee Minutes of Meeting Held 18 April 1945," Friedman Documents, NSA Website.

60 *clerks for seven:* AH Personnel Organization, 13; Personnel Organization, 1942, 1943, 1944; Box 1007; Historic Cryptographic Collection Pre-World War I Through World War II (hereafter Historic Cryptographic Collection); Records of the National Security Agency/Central Security Service 1917–1998, Record Group 457 (hereafter Record Group 457); National Archives at College Park.

61 *"we got through without any bad luck":* Rowlett, 356–366.

61 *A blue bar with a red-white-and-blue star insignia:* "War Department Civilian Service Emblems," *Philadelphia Enquirer*, 15 July 1945.

62 *One of those codes is called JAH:* The name "JAH" is randomly assigned. Most Japanese codes start with "JA" and the third letters are assigned alphabetically. Other diplomatic codes include JAI, JAJ, and JAK. Desmond Ball and Keiko Tamura, eds., *Breaking Japanese Diplomatic Codes: David Sissons and D Special Section During the Second World War*, 53–62.

62 *Sometimes called LA or "L," it's a diplomatic trade code:* Information on JAH codebreaking in this section comes from Worksheets Used in the Exploitation of JAH, a Japanese Commercial System, 1944–1945; Box 1003; Historic Cryptographic Collection.

62 *For content they "merely wish to keep from post office officials":* Ball and Tamura, 61.

62 *breaking it wasn't "too much of a job":* Rowlett, 193–194.

63 *Their indexing system makes finding even the rarest codes easy:* Benson Buffham, *Oral History Interview 1999–51,* 5.

64 *One battleship—seventy-five tons: United States Synthetic Rubber Program, 1935–1945,* American Chemistry Society, 1998.

64 *Lose the latex, lose the war:* Alexander J. Field, "The U.S. Synthetic Rubber Program and the Fall of Singapore," *Yale University Press Blog,* 9 February 2024.

Chapter 5: Victory and Defeat

66 *"We must heed the civil liberties program of the national YWCA":* "Mrs. Just Speaks," *Baltimore Afro-American,* 8 February 1941, 16.

66 *beloved by students for her enthusiasm and interest in their work:* "Ein Knopf," *Academy Herald,* 26.

67 *even when traveling great distances:* Mary Church Terrell, *A Colored Woman in a White World,* 287–307; Mia Bay, *Traveling Black,* 63–106.

68 *to cut down on overall costs:* Perry Molstad, "Operating Services Division, Executive Committee, Minutes of the Meeting Held 8 August 1945," Friedman Documents, NSA Website.

68 *urgency compelled the government to hire Black women for office work:* "Capable Office Staff; Bookkeeping Department; National Benefits Association; Washington, D. C.," *New York Public Library Digital Collections,* 1917.

68 *even when higher-paying ones were available:* Emmet J. Scott, *Scott's Official History of the American Negro in the World War,* 462–463.

70 *branding themselves as anti-communist:* "Klan Tries Revival," *Washington Afro American,* October 1945, 1, 27; "Klan to Ride Again Tennessee: Daily Heralds Its Revival," *Washington Afro American,* 23 March 1946, 16.

70 *A bill creating a permanent Fair Employment Practices Committee:* "The Civil Rights Act of 1964: A Long Struggle for Freedom, World War II and Post War (1940–1949)," Library of Congress Exhibition, 2016.

71 *prove to the Russians that America is serious about democracy:* "Civil Rights Best Defense Against Reds," *Washington Afro American,* 13 March 1948, 25.

74 *a top secret clerical operation:* Buffham, 11.

75 *"NO DESIRE TO SEVER CONNECTION WITH ASA":* Application for Federal Employment, 8 May 1947; Ethel Just; Official Personnel Folders—Department of the Army (hereafter Ethel Just, Official Personnel Folders); Record Group 146; National Archives at St. Louis.

75 *"From Stettin in the Baltic":* Winston Churchill, "The Sinews of Peace," America's National Churchill Museum Website, 5 March 1946.

75 *"the black peril" and "the rising tide of color":* Ethel Just, "The Folk Plays of Paul Green," 43.

76 *he's put in charge of a new typing unit:* Buffham, 9–11; Williams, 19. Williams states that Coffee went to Vint Hill Farms to lead a typing unit in the Intercept Control Branch there.

77 *Weisband is an NKVD spy:* Benson and Warner, 60.

78 *The FBI buzzes around Amtorg:* J. M. Flagler, "Visit to Amtorg," *New York Times*, 9 May 1954.

Chapter 6: Scared New World

79 *The postwar economy slowed—then reversed:* Michael L. Peterson, *BOURBON to Black Friday*, 79.

80 *drawing red lines tighter:* Zachary Leiter, "250 Years of Segregation," *Chicago Reporter*, 30 August 2023.

81 *"What the Young Negro Wants":* "Brookport," *Chicago Defender*, 22 February 1947.

82 *"raise your nuclear secrecy curtain":* Bertrand Goldschmidt, "A Forerunner of the NPT? The Soviet Proposals of 1947," *IAEA Bulletin*, 63.

82 *"Task #1," Lavrentyi Beria calls it:* Goldschmidt, 60.

82 *Zero to fission in under three years:* Goldschmidt, 60.

82 *"But a monopoly on the bomb cannot last long":* "Memorandum by Mr. Edmund A. Guillon, Special Assistant to the Under Secretary of the State, to Messrs. Lovett and Kennan, Subject: Molotov's Remarks of November 6, 1947, on Atomic Bomb 'Secret,' 13 November 1947," in Ralph E. Goodwin et al., eds., *Foreign Relations of the United States, 1947, General; The United Nations*, Vol. 1.

83 *even data on key players: Summary Annual Report of the Army Security Agency Fiscal Year 1947* (hereafter *ASA FY 1947*), 41.

83 *Black life expectancy of fifty-four:* Douglas C. Ewbank, "History of Black Mortality and Health Before 1940," *Millbank Quarterly*, 1987, 11.

83 *Her mother was long-lived:* Kenneth Manning, *Black Apollo of Science*, 267.

83 *a better division of labor:* ASA FY 1947, 5–6, 43.

84 *they are still responsible for mundane tasks:* ASA FY 1947, 6–7.

85 *Black men run the all-Black units or get stuck in the mail room and quit:* Minnie Kenny, *Oral History Interview 1999–27* (hereafter Kenny), 24–25.

85 *A week later, she resigns:* Notification of Personnel Action, 11 December 1946; Audrey Fox Anderson; Official Personnel Folders—Department of the Army (hereafter Audrey Fox Anderson, Official Personnel Folders); Record Group 146; National Archives at St. Louis.

86 *"Somebody had to do it":* Buffham, 10.

86 *a Soviet spy has infiltrated the War Department's General Staff:* Benson and Warner, xxi.

87 *The United States has its own double agents:* Benson and Warner, xxxi.

87 *argue for a "harsh peace" with Germany:* Steven Casey, "The Campaign to Sell a Harsh Peace for Germany to the American Public, 1944–1948," *History*, 2005, 28.

88 *"they will love one another the rest of their lives":* "LeDroit Park Civic Association Holds Appreciation Service for Pvt. Cowan," *Washington Afro American*, 27 March 1948, 14.

88 *Ethel grew up speaking German among classmates, friends, and neighbors:* Manning, 45.

89 *The Agency needs new sources of SIGINT: Post War Transition Period: The Army Security Agency, 1945–1948,* 111.

89 *they bury it inside the Pentagon:* Carol B. Davis, *Candle in the Dark: COMINT and Soviet Industrial Secrets, 1946–1956,* 17.

89 *translate anything "with intelligence value":* Williams, 23.

89 *Anything to get away from the Flex machines:* Williams, 24.

90 *"If it were important, the Russians would encipher it":* Jacob Gurin, *Oral History Interview 2003–07,* 1–2.

90 *"We didn't know anything about the Soviet economy":* Gurin, 4.

90 *plaintext is a full-fledged operation:* Gurin, 2–3.

90 *The clerks are Black, transferred from the Census Bureau:* Williams, 24.

90 *David Bryant, a Navy veteran and former statistical clerk:* "David Bryant," *NSA Historical Figures.*

90 *They're stationed in the "Flex room":* Comments made to the author, Zoom conference, 10 July 2025.

90 *Task I, just like the bomb it aims to destroy:* It's not known when Russian plaintext gets the codename "Task I," but this is its designation on the only organizational charts available. "Symbols and Titles of AFSA Activities, 14 December 1951," Friedman Documents, NSA Website.

90   *a consistent, accurate stream of intelligence from behind the Iron Curtain:* Summary Annual Report of the Army Security Agency, Fiscal Year 1948 (hereafter *ASA FY 1948*), 42.

91   *They have numbers. Names. Nuclear data:* Gurin, 3; C. B. Davis, 14.

91   *Soviet extraction teams descend on northern Korea:* Lavrentyi Beria, "Special Dossier to Members of the Special Committee," 25 April 1947, Wilson Center Digital Archive.

91   *the Soviets' first secret nuclear city:* Samira Goetschel, "The Graveyard of the Earth: Inside City 40, Russia's Deadly Nuclear Secret," *The Guardian*, 20 July 2016.

91   *thanks to blueprints stolen by Beria's spies:* Kate Brown, *Plutopia: Nuclear Families, Atomic Cities, and the Great Soviet and American Plutonium Disasters*, 78–119.

92   *its hands poised at seven minutes to midnight:* Martyl Langsdorf, cover design, *Bulletin of the Atomic Scientists*, June 1947; Martyl Langsdorf, *The History of the Bulletin's Clock*, 1947.

93   *the organization blocks Terrell's membership:* Janice Leon, "Integrating the American Association of University Women, 1946–1949," *The Historian*, 1989, 423, 426.

93   *when their race is discovered, they are expelled:* Terrell, 288–289.

93   *"I can remember when I had no trouble whatsoever":* Mable Alson, "The Eternal Feminist," *Baltimore Afro-American*, 2 August 1947, 22.

94   *Labeling civil rights groups "communist" is the same as labeling them "un-American":* Charisse Burden-Stelly, *Black Scare / Red Scare: Theorizing Capitalist Racism in the United States*, 233.

94   *"An Appeal to the World!":* W. E. Burghardt Du Bois, *An Appeal to the World: A Statement on the Denial of Human Rights to Minorities in the Case of Citizens of Negro Descent in the United States of America and an Appeal to the United Nations for Redress*, 1947.

94   *"domestic jurisdiction":* Adam Dahl, "Constructing Colonial Peoples: W. E. B. Du Bois, the United Nations, and the Politics of Space and Scale," *Modern Intellectual History*, 858.

Chapter 7: Escalation

96   *"You can't lose this job; it's all you have":* Julian McConnell and [Redacted] McConnell, *Oral History Interview 1999-37*, 9. "Shirley" is a pseudonym; the employee's first name is redacted.

97 *"it was like keeping you in your place"*: McConnell and McConnell, 9.

97 *the machines of the second floor of A Building*: Williams, 22.

97 *far fewer employees than they did during the war*: ASA FY 1948, 68–69.

97 *"you weren't permitted to sit on stools"*: McConnell and McConnell, 2, 9.

98 *two hundred staff members working round-the-clock shifts*: McConnell and McConnell, 9.

98 *and carry them back to their desks*: Williams, 22, 31–32.

98 *the office becomes less integrated*: Williams, 23.

99 *Plaintext volume is up 500 percent from the previous year*: ASA FY 1948, 41.

100 *leaving valuable material unread*: C. B. Davis, 14–15.

101 *The clerks separate them into seventy categories*: C. B. Davis, 13.

102 *"a predatory and ruthless enemy"*: Summary Annual Report of the Army Security Agency, Fiscal Year 1946, 66.

102 *All CIA attempts to gather human intelligence*: Woodrow Kuhns, "The Beginning of Intelligence Analysis in CIA," *Studies in Intelligence*, 2022, 1–5.

102 *top secret research behind the Iron Curtain*: TICOM Document #646; Russian—Preambles and Endings of W/I Soviet Messages, 1945; Box 21; Archival and Historian's Source Files, 1952?–ca. 2007 (hereafter Archival and Historian's Source Files); Record Group 457; National Archives at College Park.

103 *He doesn't do it alone*: Liza Mundy, "The Women Code Breakers Who Unmasked Soviet Spies," *Smithsonian Magazine*, September 2018.

105 *"In the time it takes to read this report"*: To Secure These Rights: The Report of the President's Committee on Civil Rights, Harry S. Truman Library and Museum, 29 October 1947, 3–16.

105 *Whiteness also can ensure immunity*: To Secure These Rights, 24–31.

106 *John Marshall's "liberal construction" of the Constitution*: To Secure These Rights, 107.

106 *achieve world peace and economic security abroad*: Harry S. Truman, "Annual Message to the Congress on the State of the Union," 7 January 1948.

106 *have their evacuation claims settled*: Harry S. Truman, "Special Message to Congress on Civil Rights," 2 February 1948.

107 *individuals can create and modify codes as they please*: Post War Transition Period, 83.

107 *commercial messages can be much shorter*: William F. Friedman and Lambros D. Callimahos, *Military Cryptanalytics Part I*, 38.

108 *her industry and output are merely "adequate"*: Report of Efficiency Rating, 31 March 1948; Ethel Just, Official Personnel Folders.

109 *which brings her salary to $3,476.40*: As of writing, $3,476.40 in 1948 is about $46,000 in 2025. "CPI Inflation Calculator," U.S. Bureau of Labor Statistics

Website, 16 September 2025; Notification of Personnel Action, 29 September 1948; Ethel Just, Official Personnel Folders.

109 *the median income for a white urban-dwelling person is $3,300:* As of writing, $3,300 is 1948 is about $44,000 in 2025; $1,800 is $24,000; $900 is $12,000. "CPI Inflation Calculator," U.S. Bureau of Labor Statistics Website, 16 September 2025. *Current Population Reports: Income of Families and Persons in the United States: 1948,* 15 February 1950, 2.

109 *Galina Dunaeva, daughter of an NKVD general: Post War Transition Period,* 128–129.

110 *taking hundreds of classified documents and top secret knowledge with him:* "Military Myths and Legends: The American NCO That Started the Korean War," *Marines Dispatches,* 2022.

110 *the world's worst grocery list: Post War Transition Period,* 129.

110 *the "Bogotazo":* CIA, 1996.

110 *All its codes, ciphers, and intelligence missing:* ASA FY 1948, 26.

111 *which runs on a grid separate from both West Germany and the GDR:* Rachel Wolpert, "Times of Surge," *Vattenfall,* 18 November 2013.

112 *almost a year later in May 1949:* "The Berlin Airlift 1948–1949," *Milestones in the History of U.S. Foreign Relations.* Office of the Historian, U.S. Department of State Website, 2017.

112 *Bernice spreads the Good News:* "Campbell Plays Host to AME Mission Unit," *Washington Afro American,* 24 September 1949, 31; Bernice Mills, *Oral History Interview 1999–92,* 10 November 1999, 2.

113 *some of the terms the unit has to recognize by sight:* The Traffic Processing Branch's keyword and subject lists remain classified, but these words appear frequently in Soviet telegrams concerning the atomic program. L. D. Ryabev, ed., *USSR Atomic Project: The Atom Bomb 1945–1954,* Vol. 2, 2003 (Рябева, Л. Д., ред., Атомный проект СССР: Атомная бомба *1945–1954,* Том *II,* 2003); C. B. Davis, 12.

113 *The average word in Russian plaintext is 6.4 letters:* Friedman, "Appendix 5, Section F: Russian Letter Frequency Data," in *Military Cryptanalytics Part I,* 5–26.

113 *She'll even miss the Halloween party:* "Southeast Settlement House," *Washington Afro American,* 25 October 1947, 18.

113 *A Building's basement is an aboveground foundation:* Descriptions of A Building's layout and construction are from "Arlington Hall Station Building No. 401," *Historic American Buildings Survey,* Library of Congress Prints and Photographs Division Website.

113 *scans her first tape:* TICOM Document #646. This translation is from German

documents captured during World War II, so it's dated 7 February 1945. The Traffic Processing Unit scanners would be looking at current telegrams, in this case, from 1948, but those documents remain classified.

114 *but they do not allow Black hires to take these courses during training:* C. B. Davis, 13–14.

114 *learning the language by rote:* Iris Carr, *Oral History Interview 1999–52*, 11–16.

115 *make sure she doesn't miss anything:* Plaintext categories based on the Task I Plaintext Branch section titles found in "Symbols and Titles of AFSA Activities," 10.

115 *Time's up! On to the next tape:* Based on firsthand accounts of working in the Traffic Processing Unit found in Williams, 24–30, and Carr, 9–14.

115 *all of whom need to know at least some of the language:* ASA FY 1948, 42.

116 *"The Agency hurt itself":* McConnell and McConnell, 10.

116 *This is only one of Bernice's jobs:* Carr, 2.

116 *which are capable of carrying atomic weapons, just in case:* Defense's Nuclear Agency 1947–1997, 53.

116 *the officers think the AEC people are "damn crooks":* Defense's Nuclear Agency, 57–58.

117 *Sverdlovsk-45 produces highly enriched uranium:* "Elektrokhimpribor Combine," NTI Website.

Chapter 8: Black Friday

118 *"familiarity with the specific target or targets":* C. B. Davis, 10.

119 *"selecting what should be printed out":* C. B. Davis, 12, 16. By 1951 the punched tapes included Cyrillic text, but this was often not readable.

119 *"Their burn bags were checked periodically":* C. B. Davis, 12.

119 *"that effort was not doing very well":* Matthew Aid, *The Secret Sentry: The Untold History of the National Security Agency*, 23.

119 *tactical intelligence on Soviet defense:* C. B. Davis, 6.

119 *pouring its resources into plaintext:* C. B. Davis, 45.

120 *people at the lower grades are considered "lower creatures":* Milton Zaslow, *Oral History Interview 1999–89*, 5–6.

120 *She "cannot sit next to a colored person at work":* Jeannette Williams and Yolande Dickerson, *The Invisible Cryptologists*, 33.

121 *one man, who "made himself in charge," and four women:* Gurin, 3.

121 *it "made the difference between success and failure":* Milton Zaslow, *Oral History Interview 1999–20*, 3.

121 *Bernice is interested in the wider world:* "African Culture Program Feature," *Washington Afro American*, 12 March 1955, 3.

121 *"there were no advancements out":* James Pryde, *Oral History Interview 1998–26*, 5, 10.

121 *"If you were brown, [the plantation] is where you went":* Pryde, 10.

122 *"Some job boards were 'white only,' some boards were 'Colored'":* Pryde, 11.

122 *"without regard to race, color, religion, or national origin":* Harry S. Truman, Executive Order 9981, 26 July 1948; Executive Orders 1862–2020; Box 14; General Records of the United States Government, 1778–2006, Record Group 11; National Archives Building, Washington, DC.

123 *"I was the first to get hired":* Williams, 36.

123 *"The best jobs for blacks at that time were with the post office":* Williams, 36.

123 *no Black officer shall ever command white troops: Policy for Utilization of Negro Manpower in the Post-War Army,* 7.

124 *the Soviet Union is still years away from building the bomb:* R. H. Hillenkoetter, "Memorandum to Senator Bourke B. Hickenlooper, Status of USSR Atomic Energy Project," *Management of Officially Released Information #136351,* January 1949.

124 *Their assumptions are dangerously flawed:* "Memorandum for: The Director, Subject: Policy Concerning the CIA Weekly Summary," CIA, 1–2.

124 *Stalin does something no one expects:* C. B. Davis, 24.

124 *one of the most devastating offensives in military history:* Effects of Russian Radio Silence on German Intelligence, May 1944; Box 33; Archival and Historian's Source Files.

124 *Like the Nazis, they are sitting ducks:* Williams, 25.

125 *Better to stick with what the Agency knows:* C. B. Davis, 6.

125 *British success on other systems dries up:* Aid, 23.

126 *providing more than a glimpse behind the Iron Curtain: TASS: Its Role, Structure and Operations,* CIA, 1; C. B. Davis, 10.

126 *"commodities in exchange for coal and raw materials":* Weekly Summary, CIA, 5 November 1948, 5.

126 *sixty-eight top-level policymakers:* Weekly Summary, 14.

128 *No other agency produces real-time intel at this rate:* Peterson, 89.

128 *the Agency ties one hand behind its back:* Peterson, 234.

128 *The war began a "revolution" in cryptanalysis, but now it's stalled:* Thomas Johnson, *American Cryptology During the Cold War, 1945–1989,* Book 1, *The Struggle for Centralization, 1945–1960,* 1.

128   *Plaintext is a "new and unusual" project:* C. B. Davis, 17.

128   *the "Dark Ages" of COMINT: The History of SIGINT in the CIA, 1947–1970,* Vol. 2, 1; Williams, 25.

128   *"little experience, less money, and no expertise":* Johnson, 61.

128   *plaintext is a "candle [in] the darkness of the early Cold War":* C. B. Davis, 48.

128   *"like a phoenix" out of the ashes of Black Friday:* Peterson, 223.

128   *Racism is the "dark side" of plaintext:* Williams, 25.

128   *creating the new working models the changing moment demands:* Richard C. Raymond, "Challenge to SIGINT: Change or Die," *Cryptologic Symposium,* 11.

128   *"they all have some kind of brains":* Williams, 28.

129   *the FBI can't use Venona to publicly corroborate Bentley's or anyone else's testimony:* Aid, 23.

130   *Communism isn't just a "red herring," as he claims:* Harry S. Truman, "The President's News Conference," Truman Library and Museum, 5 August 1948.

130   *where states have no say:* "Thurmond Hits Truman, Dewey, Wallace As Leading U.S. to 'Rocks of Totalitarianism,'" *New York Times,* 12 August 1948.

131   *The Chicago Defender runs two headlines: The Chicago Defender National Edition 44,* 31 July 1948, 1.

131   *with 50 percent supporting Dewey to Truman's 45 percent:* 1948 Campaign Trends Survey, Gallup.

131   *Truman grinningly displays the Chicago Daily Tribune headline that prematurely announced his defeat:* "The Election of 1948," photo, Harry S. Truman Library and Museum Website.

132   *who Clifford claims will make or break the election:* Clark Clifford to Harry S. Truman, 19 November 1947; Harry S. Truman Library and Museum Website.

Chapter 9: Forearmed But Not Forewarned

133   *"Very Good":* Ethel Just, "Report of Efficiency Rating, 31 March 1949," Ethel Just, Official Personnel Folders.

135   *advocates for a socialist revolution:* Paul Robeson Jr., *The Undiscovered Paul Robeson: Quest for Freedom, 1939–1976,* 143; Martin Duberman, interview, *American Masters,* 30 September 1999.

135   *reprinting the inflammatory remarks without checking their authenticity:* Gilbert King, "What Paul Robeson Said," *The Smithsonian Magazine,* 2011.

135   *"the Most Dangerous Man in the World":* Robert H. Keller, "Paul Robeson at Blaine: Singing for Freedom at the Peace Arch," *Columbia Magazine,* 2005–06, 2.

136 *the "good" Americans from the bad "Commies"*: Matthew Schuerman, "The Peekskill Riots Revealed the Racism and Antisemitism Hidden Beneath the Surface of the Anti-Communist Movement," *Smithsonian Magazine*, 27 August 2024.

136 *the evil that causes so many to suffer in silence*: Martin Duberman, *The Martin Duberman Reader: The Essential Historical, Biographical, and Autobiographical Writings*, 114–116.

137 *communist infiltration in the highest levels of government*: John F. Fox Jr., "In the Enemy's House: Venona and the Maturation of America's Counterintelligence," *History Reports & Publications*, FBI Website, 27 October 2005.

138 *citizens who might "subvert national security"*: Daniel Patrick Moynihan et al., "The Cold War," *Report of the Commission on Protecting and Reducing Government Secrecy*.

138 *can spy on whomever they want*: Frank Church et al., *Intelligence Activities and the Rights of Americans*, Book 2, 105.

138 *not that anything criminal will happen*: Dougald D. McMillan, *Report on Inquiry into CIA-Related Electronic Surveillance Activities*, 32.

138 *"in the highest interests of national security"*: Church, 145–146.

139 *Copies circulate beyond the Agency into Pentagon boardrooms*: Rowlett, 359–361.

140 *More than five hundred people walk out in less than a year*: History of the Army Security Agency and Subordinate Units, 1 July 1949–30 June 1950, Fiscal Year 1950 (hereafter *ASA FY 1950*), 1.

141 *arguing and angling for control*: Thomas L. Burns, *The Origins of the National Security Agency 1940–1952*, 59.

142 *to do the most work with the fewest people*: Efficiency and Economy—AFSA Personnel Survey, 13 February 1950, 1; AFSA Personnel Survey, 14 February 1949; Box 2; General Records, 1948–1969; Record Group 457; National Archives at College Park.

142 *The workspace is cramped, the air stale, and the floor littered with papers*: Comments made to the author, Zoom conference, 17 January 2025.

142 *next it's a cluster of names she's never heard*: ASA FY 1948, 3.

142 *working overtime to clear the backlog caused by Black Friday*: Summary Annual Report, Army Security Agency, 1 July 1948–30 June 1949, Fiscal Year 1949, 41.

143 *"housing, transportation, and innumerable items" that could improve morale*: "Responsibilities and Ideals," Responsibilities and Ideals, 2; Signal Security Agency & Army Security Agency Organization, 1945; Box 2; Organization Mission Files; Record Group 457; National Archives at College Park.

144 *tightened their security to keep Joe-1 a surprise*: C. B. Davis, 24.

144 *they're not producing HUMINT, and their research is spotty:* David Robarge, *John McCone as Director of Central Intelligence 1961–1965*, 229–230.

145 *nothing can stop him from creating a communist world order:* "Estimate of the Effects of the Soviet Possession of the Atomic Bomb upon the Security of the United States and upon the Probabilities of Direct Soviet Action," *ORE 49–91 CIA*, 5–6.

145 *with the CIA as well as with one another:* ORE 49–91, 1.

145 *Stalin calls it a "peace offensive":* ORE 49–91, 17.

145 *a few uranium bombs like the one dropped on Hiroshima:* Hans M. Kristensen and Robert Norris, "Global Nuclear Weapons Inventories, 1945–2013," *Bulletin of the Atomic Scientists*, 2013, 75–81.

146 *Or an alliance with their Russian neighbors:* ORE 49–91, 7–9.

146 *"be prepared for grave decisions":* Eugene Rabinowitch, "Forewarned—but Not Forearmed," *Bulletin of the Atomic Scientists*, 1949, 273.

146 *Compared to the US arsenal, it's "amateur handiwork":* Rabinowitch, 273.

Chapter 10: The Last Station

147 *Six years at the Recorder of Deeds Office is enough:* Background on Iris Carr in this section comes from Carr.

149 *He misses his band, the Royal Aces:* "Joint Hostesses," *San Antonio Register*, 5 May 1933, 2.

150 *General John R. Hodge, who's in charge of the transition, would rather be on the battlefield:* Andrew Salmon, "John Hodge: First US Forces Commander in Korea," *Korea Times*, 18 January 2012.

150 *"cleaner than in some of the towns in the States":* Robert Neff, "Yanks Welcomed on Their Arrival in Newly Liberated Korea," *Korea Times*, 15 August 2021.

151 *nurturing his cult of personality and suppressing rivals:* Vasilii Lebedev, "War and Peace in Liberated North Korea," *International Journal of Asian Studies*, 2021, 1–2.

151 *Korea has always been racially and culturally homogeneous:* Neff.

152 *they hole up in a new headquarters in Pyongyang:* Post War Transition Period, 112.

153 *"Not many people have heard of it, but I'll take your application in":* Carr, 2.

154 *For ASA Pacific, Korea is a miserable post:* ASA FY 1949, 31–32.

154 *After two and a half years, the 111th Signal Service Company is at a breaking point:* Information on ASA Pacific's mission in Korea comes from *Post War Transition Period*, 131–132.

155 *troops march into villages to arrest several "ringleaders":* Post War Transition Period, 132.

155 *turn the rest over to the Korean Military Advisory Group:* ASA FY 1949, 101.

155 *lingering Red Army troops in the North:* Post War Transition Period, 112.

157 *a small pawn firmly under Stalin's thumb:* Condensed and excerpted from "Notes of the Conversation Between Comrade I. V. Stalin and a Governmental Delegation from the Democratic People's Republic of Korea Headed by Kim Il Sung," Wilson Center Digital Archive; Kathryn Weathersby, "'Should We Fear This?' Stalin and the Danger of War with America," Woodrow Wilson International Center for Scholars, 4.

157 *"Well, looky here!":* Conversation quoted from Carr, 4.

Chapter 11: The Forgotten War

160 *"what with people working and printing stuff out":* Gurin, 11.

160 *She's one of 167 workers staffing the division:* Peterson, 269.

160 *The data feed two series of reports:* Gurin, 3; C. B. Davis, 56.

161 *even the smallest factories must keep their "masters" in Moscow informed of their progress if they want to stay in operation:* C. B. Davis, 37.

161 *Everyone wants a slice of plaintext:* Gurin, 4–5.

162 *for now—no Red flags:* Clayton Laurie, "The Korean War and the Central Intelligence Agency," FOIA Electronic Reading Room, Central Intelligence Agency Website, 1 May 2010, 9.

162 *The US sends South Korea $100 million ($50 million less than requested) and hopes the problem goes away:* Laurie, 13.

162 *they won't lift a finger when Kim rolls his tanks into Seoul:* Weathersby, 9–11.

166 *destroyed all their crypto equipment with thermite:* ASA FY 1950, 87–88.

167 *A shamefully low grade for six years of exceptional service:* Request for Personnel Action, 15 November 1950; Ethel Just, Official Personnel Folders.

167 *now a supervisor "down in the hole":* Kenny, 31.

167 *Visiting Fulbright Professor in the humanities at the universities of Lyon and Grenoble Alpe in France:* Otis Alexander, "Margaret Just Butcher (1913–2000)," *BlackPast.*

168 *safe, affordable spaces in a city of vanishing possibilities:* Loretta Brown, "Growing Up in LeDroit Park in the 1950s," *Washington Post,* 21 March 1985.

169 *He'll fill the opening Ethel leaves behind:* Williams, 35–44.

Chapter 12: A New Generation

171 *Iris is going to do her best:* Carr, 11.

171 *"really top-level, really sensitive COMINT":* Comment on USCIB 13/195, "Mea-

sures for Increased Security of COMINT," 18 July 1951; Measures to Increase COMINT Security, 1950–1954; Box 40; Archival and Historian's Source Files Related to William F. Friedman, ca. 1952–1974 (hereafter Friedman Collection); Record Group 457; National Archives at College Park.

172 *Someone writes "Good!" with a big arrow next to this point in the margin:* Statement by the USCIB Coordinator of USCIB 13/195, 2; Measures to Increase COMINT Security, 1950–1954; Box 40; Friedman Collection.

173 *"an approach to the plaintext problem which may not yet have been adequately investigated":* J.N. Wegner to General Canine, "Measures for Increased Security for COMINT," 29 July 1952, 4; USCIB Miscellaneous 1951–1952; Box 30; Friedman Collection.

173 *its potential value is "incalculable":* J.N. Wegner to General Canine, "Re: My memo of 29 July 1952 on the same subject," 19 September 1952, 2; USCIB Miscellaneous 1951–1952; Box 30; Friedman Collection, 2.

174 *A shipment with an address:* Carr, 19.

176 *in some cases, more than a year:* C. B. Davis, 40.

176 *"it is believed the music will be well received":* Williams, 30–31.

176 *who can command higher salaries at other agencies or in private industry:* Carter Clarke to Assistant Secretary of the Army, "Effect of Critical Grade Limitations on Operations of the Army Security Agency," 22 April 1949, 1–8 (hereafter Clarke); Personnel, ASA Historical, 1949–1952; Box 43; Friedman Collection.

176 *"they could receive no credit or corresponding pay":* Clarke, 1–2.

177 *"in those grades, Government service is more attractive":* Clarke, 8.

177 *they'll be brought in at the lowest step in their grade:* AFSA Memorandum Number 32–66, 27 March 1951, and AFSA Memorandum Number 32–26/2, 25 September 1952; AFSA Civilian Personnel Policy Memoranda; Box 1; General Correspondence Files, 1944–1969; Record Group 457; National Archives at College Park.

178 *any Black person the Agency hires is going "down in the hole":* Williams, 44.

179 *So Minnie finds her friendships elsewhere:* Background on Minnie Kenny in this section comes from Kenny, 5–12.

180 *"I didn't come through the garden door, I came in the front door":* Kenny, 10.

181 *Washington's Black society has its own politics:* Kenny, 8–9.

182 *a major city, with a network of resources and a "reasonably equable climate":* "The Move to Fort Meade," *Cryptologic Almanac 50th Anniversary Series,* 1.

182 *"Nobody wants houses looking like that":* Delores Watts, Warner Parsons, and [Redacted], *Oral History Interview 1999-19,* 25–27.

183 *"It was a burden"*: Kenny, 15.

183 *a personnel race war that mirrors the world outside:* Kenny, 24, 16.

183 *"You had to send people overseas, to Europe, to the Far East"*: Zaslow, *Oral History Interview 1999–89*, 11.

183 *some have never seen the Baltimore-Washington Parkway:* McConnell and McConnell, 7.

183 *she has to simplify her English so they can understand:* Kenny, 16.

Chapter 13: The Digital Plantation

186 *They train white people as programmers to head up the units when the time comes:* McConnell and McConnell, 6–9.

189 *"then your whole career changes"*: McConnell and McConnell, 6.

189 *"there could be no such thing as too much intelligence data"*: Walter Laqueur, *The Limits and Uses of Intelligence*, 1995, 32, 36.

190 *"a device that will automatically record the presence of preselected words in teletypewriter text"*: Miles A. Merkel, "A 'Word Spotter,'" *NSA Technical Journal*, 1959, 91–100.

190 *even those are rather challenging for the nonspecialist to follow:* Merkel, 91.

190 *when the first IBM punch card machines came into use:* Samuel S. Snyder, "Influence of US Cryptologic Organizations on the Digital Computer Industry," *Cryptologic Quarterly*, 1987–1988, 67.

191 *"machine scanning of messages, which was beyond the reach of available technology at the time"*: "Data Handling Survey—First Report, 27 February 1951," quoted in C. B. Davis, 16.

191 *this time to the Dutch, who are working with the Russians:* "Memorandum for the Members of USCIB: The Petersen Case," CIA, 5 May 1955.

192 *It effectively does what the Russian plaintext scanners do by hand, only much faster:* Cecil Phillips, *Oral History Interview 1993–23*, 45–46.

193 *Further ahead than any commercial or industrial technology:* "Before Super-Computers: NSA and Computer Development," *Cryptologic Almanac 50th Anniversary Series*, 5.

193 *the Agency's desperate need to process its increasing stream of intelligence:* Colin B. Burke, *It Wasn't All Magic: The Early Struggle to Automate Cryptanalysis, 1930s–1960s*, 274.

193 *leaving one hundred women jobless:* Phillips, Cecil and Blair Hall. *Oral History Interview 1993–14*, 4.

194 *a new class of clerical worker emerges: the "communicator"*: Phillips, 85.

194 *"unbelievable enmity" between the groups hampers collaboration:* Zaslow, 1999–89, 5–6.

194 *as does a declassified study from 1986:* Douglas Hogan, *General and Special Purpose Computers: A Historical Look and Some Lessons Learned.* The declassified version redacts all mention of Soapflakes.

194 *This makes Soapflakes sound more like legend than fact:* Thomas R. Johnson, *American Cryptology During the Cold War, 1945–1989,* Book 1, *The Struggle for Centralization,* 205. This volume cites Phillips's interview and Hogan's study as sources of information on Soapflakes.

195 *saving "thousands of hours of analyst time":* Burke, 286.

195 *"the recognition of . . . noncryptanalytic functions" should not be accompanied by "cryptanalytic defeatism":* Burke, 285–286.

196 *"There should have been more opportunities for me to excel at the things I knew":* McConnell and McConnell, 6.

196 *commands aren't always unilateral:* Ron Eglash, "Broken Metaphor: The Master-Slave Analogy in Technical Literature," *Technology and Culture,* 1–3.

197 *its central processing unit, "Plantation":* Samuel S. Snyder, *History of NSA General-Purpose Electronic Digital Computers,* 1964, 41.

197 *the need for "messy" human intervention in selecting and mounting data:* Burke, 293, 295, 297–298; Phillips, 14.

197 *a greater speed and scale than a legion of traffic processors:* Burke, 277.

197 *Data clerks encode data streams several times per job:* Snyder, *History of NSA General-Purpose Electronic Digital Computers,* 4.

198 *"Supervisors would change, and they would reorganize, but you just stayed":* Williams, 23, 32.

199 *"credibility is the scarcest resource":* Joseph Nye, "China's Soft Power Deficit," *Wall Street Journal,* 8 May 2012.

199 *"What's in it for me?":* Kenny, 33.

199 *"they would see to it getting straightened out":* Carr, 17.

199 *she raises awareness and makes it harder to get away with:* Carr, 24.

200 *She walks out of the interview—and gets the promotion:* Carr, 31–32.

200 *"You can't talk to me like that":* Carr, 33–34.

201 *"It speaks of the East, and like the East, it suggests much, says little":* Minnie Kenny et al., "This Is Dragon Seeds," *Dragon Seeds,* 1973, 1.

201 *The Agency's personnel policies are a "myth world . . . prodigious in their complete divorce from operational needs":* Tom Glenn, "Time to Look at People," *Dragon Seeds,* 1973, 19.

202 *"Why you'd hardly need cross-section paper and pencils!"*: Minnie M. Kenny, "Minnie's Mini," *Dragon Seeds*, 1973, 23.

203 *multipart processing systems that take up entire rooms instead of a single desk:* William P. Stivers, "B Needs Its Own Computer," *Dragon Seeds*, 1973, 24–29.

203 *her "desktop scopes with programmable keyboards and split-screen and scrolling capabilities" remain a fantasy:* Bill Crowell, "Computer Scratch-Pad at Home or at Work?" *Cryptolog*, 1978, 10; Kenny, "Minnie's Mini," p. 11.

203 *China has already developed minicomputers, machine translation, and integrated circuits:* Tom Mullaney, "The Origins of Chinese Supercomputing," *Foreign Affairs*, 2016.

203 *not for nothing does she still push for updated computer systems in B Group:* Kenny, 17.

203 *one in a series of missed opportunities:* Zaslow, *Oral History Interview 1999–89*, 2.

204 *they "seemed to be" gathering valuable information through traffic analysis and plaintext:* Burke, 280.

204 *their own designs continue to fail:* "Before Super-Computers," *Cryptologic Almanac 50th Anniversary Series.*

204 *Zaslow's gambit proves a success:* Zaslow, *Oral History Interview 1999–89*, 6.

Epilogue: After the Agency

205 *a blood vessel specialist at the Chicago Heart Association's artery bank:* "You Can Borrow Life from a Bank," *Chicago Tribune*, 22 April 1956, 234.

205 *a letter from President Bill Clinton thanking her for her service:* Marlon McElwaine, phone conversation with the author, 13 August 2025.

206 *nonprofits like the Junior Women's League and the Business and Professional Women's Club:* "Junior Women's League Plans Cabaret at Auditorium," *Charleston Daily Mail*, 3 February 1952, 17.

206 *the Book Lovers Club, which held literary events:* "BPW Club Votes to Sponsor Drive," *Beckley Post-Herald*, 26 March 1958, 8; "Book Lovers Party Hosts," *Baltimore Afro-American*, 8 January 1949, 10.

206 *a nonprofit serving Black women around the world:* "Obituary: Alberta McCray," Fielding Homes for Funerals Website, 2013.

206 *"She asserted a control in her life through choice and perseverance":* Ayin M. Adams, *African Americans in Hawai'i: A Search for Identity*, 71.

207 *"Apathy is a deadly disease—VOTE!":* "Runs for Hawaii Senate, 1974," source unknown.

207 *the university has no record of her employment:* South Carolina State Historical

Collection and Archives, South Carolina State University, email correspondence with the author, 8 July 2025.

207 *matrons from "the old established families of tradition"*: Francesca Morgan, *A Nation of Descendants: Politics and the Practice of Genealogy in U.S. History*, 101. "Washington's 400" references Gilded Age socialite Ward McAllister, whose list "The Four Hundred" was a who's who of New York's old money elite. The number wasn't arbitrary: Four hundred was the maximum capacity of a ballroom. See also Morgan, 218.

209 *distributed intelligence reports on Red Army Ground Forces*: "William Coffee," Cryptologic Hall of Honor; Buffham, 9–10, 28–29; Watts, 43–44.

209 *a men's club for "local gentlemen of merit and distinction"*: "Margaret Muses on the Capital Scene: July Rivals June as Month for Weddings," *Baltimore Afro-American*, 8 August 1959, 16.

210 *and to create space for those coming up behind her*: "Minnie Kenny: Champion with a Red Carnation," *Cryptologic Almanac 50th Anniversary Series*.

210 *"She's competent. She's very competent"*: Zaslow, *Oral History Interview 1999–20*, 7.

210 *she used that tokenism as a tool for change*: Stella Adams, "Focus on . . . Minnie Kenny," *Be Communique*, 1983, 4–5.

211 *"So you had your recruitment, your personnel, administration from top to bottom in the hands of whites"*: Eugene Becker, *Oral History Interview 1999–06*, 11.

211 *Helen Eagleson, a Black mathematician and cryptographer*: Very little information is available on Eagleson. Her master's thesis, "Corrections for Moments of Grouped Data," was completed at Atlanta University in 1943. She taught at Morehouse College until 1947, when she moved to Washington, DC. "Obituary: Helen Eagleson," *Washington Post*, 18 October 2007; Helen Clark Eagleson "Corrections for Moments of Grouped Data," master's thesis, Department of Mathematics, Atlanta University, 1943.

211 *The hierarchy "balked"*: "Minnie Kenny: Champion with a Red Carnation," *Cryptologic Almanac 50th Anniversary Series*, 3.

212 *"even if you have to get training on your own"*: S. Adams, 4.

213 *there was a "rationale" for putting the Black women on the project*: Buffham, 9.

214 *"In the early days, we had joyous things happening"*: Kenny, 28.

Profiles: Life Before the Agency

216 *After completing his service, he hopes to continue his education*: William Daniel Coffee, Individual Record—Civilian Conservation Corps; Reel 2136; Civilian

Conservation Corps, Individual Records CCC Enrollees, 1933–1943; Record Group 146; National Archives at St. Louis.

217 *doesn't have time to finish his degree:* Williams, 13.

217 *when it becomes the Prince Edward State Park for Negroes:* Christian Miller, "History of a Pre–Civil Rights Era State Park," Virginia State Parks.

218 *Langston Terrace, a 274-unit complex designed to curb DC's affordable housing shortage:* Chris Myers Asch and George Derek Musgrove, *Chocolate City*, 249.

218 *built by skilled labor under the New Deal:* Asch and Musgrove, 251.

219 *thousands of freedom seekers headed north to Canada:* Details about Ethel's early life and history come from Manning. Details about her teaching career and life after 1940 are found in Howard University's digital archive, newspapers, and manuscript papers.

220 *Goethe's* Herman und Dorothea; *and Storm's* Immensee: "The School of Liberal Arts Faculty," *Howard University Record*, 1908, 36.

220 *keep Black families out to protect their property values:* Asch and Musgrove, 188–192.

221 *translates Ernest's papers into German:* Lillie R. Jenkins, "Black Apollo of Science: The Life of Ernest Everett Just—Summarizing Timeline, Sumitography and Concept Poster," Perkins Faculty Research and Special Events 27, 31.

221 *she's suspended for "failure to report for duty and insubordination":* "Sustains Suspension of Mrs. Ethel Just," *Washington Afro American*, 15 November 1930, 3.

221 *It's a bizarre math, but the suspension is upheld:* "Mrs. Ernest E. Just Loses D.C. School Suit," *Washington Afro American*, 14 January 1933, p. 11.

221 *Ethel deserved to lose her case because she set a "bad example":* Richard W. Tillman, "This Reader Thinks Mrs. Just Deserved to Lose Her Case Because She Set a Bad Example," *Washington Afro American*, 21 January 1933, 6.

222 The Biology of the Cell Surface, *which Hedwig partly authors:* Manning, 240–248.

223 *they visit friends like Alain Locke:* "Ethel Just correspondence, June 4," Alain Locke Papers, Moorland Springarn Research Center, Howard University.

223 *Ethel's master's degree is one of four graduations in her family:* "Mrs. Ethel Just Gets Boston M.A.," *Washington Afro American*, 22 August 1936.

223 *she is too tired:* Mildred Hamilton, "A Lifelong Opponent of Injustice," *San Francisco Examiner*, 3 September 1974, 23.

223 *preparing teens for war work and civic engagement:* "YWCA News," *Washington Afro American*, 27 May 1939.

224 *who grabs a steer's horns and wrestles it to the ground:* Clara Stearns Scarbrough, *Land of Good Water, Takachue Pouetsu: A Williamson County, Texas, History*, 12, 15, 214.

224 *Oliver passes the fire for education and advocacy on to his children:* "Mrs. Price Celebrates 90th Birthday in Dallas," *Taylor Daily Press,* 21 February 1977, 2; "Taylor Principal, Victim of Sudden Illness, Buried," *San Antonio Register,* 26 March 1948, 1.

225 *"decades before the Pullman porters":* Scarbrough, 318.

227 *"severe and constant struggle":* Julius Carter, "If We Want Progress—We Must Produce," *The Informer,* 22 April 1939.

Afterword

233 *"by turns infuriating and inspiring":* Williams, viii.

234 *Then, the report "suddenly disappeared":* Becker, 14.

234 *the report is still missing:* Comments made to the author. Zoom conference, 10 July 2025.

235 *along with translators Audrey Fox and Eloise Daniels:* SSA History, Vol. 2, 231. Audrey's name is recorded incorrectly as "Aubrey."

235 *"several" Black people worked in that operation:* Buffham, 5.

235 *there were six major divisions:* This is true in 1943–1944. The Agency underwent several organizational restructurings during the war years, and the number of divisions fluctuated; at times there were up to eight. *SSA History,* Vol. 1, 274–275a.

236 *there are no details about their numbers:* Pryde, 3; Williams, 25, 31; Snyder, *History of NSA General-Purpose Electronic Digital Computers,* 1964, 1.

Appendix 1: Glossary

250 *"a big brute, but not very smart":* James Bamford, *Body of Secrets: Anatomy of the Ultra-Secret National Security Agency,* 582.

BIBLIOGRAPHY

"140 Years of Service: Women an Important Part of American Red Cross History." American Red Cross Website, 10 June 2021. https://www.redcross.org/about-us/news-and-events/news/2021/women-an-important-part-of-american-red-cross-history.html.

1948 Campaign Trends Survey. Gallup. https://www.trumanlibrary.gov/sites/default/files/1948Campaign_Trends.pdf.

Adams, Ayin M. *African Americans in Hawai'i: A Search for Identity*. Maui: Delane Publishing, 2014.

Adams, Stella. "Focus on . . . Minnie Kenny." *Be Communique*, April 1983: 4–5.

"African American in the 'Forgotten Theater' of World War II." *Folklife Today*. Library of Congress Website, 2019. https://blogs.loc.gov/folklife/2019/07/african-americans-in-the-forgotten-theater-of-world-war-ii/.

"African Culture Program Feature." *Washington Afro American*, 12 March 1955: 3.

AFSA Memorandum Number 32–26/2, 25 September 1952; AFSA Civilian Personnel Policy Memoranda; Box 1; General Correspondence Files, 1944–1969; Records of the National Security Agency/Central Security Service 1917–1998, Record Group 457; National Archives at College Park, College Park, MD.

AFSA Memorandum Number 32–66, 27 March 1951; AFSA Civilian Personnel Policy Memoranda; Box 1; General Correspondence Files, 1944–1969; Records of the National Security Agency/Central Security Service 1917–1998, Record Group 457; National Archives at College Park, College Park, MD.

AH Personnel Organization, 13; Personnel Organization, 1942, 1943, 1944; Box 1007; Historic Cryptographic Collection Pre–World War I Through World War II; Records of the National Security Agency/Central Security Service 1917–1998, Record Group 457; National Archives at College Park, College Park, MD.

Aid, Matthew. *The Secret Sentry: The Untold History of the National Security Agency.* New York: Bloomsbury Press, 2009. https://archive.org/details /secretsentryunto0000aidm/page/22/mode/2up.

Alexander, Otis. "Margaret Just Butcher (1913–2000)." *BlackPast,* 29 May 2021. https://www.blackpast.org/african-american-history/people-african -american-history/margaret-just-butcher-1913-2000/.

Alson, Mable. "The Eternal Feminist." *Baltimore Afro-American,* 2 August 1947: 22.

"An American Legacy with Boilermaker Roots." *Purdue University News Archive,* October 13, 2021. https://www.purdue.edu/newsroom/archive/releases /2021/Q4/an-american-legacy-with-boilermaker-roots.html.

Anderson, Audrey Fox. Official Personnel Folders—Department of the Army; Records of the U.S. Civil Service Commission, Record Group 146; National Archives, St. Louis, MO.

Archival and Historian's Source Files Related to William F. Friedman, ca. 1952– 1974; Records of the National Security Agency/Central Security Service, 1917–1998, Record Group 457; National Archives at College Park, College Park, MD.

"Arlington Hall Station, Building No. 401, 4000 Arlington Boulevard, Arlington, Arlington County, VA." *Historic American Buildings Survey.* Washington, DC: Library of Congress Prints and Photographs Division Website, n.d. https:// www.loc.gov/pictures/collection/hh/item/va1582/.

"Arlington Hall Station Photographs: Written and Descriptive Data." *Historic American Buildings Survey: Mid-Atlantic Region,* Philadelphia: National Park Service, Department of the Interior, 1989.

Asch, Chris Myers, and George Derek Musgrove. *Chocolate City: A History of Race and Democracy in the Nation's Capital.* Chapel Hill, NC: University of North Carolina Press, 2017.

Ball, Desmond, and Keiko Tamura, eds. *Breaking Japanese Diplomatic Codes: David Sissons and D Special Section During the Second World War.* Canberra, AUS: Australian National University E Press, 2013.

Bamford, James. *Body of Secrets: Anatomy of the Ultra-Secret National Security Agency.* New York: Anchor Books, 2002.

Bay, Mia. *Traveling Black.* Cambridge, MA: Belknap Press of Harvard University Press, 2021.

Becker, Eugene. *Oral History Interview 1999–06.* National Security Agency, 19 January 1999.

"Before Super-Computers: NSA and Computer Development." *Cryptologic Alma-*

nac 50th Anniversary Series. National Security Agency, 2003. https://www.nsa.gov/portals/75/documents/news-features/declassified-documents/crypto-almanac-50th/NSA_Before_Super_Computers.pdf.

Bellovin, Steven M. "Compression, Correction, Confidentiality, and Comprehension: A Modern Look at Telegraphic Codes." *Cryptologia* (2020): 1–37.

Benson, Robert Louis, and Michael Warner, eds. *Venona: Soviet Espionage and the American Response 1939–1957*. Washington, DC: National Security Agency, 1996.

Beria, Lavrentyi. "Special Dossier to Members of the Special Committee, Moscow, Kremlin." Wilson Center Digital Archive, 25 April 1947. https://digitalarchive.wilsoncenter.org/document/protocol-no-36-meeting-special-committee-under-council-ministers-soviet-union-excerpt.

"The Berlin Airlift, 1948–1949." *Milestones in the History of U.S. Foreign Relations*. Office of the Historian, US Department of State Website, 2017. https://history.state.gov/milestones/1945-1952/berlin-airlift.

The Bogotazo. Historical Review Program, Central Intelligence Agency, 2 July 1996. https://www.cia.gov/resources/csi/static/The-Bogotazo.pdf.

"Boilermakers at War: The Involvement of Purdue University in the Second World War." *Purdue Historian* 9 (2021).

"Book Lovers Party Hosts." *Baltimore Afro-American*, 8 January 1949: 10. https://www.newspapers.com/image/1134971054.

"BPW Club Votes to Sponsor Drive." *Beckley Post-Herald*, 26 March 1958: 8. https://www.newspapers.com/image/15774470.

"Brookport." *Chicago Defender*, 22 February 1947: 1. https://www.newspapers.com/image/1136015547/.

Brown, Kate. *Plutopia: Nuclear Families, Atomic Cities, and the Great Soviet and American Plutonium Disasters*. New York: Oxford University Press, 2013.

Brown, Loretta. "Growing up in LeDroit Park in the 1950s." *Washington Post*, 21 March 1985. https://www.washingtonpost.com/archive/local/1985/03/21/growing-up-in-ledroit-park-in-the-1950s/8174386a-9490-414f-8b29-784dde267090/.

Buffham, Benson. *Oral History Interview 1999–51*. National Security Agency, 15 June 1999.

Burden-Stelly, Charisse. *Black Scare / Red Scare: Theorizing Capitalist Racism in the United States*. Chicago: University of Chicago Press, 2023.

Burke, Colin B. *It Wasn't All Magic: The Early Struggle to Automate Cryptanalysis, 1930s–1960s*. Center for Cryptologic History, National Security Agency, 2002.

Burns, Thomas L. *The Origins of the National Security Agency 1940–1952*. Center for Cryptologic History, National Security Agency, 1990.

"Campbell Plays Host to AME Mission Unit." *Washington Afro American*, 24 September 1949: 31.

"Capable Office Staff; Bookkeeping Department; National Benefits Association; Washington, D.C." New York Public Library Digital Collections, 1917. https://digitalcollections.nypl.org/items/127b45b0-c6db-012f-182e-3c075448cc4b#/?uuid=510d47de-4d02-a3d9-e040-e00a18064a99.

Carr, Iris. *Oral History Interview 1999–52*. National Security Agency, 16 June 1999.

Carter, Julius. "If We Want Racial Progress—We Must Produce." *The Informer*, 22 April 1939: 2. https://texashistory.unt.edu/ark:/67531/metapth1655458/m1/10/zoom/print/?resolution=4&lat=5820.73555282941&lon=2847.5148801435344.

Casey, Steven. "The Campaign to Sell a Harsh Peace for Germany to the American Public, 1944–1948." *History* 90, no. 297 (2005): 62–92. https://eprints.lse.ac.uk/736/1/Campaign_Harsh_Peace_History.pdf.

Chicago Defender, National Edition, 31 July 1948: 1.

Church, Frank, et al. *Intelligence Activities and the Rights of Americans*, Book 2, *Final Report of the Select Committee to Study Governmental Operations with Respect to Intelligence Activities*. US Government Printing Office, 26 April 1976. https://www.intelligence.senate.gov/wp-content/uploads/2024/08/sites-default-files-94755-ii.pdf.

Churchill, Winston S. *The Grand Alliance*. Boston: Houghton Mifflin, 1950.

Churchill, Winston S. "The Sinews of Peace." America's National Churchill Museum Website, 5 March 1946. https://www.nationalchurchillmuseum.org/sinews-of-peace-iron-curtain-speech.html.

"The Civil Rights Act of 1964: A Long Struggle for Freedom, World War II and Post War (1940–1949)." Library of Congress Exhibition, 2016. loc.gov/exhibits/civil-rights-act/world-war-ii-and-post-war.html#obj058.

"Civil Rights Best Defense Against Reds." *Washington Afro American*, 13 March 1948: 25.

Clarke, Carter. Memorandum to the Assistant Secretary of the Army, "Effect of Critical Grade Limitations on Operations of the Army Security Agency," 22 April 1949; Personnel, ASA Historical, 1949–1952; Box 43; Archival and Historian's Source Files Related to William F. Friedman, ca. 1952–1974; Records of the National Security Agency/Central Security Service 1917–1998, Record Group 457; National Archives at College Park, College Park, MD.

Clifford, Clark. "Memorandum to Harry S. Truman." Political File, Clifford Papers, Harry S. Truman Library and Museum Website, 19 November 1947. https://www.trumanlibrary.gov/sites/default/files/1948Campaign _CliffordMemo.pdf.

Cochrane, Dorothy. "Meet the Curtiss-Wright Aeronautical Engineering Cadettes." National Air and Space Museum Website, 2013. https://airandspace.si.edu /stories/editorial/meet-curtiss-wright-aeronautical-engineering-cadettes.

Coffee, William Daniel. Individual Record—Civilian Conservation Corps; Reel 2136; Civilian Conservation Corps, Individual Records CCC Enrollees, 1933–1943; Records of the U.S. Civil Service Commission, Record Group 146; National Archives, St. Louis, MO. https://catalog.archives.gov /id/495040589?objectPage=2116.

Collins, Samuel P. "Introduction, 'The Office of Censorship at War.'" In Joseph C. Grew et al., *Lecture Series "This Is Our War" Delivered at Arlington Hall Station in the Autumn of 1943*. Washington, DC: Army Security Agency, 1947: 89–91.

Cook, Earle F. "Operating Services Division Executive Committee Minutes of Meeting Held 13 December 1944." William F. Friedman Collection of Official Papers, National Security Agency Website. https://www.nsa.gov/portals/75 /documents/news-features/declassified-documents/friedman-documents /panel-committee-board/FOLDER_140/41727869076712.pdf.

Cook, Earle F. "Operation Services Division Executive Committee Minutes of Meeting Held 18 April 1945." William F. Friedman Collection of Official Papers, National Security Agency Website. https://www.nsa.gov/portals/75 /documents/news-features/declassified-documents/friedman-documents /panel-committee-board/FOLDER_140/41727399076665.pdf.

"Cosmopolitan Club." *Debris* (1942): 285.

"Cosmopolitan Club to Hold Convention on Campus Sunday." *Purdue Exponent*, 12 December 1941: 1.

"CPI Inflation Calculator." U.S. Bureau of Labor Statistics Website. 15 September 2025. https://www.bls.gov/data/inflation_calculator.htm.

Crowell, Bill. "Computer Scratch-Pad at Home or at Work?" *Cryptolog* (June 1978): 10.

Current Population Reports: Income of Families and Persons in the United States: 1948. Washington, DC: U.S. Department of Commerce, 15 February 1950.

Dahl, Adam. "Constructing Colonial Peoples: W. E. B. Du Bois, the United Nations, and the Politics of Space and Scale." *Modern Intellectual History* 20, no. 3 (2023): 858–882. https://doi.org/10.1017/S1479244322000464.

"David Bryant." NSA Historical Figures. National Security Agency / Central Security Service Website. https://www.nsa.gov/History/Cryptologic-History /Historical-Figures/Historical-Figures-View/Article/1618636/david -bryant/.

Davis, Carol B. *Candle in the Dark: COMINT and Soviet Industrial Secrets 1946–1956.* Center for Cryptologic History, National Security Agency, 2017.

Davis, John A., and Cornelius L. Golightly. "Negro Employment in the Federal Government." *Phylon (1940–1946)* 6, no. 4 (1945): 337–346.

Defense's Nuclear Agency 1947–1997. Washington, DC: Defense Threat Reduction Agency, US Department of Defense, 2002. https://www.dtra.mil/Portals/61 /Documents/History/Defense's%20Nuclear%20Agency%201947-1997.pdf.

"Dies Committee Uncovers Nazi Propaganda Network in US." *Purdue Exponent*, 3 December 1941: 1.

Donovan, William J., to Franklin D. Roosevelt, President, New York, December 24, 1941; Office of Strategic Services—Reports, December 22, 1941–January 15, 1942, 105; Box 163; Subject Files 1933–1945; President's Secretary's File (Franklin D. Roosevelt Administration), 1933–1945; Franklin D. Roosevelt Library, Hyde Park, New York. http://www.fdrlibrary.marist.edu/_resources /images/psf/psf000767.pdf.

Du Bois, W. E. Burghardt. *An Appeal to the World: A Statement on the Denial of Human Rights to Minorities in the Case of Citizens of Negro Descent in the United States of America and an Appeal to the United Nations for Redress.* New York: National Association for the Advancement of Colored People, 1947. Civil Rights Modern Archive Website. https://www.crmvet.org/info/470000 _naacp_appeal_un-r.pdf.

Duberman, Martin. "Paul Robeson: Here I Stand," *American Masters Digital Archive (WNET),* Public Broadcasting Station, 30 September 1998, https:// www.pbs.org/wnet/americanmasters/archive/interview/martin-duberman/.

Duberman, Martin. *The Martin Duberman Reader: The Essential Historical, Biographical, and Autobiographical Writings.* New York: The New Press, 2013.

Eagleson, Helen Clark. *Corrections for Moments of Grouped Data.* Master of Science Thesis. Atlanta: Atlanta University, 1943. https://radar.auctr.edu /corrections-moments-grouped-data-1943.

Effects of Russian Radio Silence on German Intelligence, May 1944; Box 33; Archival and Historian's Source Files, 1952?–ca. 2007; Records of the National Security Agency/Central Security Service 1917–1998, Record Group 457; National Archives at College Park, College Park, MD.

Efficiency and Economy—AFSA Personnel Survey, 13 February 1950, 1; AFSA Personnel Survey, 14 February 1949; Box 2; General Records, 1948–1969; Records of the National Security Agency/Central Security Service 1917–1998, Record Group 457; National Archives at College Park, College Park, MD.

Eglash, Ron. "Broken Metaphor: The Master-Slave Analogy in Technical Literature." *Technology and Culture: The Journal of the Society for the History of Technology* 48, no. 2 (2007): 1–10.

"Ein Knopf." *Academy Herald* 2, no. 2 (1910): 26. https://dh.howard.edu/academy_herald/vol2/iss2/16.

"The Election of 1948." Harry S. Truman Library and Museum Website. https://www.trumanlibrary.gov/education/presidential-inquiries/election-1948.

"Elektrokhimpribor Combine." NTI (Nuclear Threat Initiative) Website. https://www.nti.org/education-center/facilities/elektrokhimpribor-combine/.

"Estimate of the Effects of the Soviet Possession of the Atomic Bomb upon the Security of the United States and upon the Probabilities of Direct Soviet Action." *ORE 49–91.* Central Intelligence Agency, 6 April 1950. https://www.cia.gov/readingroom/docs/DOC_0000258849.pdf.

"Ethel Just Correspondence." Alain Locke Papers. Moorland Springarn Research Center, Howard University, 4 June [year unknown].

Ewbank, Douglas C. "History of Black Mortality and Health before 1940." *Millbank Quarterly* 65, no. 1 (1987): 100–128.

Ferraz, Francisco Cesar Alves, and Henry Granville Widener. "Brazil-U.S. Relations: Brazil in World War II." Library of Congress Website, 2024. https://guides.loc.gov/brazil-us-relations/brazil-world-war-ii.

Field, Alexander J. "The U.S. Synthetic Rubber Program and the Fall of Singapore." *Yale University Press Blog*, 9 February 2024. https://yalebooks.yale.edu/2024/02/09/the-u-s-synthetic-rubber-program-and-the-fall-of-singapore.

Finch, Lynette. "Psychological Propaganda: The War of Ideas on Ideas During the First Half of the Twentieth Century." *Armed Forces & Society* 26, no. 3 (2000): 367–386.

Flagler, J. M. "Visit to Amtorg: The Soviet Trading Agency, Long Quiescent, Looks for an Upturn as U. S. Talks of Easing Restrictions." *New York Times*, 9 May 1954. https://www.nytimes.com/1954/05/09/archives/visit-to-amtorg-the-soviet-trading-agency-long-quiescent-looks-for.html.

Fox, John F. Jr. "In the Enemy's House: Venona and the Maturation of American Counterintelligence." *History Reports & Publications*, FBI Website, 27 October 2005.

https://www.fbi.gov/history/history-publications-reports/in-the-enemys
-house-venona-and-the-maturation-of-american-counterintelligence.

Friedman, William F., and Lambros D. Callimahos. *Military Cryptanalytics Part I*.
Washington, DC: National Security Agency, 1952.

"From Freedman's Village to Queen City." Arlington Virginia Library Website,
January 31, 2018. https://library.arlingtonva.us/2018/01/31/from-freedmans
-village-to-queen-city-one-communitys-evolution/.

Gioe, David V., and Nicholas Reynolds. "Capturing Wartime History to Forge
Postwar Intelligence Liaison: Telford Taylor's Battle with the US Navy over
the Future of Anglo-American Signals Intelligence." *Journal of Intelligence History* 23, no. 4 (2024): 225–235.

Glenn, Tom. "Time to Look at People." *Dragon Seeds*, December 1973: 19–20.

Goetschel, Samira. "'The Graveyard of the Earth': Inside City 40, Russia's Deadly
Nuclear Secret." *The Guardian*, 20 July 2016. https://www.theguardian.com
/cities/2016/jul/20/graveyard-earth-inside-city-40-ozersk-russia-deadly
-secret-nuclear.

Goldberg, Alfred. *The Pentagon: The First Fifty Years*. Washington, DC: Historical
Office, Office of the Secretary of Defense, 1992.

Goldschmidt, Bertrand. "A Forerunner to the NPT? The Soviet Proposals of 1947."
IAEA Bulletin (Spring 1986): 58–64. https://www.iaea.org/sites/default
/files/publications/magazines/bulletin/bull28-1/28103595864.pdf.

Gonzalez, Naiomi. "William Weisband." *The Intelligencer: Journal of U.S. Intelligence Studies* 26, no. 1 (2020): 49.

Goodwin, Ralph E., et al., eds. "Memorandum by Mr. Edmund A Gullion, Special
Assistant to the Under Secretary of State, to Messrs. Lovett and Kennan, 13
November 1947, Subject: Molotov's Remarks of November 6, 1947, on Atomic
Bomb 'Secret.'" In *Foreign Relations of the United States, 1947, General, The
United Nations*, Volume 1. Washington, DC: US Government Printing Office,
US Department of State, 1973. https://history.state.gov/historicaldocuments
/frus1947v01/d437.

Grew, Joseph C. "The Japanese, Our Enemy." In Joseph C. Grew et al., *Lecture Series
"This Is Our War" Delivered at Arlington Hall Station in the Autumn of 1943*.
Washington, DC: Army Security Agency, 1947: 128–142.

Gurin, Jacob. *Oral History Interview 2003–07*. National Security Agency, 30 April
2003.

Hamilton, Mildred. "A Lifelong Opponent of Injustice." *San Francisco Examiner*, 3
September 1974: 23.

Heller, Steven. "RCA Victor's Victory Lap." *PRINT*, 10 May 2016. https://www.printmag.com/daily-heller/rca-victors-victory-dance.

"The Heritage of Racism and Medicine in Indiana." *Invisible Indiana*, 9 August 2020. https://invisibleindianapolis.wordpress.com/.

Hillenkoetter, R. H. "Memorandum to Senator Bourke B. Hickenlooper, Status of the USSR Atomic Energy Project." *Management of Officially Released Information #136351*. Central Intelligence Agency, January 1949.

Hinsley, Francis Harry, et al. *British Intelligence in the Second World War: Its Influence on Strategy and Operations*, Volume 1. Cambridge, UK: Cambridge University Press, 1979.

The History of SIGINT in the CIA, 1947–1970, Volume 2. Historical Staff, Central Intelligence Agency, 1971.

History of the Army Security Agency and Subordinate Units, 1 July 1949–30 June 1950, Fiscal Year 1950. Washington, DC: Historical Section, Army Security Agency, 1953.

The History of the Signal Security Agency, Volume 1, *Organization*. Washington, DC: Army Security Agency, 13 April 1948.

The History of the Signal Security Agency, Volume 2, *The General Cryptanalytic Problem*. Washington, DC: Army Security Agency, 15 January 1947.

Hogan, Douglas. *General and Special Purpose Computers: A Historical Look and Some Lessons Learned*. National Security Agency, 1986.

Hollmuller, Anne. "'Right Out Our Front Door': The Construction of the Pentagon Destroyed a Black Neighborhood in Arlington." *Boundary Stones*, 23 March 2018, updated 9 April 2024. https://boundarystones.weta.org/2018/03/23/right-out-our-front-door-construction-pentagon-destroyed-black-neighborhood-arlington.

Holloway, David. *Stalin and the Bomb: The Soviet Union and Atomic Energy, 1939–1956*. New Haven: Yale University Press, 1994.

Holmes, Brenda L. "RCA: Bloomington Boom: RCA Delivers for Nearly 50 Years." *BizVoice: Magazine of the Indiana Chamber of Commerce*, 2020: 60–62.

"Howard University Course Catalog." Howard University, 1908.

Invisible Warriors: African American Women in World War II. Dir. Gregory S. Cooke. Charlie Horse Productions, 2020.

Jenkins, Lillie R. "Black Apollo of Science: The Life of Ernest Everett Just—Summarizing Timeline, Sumitography and Concept Poster." Perkins Faculty Research and Special Events 27, 2021. https://scholar.smu.edu/theology_research/27.

Johnson, Thomas. *American Cryptology During the Cold War, 1945–1989*, Book 1, *The Struggle for Centralization 1945–1960*. Center for Cryptologic History, National Security Agency, 1995.

Johnson, Thomas R. "Purdue University in the War." *Purdue Alumnus* 30 (1942): 5–12.

"Joint Hostesses." *San Antonio Register*, 5 May 1933: 2.

"Junior Women's League Plans Cabaret at Auditorium." *Charleston Daily Mail*, 3 February 1952: 17.

Just, Ethel. "Negro American Folk-Plays of Paul Green with Special Reference to Their Sociological Value." Master of Arts Thesis. Boston University, 1936. https://open.bu.edu/bitstream/2144/18194/1/negroamericanfol00just.pdf.

Just, Ethel. Official Personnel Folders—Department of the Army. Records of the U.S. Civil Service Commission, Record Group 146, National Archives, St. Louis, MO.

Kahn, David. *The Codebreakers: The Comprehensive History of Secret Communication from Ancient Times to the Internet*. Scribner, 1996.

Keller, Robert H. "Paul Robeson at Blaine: Singing for Freedom at the Peace Arch." *Columbia Magazine* 19, no. 4 (2005–06): 1–7. https://www.washingtonhistory.org/wp-content/uploads/2020/04/winter-2005-06_001.pdf.

Kenny, Minnie M. "Minnie's Mini." *Cryptolog* (June 1978): 11.

Kenny, Minnie M. "Minnie's Mini." *Dragon Seeds*, December 1973: 23.

Kenny, Minnie M. *Oral History Interview 1999–27*. National Security Agency, 30 March 1999.

Kenny, Minnie M., et al. "This Is Dragon Seeds." *Dragon Seeds*, December 1973: i.

King, Gilbert. "What Paul Robeson Said." *Smithsonian Magazine*, 13 September 2011. https://www.smithsonianmag.com/history/what-paul-robeson-said-77742433/.

"Klan to Ride Again Tennessee: Daily Heralds Its Revival." *Washington Afro American*, 23 March 1946: 16.

"Klan Tries Revival." *Washington Afro American*, 27 October 1945: 1, 27.

Kristensen, Hans M., and Robert S. Norris. "Global Nuclear Weapons Inventories, 1945–2013." *Bulletin of the Atomic Scientists* 69, no. 5 (2013): 75–81. https://doi.org/10.1177/0096340213501363.

Kuhns, Woodrow. "The Beginning of Intelligence in CIA. The Office of Reports and Estimates, CIA's First Center for Analysis." *Studies in Intelligence* 66, no. 3 (2022): 1–20. https://www.cia.gov/resources/csi/static/ORE-First-Center-of-Analysis-at-CIA-Sep2022.pdf.

Langsdorf, Martyl. "Cover Design." *Bulletin of the Atomic Scientists* 3, no. 6 (1947).

Langsdorf, Martyl. "The History of the Bulletin's Clock," 1947. https://thebulletin .org/wp-content/uploads/2013/05/The-History-of-Martyls-Clock.pdf.

Laqueur, Walter. *The Limits and Uses of Intelligence.* New York: Routledge, 1995. https://archive.org/details/useslimitsofinte0000laqu.

Laurie, Clayton. "The Korean War and the Central Intelligence Agency." FOIA Electronic Reading Room, Central Intelligence Agency Website, 1 May 2010: 1–27. https://www.cia.gov/readingroom/docs/2010-05-01.pdf.

Lebedev, Vasilii. "War and Peace in Liberated North Korea: Soviet Military Administration and the Creation of North Korean Police Force in 1945." *International Journal of Asian Studies* 19, no. 1 (2021): 1–17.

"LeDroit Park Civic Association Holds Appreciation Service for Pvt. Cowan." *Washington Afro American,* 27 March 1948: 14.

Leiter, Zachary. "Chicago's 250 Year History of Segregation." *Chicago Reporter,* 30 August 2023. https://www.chicagoreporter.com/chicagos-250-year-history -of-segregation/.

"Lend-Lease Shipments, World War II." *Quantities of Lend-Lease Shipments: A Summary of Important Items Furnished Foreign Governments,* 31 December 1946. https://www.ibiblio.org/hyperwar/USA/ref/LL-Ship/LL-Ship-3B.html.

Lenin, Vladimir I. *Lenin's Collected Works,* Volume 28. Moscow: Progress Publishers, 1965.

Leon, Janice. "Integrating the American Association of University Women, 1946–1949." *The Historian* 51, no. 3 (1989): 423–445. https://www.jstor.org /stable/24447356.

Manning, Kenneth. *Black Apollo of Science: The Life of Ernest Everett Just.* New York: Oxford University Press, 1983.

"Margaret Muses on the Capital Scene: July Rivals June as Month for Weddings." *Baltimore Afro-American,* 8 August 1959: 16.

McCarthy, Melba. *Oral History Interview 1999–32.* National Security Agency, 15 April 1999.

McConnell, Julian, and [Redacted] McConnell. *Oral History Interview 1999–37.* National Security Agency, 27 April 1999.

McElwaine, Marlon. Phone Conversation with the author, 13 August 2025.

McElwaine, Naomi. Official Personnel Folders—Department of the Army; Records of the U.S. Civil Service Commission, Record Group 146; National Archives, St. Louis, MO.

McElwaine, Naomi Kate. Official Transcript. Lafayette: Purdue University, 1944.

McMillan, Dougald D. *Report on Inquiry into CIA-Related Electronic Surveillance Activities.* Washington, DC: US Department of Justice, 1976. https://nsarchive.gwu.edu/sites/default/files/documents/rd5srh-6d4a/ciasignals_25.pdf.

McWatt, Martha. Official Personnel Folders—Department of the Army; Records of the U.S. Civil Service Commission, Record Group 146; National Archives, St. Louis, MO.

"Memorandum for: the Director, Subject: Policy Concerning the CIA Weekly Summary." Central Intelligence Agency, 27 March 1950. https://www.cia.gov/readingroom/docs/CIA-RDP80R01731R003600030009-5.pdf.

"Memorandum for the Members of USCIB: The Petersen Case." Central Intelligence Agency, 5 May 1955.

Merkel, Miles A. "A 'Word Spotter.'" *NSA Technical Journal* 4, no. 4 (1959): 91–100. https://www.nsa.gov/portals/75/documents/news-features/declassified-documents/tech-journals/a-word-spotter.pdf.

"Military Myths and Legends: The American NCO That Started the Korean War." *Marines Dispatches*, 2022. https://marines.togetherweserved.com/dispatches-articles/107/1234/Military+Myths+and+Legends%3A+The+American+NCO+That+Started+the+Korean+War.

Miller, Christian. "History of a Pre–Civil Rights Era State Park." Virginia State Parks, 19 February 2019. https://www.dcr.virginia.gov/state-parks/blog/black-history-month-prince-edward-state-park-for-negroes-a-refuge-for.

Mills, Bernice. *Oral History Interview 1999–92.* National Security Agency, 10 November 1999.

"Minnie Kenny: Champion with a Red Carnation." *Cryptologic Almanac 50th Anniversary Series*, 2003. https://www.nsa.gov/portals/75/documents/news-features/declassified-documents/crypto-almanac-50th/Minnie_Kenney.pdf.

Molstad, Perry. "Operating Services Division, Executive Committee, Minutes of the Meeting Held 8 August 1945." William F. Friedman Collection of Official Papers, National Security Agency Website. https://www.nsa.gov/portals/75/documents/news-features/declassified-documents/friedman-documents/panel-committee-board/FOLDER_140/41726999076625.pdf.

Molstad, Perry. "Operating Services Division Minutes of Meeting Held 13 June 1945." William F. Friedman Collection of Official Papers, National Security Agency Website. https://www.nsa.gov/portals/75/documents/news-features/declassified-documents/friedman-documents/panel-committee-board/FOLDER_140/41727219076647.pdf.

Morgan, Francesca. *A Nation of Descendants: Politics and the Practice of Genealogy in U.S. History*. Chapel Hill: University of North Carolina Press, 2021.

"The Move to Fort Meade." *Cryptologic Almanac 50th Anniversary Series*. National Security Agency, 28 February 2003. https://media.defense.gov/2021/Jun/29/2002751983/-1/-1/0/THE_MOVE_TO_FORT_MEADE.PDF.

Mowry, David P. *The Cryptology of the German Intelligence Service*. Washington, DC: National Intelligence Service, 1989.

Moynihan, Daniel Patrick, et al. "Appendix A, Section 7: The Cold War." *Report on the Commission on Protecting and Reducing Government Secrecy*. Washington, DC: US Government Printing Office, 1997. https://sgp.fas.org/library/moynihan/appa7.html.

"Mrs. Ernest E. Just Loses D.C. School Suit." *Washington Afro American*, 14 January 1933: 11.

"Mrs. Ethel Just Gets Boston M.A." *Washington Afro American*, 22 August 1936.

"Mrs. Just Speaks." *Washington Afro American*, 8 February 1941: 16. https://www.newspapers.com/image/1133894684/.

"Mrs. Price Celebrates 90th Birthday in Dallas." *Taylor Daily Press*, 21 February 1977: 2.

Mullaney, Tom. "The Origins of Chinese Supercomputing." *Foreign Affairs*, 4 August 2016. https://www.foreignaffairs.com/articles/china/2016-08-04/origins-chinese-supercomputing#:~:text=By%201970%2C%20the%20institute%20in,development%20of%20a%20computing%20industry.

Mundy, Liza. *Code Girls: The Untold Story of the American Women Codebreakers of World War II*. New York: Hachette Books, 2017.

Mundy, Liza. "The Women Code Breakers Who Unmasked Soviet Spies." *Smithsonian Magazine*, September 2018. https://www.smithsonianmag.com/history/women-code-breakers-unmasked-soviet-spies-180970034/.

namnoiz, "Pearl Harbor Radio Broadcasts—December 7, 1941," YouTube, 7 December 2012. http://youtube.com/watch?v=ZbKLkJymyQE.

"Naomi McElwaine Will Speak to Club in Union Tonight." *Purdue Exponent*, 13 April 1943: 1.

Neff, Robert. "Yanks Welcomed on Their Arrival in Newly Liberated Korea." *Korea Times*, 15 August 2021. https://www.koreatimes.co.kr/opinion/20210815/yanks-welcomed-on-their-arrival-in-newly-liberated-korea.

Negro Press Report, October 12, 1942, 6; Negro Press; Press Items, Re: Negro Newspapers 1944–1946; Assistant Secretary of Defense (Legislative & Public Affairs) Office of Public Information, Analysis Branch; Box 266, Subversives;

Records of the Office of the Secretary of Defense 1921–2008, Record Group 330; National Archives at College Park, College Park, MD.

Negro Press Report, October 26, 1942, 2–4; Negro Press; Press Items, Re: Negro Newspapers 1944–1946; Assistant Secretary of Defense (Legislative & Public Affairs) Office of Public Information, Analysis Branch; Box 266, Subversives; Records of the Office of the Secretary of Defense 1921–2008, Record Group 330; National Archives at College Park, College Park, MD.

"New Research Leads to West Lafayette Apology for Past Racial Covenants." *Based in Lafayette, Indiana*, 20 June 2024. https://www.basedinlafayette.com/p /new-research-leads-to-west-lafayette.

"News of the Colored People: Officers Chosen." *Lafayette Journal and Courier*, 1 November 1941: 8.

Nissan, Regene. Interview, Bletchley Park Website, n.d. https://bletchleypark.org .uk/wp-content/uploads/record_attachments/2032.pdf.

Norberg, John. "African Americans Apply to Purdue's Residence Halls 1944– 1947." Excerpted from *Ever True: 150 Years of Giant Leaps at Purdue University* (2019). Purdue Libraries and School of Information Studies News Online, 4 February 2021. https://blogs.lib.purdue.edu/news/2021/02/04/excerpts-of -black-history-at-purdue-university-part-1-ever-true/.

"Notes of the Conversation Between Comrade I. V. Stalin and a Governmental Delegation from the Democratic People's Republic of Korea Headed by Kim Il Sung." History and Public Policy Program Digital Archive. Wilson Center Digital Archive, 5 March 1949. http://digitalarchive.wilsoncenter.org/document/112127.

"Notices." *Purdue Exponent*, 7 December 1941: 4.

Nye, Joseph. "China's Soft Power Deficit." *Wall Street Journal*, 8 May 2012. https:// www.wsj.com/articles/SB10001424052702304451104577389923098678842.

"Obituary: Alberta McCray." Fielding Homes for Funerals Website, 21 March 2013. https://obits.postandcourier.com/us/obituaries/charleston/name/alberta -mccray-obituary?id=20394169 1/.

"Obituary: Helen Eagleson." *Washington Post*, 18 October 2007.

"Ornaments, Fir Trees Festoon Union as First Signs of Christmas Hit Campus." *Purdue Exponent*, 7 December 1941: 1.

Penney, Elizabeth. Elizabeth Penney Interview. Archives and Special Collections, Purdue University Libraries, 6 May 2019.

Peterson, Michael L. *BOURBON to Black Friday: The Allied Collaborative COMINT Effort against the Soviet Union, 1945–1948*. Center for Cryptologic History, National Security Agency, 1995.

Phillips, Cecil. *Oral History Interview 1999–23.* National Security Agency, 12 March 1999.

Phillips, Cecil, and Blair Hall. *Oral History Interview 1999–23.* National Security Agency, 5 May 1993.

Policy for Utilization of Negro Manpower in the Post-War Army: Supplemental Report. Special Board on Negro Manpower, War Department, 26 January 1946. https://apps.dtic.mil/sti/trecms/pdf/AD1117235.pdf.

Post War Transition Period: The Army Security Agency, 1945–1948. Washington, DC: Army Security Agency, 1952.

Price, Byron. "The Office of Censorship at War." In Joseph Grew et al., *Lecture Series "This Is Our War" Delivered at Arlington Hall Station in the Autumn of 1943.* Washington, DC: Army Security Agency, 1947: 88–110.

Pryde, James. *Oral History Interview 1998–26.* National Security Agency, 26 March 1999.

Pryor, Elizabeth Stordeur. "The Etymology of Nigger: Resistance, Language, and the Politics of Freedom in the Antebellum North," *Journal of the Early Republic* 36, no. 2 (Summer 2016): 203–245. https://muse.jhu.edu/article/620987.

Rabinowitch, Eugene. "Forewarned—But Not Forearmed." *Bulletin of the Atomic Scientists* 5, no. 10 (1949): 273–292. https://thebulletin.org/wp-content/uploads/2013/05/1949-Clock-Statement-1.pdf.

"Racism in Anti-Japanese Propaganda." Anti-Japanese Propaganda Informational Sheet (n.d.). https://www.history.navy.mil/content/dam/museums/hrnm/Education/EducationWebsiteRebuild/AntiJapanesePropaganda/AntiJapanesePropagandaInfoSheet/Anti-Japanese%20Propaganda%20info.pdf.

"Radio Corporation to Train Cadettes in Engineering." *Purdue Exponent*, 22 January 1943: 1.

Raymond, Richard C. "Challenge to SIGINT: Change or Die." *Cryptologic Symposium* (1969): 11–13.

"RCA's 'soldiers of production.'" *24th Annual Report*, Radio Corporation of America, 31 December 1943.

Rehman, Azreen. "The Black History of Purdue University." *The Odyssey Online*, 24 January 2019. https://www.theodysseyonline.com/black-history-of-purdue-university.

Responsibilities and Ideals, 2; Signal Security Agency & Army Security Agency Organization, 1945; Box 2; Organization Mission Files; Records of the National Security Agency/Central Security Service 1917–1998, Record Group 457; National Archives at College Park, College Park, MD.

Robarge, David. *John McCone as Director of Central Intelligence 1961–1965*. Central Intelligence Agency, 2005.

Robeson, Paul Jr. *The Undiscovered Paul Robeson: Quest for Freedom, 1939–1976*. New York: John Wiley & Sons, 2009.

"Rosie the Engineer: RCA Cadettes." *Lockheed Martin News*, 2020. https://www .lockheedmartin.com/en-us/news/features/history/rca-cadettes.html.

Rowlett, Frank. *Oral History Interview 1976–01*. National Security Agency, 31 August 1976.

"Runs for Hawaii Senate, 1974." Source unknown, 1974.

Salmon, Andrew. "John Hodge: First US Forces Commander in Korea." *Korea Times*, 18 January 2012. https://www.koreatimes.co.kr/lifestyle/people -events/20120118/23-john-hodge-first-us-forces-commander-in-korea.

Scarbrough, Clara Stearns. *Land of Good Water: Takachue Pouetsu: A Williamson County, Texas, History*. Georgetown, TX: Williamson County Sun Publishers, 1973.

"The School of Liberal Arts Faculty." *Howard University Record*, 1908: 36–40. https://dh.howard.edu/hurecord/vol2/iss2/1.

Schuerman, Matthew. "The Peekskill Riots Revealed the Racism and Antisemitism Hidden Beneath the Surface of the Anti-Communist Movement." *Smithsonian Magazine*, August 27, 2024. https://www.smithsonianmag.com/history/the -peekskill-riots-revealed-the-racism-and-antisemitism-hidden-beneath-the -surface-of-the-anti-communist-movement-180984936/.

Scott, Emmet J. *Scott's Official History of the American Negro in the World War*. Chicago: Homewood Press, 1919. https://www.loc.gov/resource/gdcmassbookdig .scottsofficialhi01scot/?sp=473&st=pdf&r=-0.244%2C0%2C1.487%2C1.487 %2C0&pdfPage=565.

Sherman, David J. "Ann's War: One Woman's Journey to Codebreaking Victory over Japan." *Cryptologic Quarterly* 36, no. 3 (2017): 41–49.

Sherry, Gretchen, and Ann Hathaway. "Cadettes on Campus." *Purdue Engineer* 39, no. 9 (1 August 1943): 244–246. https://historicalnewspapers.lib.purdue .edu/?a=d&d=EGR19430901-01.2.20.

Snyder, Samuel S. *History of NSA General-Purpose Electronic Digital Computers*. Washington, DC: US Department of Defense, 1964.

Snyder, Samuel S. "Influence of U.S. Cryptologic Organizations on the Digital Computer Industry." *Cryptologic Quarterly* 8, nos. 3–4 (1987–1988): 65–82.

"Southeast Settlement House." *Washington Afro American*, 25 October 1947.

St. Paul Recorder, 1938–1944.

Stivers, William P. "B Needs Its Own Computer." *Dragon Seeds*, December 1973.

"A Storied History: Purdue University and the Military." Purdue University Press Website, 4 December 2024. https://www.press.purdue.edu/blog/2024/12/04/a-storied-history-purdue-university-and-the-military-a-q-a-with-author-john-norberg.

Summary Annual Report, Army Security and Subordinate Units, 1 July 1948–30 June 1949, Fiscal Year 1949. Washington, DC: Historical Section, Army Security Agency, 1952.

Summary Annual Report of the Signal Security Agency, Fiscal Year 1946. Washington, DC: Army Security Agency, 1947.

Summary Annual Report of the Army Security Agency Fiscal Year 1947. Washington, DC: Army Security Agency, 1950.

Summary Annual Report of the Army Security Agency, Fiscal Year 1948. Washington, DC: Army Security Agency, 1950.

"Sustains Suspension of Mrs. Ethel Just." *Washington Afro American*, 15 November 1930: 3.

"Symbols and Titles of AFSA Activities." 14 December 1951. William F. Friedman Collection of Official Papers, National Security Agency Website. https://www.nsa.gov/portals/75/documents/news-features/declassified-documents/friedman-documents/correspondence/FOLDER_034/41711309075061.pdf.

"TASS: Its Role, Structure and Operations." Central Intelligence Agency, June 1959.

Taylor, Telford. "Brigadier Telford Taylor from the American Embassy in London to Colonel Corderman at Arlington Hall Station, Arlington," 25 May 1943.

Taylor, Telford. "Brigadier Telford Taylor from the American Embassy in London to Colonel Corderman at Arlington Hall Station, Arlington," 27 May 1943.

"Taylor Principal, Victim of Sudden Illness, Buried." *San Antonio Register*, 26 March 1948: 1.

Terrell, Mary Church. *A Colored Woman in a White World*. New York: Simon and Schuster, 1996.

"This Reader Thinks Mrs. Just Deserved to Lose Her Case Because She Set a Bad Example." *Washington Afro American*, 21 January 1933: 6.

"Thurmond Hits Truman, Dewey, Wallace as Leading U.S. to 'Rocks of Totalitarianism." *New York Times*, 12 August 1948. https://www.nytimes.com/1948/08/12/archives/thurmond-hits-truman-dewey-wallace-as-leading-us-to-rocks-of.html.

TICOM Document #646; Russian—Preambles and Endings of W/I Soviet Messages, 1945; Box 21; Archival and Historian's Source Files, 1952?–ca. 2007; Records of the National Security Agency/Central Security Service 1917–1998, Record Group 457; National Archives at College Park, College Park, MD.

To Secure These Rights: The Report of the President's Committee on Civil Rights. Harry S. Truman Library and Museum, 29 October 1947. https://www.truman library.gov/library/to-secure-these-rights.

"Town Girls Discuss Formation of Club at Initial Meeting." *Purdue Exponent*, 19 December 1941: 1.

Truman, Harry S. "Annual Message to the Congress on the State of the Union." The American Presidency Project, 7 January 1948. https://www.presidency .ucsb.edu/documents/annual-message-the-congress-the-state-the-union-14.

Truman, Harry S. Executive Order 9981, 26 July 1948; Executive Orders 1862– 2020; Box 14; General Records of the United States Government, 1778–2006, Record Group 11; National Archives Building, Washington, DC. https:// catalog.archives.gov/id/300009

Truman, Harry S. "The President's News Conference." Harry S. Truman Library and Museum Website, 5 August 1948. https://www.trumanlibrary.gov /library/public-papers/170/presidents-news-conference.

Truman, Harry S. "Special Message to Congress on Civil Rights." Harry S. Truman Library and Museum Website, 2 February 1948. https://www.trumanlibrary .gov/library/public-papers/20/special-message-congress-civil-rights.

The United States at War: Development and Administration of the War Program by the Federal Government. Washington, DC: Bureau of the Budget, US War Department, 1946.

United States Synthetic Rubber Program, 1935–1945. Washington, DC: National Historic Chemical Landmarks program of the American Chemical Society, 1998. https://www.acs.org/education/whatischemistry/landmarks/synthetic rubber.html.

"War Department Civilian Service Emblems." *Philadelphia Enquirer*, 15 July 1945. https://www.frontiernet.net/~ericbush/US/Gov/WW2GovCivRibbons .html.

Watts, Delores, Warner Parsons, and [Redacted]. *Oral History Interview 1999–19.* National Security Agency, 26 February 1999.

Weathersby, Kathryn. "'Should We Fear This?' Stalin and the Danger of War with America." Washington, DC: Woodrow Wilson International Center for Scholars, July 2002. https://www.wilsoncenter.org/sites/default/files/media /documents/publication/ACFAEF.pdf.

Weekly Summary. Central Intelligence Agency, 5 November 1948.

"West Lafayette," *Sundown Towns Database.* History and Social Justice Website, Tougaloo College (n.d.). https://justice.tougaloo.edu/sundowntown/west-lafayette-in/.

Wharton-Beck, Aura. "Interrupted Labour by Another Name: Resistance." *Feminist Review* 132, no. 1 (2022): 10–23.

Wiley, Bell I. *The Training of Negro Troops.* Historical Section, Army Ground Forces, US War Department Special Staff, 1946.

"William Coffee." Cryptologic Hall of Honor, National Security Agency Website. https://www.nsa.gov/DesktopModules/ArticleCS/Print.aspx?PortalId=75&ModuleId=15049&Article=1621571.

Williams, Jeannette, and Yolande Dickerson. *The Invisible Cryptologists: African Americans, WWII to 1956.* Center for Cryptologic History, National Security Agency, 2001.

Williams, Jeannette, and Yolande Dickerson. *The Invisible Cryptologists: African Americans, WWII to 1956,* revised ed. Center for Cryptologic History, National Security Agency, 2024.

Wolpert, Rachel. "Times of Surge." Vattenfall, 2013. https://group.vattenfall.com/press-and-media/newsroom/2/times-of-surge.

"Women's Residence Halls." *Debris,* 1943: 334.

Worksheets Used in the Exploitation of JAH, a Japanese Commercial System; Box 1003; Historic Cryptographic Collection Pre–World War I Through World War II; Records of the National Security Agency/Central Security Service 1917–1998, Record Group 457; National Archives at College Park, College Park, MD.

"World War II." *Encyclopedia of Indianapolis* (2001). https://indyencyclopedia.org/world-war-ii/.

"You Can Borrow Life from a Bank." *Chicago Tribune,* 22 April 1956: 234.

"YWCA News." *Washington Afro American,* 27 May 1939.

Zaslow, Milton. *Oral History Interview 1999–20.* National Security Agency, 25 February 1999.

Zaslow, Milton. *Oral History Interview 1999–89.* National Security Agency, 9 November 1999.